War & Peace
In Our Time

War & Peace In Our Time

MORMON PERSPECTIVES

Edited by Patrick Q. Mason, J. David Pulsipher,
and Richard L. Bushman

GREG KOFFORD BOOKS
SALT LAKE CITY 2012

"War and the Gospel: Perspectives from Latter-day Saint National Security Practitioners" was originally published in *SquareTwo* 2, no. 2 (2009). Reprinted here with permission.

2015   14   13   12   11   5   4   3   2   1

Greg Kofford Books, Inc.
P.O. Box 1362
Draper, UT 84020
www.koffordbooks.com

Library of Congress Cataloging-in-Publication Data

War & peace in our times : Mormon perspectives / edited by Patrick Q. Mason, J. David Pulsipher, and Richard L. Bushman.
    pages cm
  Includes index.
  ISBN 978-1-58958-099-2
  1. War—Religious aspects—Church of Jesus Christ of Latter-day Saints. 2. Church of Jesus Christ of Latter-day Saints—Doctrines. 3. Mormon Church—Doctrines. I. Mason, Patrick Q., editor. II. Pulsipher, J. David (John David), 1967- editor. III. Bushman, Richard L., editor. IV. Title: War and peace in our times.
  BX8643.W3W37 2012
  261.8'730882893—dc23
              2012029036

Contents

Introduction   ix
    Patrick Q. Mason

Part I. Scriptural & Doctrinal Interpretations

1. The Ammonite Conundrum   1
    J. David Pulsipher

2. A Non-Violent Reading of the Book of Mormon   13
    Joshua Madson

3. Offensive Warfare in the Book of Mormon
   and a Defense of the Bush Doctrine   29
    Morgan Deane

4. Imagining Peace: The Example of the Nephites
   following Christ's Visit to the New World   41
    Robert A. Rees

5. Pax Sanctorum   57
    F. R. Rick Duran

Part II. Historical & Cultural Perspectives

6. Zion as a Refuge from the Wars of Nations   83
    Mark Ashurst-McGee

7. Fall from Grace: Mormon Millennialism,
   Native Americans, and Violence   93
    Jennifer Lindell

8. Negotiating War and Peace in Korea: A Comparison
   of U.S. Military and Korean Latter-day Saints   101
    Ethan Yorgason

9. Nonviolent Responses and Mormon Attitudes:
   Reasons and Realities   115
    Jesse Samantha Fulcher

Part III. Notable & Prophetic Voices

10. General Conference Addresses during Times of War   127
    Robert H. Hellebrand

11. Pacifist Counselor in the First Presidency:
    J. Reuben Clark Jr., 1933–1961   141
    D. Michael Quinn

12. The Work of Death: Hugh Nibley as Scholar,
    Soldier, Peace Activist   161
    Boyd Jay Petersen

13. Eugene England's Theology of Peace   171
    Loyd Ericson

Part IV. Personal & Professional Observations

14. An LDS Chaplain's Perspective on Current Conflicts   191
    Eric A. Eliason

15. "Renounce War and Proclaim Peace": Personal Reflections
    on Mormon Attempts at Peacemaking   203
    Gordon Conrad Thomasson

16. Doctrine and Covenants 98:
    The "Immutable" Rejected Covenant of Peace   219
    Ron Madson

17. War and the Gospel: Perspectives from Latter-day Saint
    National Security Practitioners   235
    Mark Henshaw, Valerie M. Hudson, Eric Jensen, Kerry M.
    Kartchner, and John Mark Mattox

Aftermath   267
    Richard Lyman Bushman

Contributors   273

Index   279

Scripture Index   285

For followers of the Prince of Peace

Introduction

Patrick Q. Mason

We live in a world of war. Though most people—especially those in developed nations—are sheltered from the direct brutalities and horrors of war, the fact is that most nations around the world have been engaged in violent conflict at some point over the past thirty-five years. Global violence has actually decreased in recent years but hardly disappeared: according to one respected measure there were thirty armed conflicts around the globe in 2010.[1] At least eight additional conflicts have sprung up since the beginning of 2011, many of which are related to the uprisings in the Arab world and the embattled independence won by South Sudan.[2] Whether one sees the world through a Machiavellian or millenarian lens, it is doubtful that the world will witness an end to war anytime soon.

Of course, this state of affairs is hardly new. The Bible traces the origins of deadly violence to the first sibling rivalry between Cain and Abel. Joseph Smith's revelations placed the origins of conflict even earlier, with the premortal "war in heaven" between the followers of Jesus and Satan. Humans' seemingly inexhaustible capacity for violence is documented in

---

1. The Uppsala Conflict Data Program website hosts a wealth of statistics, maps, charts, and graphs tracking armed conflicts around the globe since 1975. See http://www.ucdp.uu.se/gpdatabase/search.php and http://www.pcr.uu.se/research/ucdp/charts_and_graphs/ (last accessed May 2, 2012). Other helpful websites include the Correlates of War project, http://www.correlatesofwar.org/; the Peace Research Institute Oslo (PRIO), http://www.prio.no/; and the Stockholm International Peace Research Institute (SIPRI), http://www.sipri.org/.

2. See http://en.wikipedia.org/wiki/List_of_wars_2011%E2%80%93present (last accessed May 2, 2012). Since statistical information typically takes one to two years to appear in the more rigorous scholarly databases, sites like this help keep informal track of new and ongoing conflicts.

both secular and sacred history: the Hebrew Bible is a famously bloody text, and the Book of Mormon begins with threats of murder and a decapitation, culminating in not one but two civilizational holocausts.

The doctrine of the incarnation—or, as the Book of Mormon prophet Nephi puts it, "the condescension of God"—encourages followers of Jesus to take seriously their sojourn "among the children of men," in all its political, economic, social, cultural, and religious particularity (1 Ne. 11:24, 26). From the very beginning, Mother Eve recognized that this fallen world would bring about both good and evil, joy and pain. Surely no one sorrowed more than she did when, in fact, violence entered the world as one of her sons took the life of another (see Moses 5, esp. v. 11). Ever since then, believers have been forced to consider the appropriate, even godly, responses to suffering, violence, and sin. Should Abel have used violent, even lethal, force to stop Cain's assault? Or, if Adam had happened upon them, would violence against his aggressor son be justified to protect and preserve his victim son? Is at least some degree of violence a tragic but necessary evil in a world of sin, or a symptom of human fallenness that should be rejected outright?

The question of justifiable violence is complicated—indeed, precipitated—by the fact that scripture seems to give mixed messages as to how the believer is to behave in the face of violence. God announces himself to the prophets as both the Lord of Hosts and Prince of Peace. The Gospels record Jesus as offering seemingly conflicting advice. On the one hand there is the Sermon on the Mount: "Blessed are the peacemakers: for they shall be called the children of God. . . . Whosoever will smite thee on thy right cheek, turn to him the other also" (Matt. 5:9, 39). But a few chapters later Jesus sounds downright bellicose: "Think not that I am come to send peace on earth: I came not to send peace, but a sword" (10:34). And then on the night before his crucifixion: "Put up again thy sword into his place: for all they that take the sword shall perish with the sword" (26:52). This paradox, with passages apparently endorsing both violence and nonviolence within earshot of one another, can be readily found throughout the scriptures; this is true not just of Christian and Mormon scriptures but the sacred texts of virtually every religious tradition.

This tension—inherent and internal to every faith—belies popular notions that religion is either intrinsically peaceful or fundamentally violent in nature. To say that all religion—or even any particular religious tradition—is entirely loving and nonviolent on the one hand or intolerant and crusading on the other is irresponsibly reductionistic. It is to capture one strand of belief and behavior while neglecting a considerable amount of historical and theological nuance, complexity, and richness. The fact that both civil rights workers and Ku Klux Klansmen were churchgoing southern evangelical Christians in the 1960s is only one example of how the same religious tradition can be pulled in opposite directions by people who sincerely believe they are doing God's will.[3]

In contests over the correct interpretation of a particular religious tradition, people on either side often accuse the other of manipulating the true essence of the faith. In fact, religion is always multilayered, internally pluralistic, and contested—especially when it comes to questions of peace and violence. Scott Appleby, one of the preeminent scholars in the emerging field of religion, conflict, and peacebuilding, has memorably labeled this phenomenon "the ambivalence of the sacred." Appleby contends that religion, precisely because it deals with matters of the divine, calls on its adherents to make (or be prepared to make) the ultimate commitment and sacrifice on behalf of what is perceived as the godly cause. In its unmoderated form, religion naturally produces what he terms "militants." Appleby's key insight is that religious militancy takes different forms, ranging from mass violence to self-sacrificing nonviolence: "Militant religion, in short, produces a broad spectrum of religious actors with differing attitudes toward the pursuit of political power and the use of violence." He continues:

> Both the extremists and the peacemaker are militants. Both types "go to extremes" of self-sacrifice in devotion to the sacred; both claim to be "radical," or rooted in and renewing the fundamental truths of their religious traditions. In these ways they distinguish themselves from people not motivated by religious commitments—and from the vast middle ground of believers. Yet the peacemaker renounces violence as an acceptable extreme and restricts the war against oppressors and injustice to noncoercive means. The extremist, by contrast, exalts violence as a religious prerogative or even as a spiritual *imperative* in the quest for justice.

The ultimate difference between religious peacemakers and extremists, Appleby concludes, is not in their commitment but rather in their orientation. The peacemaker is motivated by and seeks "reconciliation or

---

3. See Charles Marsh, *God's Long Summer: Stories of Faith and Civil Rights* (Princeton, N.J.: Princeton University Press, 1997).

peaceful coexistence with the enemy [as] the ultimate goal," whereas the extremist "is committed primarily to victory over the enemy," and thus may sanction the use of violence as a godly means of achieving his or her sacred ends.[4]

Naturally, not every religious person who engages in any form of violence is rightly labeled an "extremist." There are clearly qualitative distinctions to be made between the genocidaire and the proponent of a strict just war theory—let alone someone acting in pure self-defense to preserve either her own life or that of an innocent bystander. Many religious peacemakers would allow for some violence in some situations, just as most religious people who employ violence do so grudgingly, for specific and limited purposes, and with the hope that it will effectively secure a greater and more lasting peace. We are handicapped by what Joseph Smith called "the little, narrow prison . . . [of] a crooked, broken, scattered and imperfect language,"[5] but we should not allow our analysis of so weighty a topic to be as wooden, clunky, and two-dimensional as the simple terms "war" and "peace," or even "violence" and "nonviolence." Our analyses should always be cognizant of the complexity, even messiness, of the human condition.

---

4. R. Scott Appleby, *The Ambivalence of the Sacred: Religion, Violence, and Reconciliation* (Lanham, M.d.: Rowman & Littlefield, 2000), 7, 11, 13. Appleby's argument builds on foundational insights in Paul Tillich, *Dynamics of Faith* (New York: Harper & Brothers, 1957); and Charles S. Liebman, "Extremism as a Religious Norm," *Journal for the Scientific Study of Religion* 22 (March 1983): 75–86. Martin Luther King Jr. offered a parallel insight when he accepted the label "extremist" in his classic "Letter from a Birmingham Jail" (King uses the word "extremist" where Appleby uses "militant"): "But though I was initially disappointed at being categorized as an extremist, as I continued to think about the matter I gradually gained a measure of satisfaction from the label. Was not Jesus an extremist for love. . . . Was not Amos an extremist for justice. . . . Was not Paul an extremist for the Christian gospel. . . . So the question is not whether we will be extremists, but what kind of extremists we will be. Will we be extremists for hate or for love? Will we be extremists for the preservation of injustice or for the extension of justice?" Martin Luther King Jr., *Why We Can't Wait* (New York: Signet Classics, 2000 [1963]), 76–77.

5. Joseph Smith Jr., *History of The Church of Jesus Christ of Latter-day Saints*, 7 vols., ed. B. H. Roberts (Salt Lake City: Deseret Book, 1957), 1:299. See Richard L. Bushman, "The Little, Narrow Prison of Language: The Rhetoric of Revelation," in *Religious Educator* 1, no. 1 (2000): 90–104.

The essays in *War and Peace in Our Time* reveal such "messiness"— in this case, the particular Mormon contours of "the ambivalence of the sacred" described by Appleby. The contributors reveal how the scriptures, prophetic teachings, history, culture, rituals, and traditions of Mormonism have been, are, and can be used as warrants for a wide range of activities and attitudes—from radical pacifism to legitimation of the United States' use of preemptive force against its enemies. With the exception of this introduction and the two concluding chapters, earlier versions of these essays were delivered as papers at a conference held at Claremont Graduate University, in Claremont, California, on March 18–19, 2011, with sponsorship from the School of Religion and the LDS Council on Mormon Studies at Claremont Graduate University, as well as the Joan B. Kroc Institute for International Peace Studies at the University of Notre Dame (where I worked at the time). Organized by Richard Bushman and myself, with assistance from Loyd Ericson, the conference sought to facilitate a robust discussion on issues we considered both relevant and important. As a relatively young religion that for much of its early history was simply struggling for survival, Mormonism, we felt, had not yet fully grappled with some of the pressing questions of war and peace, with all of the attendant theological, social, and political ramifications. Given the LDS Church's relative stability and measure of prominence and influence in the early twenty-first century, we thought the time was ripe to examine the historical, spiritual, and cultural resources within the tradition that provide a foundation for constructive dialogue about how individual Latter-day Saints and the institutional Church orient themselves in a world of violence. While recognizing the important contributions of previous scholars who had offered analysis and reflection on the topic, we believed there remained a pressing need for a more sustained and collaborative examination of Mormon perspectives on war and peace, drawing on both historical-social scientific research as well as more normative (theological and ethical) arguments.[6]

---

6. For a sampling of previous scholarship on the topic, see D. Michael Quinn, "The Mormon Church and the Spanish-American War: An End to Selective Pacifism," *Pacific Historical Review* 43 (August 1974): 342–66; Ronald W. Walker, "Sheaves, Bucklers, and the State: Mormon Leaders Respond to the Dilemmas of War," *Sunstone* 7, no. 4 (July/August 1982): 43–56; Eugene England, *Making Peace: Personal Essays* (Salt Lake City: Signature Books, 1995); Valerie M. Hudson and Kerry M. Kartchner, eds., *Moral Perspectives on U.S. Security Policy: Views from the*

Most of the contributors to this volume came to us by responding to an open call for papers; a few were specifically invited to participate. In all cases, we selected participants who would argue from a distinctively Mormon perspective. Certainly there are powerful arguments that can be and have been made from a variety of non-Mormon epistemological grounds, both religious and secular, but the challenge of the conference was to see what, if anything, Mormonism had to say about peace and violence on its own terms. This means that the claims made here are predicated on the assumption that Latter-day Saint scripture and prophetic teaching is normative and authoritative—though certainly the various authors' readings and interpretations of the tradition vary considerably.[7]

It will soon become apparent that the essays in this volume are decidedly weighted toward what we might oversimplify as the peace camp. (In truth, all of the authors would insist that they are dedicated to the pursuit of peace.) To some degree this reflected the balance of submissions we received from our original call for papers, but frankly it is also more intentional than that. As conference organizers and now editors we operated on the assumption that, speaking broadly, in the past century active members of the LDS Church have been inclined to support war as a legitimate and perhaps the most effective means of resolving international disputes, both as a general principle but especially when involving their home country. Though Latter-day Saints

LDS Community (Provo, Utah: David M. Kennedy Center for International Studies, Brigham Young University, 1995); Grant Underwood, "Pacifism and Mormonism: A Study in Ambiguity," in *Proclaim Peace: Christian Pacifism from Unexpected Quarters*, ed. Theron F. Schlabach and Richard T. Hughes (Urbana: University of Illinois Press, 1997), 139–56; Patrick Q. Mason, "The Possibilities of Mormon Peacebuilding," *Dialogue: A Journal of Mormon Thought* 37, no. 1 (Spring 2004): 12–45; and Kerry M. Kartchner and Valerie M. Hudson, eds., *Wielding the Sword while Proclaiming Peace: Views from the LDS Community on Reconciling the Demands of National Security with the Imperatives of Revealed Truth* (Provo, Utah: David M. Kennedy Center for International Studies, Brigham Young University, 2004).

7. As a result, this is thoroughly a LDS collection: we had only limited representation from the Community of Christ at the conference, and none of the essays in this volume hail from that tradition. Future research systematically comparing the historical and theological development of the Church of Jesus Christ of Latter-day Saints and Community of Christ on issues of war and peace would be most instructive, particularly given the Community of Christ's recent adoption of peace as a central part of their world mission.

would certainly always prefer peace to war, our sense is that they are, as a group, somewhat dubious about the efficacy of nonviolent alternatives ranging from pacifism to conscientious objection to robust internationalism. At least within the United States, Mormons serve in disproportionate numbers in the armed forces and national security apparatus. Furthermore, LDS Church leaders publicly supported every major American war in the twentieth and twenty-first centuries, which correlated with (and perhaps caused) a high level of support for war among the general Mormon public. For instance, Utah Mormons supported the recent Iraq War "almost as an article of faith," according to one report, even when the war's popularity among the general American public began to wane.[8] In putting together the conference, and then this volume, we were uninterested in encouraging yet another set of competing monologues on a subject that has seen too much of opposing camps caricaturing and dismissing one another from afar. We did, however, seek to privilege perspectives that provided a counterweight and constructive alternatives to prevailing opinions among Latter-day Saints regarding the use of violent force. What emerged was an impressive—though certainly not exhaustive—range of informed perspectives on the issue, many of which are shaped by front-line experience with either war or nonviolent activism.

The volume is organized in four parts, with an attempt to group the essays together methodologically and thematically in a way that places them in conversation with one another. We specifically avoided lumping all the "pro-peace" and "pro-war" essays together—in part because those labels are far too blunt an instrument and the authors'

---

8. In a January 2006 poll commissioned by the *Salt Lake Tribune*, 73% of self-identified Mormons in Utah supported President Bush's conduct of the war, while about 62% of non-Mormons in the state said they disapproved. Matthew D. LaPlante, "Utahns and the War: A Religious Divide," *Salt Lake Tribune*, January 29, 2006. A year later, support among Utah Mormons for the war had plummeted 21 points, to 44% (still considerably above the national and non-Mormon Utahn numbers). Some observers explained the precipitous decline in Mormon support for the war by pointing to the influence of a speech given by President Gordon B. Hinckley in October 2006 at Brigham Young University in which he reflected on the terrible costs of war, though he never specifically mentioned Iraq or President Bush. LaPlante, "Utah's LDS No Longer Firmly Back Iraq War," *Salt Lake Tribune*, March 25, 2007. The observations here focus on American Mormons—much more study is needed on the attitudes of Latter-day Saints in other nations.

thinking is far too rich to be pigeonholed that way. Even more, we wanted the volume, like the conference, to embody a model of spirited dialogue rather than the reification of entrenched positions.

The essays in the first section deal primarily with interpretations of LDS scripture and doctrine, with a particular emphasis on the Book of Mormon. David Pulsipher leads things off by employing the Book of Mormon's story of the Ammonites (or the Anti-Nephi-Lehies) to problematize both Mormon pacifism and just war doctrine. He argues that the dichotomy between pacifism and just war is a false one that should be replaced by the notion of a continuum or gradation that resonates with the doctrine of eternal progress lying at Mormonism's core. Though recognizing the legitimacy of multiple approaches to the question of violence, ultimately Pulsipher argues for the supremacy of an assertive nonviolence that he calls the "weapon of love." Joshua Madson readily dismisses the Book of Mormon's violence by applying a strong Christological reading to the text, which reading reveals it as an extended testimony against the logic of violence and favors Christian nonviolence. By employing a literary reading of scripture, he deconstructs some of the Book of Mormon's key foundational myths, particularly that of Nephi's violence against Laban. Morgan Deane, by contrast, contends that the Book of Mormon condemns violent intentions but not violence itself. Legitimizing a wider range of wartime activities than any other author in this volume, Deane argues that the Book of Mormon explicitly supports an active "offensive defensive" security strategy that relies on interventionism rather than isolationist or defense-only policies. Robert Rees counters with a lyrical essay reflecting on the books of Third and Fourth Nephi, suggesting that a profound encounter with Jesus naturally leads one to actively work for peace, justice, and equality. Much of the argument between Rees and Madson on the one hand and Deane on the other revolves around which parts of the Book of Mormon to privilege and to see as normative, and furthermore what might be the relationship of individual Christian morality to national policy. Rick Duran combines both personal morality and structural conflict on a "morality-conflict grid" onto which he charts all the instances of both peace and war narrated in the Book of Mormon. His conclusion is that the Book of Mormon is a "pacifist manifesto" that equates the highest levels of fidelity to the gospel with the highest levels of societal peace—and by contrast a state of wickedness with an increased penchant for violence.

The second section moves from the scriptural and theological to the historical and cultural—though, as has often been observed, the boundary between history and theology in Mormonism is fuzzy at best. That is certainly the case in Mark Ashurst-McGee's essay, which relies on a close and historically informed reading of Joseph Smith's early revelations to rediscover Zion as an intentionally peaceful community set apart from the wars of the nations. The early Latter-day Saints held a pessimistic view of the world as a scene of violence and imminent destruction from which Zion would provide not only spiritual but also physical refuge. Jennifer Lindell traces one strand of the persistent tension between scriptural/prophetic pronouncements versus lived reality. Although LDS scripture contains rapturous prophecies about the redemption of the Lamanites, when Mormon settlers moved onto the frontier "Lamanites" quickly became "Indians," and spiritual brothers became racialized others. Lindell's essay reminds us that religious rhetoric and lived experience do not always match, as Mormon settlers acted as typical American frontiersmen as much as they did as radically countercultural millenarians. Ethan Yorgason approaches the topic through the lens of another seemingly intractable conflict—that of present-day Korea. Yorgason interviewed native Korean Mormons and American Mormons living in Korea (typically stationed on military duty). Both groups seem to agree on the necessity of military deterrence to keep the peace, though Americans more readily cited the Book of Mormon in formulating their views on the subject. In general, Yorgason found that Mormonism had little to do with the shaping of Korean political viewpoints, even among active and doctrinally literate members of the Church. Jesse Fulcher, an Australian Latter-day Saint, provides another international perspective, with a focused argument on parallels between Gandhian nonviolence and a Mormon social ethic. Fulcher finds evidence of Mormon nonviolence not only in LDS scripture but also in Mormon history, such as the Saints' nonviolent resistance to the anti-polygamy raids of the 1880s.

The third section telescopes in on the writings and reflections of several prominent individual Latter-day Saints on issues of peace and war. Robert Hellebrand surveys the teachings of LDS prophets and apostles in General Conferences at the time of every major American armed conflict since the Mexican-American War. He charts an increasing trend toward counseling members how to live and be faithful in the midst of conflict, rather than pronouncements on the justness of the war itself or directions on whether to participate in the war. One of the Church leaders who consistently gave anti-war pronouncements from the pulpit was J. Reuben Clark Jr., who served as an influential counselor to three successive Church presidents. His main biographer, D. Michael Quinn, reveals Clark as an unlikely champion of pacifism, but one who advocated the cause with all the zeal of a late-life convert. Quinn locates Clark's pacifism less in nonviolent ideals than in a combination of pro-German and anti-British sentiment, a belief in American isolationism, and a general disdain for soldiers—thus complicating simplistic notions of a pacifism born of "pure intent."

Clark was the last major pacifist voice in the top echelons of the LDS hierarchy, but the standard was carried throughout the second half of the twentieth century by two scholars and lay Church members: Hugh Nibley and Eugene England. Boyd Petersen details Nibley's disgust with the ineptitude, greed, and cavalier disregard for human life that he observed as an intelligence officer in Europe during World War II. Nibley's personal experience with the horrors of war, paired with his mastery of scripture and ancient history, led him to produce a series of devastating critiques of war in both personal correspondence and published writings. Eugene England also served in the armed forces as a young man, but became disenchanted with America's militarism after the Gulf of Tonkin incident that led to the Vietnam War. Loyd Ericson surveys England's powerful writings calling for an "effective pacifism," which left room for a narrowly conceived just war but always insisted on taking seriously the radical political implications of the Sermon on the Mount and the other teachings of Jesus and the prophets. For both England and Nibley, violence is one of an interconnected web of sinful social practices that Latter-day Saints must seek to eradicate in their pursuit of Zion.

In the last section, we hear directly from a number of contemporaries who speak on the subject of war and peace based from the combined perspective of personal and professional experience. Eric Eliason, an English professor who served as a chaplain for a Special Forces unit in Afghanistan, argues that some wars are in fact just, especially when fought for the genuine protection of freedom in the face of tyranny and totalitarianism. Eliason asserts that violence is occasionally necessary to guarantee security and to create a space where effective peacebuilding can occur. There are multiple valid approaches to conflict, and a simple rejection of all "war" or "violence," assuming that they are always categorically evil, fails to account for the moral duty of defending other people's lives and freedoms. Gordon Thomasson provides a counternarrative to Eliason based on his decades of experience as an outspoken advocate for conscientious objection and pacifism. He calls on Mormons to make an active and concerted effort to resist war, according to the 1833 revelation that unequivocally commanded the Saints to "renounce war and proclaim peace" (D&C 98:16). Similarly, Ron Madson, who protested against the war in Afghanistan that Eliason participated in, argues that since the early days of the Church Latter-day Saints have generally failed to keep the "immutable covenant" of peace outlined in section 98 of the Doctrine and Covenants. Madson laments and condemns what he sees as Mormon capitulation to the militarism of the state. The last essay in this section comes from a group of national security practitioners who make an extended argument for the correspondence of LDS teaching and active participation in national defense—taking into consideration many of the theological and moral conundrums that they deal with on a daily basis. Two of the authors, Kerry Kartchner and Eric Jensen, offered comments as part of a panel discussion at the conference; we have decided to reprint their formal essay, previously published in the online journal *SquareTwo*, in its entirety. The paradoxes raised by these national security practitioners, along with a consideration of the tragedy of the Jaredites, help frame Richard Bushman's benedictory comments in the volume's final, poignant reflection.

While we are proud of the collection of essays offered here, and believe that the reader will find much to provoke further thinking and stir the conscience, we recognize that this volume is by no means exhaustive in its approach and findings. There are, in fact, significant gaps that we hope will be closed by future scholars. This volume does not offer a systematic Mormon theology of war and peace, nor a comprehensive history of Mormon engagement in war and/or peace movements. For the most part, this collection does not grapple with the exceedingly complicated questions related to establishing what peace scholars call "positive peace"—namely a society that not only rejects outright war but all forms of structural and cultural violence including racism, poverty, gender discrimination, and ecological destruction. With a handful of exceptions, the essays here are highly Americentric—what do Latter-day Saints in Europe, or Latin America, or sub-Saharan Africa think about these issues? The authors are without exception white, middle-class, and well-educated—in short, not the types of people who typically find themselves at the point of the spear. Furthermore, our contributors (not to mention editors) are overwhelmingly male. While that fact in itself is not necessarily discrediting, there is little here that considers the unique perspectives, attitudes, and experiences of women—whether as active supporters or opponents of war; as readers and interpreters of scripture regarding war and peace; as mothers, wives, daughters, and sisters of men who go to war (not to mention the increasing number of women who themselves go to war); or as victims of war, a tragically but increasingly relevant subject given the rising rate of gender-based violence in conflict zones. We need more gendered analyses of war and peace, including studies considering the role of violence in the construction of Mormon masculine identity. In short, while we believe the essays in this volume advance the conversation considerably, we acknowledge our limitations and invite others to build on the work done here.

This volume is dedicated to the memory of contributor Jennifer Lindell. Jen was in the final stages of completing her master's degree in history at San Diego State University when she presented her paper at our conference. Although not herself LDS, she had taken a keen interest in Mormon history and had planned to continue her study of Mormon-Indian relations in a doctoral program. Her life and career were tragically cut short, however, as she died from cystic fibrosis only two months after the conference. We all benefited from Jen's insightful analysis and had looked forward to many more conversations over the years. We're very proud, then, that her published essay in this volume will be part of the legacy she leaves behind, speaking not only historically but prophetically about the challenge for religious believers to transcend their earthbound cultures of violence and live up to their best ideals of tolerance, compassion, and peace.

Part I

Scriptural & Doctrinal Interpretations

1

The Ammonite Conundrum

J. David Pulsipher

I once participated on a panel entitled "To War or Not to War." My presentation was only tangentially related to the topic (the conference organizers apparently didn't know where to put me), but my participation afforded a front-row seat to a fierce contest of ideas, egged on in part by the dichotomous title of the panel. One panelist presented a thoughtful but scathing critique of the Mormon cultural inclination to support state-sponsored warfare. Another responded with a poignant but pointed defense of recent military action as a catalyst for positive change. Both were civil but passionate. And each believed his perspective was divinely sanctioned, appealing to latter-day scriptures and prophetic statements to bolster his position. For me, their exchange exposed two seemingly irreconcilable theories of violence within our tradition—pacifism and just warfare—and highlighted how complex such issues are for students of Latter-day Saint theology and practice, as well as how difficult it is to resolve the inevitable contradictions with appeals to simple but ultimately constraining polarities.

Latter-day Saint pacifists, for example, must exercise extraordinary agility to make their case. Crafting an argument against *any* violence—even defensive warfare—requires navigating a scriptural minefield, dodging or diffusing potentially explosive verses. The Book of Mormon, with its iconic and popular warrior-prophets, contains the most hazards. Compiled by a seasoned general, the text often exudes a just war sensibility. To diffuse the power of that story, Latter-day Saint pacifists resort to close and complex readings of the text—arguing that a careful observation of the larger Book of Mormon narrative speaks to the futility of violence, its endless cycles, and its inability to achieve lasting peace. Book of Mormon battles are *descriptions* of calamities that befall immoral societies rather than *prescriptions* for righteous defense. Thus, by such interpretations, the text is clearly anti-war—in spirit if not always in letter.[1]

Such interpretations are instructive, even persuasive. But the extreme care with which they must be articulated is similar to the arguments of some nineteenth-century abolitionists who were forced to appeal to a "general principle of the Bible" to counter specific verses that condoned slavery. Such unorthodox interpretations left abolitionists vulnerable to charges of being "unscriptural"—even heretical—and of appealing to reason rather than revelation.[2] Latter-day Saint pacifists are likewise vulnerable to similar accusations of ignoring seemingly straightforward interpretations in favor of overly complex analysis. Indeed, the careful attention necessary to understand a pacifist interpretation of the Book of Mormon is probably too much for the average reader. And even with such care, the text may not support a strictly pacifist analysis.[3]

Both the potential and problems of pacifist interpretations are clearly expressed in the story of the Ammonites (also known as the Anti-Nephi-Lehies or people of Ammon). Their decision to eschew violence, bury their weapons, and confront their enemies with loving prayer—along with the powerful effect those actions had on their enemies—is one of the most remarkable and moving accounts in the Book of Mormon. Taken in isolation, these events seem clearly pacifist.[4] But subsequent developments cloud the waters. The Ammonites later accepted Nephite military protection and even helped fund it. During

---

1. See Joshua Madson's and Rick Duran's essays in this volume for excellent and compelling arguments for reading the Book of Mormon as an anti-war text.

2. Mark Noll, *The Civil War as a Theological Crisis* (Chapel Hill: University of North Carolina Press, 2006), 31–50.

3. This is not to imply that Latter-day Saint pacifists are wrong in their principled opposition to all forms of warfare. As was the case with their abolitionist counterparts, absolute pacifists probably hold the moral high ground. But in an appeal to scripture—as Latter-day Saints are wont to do—the Book of Mormon seems only occasionally friendly to their cause, and just as often at odds with it.

4. Hugh Nibley was the most prominent scholar to regularly apply the term "pacifism" to the Ammonites. See, for example, *Since Cumorah* (Salt Lake City: Deseret Book, 1988), 295–96. This term was repeated and endorsed by Eugene England. See, for example, "Hugh Nibley as Cassandra," *BYU Studies* 30, no. 4 (1990): 112. More recently, Grant Hardy also employed the term in *Understanding the Book of Mormon: A Reader's Guide* (New York: Oxford University Press, 2010), 118.

the extremities of another war, they offered to break their nonviolence vows and engage in violent resistance (although they were talked out of it). And, most importantly, they did not seem to transfer pacifist convictions to their sons, who became some of the most celebrated war heroes in the Book of Mormon. Tellingly, it is these young men, rather than their parents, that have captured the Latter-day Saint imagination. Pacifists may rightly criticize this bias, but there is power—and goodness, purity, and justice—in the young men's story that cannot be overlooked. Consequently, their principled warfare introduces nettlesome difficulties for anyone who would appeal to the Ammonites as clear-cut models for absolute pacifism.[5]

Such difficulties are fostered by a sharp dichotomy at the heart of pacifism. By condemning *all* violence, even defensive warfare, pacifism draws a line that is unnecessarily constraining.[6] While all violence is lamentable, not all forms are equal. The ambitious, enraged, and vengeful violence of some Book of Mormon personalities (the Amalekites, for example) is qualitatively different from the reluctant, selective, and protective violence of the young Ammonite army. An absolute pacifist position, however, creates a distorted moral calculus by which *all* warfare is immoral, abusive, and savage; while pacifism, by contrast, is virtuous, peaceful, and civilized. According to this dichotomy, the Ammonite sons were on the wrong side of the line, participating in immoral, abusive, and savage behavior—a characterization most Latter-day Saints would find illogical, unscriptural, and troubling.

This is because most Latter-day Saints embrace an informal just war theory as the lens through which they evaluate violence (although they are generally unfamiliar with the *formal* theory's intricacies, controls, and nuances).[7] Captain Moroni's typical code of military conduct—reluctant-

---

5. For a good overview of the challenges of applying absolute pacifism to the Ammonites, see Duane Boice, "Were the Ammonites Pacifists?" *Journal of the Book of Mormon and Other Restoration Scripture* 18, no. 1 (2009): 32–47.

6. Technically, not all varieties of pacifism eschew violence in all circumstances. But as the term is popularly understood and applied, pacifism implies a principled position against violence in all its forms.

7. At first glance, just war theory seems a close fit with the actions and intentions of many Book of Mormon warrior-prophets, notably Captain Moroni, Helaman, Gidgidonni, and Mormon (see Alma 48:11–14, 55:19, 56:46, 3 Ne. 3:20–21, and Morm. 3:10–16 for examples). On closer inspection and comparison, however, Book of Mormon standards for appropriate warfare might be even more

ly engaging in strictly defensive war, eagerly seeking the earliest opportunity for resolution, generously treating prisoners of war, and avoiding civilian casualties—essentially captures the broad outlines of just war theory, as does the behavior of the Ammonite sons.[8] Nevertheless, just war theory has its own scriptural hazards and discomfiting dichotomies.[9] Popular applications of the theory sometimes overestimate the effectiveness of warfare, considering violent resistance to be the most sensible response to aggression—indeed, the *only* moral and effective response. Pacifism, by this moral calculus, is on the wrong side of the dichotomy and is reprehensible because it does not seem to resist atrocities such as conquest or genocide. It is weak, naïve, even cowardly. Just warfare, by contrast, is strong, wise, and brave—effectively holding evil at bay while more feeble strategies fail.

Again, a comparison to the antebellum slave debate is illuminating. During the first decades of the nineteenth century, most southerners saw slavery as a "necessary evil"—a shameful but essential

---

restrictive than those imposed by traditional just war theory. See Kyle McKay Brown, "Whatsoever Evil We Cannot Resist With Our Words: An Exploration of Mormon Just War Theory" (master's thesis, University of Edinburgh, 2007).

8. However, even Captain Moroni did not always adhere to such standards—as when he summarily executed the rebellious Amalickiahites (Alma 46:34–35) or compelled his Lamanite prisoners to bury the dead and construct their own prison camp (Alma 53:1–6). As Grant Hardy suggests, Moroni is a "complex, somewhat problematic character," for despite Mormon's ringing endorsement of the Nephite general's essential character, "there is much in his actions and personality that may strike some observers as less than sympathetic." See Hardy, *Understanding the Book of Mormon*, 174–77.

9. Traditional just war theory, for example, carefully distinguishes between standards for going to war (*jus ad bellum*) and standards for conducting a war (*jus in bello*), because once violence has been engaged—even for just causes—it is easy to excuse "any means necessary" to win. The Book of Mormon almost seems to endorse this idea when it notes that the "only desire of the Nephites was to preserve their lands, and the liberty, and their church" (*jus ad bellum*) so they "felt it no sin" to resort to "stratagem" (Alma 43:30). The fact that the author (Mormon) felt the need to justify Nephite "stratagem" is itself a tacit admission that the conduct of warfare ought to have limits (*jus in bello*). Furthermore, the overall actions of the warrior-prophets speak to strict standards of restraint in warfare. Unfortunately, such distinctions and standards are not always observed or endorsed by the general populace (including Latter-day community), which too often resorts to an "ends justify the means" attitude once war is declared.

institution.[10] But as the southern economy became more dependent on slavery, and as militant abolitionism attacked the moral character of slave owners, southerners increasingly embraced slavery as a "positive good"—the foundation of (white) political liberty.[11] Likewise, in its most morally persuasive forms, just war theory acknowledges war is "evil"—occasionally necessary perhaps, but always evil. However, as the economy has become more dependent on military industries, and as militant pacifism has disparaged the moral character of war, many just war advocates, including many Latter-day Saints (several of whom are employed in defense industries), have increasingly downplayed the "evil" nature of war and instead celebrated it as a "positive good," spreading political and economic freedom—even the restored gospel of Jesus Christ—throughout the world.[12] This perspective has never been an official position of the Church, but it represents a popular sentiment among certain Latter-day Saint populations.[13]

---

10. Thomas Jefferson famously described slavery as holding "the wolf by the ear, and we can neither hold him, nor safely let him go." Letter to John Holmes, April 22, 1820, as quoted in *The American Whig Review*, vol. 8 (Wiley and Putnam, 1848), 123.

11. John C. Calhoun declared: "I fearlessly assert that the existing relation between the two races in the South, against which these blind fanatics are waging war, forms the most solid and durable foundation on which to rear free and stable political institutions." *The Congressional Globe*, 46 vols. (Washington: Gales and Seaton, 1833–73), 28:2187.

12. The most famous example of this philosophy was articulated by Hartman Rector Jr.: "In both Japan and Korea, when the troops moved out, the mission president and the missionaries moved in. . . . It works the same way wherever you look. The same thing is happening in Vietnam, Thailand, Hong Kong, Singapore, Southeast Asia, and Taiwan. Mormon servicemen have established the kingdom, so when the military goes out, the mission president and the missionaries go in. And the Lord's kingdom rolls forth." See "The Land Choice Above All," presented at Brigham Young University, June 30, 1974, available at http://speeches.byu.edu/reader/reader.php?id=6089 (accessed February 2, 2012). Over a quarter century later, Rector repeated and updated these sentiments in light of more recent conflicts in Afghanistan and Iraq, predicting the pattern would be the same. See his address to Phi Alpha Theta, Brigham Young University–Idaho, January 28, 2004, video in possession of the author.

13. First Presidency statements are much more akin to a "necessary evil" argument for just warfare. In the first months of American involvement in the Second World War, for example, the First Presidency noted that "the Church is and must be against war. . . . It cannot regard war as a righteous means of settling international disputes. . . . But the Church membership are citizens or subjects

The Ammonite *parents* thus present a challenge for just war advocates in ways that are similar to the difficulties their *sons* create for pacifists. If just warfare is a moral duty, let alone the best practical approach to aggression, how should we understand the Ammonites' decision to bury their weapons and confront their enemies with prayer? And what lessons ought to be drawn from the relative effectiveness of their nonviolence? Does such success suggest alternative strategies or moral principles that ought to be studied and emulated? Just war theory has difficulty embracing such possibilities. Consequently, Latter-day Saints with just war inclinations are often at pains to explain the Ammonite behavior as anomalous and therefore not prescriptive. It may be commendable, they say, even extraordinary as an example of extreme repentance by depraved sinners, but it has no explicit lessons for modern saints living in a violent world.[14]

An "Ammonite Conundrum" thus afflicts both camps. Pacifists cannot accommodate the noble warfare of the sons, and just war advo-

---

of sovereignties over which the Church has no control. . . . When, therefore, constitutional law, obedient to these principles, calls the manhood of the Church into the armed service of any country to which they owe allegiance, their highest civic duty requires that they meet that call." See "First Presidency Message," *Report of the Semi Annual Conference of the Church of Jesus Christ of Latter-day Saints*, April 1942, 88–97.

14. The basic logic of such advocates is that the People of Ammon were highly anomalous because of their deeply sinful and murderous past. Having achieved a hard-won forgiveness, they feared to jeopardize it. Therefore, their decision to bury their weapons could not and should not be interpreted as having any broad application, because most people do not have to repent of such depravity nor fear such relapse. These explanations gained traction during the Cold War until they became relatively standard to Church curriculum materials and other commentaries, although there have been some notable variations. In their *Doctrinal Commentary on the Book of Mormon*, for example, Joseph Fielding McConkie and Robert L. Millet articulated the essential logic as stated above, but nonetheless expressed a certain ambivalence about the fact that the story cannot be interpreted as prescriptively pacifist, concluding their commentary with a call to peace: "Eventually, men and women must learn the lesson of the ages, a lesson stressed by Mormon just prior to his death, a message he could offer with over a thousand years of Nephite perspective before him: 'Know ye,' he said to the future remnants of Israel, 'that ye must lay down your weapons of war, and delight no more in the shedding of blood, and take them not again, save it be that God shall command you.'" See *Doctrinal Commentary on the Book of Mormon* (Salt Lake City: Bookcraft, 1991), 170.

cates cannot fully embrace the principled and effective nonviolence of the parents. Both camps encourage false dichotomies from which the conundrum springs. Both camps often represent the choice between absolute pacifism and just warfare as a choice between right and wrong (or vice versa)—each portraying the other as being on the "wrong" side of the dichotomy. Both camps often engage in analytical acrobatics to dance around or defuse their own scriptural landmines, thus appearing to resolve the conundrum in their favor.

While such contorted "resolutions" may bolster the faithful of each camp, the flawed dichotomies upon which they are built begin to dissolve in light of the restored gospel of Jesus Christ. For the gospel embraces continuums more often than polarities, and gradations more than sharp contrasts. Take the traditional Christian dichotomy of heaven and hell. Latter-day revelations replace it with increasing intensities of divine light and glory. Moreover, each succeeding realm of being encompasses and subsumes the "lesser"—or, more accurately, "partial"—realms of glory.

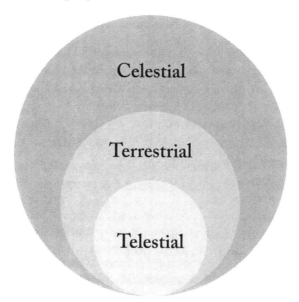

This spectrum is not unique within Latter-day Saint theology. Other doctrines brim with similar notions of progression—moving from partial truths (or experiences or practices or states of being) to greater and greater fullness. The Aaronic and Melchizedek Priesthoods, for example, are both expressions of the same divine power—the first being only a partial (or preparatory) version of the second.

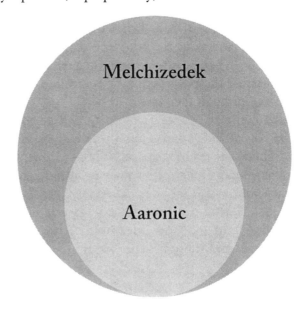

Similar principles apply to the two main loci of Latter-day Saint worship—meetinghouses and temples—the rites of the former preparing individuals for greater communion in the latter. Indeed, the core Latter-day Saint theological narrative involves a divine Father urging His children—both individually and collectively—into progressively higher orders of being, moving from partial to full divinity. Such progressive theology implies that many (if not most) strategies and behaviors are more appropriately evaluated as *higher/lesser*—or, even better, as *full/partial*—rather than simply *good/evil* or *right/wrong*. They constitute a continuum of possibilities that are increasingly "more." More moral. More effective. More complete. In short, more divine.

The principle of progression may provide a key to resolving the Ammonite Conundrum. Confronted with violence and evil, individuals and societies choose from a range of possible responses. Wrathful, vengeful, or cowardly responses contain little if any virtue, light, or truth; but other responses might be characterized as increasingly more divine. Consider just warfare, which was at times the principal (and principled) strategy of the Nephites. While they did not always exhibit honorable attitudes towards violence, at their best the Nephites "were sorry to take up arms . . . because they did not delight in the shed-ding of blood. . . . Nevertheless, they could not suffer to lay down their lives, that their wives and their children should be massacred" (Alma 48:21–25. See also 56:46–47). Such reluctant but firm protection of the innocent bespeaks a spark of divine character. To a great extent, such character and behavior effectively protected the Nephite nation.[15] And through their scrupulous application of just war principles, several Book of Mormon personalities earned high praise for their valor and virtue. Among these were the Ammonite sons (more popularly labeled as "stripling warriors") who, according to just war principles, declared: "we would not slay our brethren if they would let us alone" (56:46). Nevertheless, "moved with compassion" by the "many afflictions and tribulations which the Nephites bore for them," they subsequently took up arms to "protect the Nephites and themselves from bondage" (53:10–17). Such attitudes and actions earned them high praise from Mormon and Helaman—the former describing them as "exceedingly valiant" and "true at all times," and the latter implying they enjoyed divine favor and protection (53:20; 56:46, 56; 57:26). Thus, while it generally condemns the terrible fruits of war, the Book of Mormon also explicitly suggests just warfare, rightly applied, is a divine strategy for resisting violence.

But the text never suggests that just warfare is the *only* or even *most* divine resistance strategy. In keeping with principles of progression,[16] the Book of Mormon is replete with descriptions of less violent, more effective, more sanctifying strategies. Consider the parents of the strip-

---

15. However, just war strategies did not provide perfect protection. Such actions achieved, at best, extended armistices. The long trajectory of Nephite history entails continuous cycles of violence ending in complete annihilation; and it is in analyzing the persistence of these cycles that the pacifist argument has the most to teach us.

16. The Book of Mormon demonstrates principles of progression in some of its key narrative structures. Grant Hardy notes that the Book of Mormon offers several sets of parallel narratives—the separate escapes of Limhi and Alma the Elder, the separate missions of Alma the Younger and the Sons of Mosiah, and the separate military campaigns of Moroni and Helaman—that delineate "a distinction between faithful, ordinary competence and miraculous, blessed achievement." Rather than contrasting right and wrong options, the text emphasizes "both modes of action as virtuous and acceptable before God" and "praiseworthy," although one narrative from each set is clearly more "extraordinary" than its companion piece. See Hardy, *Understanding the Book of Mormon*, 166 and 178.

ling warriors. At first glance, their strategy—in contrast to their sons' forceful resistance—may appear to be "submission." But with closer inspection, it seems better described as an unusual but *assertive* form of resistance. Analysis of the Ammonites too often concentrates on their decision to bury their weapons—on what they would *not do*—rather than on what they *did do*. True, they would not kill their opponents, nor even lift a hand in defense. But neither did they flee, nor submit to their enemies' demands, nor surrender their position. Rather, they went out and *met* their enemies—confronted them—armed only with love and prayer, which turned out to be strong and effective weapons. They *converted* their enemies, in large numbers. The aggression *stopped*. And not just for a few days. A careful reading of the text indicates their strategy of love and prayer prevented further aggression for at least four years, a remarkable stretch by Book of Mormon standards.[17]

What then should this resistance strategy be called? The term "pacifism" does not capture it. Neither does "flight," "surrender," or "just warfare." The Ammonite behavior seems even more courageous, more effective, and more divine. Here we are constrained by the limits of language and culture. We might call it "nonviolence," but even that term does not capture its potency, because it implies an *absence* of violence rather than the *presence* of a dynamic that is more powerful. We need better words. We need more imagination. Gandhi, a master of such strategies, struggled to find a better phrase to express the power he instinctively felt in these methods. He called it *satyagraha*—"truth force." Others have called it "soul force." My personal favorite is the "weapon of love."

Such "weapons" are not mystical or misty-eyed. They are not impractically idealistic approaches to violence in the modern world. Rather—as the Ammonite experience, and the early Civil Rights Movement, and the best moments of the Arab Spring have demonstrated—they can be clear-headed, pragmatic responses to aggression.

---

17. This four-year peace is determined by dating the Lamanite attack on Ammonihah (in the beginning of the eleventh year of the reign of the judges, about 81 BC), which occurred *after* the Ammonite's initial confrontation with their enemies (see Alma 25:1–2), and comparing it with the time of the next attack on the Ammonites, which seems to have occurred shortly *before* the Sons of Mosiah met up with Alma (about 77 BC; see Alma 17:1). This indicates that the Ammonite strategy was more effective than is generally recognized. Captain Moroni, by comparison, was able to achieve only slightly longer armistices—about five or six years at best.

The proof is in the results. If such strategies really are more divine, they should not only be more moral at their core, they should also be more effective (recognizing that divine measures of success may sometimes be beyond our limited perspective). Such strategies should be both principled and pragmatic. And in this regard, "weapons of love"—or whatever we choose to call them—have been remarkably understudied, underappreciated, and underestimated.

Space does not permit a more thorough description of these theories and practices, nor an exploration of how integral they are to Latter-day Saint theology. The essential point for now is this: the Book of Mormon and other latter-day revelations indicate that there are *many* options for resisting violence and evil—some partial and others more fully divine—and embracing the latter does not necessarily mean rejecting the former. Latter-day Saints do not abandon the lesser priesthood when they obtain the higher. Nor do they cease to attend Sabbath-day meetings because they are not as sublime as temple worship. So it is with just warfare and the weapon of love. The former may be foundational for the latter. Some individuals and societies may need to first learn to justly resist aggression—even with violence—before they can muster still greater courage and skill to resist such threats with assertive love. A divine just war inclination to resist evil is thus encompassed and subsumed within a more effective, more complete arsenal of divine options.[18]

Consequently, embracing one generation of Ammonites does not mean dismissing or rationalizing the behavior of the other. As a Latter-day Saint community, we ought not divide ourselves over false dichotomies. We should be wiser than that—wise enough to embrace the complexity of possibilities and expansive array of divine options

---

18. The range of divine resistance strategies may include, paradoxically, some forms of "surrender" or "flight." Both the peoples of Limhi and Alma, for example, decided against violence (although it took several military defeats for Limhi's people to settle on this option). But they didn't fully submit to their oppressors. In effect, both groups launched successful resistance strategies. Alma's people continued to pray despite orders to the contrary. And both groups ultimately escaped the grasp of their captors. From a strictly dichotomous worldview, such responses might be judged as weak or cowardly—surely, a just war position states, it is better to fight evil than to appear to submit to or flee from it. Given the full range of divine options for resistance, these strategies were prudent, moral, and effective. Their oppressors did not prevail—they *were* thwarted—and no one died (on either side). See Mosiah 19–24.

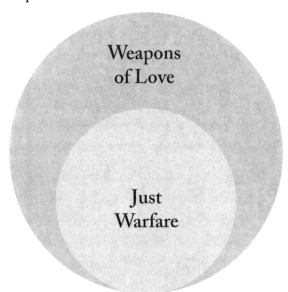

available in any struggle against violence and oppression. Indeed, we ought to have the breadth of vision to imagine stronger and more divine options than the beggarly choices our world most often emphasizes. Embracing the implications and advantages of our progressive theology, the Latter-day Saint community should permanently retire the Ammonite Conundrum, casting it into a philosophical pit with other sharp yet defunct dichotomies such as heaven and hell. Only then can we approach our responses to violence and evil with greater deliberation, carefully weighing the relative morality and effectiveness of various strategies, as well as our individual and collective capacity to implement them. We may then discover, to our delight, that we are similar to the Ammonites—capable of unique responses that are remarkably divine.

2

A Non-Violent Reading of the Book of Mormon

Joshua Madson

Through violence you may murder the liar, but you cannot murder the lie, nor establish the truth.
Through violence you may murder the hater, but you do not murder hate . . .
Darkness cannot drive out darkness: only light can do that.
Hate cannot drive out hate: only love can do that.

— Dr. Martin Luther King Jr.[1]

The Book of Mormon begins with the destruction of Jerusalem and ends with a horrible scene of blood and carnage. Within its pages we find sibling rivalries turned national rivalries, self-justifying national narratives, assassinations, political insurrections and coups, corruption, secret societies, economic and social collapse, the rise of class distinctions, gross economic and social inequalities, murder for gain, the slaughter of children and murder of defenseless individuals and communities, the sacrifice of individuals and communities by fire, torture and even cannibalism, and finally, the eventual collapse and destruction of two civilizations. With this overview of the book, we may find ourselves questioning how it is what it purports to be—a testament of Christ—when it also offers such a poignant testament of a civilization's relentless blood-soaked drive to extinction fueled by its lust for wealth, power, and the satisfaction of carnal desires.

---

1. Martin Luther King Jr., *A Testament of Hope: The Essential Writings and Speeches of Martin Luther King, Jr.*, ed. James M. Washington (San Francisco: HarperCollins, 1986), 594.

What sort of testament is this book that spends the majority of its pages chronicling a civilization's death struggle? Is this the witness of the survivors? Or is this the witness of the bodies crushed under the weight of their own civilization? Despite all these voices of violence and death, let me suggest that the Book of Mormon is in fact an anti-war text. From its opening pages until its conclusion its authors plead with us to be wiser, to learn from their imperfections, and to come unto Christ. The book is not simply a collection of stories or morals for us to emulate—it is a tragedy, a warning, and a voice crying from the dust. To the extent that we ignore the warning, we not only fail to understand fully the text but also risk repeating the tragedy.

The Book of Mormon as Narrative

Too often Latter-day Saints read the Book of Mormon as a set of proof texts confirming what we already hold true. Quotations ripped from historical and textual context are memorized as a form of "scripture mastery." In Sunday School classes, isolated sections of scripture are correlated with predetermined doctrinal positions, missing the larger patterns and themes that are only understood with context, depth, and breadth of reading. The danger here is that a text interpreted without its context can become a pretext to divert attention away from the larger message, thus stripping the scripture of any truly prophetic quality.

In discovering the anti-war message of the Book of Mormon, I have tried to read the text as a narrative. New Testament scholar N. T. Wright has suggested that the Bible should be read as a narrative. Specifically, he suggests seeing the Bible as a five-act play where

> [t]he earlier parts of the story are to be told precisely as the earlier parts of the story. We do not read Genesis 1 and 2 as though the world were still like that; we do not read Genesis 3 as though igno-rant of Genesis 12, of Exodus, or indeed of the gospels. Nor do we read the gospels as though we were ignorant of the fact that they are written precisely in order to make the transition from Act 4 to Act 5, the Act in which we are now living and in which we are to make our own unique, unscripted and yet obedient improvisation.[2]

---

2. N. T. Wright, "How Can the Bible be Authoritative? (The Laing Lecture for 1989)," *Vox Evangelica* 21 (1991): 7–32. Grant Hardy asserts that "the starting point for all serious readers of the Book of Mormon has to be the recognition that

In a more direct literary example, to understand the tragedy of *Hamlet* we must finish the play and see the results of violence and vengeance in the dead bodies of Ophelia, Polonius, Laertes, and even Hamlet. To focus only on the violence without its consequences and resolution is to miss not only the literary trajectory of the narrative but also its underlying message.

Narratives are how we perceive and relate to the world. They typically follow a basic structure, having a beginning, middle, and end. When reading a story or play we do not fully form our conclusions about the work's theme and intent until the end. This is reading the text *literarily* instead of simply reading it *literally*. The Book of Mormon is a narrative by design and is meant to be read as a whole. Mormon, the primary narrator, confirms that there is an intent and theme to his work.[3] A rough outline of the Book of Mormon history would consist of the following acts: (1) Creation of Lehites, (2) Fall of Lehites and their division, (3) Nephite and Lamanite conflict, (4) Jesus and Zion, (5) Apocalypse.[4] These acts form parts of a larger narrative—and although there are "multiple smaller narratives, some of them pulling this way and that within the larger one, sometimes even seemingly in opposite directions" within this grand narrative, this is to be expected and only a problem if we shrink the grand narrative from its full implications.[5] Therefore, justifications for violence taken from teachings and actions in the third act of the Book of Mormon should not trump the corrective teachings of Jesus in Act 4 and the results of continuing to live as if he never came in Act 5. It is not to Captain Moroni, for example, that we should look for our views on war but to the larger narrative and subsequent acts, especially as they resolve or explain the

---

it is first and foremost a narrative, offered to us by specific, named narrators." Grant Hardy, *Understanding the Book of Mormon* (New York: Oxford University Press, 2010), xv.

3. See Mormon 7 and Mormon 8:5; see also the title page of the Book of Mormon, composed by Mormon's son Moroni.

4. "'Apocalyptic' is not about a god doing something and humans merely spectating. It invests human political and social action with its full theological significance." N. T. Wright, *Jesus and the Victory of God* (Minneapolis: Fortress Press, 1996), 57.

5. N. T. Wright, "Reading Paul, Thinking Scripture," in *Scripture's Doctrine and Theology's Bible*, ed. Markus Bockmuehl and Alan J. Torrance (Grand Rapids, Mich.: Baker Academic, 2008), 61.

problem of violence. The reality is that certain parts—or acts—of this story are no longer morally determinative for us today.[6]

When read in this manner, the Book of Mormon presents a strong critique of violence as a solution to conflict. It presents us with a thousand-year case study and addresses the question: how should we respond to our enemies? Ultimately it presents us with two options: we can either imitate Christ in loving our enemies and seek at-one-ment with them, or we can resort to violence, which leads to individual and communal annihilation. As literary theorist René Girard argues, "the gospel simply shows us two options, which is exactly what ideologies never provide. Either we imitate Christ, or we run the risk of self-destruction."[7] In other words, will we sacrifice others for our own benefit, or are we willing to sacrifice self for others? Will we follow the sacrificial economy of Satan, or will we imitate Christ in his voluntary self-giving for others?[8] In the case of the Book of Mormon, both options are presented and the consequences of choosing violence are shown in Nephite destruction. Mormon concludes that "it is by the wicked that the wicked are punished," and that we must "lay down our weapons of war" (Morm. 4:5, 7:4). Or as Girard states, "Jesus doesn't need to finish off all the bad guys. They finish each other off."[9]

---

6. This is largely a question of evaluating truth claims. This approach takes the maxim "by their fruits" and gives it its full theological weight. The truthfulness of authoritative claims are subject to the fruits or consequences of following them, or in more colloquial terms: the "proof is in the pudding." The Book of Mormon history, when read as a narrative, deconstructs claims in support of violence by showing the eventual results of living in such a manner. This reading also values God's nature as revealed through Jesus above others' claims in the text. Claims in support of violence are inherently suspect because they are not in harmony with the life, words, and death of Jesus of Nazareth.

7. Mack C. Stirling and Scott Burton, "Scandals, Scapegoats, and the Cross: An Interview with René Girard," *Dialogue: A Journal of Mormon Thought* 43, no. 1 (2010): 130. René Girard is a French historian, literary critic, and philosopher known for his work on the scapegoat mechanism, origins of religion, and the foundations of human culture.

8. Mack C. Stirling, "Violence in the Scriptures: Mormonism and the Cultural Theory of René Girard," *Dialogue: A Journal of Mormon Thought* 43, no. 1 (2010): 72–73.

9. Stirling and Burton, "Scandals, Scapegoats, and the Cross," 130.

Foundational Narratives

One prominent theme in the Book of Mormon is the power of foundational narratives. To a large degree, Nephites and Lamanites were defined by belief in specific traditions. Those who rejected the "tradition of the Lamanites" and instead accepted the traditions of Nephi were called Nephites (Alma 3:11), whereas those who believed the foundational narratives of Laman and Lemuel were called Lamanites. Narratives are more than just stories that explains why the world exists and we exist as we do—a *retrospective* kind of telling. They also influence what we do in the future—as a *prospective* guide.[10]

The Lamanites' foundational narrative, for example, trapped them in their hatred of Nephites (see Alma 9:16, 60:32; Hel. 15:15). In the Lamanite narrative, Nephites were liars, deceivers, and thieves who had wronged their ancestors multiple times (Mosiah 12:13–17). According to Richard Bushman, Lamanite hatred of the Nephites was so ingrained into their national identity that "[w]ars against the Nephites were to the Lamanites like fighting for freedom and equality is to us. . . . One could not expect them to stop the wars any more than we can be expected to renounce the idea of equality enunciated in the Declaration of Independence. They would not be Lamanites, nor we Americans, if this occurred."[11] It is no coincidence that conversion to the gospel included the abandonment of those same narratives (see Alma 9:17, 21:17, 23:5; Hel. 5:51).[12]

Despite assurances that their traditions were "correct" (Alma 3:11), the Nephite inability to escape founding narratives also shaped their reality by acting as a prospective guide for future interactions with Lamanites. Nephite civilization was founded upon a violent act: the slaying of Laban. This "founding murder" marked Nephi and his family as a separate and distinct people, differentiating the group from the people in Jerusalem and differentiating Nephi, individually, from his brothers as their king.[13] Nephi's own account begins with divine

---

10. Arthur Silber, "The Power of Narrative, and the Myth that Justifies the Horrors," *Once Upon a Time . . .* http://powerofnarrative.blogspot.com/2006/03/power-of-narrative-and-myth-that.html (accessed February 6, 2012).

11. Richard Bushman, "The Lamanite View of Book of Mormon History," in *Believing History: Latter-day Saint Essays*, ed. Reid Larkin Neilson and Jed Woodworth (New York: Columbia University Press, 2004), 88.

12. See Alma 9:17; 21:17; 23:5; Helaman 5:51.

13. As René Girard explains, "to talk in terms of 'founding' is to talk in terms

messengers indicating he would be ruler if he kept God's command-ments (1 Ne. 2:22), followed by divine commands to get the brass plates (3:1–4), and culminating in Nephi following what he asserts is God's command in slaying Laban (4:1–26).

The significance of this foundational act cannot be understated. Not only did this act create a new separate society, it also became the theological and historical foundation for Nephite ideology and traditions about one's enemies. This tradition held that violence can be redemp-tive and serve righteous ends—that it is better to kill your enemies than lose your culture and civilization—and memorialized this into Nephite thought with the use of Laban's sword as an emblem of their nation and power. This same sword was used as a facsimile by Nephi to create more weapons of war (2 Ne. 5:14), and was carried by subsequent Nephite rul-ers into conflict (Jacob 1:10, Mosiah 1:16, W of M 1:13).

In endorsing Nephi's actions, some have argued that "sacrificing one person to save many others is the ultimate reason of state" and that "every society must invest in the sovereign the power to sacrifice the few to save the many, if occasion requires . . . even if he must act on foreign territory against the citizens of other nations."[14] If the sacrificial logic of one in place of the many defines the state and in turn the Nephite nation, it should be no surprise when Nephite leaders later carry out "executions of subjects who committed capital crimes or leading [their] people into battle against brothers and cousins and nephews."[15] Independent of the morality of Nephi slaying Laban, this foundational act became a prospec-tive guide for future Nephite actions.

This belief was married to narratives of Lamanites as a wild and fe-rocious, bloodthirsty people who delighted in murdering, robbing, and plundering the Nephites (Mosiah 10:12, 17). Lamanites, the caricature held, were incapable of virtuous actions. It is hard to ignore the language of demonization and scapegoating here. Lamanites are painted as dark,

---

of 'differentiating.'" René Girard, *Things Hidden Since the Foundation of the World* (Stanford, Calif.: Stanford University Press, 1987), 146. Val Larsen suggests that "[i]nsofar as sovereignty and group membership is concerned, the critical moment for the Nephites must be the moment when Nephi became the rightful king," and "[H]e became prophet leader and king when he killed Laban, acquired the sword of Laban and the brass plates." Val Larsen, "Killing Laban: The Birth of Sovereignty in the Nephite Constitutional Order," *Journal of Book of Mormon Studies* 16, no. 1 (2007): 29.

14. Larsen, "Killing Laban," 36–37.

15. Ibid., 38.

loathsome, indolent, violent, criminal in nature, savage, and lusting after others' wealth so that they wouldn't need to labor with their own hands (2 Ne. 5:21–22; Alma 3:6, 17:14–15). This one-sided propaganda piece, written by and for Nephites, memorialized Lamanite degeneracy and Nephite chosenness into sacred history and acted as a prospective guide for future interactions with Lamanites. This narrative encouraged future Nephite generations to trust in the sword over the word.[16]

In effect, any threat to future Nephite society could be recast into the foundational framework provided by Nephi: just as it was better that the one man perish rather than lose their culture and civilization, so were later Nephites justified in killing Lamanites or others who were now demonized as enemies and existential threats. Appeals to foundational events in justifying violence are not unique to the Nephites, but the Book of Mormon does provide a powerful example of this phenomenon.[17]

Myths, Reality, and Violence

Salman Rushdie observed that "those who do not have power over the story that dominates their lives, the power to retell it, rethink it, deconstruct it, joke about it, and change it as times change, truly are powerless, because they cannot think new thoughts."[18] Nephite and Lamanite political narratives were based, respectively, on the myth of their own innocence and used to maintain that innocence by making their violence become God's violence.[19] Lamanite traditions covered up truths about Laman, Lemuel, Nephi, and God's plan. Nephite political

---

16. It is fortuitous that we have Nephi's record which gives insight into the foundational narratives that Mormon's text may have glossed over. Along with great sermons and spiritual insights, Nephi's writings are also a self-conscious political narrative meant to explain Nephite/Lamanite division by justifying Nephi and in turn Nephite civilization. It emphasized "Nephi's role in his family and especially his superiority to his two older brothers: they were unbelieving, he was faithful; they were terrified, he had courage; they received an angelic rebuke, he enjoyed divine favor; they failed, he succeeded." Hardy, *Understanding the Book of Mormon*, 17.

17. For an examination of how America's foundational narratives contribute to violence, see Silber, "Power of Narrative."

18. Salman Rushdie, *Imaginary Homelands: Essays and Criticism 1981–1991* (New York: Penguin Books, 1992), 430–39.

19. Stirling, "Violence in the Scriptures," 67. See also Girard, *Things Hidden*, wherein he explains the scapegoat mechanism in detail and how the unanimous voice of a community can become, unbeknownst to them, the voice of God.

narratives also hid the truth, disguising the violence at the foundation of Nephite culture and allowing the Nephites—even the most righteous among them—to "unconsciously slide into scapegoating, into the unjustified blaming of another for one's or society's problems . . . maintaining a myth of personal sanctity purchased by means of self-deception about [their] own violence or that of [their] culture."[20]

These narratives were often at odds with reality. Laman and Lemuel were not Nephi's simple caricatures. Note the irony in Nephi's portrayal of himself as one who has killed, though not a murderer—while Laman and Lemuel who have not killed are "murderers in [their] hearts" (1 Ne. 17:44). Grant Hardy notes that "they seem to be rather halfhearted assassins. . . . [T]hey never kill him or even wound him, despite numerous opportunities and provocations." When describing their sins, Nephi "never accuses them of idolatry, false swearing, Sabbath breaking, drunkenness, adultery, or ritual uncleanness. . . . [T]he worst he can come up with is 'rudeness.'"[21]

Laman and Lemuel also show signs of great affection and tenderness toward their wives and children, which seemed to have passed on to their descendants. Jacob notes Lamanites were better husbands and fathers than Nephites, and that "their hatred" was not innate but rather came "because of the iniquity of their fathers" (Jacob 3:7).[22] One could argue that the Lamanites were just as civilized, decent, and receptive of truth as the Nephites: "They had highways, transportation, government, religious buildings, planned cities, various religious customs, government officials, soldiers, outlaws and renegades, and kings and subkings (or 'chiefs'), just as the Nephites had, and were not quite as uncivilized as the Nephites originally feared."[23]

Despite clear textual cues, modern readers, perhaps held captive to founding myths, rarely note one of the more significant truths

---

20. Stirling, "Violence in the Scriptures," 94. One example of this is shown in Zeniff's statement in Mosiah 10. In verse 17 he speaks of Lamanite hatred and bloodthirsty nature. It is only three verses later (v. 20) when without any sense of irony he states, "And it came to pass that we did drive them again out of our land; and we slew them with a great slaughter, even so many that we did not number them."

21. Hardy, *Understanding the Book of Mormon*, 39.

22. See also Hardy, *Understanding the Book of Mormon*, 7; Bushman, "Lamanite View," 85.

23. J. Christopher Conkling, "Alma's Enemies: The Case of the Lamanites, Amlicites, and Mysterious Amalekites," *Journal of Book of Mormon Studies* 14, no. 1 (2005): 115.

about Lamanite and Nephite conflict. Contrary to popular belief, the Lamanites were not the instigators of most conflicts. In fact, nearly all of the major wars can be traced back to prior Nephite acts of violence and Nephite dissidents.[24] The Book of Mormon shows repeatedly that it was Nephite dissenters who manipulated Lamanite hatred toward Nephites and "continually stirred up, recruited, and inspired the reluctant Lamanites to go into battle."[25] After Laman and Lemuel, the truly vicious villains came almost exclusively from the Nephite groups.[26] In other words, the cause of Nephite-Lamanite conflict was as much a Nephite problem as it was a Lamanite one.

The case of Nehor is an illustrative, though less obvious, example. By reading literally we can more accurately evaluate Alma's statement that sparing Nehor's life would cause Gideon's blood to come upon them in vengeance. Alma's record begins and ends in the same place: confronting Nehorite dissidents. Nehor's public execution spirals into more violence with his Amlicite followers reacting violently in persecuting the Church of God, inciting warfare, and burning women and children alive. The Amlicites join with Amulonites and Zoramites, other renegade Nephites, in an effort to destroy the Nephite nation.[27] Alma's solution in

---

24. Conkling notes, "The great battles during Alma's reign were against Lamanite armies allied with or led by Nephite apostates such as the Amlicites (Amalekites), half-Nephite Amulonites (see Alma 21:2–25:9), or Zoramites (see Alma 30:59–43:44)." In fact, the dissenters were of such a murderous disposition that Alma 43:6 states they were "appointed chief captains over the Lamanites." Ibid., 113.

25. Ibid., 116.

26. "Nephite groups: Sherem, Noah and his priest Amulon, Nehor, Amlici, the people of Ammonihah, Korihor, the Zoramites in the book of Alma, Amalickiah, Ammoron, Jacob, Pachus and the king-men, Morianton, Kishkumnen, Paanchi, Gadianton, and probably Zerahemnah. Even when the record calls some of these lesser-known villains such as Tubaloth and Coriantumr 'Lamanites' or even 'bold Lamanites,' we have already been told that their true parentage was Nephite or Mulekite." Conkling, "Alma's Enemies," 116. See also Alma 21:3, 23:13–15, 24, 27:2–3, 43:44, 47:1–6, 48:1–3, 52:1–4, 62:35–38, 63:14–15; Helaman 1:14–33, 4:4.

27. Royal Skousen explains that "the apostate groups in the book of Alma currently spelled *Amlicites* and *Amalekites* are most likely the same group of dissenters, founded by Amlici, and that the names should be spelled identically." Cited in Conkling, "Alma's Enemies," 111. Conkling also makes a strong case that, along with Skousen's observations, the internal textual evidence points strongly to the fact that the Amlicites and Amalekites are one and the same. Conkling, "Alma's Enemies," 110–11.

using violence to end the Nehor problem fails to bring peace and instead only deepens the divisions already begun by Nehor. We are told explicitly that "the greatest number of those of the Lamanites who slew so many of their brethren" were in fact from renegade Nephite groups "after the order of the Nehors" (Alma 24:28). Ironically, Alma's actions led to more violence; his "earliest battle and his final battle 18 years later end with the same story: the dead bodies of the enemy soldiers being thrown into the River Sidon, which carried them to 'the depths of the sea.'"[28] This is the power of "story authority" that looks beyond individual propositions or statements to the fruits or consequences of actions, revealing patterns and themes that we may have missed if we had only read the scriptures literally rather than literarily.[29]

This is but one of many instances of how "justified" violence, no matter how correct it may seem, led to more violence and conflict in the Book of Mormon. Instead of resolving conflict, violence reinforced Nephite and Lamanite traditions and narratives, reducing each "other to objects—eventually in the form of corpses."[30] For one group, the inability to change their traditions led to extinction. For the other, we are left with this ominous statement from Moroni: "the Lamanites are at

---

28. Conkling, "Alma's Enemies," 113. See Alma 3:3, 44:22.

29. "Story Authority" is a term used by N. T. Wright to describe how authority in scripture ultimately does not come from propositions but from larger structures. "Story Authority" recognizes the genre of the text and looks to the meaning of the story rather than atomistic readings of texts as sets of propositions. In such a reading, the story is primary and statements and propositions ultimately serve the story and are to be understood in light of the import of the larger narrative.

30. Chris Hedges, *War is a Force that Gives Us Meaning* (New York: Anchor Books, 2003), 21. Hedges describes this process: "We imbue events with meanings they do not have. We see defeats as signposts on the road to ultimate victory. We demonize the enemy so that our opponent is no longer human. We view ourselves, our people, as the embodiment of absolute goodness. Our enemies invert our view of the world to justify their own cruelty. In most mythic wars this is the case. Each side reduces the other to objects—eventually in the form of corpses." George Orwell also noted this link between false narratives and violence: "war damages the fabric of civilization by . . . stimulating hatred and dishonesty. By shooting at your enemy you are not in the deepest sense wronging him. But by hating him, by inventing lies about him and bringing children up to believe them, by clamoring for unjust peace terms which make further wars inevitable, you are striking not at one perishable generation, but at humanity itself." George Orwell, "As I Please," *Tribune*, August 4, 1944.

war one with another; and the whole face of this land is one continual round of murder and bloodshed; and no one knoweth the end of the war" (Morm. 8:8). Ultimately, the Book of Mormon powerfully demonstrates how violence stems from and perpetuates the fundamental values of a society that are both rooted in mythic accounts of national beginnings and essential to national identity.[31]

Another Way

As we have seen, stories are powerful. They have the ability to shape our reality by influencing our ideas, thoughts, feelings, and even our actions. When stories act as a barrier to change and as a barrier to peace there is only one real option: the two estranged stories must be reconciled through at-one-ment.[32] Separate and conflicting stories were at the foundation of Nephite and Lamanite violence, and it is precisely this barrier that had to be overcome in reaching peace. Because these narratives involved forms of scapegoating, they present a unique challenge. Book of Mormon wars, no matter how justified, rarely ended in lasting peace. In nearly every case, peace lasted briefly, no more than a short period of time.[33] Even Captain Moroni's efforts ultimately resulted in only eight years of peace before violence and conflict renewed.[34] The Book of Mormon suggests this occurred because, absent wholesale genocide, violence only reinforces enemies' traditions and fails to address the underlying causes of conflict.

While violence reinforced hatred and divisive narratives, missionary work or dialogue challenged both Nephite and Lamanite narratives about the other, broke down barriers of distrust, and allowed at-one-

---

31. Bushman, "Lamanite View," 92.

32. For an example of how this operates in the Apostle Paul's writings, see John Howard Yoder, *He Came Preaching In Peace* (Eugene, Ore.: Wipf and Stock Publishers, 1998), 112.

33. The Book of Mormon suggests that wars occurred for most of their history (1 Ne. 12, Jarom 1:13, Alma 48:22). There are, however, a handful of verses indicating periods of peace that occurred usually for short periods of time. Notice Mormon's emphasis illustrating how rare these periods may have been in Alma 48:20, "*even for* the space of four years." See also Mosiah 6:7 "three years"; Mosiah 7:1 "three years"; Mosiah 19:29 "two years"; Mormon 1:12 "four years."

34. In this instance, war renews and Nephites lose half their lands. In the end, it was not Nephite just war that ended the conflict and brought peace, but the power of the word. See Alma 62:42–43, 63:14–15; Helaman 4:16, 5:50–52.

ment and peace to occur. The mission of Ammon and his brothers to the Lamanites, specifically in defiance of Nephite cultural stereotypes, ultimately demonstrates that acts of love and service can break through false cultural narratives, unite kingdoms, and convert thousands to Christianity where violence could not. While these conversions did not permanently end war, they "showed how peace was to be achieved—by conversion to Christ and to the *correct* story of the nation's founding. Their work set the pattern for later conversions by Nephi and Lehi, the sons of Helaman."[35] In the end, Nephite just wars did not bring peace, whereas those like Ammon who rejected their culture's political narratives and hatred did— thus resulting in many Lamanites giving up war entirely, and in one case ended with Lamanites voluntarily handing over land that could not be retaken through violence (Hel. 4:16–19, 5:51–52).

The only basis for lasting peace was through dialogue involving a conversion to Christ, laying down weapons of war, and giving up false narratives. Despite political narratives that trapped Book of Mormon peoples into cycles of violence, they also had another tradition that allowed them to escape their cognitive prison. What allowed the sons of Mosiah, Lehi and Nephi, and numerous Lamanites to overcome their foundational narratives and myths about each other was ultimately Christ. They talked of Christ, rejoiced in Christ, preached of Christ, and longed for the day they would hear his voice (2 Ne. 11:4, 25:25–27). They taught that when he came, his words would "be the law which ye shall do" (1 Ne. 13:40–41; 2 Ne. 26:1, 32:6).

At the center of the Book of Mormon we find a resurrected Christ who interrupts the narrative and compels us to reinterpret the entire history and future of the Lehite civilization. This was not an iconic Christ figure but a living person conveying a message in a historical context to a people with a particular cultural and national history. His words and actions were not a set of vague and universal wisdom sayings (or "chicken soup for the soul") but were applied to a specific context of Lehite history. Jesus's teachings are thus the interpretive key to understanding the Book of Mormon's overall narrative. Gil Bailie's observation about the disciples on the road to Emmaus is instructive: "[They] are lost and they don't

---

35. Bushman, "Lamanite View," 91. My reading differs from Bushman in one key aspect: while the Lamanites adopted Nephite founding stories in the most important aspects, they rejected the logic that it is better that another perish and offered their own lives instead.

have a story and Jesus intercepts them and with a few depth-strokes of his brush paints them the picture, tells them the story, which includes the cross, and therefore the story not only can go on, but now has a center."[36] The fourth act of the Book of Mormon—Christ's words, teaching, and establishment of Zion—is that center. This center helps us to understand the broader narrative, including the earlier acts of violence and the final apocalypse to come.[37]

Jesus denounces all sacrificial violence, including war, and references Lamanite conversion and abandonment of war as the quintessential Christian act.[38] As the interpretive key or center of the Book of Mormon, Christ reveals a profound truth about Lamanite conversion. Although they rejected their own traditions for Nephite traditions when converted to the gospel, they did not accept Nephite foundational narratives in one significant way: they rejected the foundational narrative that it was better for another to perish (Alma 9:17, 21:17, 23:5; Hel. 5:51). As part of their conversion, "they took their swords, and all the weapons which were used for the shedding of man's blood, and they did bury them up deep in the earth" (Alma 24:25, Hel. 5:51).[39]

This was not an isolated event but a pattern followed by generations of Lamanite converts who would rather "be trodden down and slain by their enemies" than use violence (Hel. 15:9). The foundational narrative of Christian Lamanites was not *better another die than me and my culture*. Instead it was *rather than shed the blood of my brethren I will give up my own life* (Alma 24:18). In other words, in a perfect imitation

---

36. Gil Bailie, "Entering the Biblical Story at the Eucharistic Table," *Aramis of the 4 Mass'keteers*, http://aramis3massketeers.blogspot.com/2007/10/entering-biblical-story-gil-baile.html (accessed February 6, 2012). See Luke 24:13–32.

37. Not only does a belief in Christ compel such an approach, but the Book of Mormon also argues that we should approach the entirety of the narrative through the prism of Christ.

38. Some have suggested that Jesus's claiming responsibility for natural disasters earlier in this chapter work against this conclusion. Whatever the rationale for a divine resurrected beings actions, it seems clear that as it pertains to us we are asked to forgive our enemies and in this instance to end all forms of shedding blood. Mack Stirling has addressed this issue in more detail in Stirling, "Violence in the Scriptures," 80–81.

39. This pattern was followed by later Lamanite converts on at least two more occasions as converts "did lay down their weapons of war, and also their hatred and the tradition of their fathers." This change was so pronounced that even Gadiantons were destroyed or converted through preaching the word of God rather than violence (Hel. 6:37).

of Christ they chose to sacrifice self rather than others. By refusing to shed blood and offering instead an acceptable sacrifice, "a broken heart and a contrite spirit," these remarkable Lamanite converts were "baptized with fire and with the Holy Ghost" long before Nephites received such a blessing. And this occurred "because of their faith in [Christ] at the time of their conversion" (3 Ne. 9:20, Hel. 15:9).

Fourth Nephi demonstrates the decisive event in how lasting peace can be established, in which both Lamanites and Nephites reject the myth of redemptive violence and are baptized with fire and the Holy Ghost. This seminal two hundred-year period in their history comes as they follow Jesus's teachings by rejecting foundational narratives and ideology about the *other*. Rather than the false divisions based upon class, ethnic, cultural, or even national identities, they saw all humanity as one, held all things in common without rich or poor, and had no contentions but rather the love of God. Here, Jesus "has made both groups into one and has broken down the dividing wall, that is, the hostility between [them] . . . that he might create in himself one new humanity in place of the two, thus making peace, and might reconcile both groups to God in one body through the cross, thus putting to death that hostility through it" (Eph. 2:13–20 NRSV).

Conclusion

The real tragedy of the Book of Mormon is that, despite the Lehite culture of violence, there was always another way. The failure of Nephi and his brothers to find at-one-ment gave rise to political narratives based in myth, and trapped two cultures into a multi-generational cycle of violence spanning nearly a thousand years. One of the saddest ironies is that by taking the brass plates through violence and establishing Lehite culture on the foundation of a scapegoat, Nephi, his brothers, and their descendants were "psychosocially constituted and therefore trapped by the lie of sacred violence."[40] Because they thought in sacrificial terms that it was better that one person should die than that all should perish, they may have had great difficulty recognizing the truth of their own violence and its foundational role in their culture. And yet, it was in those very plates where they could have found examples of others who transcended rivalries and pointed to another way. Abraham

---

40. Stirling, "Violence in the Scriptures," 70.

knew that if there were even a handful of innocents living in Sodom and Gomorrah, the cost of destroying them would be too high (Gen. 18). Jacob and Esau, and then Joseph and his brothers, had violent sibling rivalries that ended in peace and reconciliation, not false narratives and generational conflict.[41] In these stories the brothers, once enemies, destroy their rivalry and become one. The pattern is reversed: neither revenge nor seeking justice, just forgiveness and reconciliation.

Conversely, the Book of Mormon narrative begins with Nephi's claim of killing a man because God commanded it and ends with Mormon pleading with whomever survives the chaos about him to lay down their weapons and delight no more in bloodshed.[42] And in between these two bookends, we find the bodies of those crushed under the weight of the "better another die than me" narrative—crying out from the dust, pleading for us to learn from their mistakes. By repeating the logic of the foundational murder, Nephites did not ultimately achieve their objective of saving their nation from perishing in unbelief. The Book of Mormon is a witness in confirming that those who live by the sword die by the sword, and that violence begets violence.

Because the Book of Mormon is a narrative we must read the "pro-war" notions of those trapped in foundational narratives in light of the good news. To the degree that we have moved Jesus's message in the Book of Mormon to the margins, we too risk supporting violence and coercion.[43] In moving Jesus and his message on violence and conflict back to center from the margins, we no longer read Nephi's narrative as though it is determinative; we do not read Captain Moroni's battles ignorant of Jesus's teachings, the Zion society in Fourth Nephi, nor

---

41. Jacob and Esau, unlike Nephi and his brothers, overcame their rivalry. Jacob transcended his sibling/mimetic rivalry, even offering to restore the patriarchal blessing. "What matters is the outcome of Jacob's thought, 'I may propitiate or atone his face with a gift.' Jacob is returning the blessing that he had stolen, and in so doing he is asking his brother for forgiveness." James G. Williams, *The Bible, Violence & The Sacred* (New York: HarperCollins, 1991), 51.

42. Whatever conclusions we may draw from Mormon 7, Mormon's words should, at a minimum, temper any temptations to use the Nephite/Lamanite war cycles as an endorsement of current military conflicts.

43. There is a parallel here to the early Christians, who lived on the margins of society and practiced nonviolence based on their interpretation of the gospel. When they moved from the margins to the center of the Roman Empire, Christians rejected their previous nonviolence and the church, no longer powerless, sanctioned violence and coercion.

the eventual Nephite destruction. Justifications for violence, taken from teachings and actions in the first three acts of the Book of Mormon, no longer trump the corrective teachings of Jesus in Act 4. By understanding and living in light of this new narrative we can thus hopefully avoid continuing to live as if Jesus never came and thereby also avoid the mass destruction detailed in the final act of the Book of Mormon narrative.

Like the Nephites, we can no longer repeat false narratives without risking destruction. We cannot justify our national sins by citing Nephite wars. If we want to emulate Book of Mormon peoples, let us emulate those who were able to escape their cultures' narratives and find another way: Nephite missionaries who repented and changed paths by not letting those stories influence their future; Lamanite converts who rejected not only their culture's traditions of hate but also the myth of redemptive violence—laying down their weapons and like Christ offering themselves instead; and ultimately those who lived in a truly Christian manner for nearly two hundred years. These voices run through the Book of Mormon offering us a second path, another choice. We can choose that better path or continue in the same path that led to the end of the Nephite civilization. If we cannot learn from their mistakes then for all intents and purposes the Book of Mormon remains a sealed book.

3

Offensive Warfare in the Book of Mormon and a Defense of the Bush Doctrine

Morgan Deane

A common assumption made by readers of the Book of Mormon is that God commanded the Nephites to assume a purely defensive posture. Relying upon a narrow strip of wilderness as a buffer, the Nephites often reacted to Lamanite aggression to defend themselves. This reactive policy, along with supposed prophetic denunciations and disastrous results from a few offensives, provide the rationale for a non-interventionist modern U.S. foreign policy. Most recently, Mormon opponents of the Iraq War have pointed to these lessons from the Book of Mormon to justify their position.[1] But through a closer examination of the Nephite decisions, dictated as they were by terrain and technology, and comparison to the modern challenges that face America, we see that this neo-isolationist foreign policy is not only dangerous, but also an incorrect application of lessons from the Book of Mormon.

---

1. See Cliff Burton, "When is Violence Justified?" *The Mormon Worker*, http://themormonworker.net/past-issues/mw-issue-6/when-is-violence-justified-the-curious-case-of-sgt-hassan-akbar/ (accessed July 5, 2011); Connor Boyack, "Preventive War and The Book of Mormon," *Connor's Conundrums*, September 13, 2009, http://www.connorboyack.com/blog/preventive-war-and-the-book-of-mormon (accessed July 5, 2011); David Payne, "US Invasion of Iraq Fails Just War Test," *Intellectual Conservative*, February 5, 2003, http://www.intellectualconservative.com/article2134.html (accessed December 3, 2011); "The Book of Mormon Does Not Justify the War in Iraq," *JinxIdoru*, September 29, 2006, http://jinxidoru.blogspot.com/2006/09/book-of-mormon-does-not-justify-war-in.html (accessed December 3, 2011).

This paper will argue that a careful reading of the Book of Mormon provides evidence to support an active defense and interventionist foreign policy. The thrust of my argument is that the Book of Mormon, where Lamanite aggression repeatedly penetrated the narrow strip of wilderness in quick and devastating attacks, persistently illustrates what military theorist Carl Von Clausewitz described as the danger of a purely passive defense.[2] Furthermore, the scriptures, which supposedly condemn offensive action, might more accurately be interpreted as condemning the unrighteous *intentions* that motivated them. Moreover, these scriptures are not conclusive, since the Nephites pursued offensive maneuvers ranging from "search and destroy" missions to preemptive action against potential enemies (Hel. 11:28, Alma 46:30). Several other passages model "up and doing" behavior with a trust in the Lord while condemning "thoughtless stupor" (Alma 60:24, 33). Indeed, the dominant strategy used by the Nephites is best characterized by military historian Russell Weigley's notion of the "offensive defensive."[3]

Thus the devastating strikes against Nephite lands should provide a reminder for modern opponents of military action. While the Lamanites and other enemies had to move by foot with primitive logistics and were limited to what they could personally smash and grab, modern nations mechanize their forces, communicate by cell phone and satellite, fund terrorists who travel the world, and have access to weapons that magnify an individual's destructive ability. The Book of Mormon's message for us today is not to avoid offensive action but rather to avoid bloodlust, trust in God, and be "up and doing" in the defense of your country. More importantly, the intent of a strategists' heart matters more than the offensive or defensive nature of his strategy.

Passive Defense in Theory and Practice

Hugh Nibley wrote an excellent article examining warfare in the Book of Mormon using the writings of Clausewitz.[4] While Nibley's

---

2. Carl Von Clausewitz, *On War* (Princeton, N.J.: Princeton University Press, 1989), 613.

3. Russell Weigley, *The American Way of War: A History of United States Military Policy and Strategy* (Bloomington: University of Indiana, 1977), 97.

4. Hugh Nibley, "Warfare in the Book of Mormon," in *Warfare in the Book of Mormon*, ed. Stephen D. Ricks and William J. Hamblin (Salt Lake City: Deseret Book, 1991), 127–45.

analysis was superb, it left out several important considerations. Clausewitz, for example, points out that the defensive is the "intrinsically" stronger form of combat; however, he also notes: "the defense enjoys the benefit of terrain, while the attack has the advantage of initiative. . . . It must be noted that [initiative is] infinitely more important and effective in strategy than in tactics . . . [and] strategic surprise has often brought the war to an end at a stroke."[5]

Clausewitz also elaborates on defensive concepts and particularly the concept of a passive defense. The passive defense might be sound if defenders "were sure that a certain number of attacks would actually wear the enemy down and make him desist. But this is not necessarily so. [In a passive defense] the defender is actually at a disadvantage." The attacker's strength may ebb. But the defender is usually the weaker party to begin with, and can less afford the losses. Also, the attacker will usually gain territory and resources. For example, Alexander the Great did not eliminate the massive Persian fleet through a naval battle, but by conquering their port cities with his land army. Thus his conquest of territory along the Eastern Mediterranean drastically altered the balance of power in favor of the attackers. We are left with the conclusion that if the attacker sustains his efforts while the defender does nothing but ward them off, the latter can do nothing to neutralize the danger that sooner or later an offensive thrust will succeed.[6]

I describe this theory so we might better understand the danger and disasters that faced the Nephite nation. In the second chapter of Alma, we read that the Nephite army had to react with "great haste, being greatly astonished," and with "much fear" (Alma 2:23). While the Nephites did defeat their enemies, the call for miraculous help by Alma the Younger in his epic duel with Amlici, the massive destruction of their crops, and generally frantic description in the text suggest this was a near defeat resembling the dangers described by Clausewitz.

The Lamanites wreaked more havoc in Alma 16, where the citizens of Ammonihah and surrounding villages were destroyed before "a sufficient army could be raised" to drive them out (vv. 2–4).[7] Likewise, the famous "war chapters" (Alma 43–63) contain the account

---

5. Clausewitz, *On War*, 363.

6. Ibid., 357, 613.

7. This should be taken with a grain of salt, since it is possible the destruction of Ammonihah was exaggerated for moral effect.

of Amalickiah's thrust along the east sea that captured many important cities in quick succession. And in Helaman 1 the Lamanite army captured Zarahemla, killed the governor, and marched to capture the rest of Nephite lands. Their army moved "so speedily" that the Nephite capital was easily taken. Nephite armies were able to recover their territory a short time later, but under the same military leadership they lost all of it again in less than a year (see Hel. 4).

A quick example from Chinese history helps further illustrate the danger of a passive defense. The Southern Song Dynasty of thirteenth-century China successfully defended their lands against the Mongol threat for almost fifty years. Their incredibly strong defensive positions and capable military families presented an impressively difficult target for the invading Mongols. But the policymakers in the capital were divided between Neo-Confucianists and northern refugees (who argued for an aggressive recapture of the northern territory) and local elites (who dominated the court and wished to keep the armies closer to home). These factions paralyzed the court and created a passive defense by default. This allowed the Mongols to concentrate their military forces at any point of their choosing. The Chinese defenders, in turn, were cut off from a comprehensive and active national strategy and had to defend every point of their territory. This allowed the Mongols to break through the Song defenses and quickly end their rule.[8]

These examples illustrate the danger of abdicating strategic initiative to your enemy. As Clausewitz outlined and Chinese history demonstrates, the Lamanites could concentrate their forces and choose their point of attack. In most cases they moved swiftly enough to quickly overcome large segments of Nephite defenses. In two generations, they attacked Nephite lands in the center, west, east, both west and east simultaneously, and finally the center again. Their offensives progressed in strength as well. The Lamanite assaults moved from a raid that ended in one battle, to concentrated assaults and semi-permanent occupation, to permanent conquests and annihilation. It may have been later rather than sooner, but as Clausewitz prescribed, the Lamanites' offensive succeeded.

But the Nephites fought back and their demise was not a foregone conclusion. They adopted active and, dare I say, preemptive measures to protect their nation. Mormon records the first instance of this in Alma 43. As

---

8. Peter Lorge, *War Politics and Society in Early Modern China: 900–1795* (New York: Routledge Press, 2005).

Moroni prepared an ambush for Lamanite forces, he "thought it no sin that he should defend them by stratagem" (v. 30). Moreover, Moroni preemptively "cut off" Amalickiah, based on the assumption that preventing his escape through military action would prevent a future war (46:30). As with the first instance, this action is presented without editorial dissent, and it is instead given as part of Moroni's stellar résumé. In the same chapter that described a period in their history that was "never happier,"[9] Moroni "cut off" the Lamanites living in the east and west wildernesses (Alma 50:11). This occurs during a time of supposed peace, but it could also be described as a lull or "cold war" between the First and Second Amalickiahite War.[10] In either case, while there were no active hostilities between the two nations, Moroni is lauded for his preemptive actions, ambushes, and active defense.

Later in Nephite history, it "was expedient" to fight the Gadianton robbers. Using terminology eerily familiar to modern readers, they sent an army to "search" and "destroy" their enemies (Hel. 11:28). The particular placement in the chapter suggests this was a righteous reaction to their problem.[11] And particular geographic considerations demanded Nephite consideration. Instead of bunkering down in their cities, or adopting a passive strategy, the Nephites actively sought their enemies as a long-term solution. These particular operations did end up failing, but not because of the supposedly evil nature of their offensive.

Still fighting the robbers a few years later, the Nephite general Gidgiddoni "cut off" their retreat (3 Ne. 4:24–25). Again, this shows the need for a combination of offensive and defensive operations instead of a passive defense. The Nephites drew the robbers out of their favorable position by gathering in their central lands, but only defeated them through a counter offensive. As with Moroni, this strategy is noteworthy since Gidgiddoni is specifically described as a prophet (3 Ne. 3:19). If the Book of Mormon really meant to condemn pre-

---

9. Mormon said there "was never a happier time" during a lull in the war chapters (Alma 50:23). R. Douglas Phillips refers to it as a "golden age" in "Why is so much of the Book of Mormon Given Over to Military Accounts?" in *Warfare in the Book of Mormon*, ed. Ricks and Hamblin (Salt Lake City: Deseret Book, 1991), 27.

10. Using the terminology of John Welch, "Why Study War in the Book of Mormon," in *Warfare in the Book of Mormon*, ed. Stephen Ricks and William Hamblin (Salt Lake City: Deseret Book, 1991), 6–15.

11. The preceding verses (Hel. 11:25–27) describe the robbing, murdering, and plundering of this band of robbers that sought out the old plans authored by the devil.

emptive attacks, this was a prime chance to do so. But instead, the prophet-general commanded a mixture of defense and offense.

The Nephites were successful and righteous in pursuing an "offensive defensive" strategy. While this strategy is complex and debated by both military leaders and historians, it remains extremely useful for our discussion of Nephite strategy. This strategy was used by the Confederacy during the American Civil War, permitting them to choose the locations where critical military confrontations should occur: "Then the confederacy might muster adequate numbers and resources at critical places despite overall inferiority of strength."[12] I contend that the Nephites were successful when they adopted this strategy. They were numerically inferior and, for much of their history, "nearly surrounded" by the Lamanites (Alma 22:29). Strategically they would receive the Lamanite attack. Once the attack entered Nephite territory they would then move offensively to force a battle at the time and location of their choosing. These tactical advantages would offset their numerical deficiency and result in victory. We see examples of this strategy throughout the Book of Mormon. In Alma 43–44, Moroni sets an elaborate ambush for the enemy army, and he prepared defensive lines in Alma 48 by forcefully removing settlers of an enemy nation. But when the Nephites failed to apply this model, they experienced swift destructions and perilous captures of their territory. Examples of such failures included improperly guarding approaches to the land (Hel. 1:18), a lack of advanced defense,[13] and a failure of effective preemptive measures (Alma 46:33).

Many times the text of the Book of Mormon credits God and not tactics for military victories. Since warfare in ancient societies was often seen as a diagnostic of the people's spiritual health, their actions on the battlefield were intimately connected to God's will. In simple modern terms the Nephite generals viewed their profession as essentially "subcontracting" Divine command. Hence Nephi was guided to an incapacitated Laban but had to physically use the latter's sword to behead him. That sword was not only an abstract symbol of divine favor and right to kingship,[14] but was actually wielded by Nephite kings in defense of their people (Jacob 1:10, W of M 1:13). Captain Moroni

---

12. Weigley, *The American Way of War*, 97.

13. Hence the Nephite's complete surprise in seeing Ammonihah destroyed.

14. Brett Holbrook, "The Sword of Laban as a Symbol of Divine Authority and Kingship," *Journal of Book of Mormon Studies* 2, no. 1 (1993): 39–72.

"prayed mightily" for his people but also thought it was both necessary and "no sin" to defend his people by his tactics (Alma 46:13, 43:30). He "prepared the minds of the people to be faithful to the Lord" and in the same breath he "strengthen[ed] their armies and fortifications" (48:7–8). Moroni explicitly condemned and invoked the wrath of God upon those that sat on their thrones in a passive "stupor" while expecting God's divine favor to save them (60:11, 21). The Chief Judge Pahoran told his comrade to trust in God, but absent any command from God to surrender, he advised that a person must then resist evil with his sword (61:13–14). And so on. To borrow a modern phrase, righteous Nephite military leaders prayed as though everything depended on God but acted as though everything depended on their swords and strategy. Hence a discussion of tactics and strategy as a means of securing God's blessings is completely appropriate here.

While the Nephites' "offensive defensive" strategy was effective when properly implemented, it still suffered from one general weakness—it relied upon first receiving an attack, the strength of which could be so great as to destroy the Nephites' ability to counterattack. As Clausewitz writes, it could "end the war at a stroke."[15] Several examples illustrate this point. Ammonihah was destroyed and many Nephites were carried away captive before an army could repel them. Even with Moroni's preemptive action, the capital was lost to the rebellious Nephite kingmen. In the next generation Moroni's son lost Zarahemla twice, and could not recover it the second time. While the earlier failures to adopt this "offensive defensive" policy resulted in deadly raids, it was the later attacks that almost destroyed the Nephite nation.

This strategy had its variations, but the exceptions still prove the rule. The original "search and destroy" missions against the Gadianton robbers attempted to fight them in their mountains and hideouts. However, the prophet general Gidgiddondi lured them out of their strongholds and then maneuvered to destroy them in battle. Earlier in Nephite history Moroni cut off the threat presented by Amalickiah. And while this was not a battle between nations, it was a use of military force to preempt a perceived threat.

---

15. Clausewitz, *On War*, 363.

Offensive Prohibitions

The Book of Mormon does, however, prohibit certain practices in warfare. For example, there seems to be several verses that forbid "preemptive war." These verses have alternate explanations that have received little attention from readers—combined with underlying military theory or broader context, they demand a more nuanced understanding of "moral" warfare. In Third Nephi, Gidgiddoni claims that the Lord forbids them from preemptively going into their opponents' lands (3:21). However, in that same campaign, Gidgiddoni maneuvered his army to cut off the robbers. His "offensive defensive" operations suggest, at least, a more flexible approach than an overly simplistic notion that offensive war is inherently immoral.

Mormon 3:15 also seems to prohibit preemptive war. However, the real sin recorded by Mormon was not the offensive tactics but rather the bloodlust and vengeance that dictated Nephite strategy (v. 14). The seemingly unequivocal anti-war sentiment expressed in 4:4 does not record any saying of the Lord, but can just as easily represent a strategic description. If this is a command against offensive action it is also contradicted by other writings of Mormon. This is most clearly seen in a reevaluation of Alma 48:14. The traditional understanding of this verse is a prohibition against offensive warfare. But a slightly different reading suggests the Nephites are commanded to never "give an offense" except "against an enemy" and "to preserve their lives" (Alma 61:3).

Finally, there is Mormon's statement that the wicked punish the wicked (Morm. 4:5). This seems to describe the inverse of the ideal to trust in the Lord and implies, unsurprisingly, that making strategic decisions while *not* "under the influence" of the Spirit results in lousy choices with equally horrible results. Here Clausewitz can again lend us assistance with his description of an essential element of leadership called *Coup De' Oeil*.[16] This term is complex, but it basically describes both a commander's ability to "see the light" and his strength to follow it. Clausewitz did not have any spiritual implications in mind, but it certainly applies here. When the Nephites were spiritually darkened, their ability to make correct military decisions were severely impaired. Thus the military prohibition described in the Book of Mormon is not against offensive or even preemptive action, but it is rather condemning

---

16. Ibid., 101–2.

passive stupor, lacking trust in the Lord, and lusting for vengeance—in short, a darkened mind.

Offensive Defensive Theory and Practice in the Modern Age

How does offensive defensive theory apply to the modern age? Put another way, how does Moroni's move to cut off his enemies apply to today's wars? Moroni's preemption operated on a much smaller scale. Pre-modern battle consisted of face-to-face encounters. The armies that travelled to these battles were limited by the primitive logistics of that age. Their logistical limits were compounded by an apparent lack of wheeled transport in pre-Colombian Mesoamerica. But even with an army's damage limited to what they could personally smash or kill, and a nation's limitations in supplying its troops, the Lamanites could quickly desolate many cities before the Nephites "could raise a sufficient army" (Alma 16:2–3). In Helaman 1:19, the Lamanites marched "with such great speed" and captured the capital city, enacting genocide with these primitive means. Today's battlefields stretch over many miles. The personal weapon of American infantrymen, the M-16, has an effective range of roughly a third of a mile. Jet fighters, stealth bombers, and cruise missiles can launch from one location and strike a thousand miles away. And Intercontinental Ballistic Missiles live up to their name, attacking from continents away. Worldwide airline and naval travel easily transport dangerous people and materials. During the Cold War the United States could nominally count on the international order to restrain the actions of the enemy.[17] Now, the United States faces regimes that explicitly reject that world order, support terrorism as an arm of foreign policy, and seek the most devastating weapons known to man. It was this triad (rogue regimes, seeking weapons of mass destruction, and supporting terror) that President George W. Bush presented as

---

17. But even this balance of power produced the Cuban Missile Crisis, with Krushchev threatening to "swat [America's] ass" with the nuclear weapons he inserted there. See Ernest May and Philip Zelikow, eds., *The Kennedy Tapes: Inside the White House During the Cuban Missile Crisis* (New York: W. W. Norton, 2002), 428.

justification for the attack on Iraq.[18] This war is another model of the "offensive defensive" principles described earlier. In Alma 46 we read how Amalickiah presented a threat to the liberty of the Nephites. The actual results of his behavior could not be seen until his treachery and murder in chapter 47, his agitation of the Lamanites in chapter 48, his devastating offensive in chapter 50, and his brother's hellish letter in chapter 54. While it is possible that Moroni acted with incomplete intelligence, I believe he correctly identified Amalickiah's intent and latent evil and followed a righteous course of action in Alma 46:30–32. In these verses Moroni did "according to his desires" and sought to "cut off" Amalickiah. Thus Moroni saw Amalickiah (using Bush's terminology) as a "gathering storm." Precise details of Moroni's specific military campaign are scarce, but the reason for his preemptive action is not far removed from Bush's removal of Saddam Hussein. And it seems fair to conjecture that the kingmen who opposed Moroni did so by labeling him as a warhawk (or its ancient equivalent).

It is difficult to justify offensive action based on possible future events or latent evil, but from the actions of Moroni in Alma 46 and several other places, it is clear that offensive, proactive, and even preemptive attacks are morally sanctioned from the righteous actors in the Book of Mormon. For example, the Nephites at times adopted vigorous counterinsurgency campaigns to actively search and destroy their enemies (Hel. 11:28). And on another occasion, the Nephite government established a military outpost in enemy territory to try and strengthen their position (Alma 50:6–16).

Modern threats are just as real and apparent as were the Lamanites marching on Zarahemla. And just like ancient times, the terror attacks of September 11, 2001, demonstrate that the United States' "narrow strip of wilderness" is surprisingly thin. But unlike ancient times, strategic surprise in the modern age may not simply represent the destruction of a small ancient city, but could take the form of a nuclear attack in a highly populated metropolis. The power of nuclear weapons increases the ability of an opponent to "end the war at a stroke."[19] Arguing for a

---

18. George W. Bush, "Full Text: Bush's Speech: A Transcript of George Bush's War Ultimatum Speech from the Cross Hall in the White House," *The Guardian*, March 17, 2003, http://www.guardian.co.uk/world/2003/mar/18/usa.iraq (accessed May 5, 2011).

19. Clausewitz, *On War*, 363.

neo-isolationist foreign policy based on *the Book of Mormon* ignores the strategic realities that the ancient Nephite and Lamanite nations faced as a result of geography and technology. The nature of modern technology, the connection of rogue regimes with terrorist organizations, the precedent established by September 11th, and the shrinking world of globalization demand that the United States pursue an "offensive defensive" like the Nephites of old. The exact nature of these actions remains complicated and outside the scope of this paper. Debates about the use of hard power versus soft power, the exact scope of our intelligence gathering activities, and which court system is supposed to try our enemies will continue. But based on a detailed reading of the Book of Mormon, the dominant message of the text implies an active defense by those that do not lust for blood.[20]

The Nephite "offensive defensive" solution was a mixture of defensive positions buttressed by offensive and preemptive action. This is especially vivid in Moroni's attempt to cut off Amalickiah and clear settlers from Nephite flanks. None of these actions are presented in the Book of Mormon as being inherently sinful. Rather it was the bloodlust and general spiritual weakness of Nephite society that caused their failure. Converted to the modern day, these principles still apply. **The dangers of a devastating surprise attack have long been clear to American military planners.**[21] This danger has only increased with the advent of nuclear weapons, the breakdown of the bipolar world order, and advances in modern transportation. As with the Nephites, the United States' best strategy is a combination of strong defenses complimented by offensives to cut off threats before others use speed and surprise to wreak havoc in American lands.

---

20. One of the difficulties in applying the Book of Mormon to a modern American context is the difference in political systems. The modern notion of separation of church and state precludes a prophet leading the United States and thus begs the question of what constitutes "righteous" leadership. Likewise, the concept of a civilian audit over the military excludes a prophet-general leading the country or even determining military policy in any significant degree.

21. As early as 1799 American strategists were incredibly worried about a naval attack and seizure of port cities such as Hong Kong by the British in the Opium War. Afterall, Washington DC was raided and burned through this very method during the War of 1812. See Allen Millet and Peter Maslowski, *For The Common Defense: A Military History of the United States* (New York: Free Press, 1994), 99.

4

Imagining Peace:
The Example of the Nephites
following Christ's Visit to
the New World

Robert A. Rees

Imagine all the people
Living life in peace

— John Lennon

Studying the scriptures over the years, I have been struck by how often writers of sacred literature use elements of drama to teach important lessons.[1] In fact, one could argue that to the extent that God inspires and directs the writing of scripture, He is himself a superb dramatist. The use of dramatic setting, plot, tension, and irony in scripture is similar to what one finds in great literature, from the Greeks to the present. The stories of both individuals and entire peoples who begin in grace and end in tragedy, or who transcend sin and evil to find redemption, make the Judeo-Christian scriptures among the great works of world literature.

By its very nature, dramatic literature has the power to engage our minds and imaginations in such a way that we are emotionally drawn into the action of the narrative. A reviewer of Paul Woodruff's *The Necessity of Theater* argues that drama is "as necessary—and as powerful—as lan-

---

1. This article is a revised version of "Children of Light: How the Nephites Sustained Two Centuries of Peace," in *Third Nephi: An Incomparable Scripture*, ed. Andrew C. Skinner and Gaye Strathearn (Provo, Utah: Neal A. Maxwell Institute for Religious Scholarship, 2012), 309–28.

guage itself. . . . [It is] an art that—at its most powerful—can change lives and (as some peoples believe) bring a divine presence to earth."[2]

I was struck by the use of such dramatic elements in my recent reading of Third Nephi, especially as I considered what happens there as illumination on the world today. Essentially, in Third Nephi there is a dramatic presentation of the archetypal conflict between the forces of darkness/war and light/peace. This conflict was central to Nephite history from the beginning as the sons of Lehi divided into opposing tribes, with the Nephites symbolizing the quest for light (as exemplified by their industry, righteousness, and striving for peace), and the Lamanites representing the powers of darkness (as exemplified by their slothfulness, wickedness, and impulse to war). At times these two groups change sides so that the Lamanites are righteous and peace-loving and the Nephites are wicked and warlike; at other times this conflict erupts within the tribes themselves.

Given the near continuous war during the first six hundred years of Nephite history, some have argued that the two hundred years of sustained peace following Christ's appearance in the New World is unrealistic, a clear indication of Joseph Smith's fictive invention.[3] It might also be unrealistic considering the place of war in the history of humankind. As the historian Will Durant noted, there have been less than thirty years in recorded history in which war has not been waged somewhere on the planet.[4] Nevertheless, I believe the Book of Mormon itself provides convincing evidence that such a sustained period of peace is attainable, and it does so by using the elements of drama.

The penultimate conflict among the Nephites between darkness/war and light/peace is symbolized by the parallel sustained period of

---

2. "Description," under the entry for Paul Woodruff, *The Necessity of Theater: The Art of Watching and Being Watched* (Oxford: Oxford University Press, 2008), *Oxford University Press*, http://www.oup.com/us/catalog/general/subject/Philosophy/?vie w=usa&ci=9780195332001 (accessed June 8, 2012). Although Woodruff's subject is live theater, as a long-time teacher of dramatic literature, I believe that the imaginative engagement with written drama can also produce such effects.

3. See, for example, http://skepticsannotatedbible.com/BoM/abs/long.html (accessed April 30, 2012).

4. As cited in Chris Hedges, *War Is A Force that Gives Us Meaning* (New York: Public Affairs, 2002), 10. Of course, this does not mean that war has been waged continuously everywhere. Some countries have been relatively free of war and some peoples have rejected war as a strategy.

light that comes at Christ's birth—"[a] day and that night and that day which should be as one day as if there were no night" (3 Ne. 1:8, see also Hel. 14:4) and the three days of darkness that come at his crucifixion (3 Ne. 8:23). It is significant that the light precedes the darkness (a reversal of Genesis), because it intensifies the darkness. In other words, having experienced the promise of endless light (symbolized by the two days without an intervening night), the Nephites later experience what must have seemed like endless night. It appears that it is the extent and intensity of the darkness during those three days that cause them to once again embrace the light when they are given the opportunity to do so. It is the bold and imaginative juxtaposition of these two archetypical symbols that gives the narrative much of its dramatic power.

Great literature always awakens and enlivens the imagination. Thus, this story compels us to try to imagine what it must have been like to have experienced those three hours in which a "terrible tempest," a "terrible thunder," and earthquakes changed the face of the whole earth—in which cities were covered with earth, destroyed by fire, or swallowed by the sea; and in which people were drowned, carried away in whirlwinds, crushed by falling buildings, and consumed by fire (3 Ne. 8:6–19). Through the technological wonders of modern media, we have a repository of graphic images and sounds of such events stored in our memories, which makes it easier for us to imagine a world turned inside out and upside down by powerful atmospheric, oceanic, and terrestrial upheavals. The violent scenes of destruction caused by the March 2011 earthquake and tsunami in Japan may give us some idea of the kinds of destruction described in Third Nephi.

We are told that following the cataclysmic destruction during Christ's crucifixion, "there was darkness upon the face of the land" (8:19). This was not an ordinary darkness but a "thick darkness," a "vapor of darkness" so heavy that "there could be no light, because of the darkness, neither candles, neither torches; neither could there be fire kindled with their fine and exceedingly dry wood, so that *there could not be any light at all*" (v. 21, emphasis added). There was a total, engulfing darkness on earth and in the heavens: "And there was not any light seen, neither fire, nor glimmer, neither the sun, nor the moon, nor the stars, for so great were the mists of darkness which were upon the face of the land" (v. 22).

Now, imagine yourself, or one of your own children or grandchildren, as a child in such darkness, not for an hour or a day but for three days, wondering if you would ever see light again. The terror you would experience is incomprehensible. No wonder "there was great mourning and howling and weeping among all the people continually; yea, great were the groanings of the people, because of the darkness and the great destruction which had come upon them" (8:23, 25). As a child completely alone in the dark hearing such lamentations, you would be aware that many children like you had perished, perhaps among them your own brothers and sisters and friends.

Imagine crying out in this encompassing darkness, not being able to find your mother or father, or perhaps any other living soul, although you grope in the darkness toward other voices also crying out in despair. You have just witnessed the death and destruction of all that you have known, seen unimaginable terror, and been thrust into the very heart of darkness. What would be your psychological state? In all wars, children especially suffer unspeakable terror.[5]

Now, imagine that after enduring three days of such dark terror, you hear a voice penetrating the darkness, speaking to you as one of the few who has survived the horrific scene of destruction:

---

5. The lead article in the April 16, 2007, of *USA Today* states, "About 70% of primary school children in a Baghdad neighborhood suffer symptoms of trauma-related stress.... Many Iraqi children have to pass dead bodies on the street as they walk to school in the morning...others have seen relatives killed or have been injured in mortar or bomb attacks." As an Iraqi psychiatrist says, "We're not certain what will become of the next generation, even if there is peace one day." James Palmer, "Trauma Severe for Iraqi Children," *USA Today*, http://www.usatoday.com/news/world/iraq/2007-04-15-cover-war-children_N.htm (accessed June 8, 2012). Of course, the destruction in Zarahemla lasted three hours while that in Iraq is now past its tenth year. Another recent article reports, "As many as one-third of children living in our country's violent urban neighborhoods have PTSD, according to recent research and the country's top child trauma experts—nearly twice the rate reported for troops returning from war zones in Iraq." Jill Tucker, "Children Who Survive Urban Warfare Suffer from PTSD, Too," *San Francisco Chronicle*, August 26, 2007, http://articles.sfgate.com/2007-08-26/news/17256954_1_ptsd-war-zone-post-traumatic-stress-disorder (accessedAugust 21, 2011). Not long after the terror attacks of September 11, 2001, I trained a group of counselors in the Stanton Island School District. The day I conducted the training, the New York City Board of Education published a report indicating that 92% of the school children in New York City had one or more symptoms of PTSD.

Behold, mine arm of mercy is extended towards you, and whosoever will come, him will I receive; and blessed are those who come unto me. Behold, I am Jesus Christ the Son of God. . . . I am the light and the life of the world. (9:14–15, 18)

Enveloped in complete darkness, you would instinctively be drawn to the voice of a personage proclaiming to be the light of the world. Nevertheless, the darkness continues and is made more intense because "there was silence in all the land for the space of many hours" (10:2). As you ponder these words from a voice of light speaking into the darkness, you hear his voice again. This time it is a tender voice that speaks of himself as a mother hen who would gather you under her wings of love if you will turn to him "with full purpose of heart" (v. 6). This metaphor is exquisitely comforting to you since you don't know if your own mother is alive, and because you long for her comforting love. After such terror, you cannot imagine what it would feel like to be sheltered in such love, but you long for it with all your heart.

When the morning finally comes, the darkness disperses and the earth ceases to shake, the "dreadful groanings did cease, and all the tumultuous noise did pass away . . . and the mourning, and the weeping, and the wailing of the people . . . did cease," replaced by expressions of joy, "praise and thanksgiving unto the Lord Jesus Christ, their Redeemer" (10:9–10). Your voice is among those expressing such paeans of praise and gratitude.

Now imagine that it is a short time later, and once again you hear the voice, "not a harsh voice, neither . . . a loud voice, [but] a small voice" that nevertheless pierces your "very soul" and causes your "heart to burn" within you (11:3). And then you see something amazing—"a Man descending out of heaven . . . clothed in a white robe" who comes down and stands near you. Once more he identifies himself as "Jesus Christ," again describing himself as "the light and life of the world" (v. 10).

As you listen to the Savior, you hear him teach the adults around you and then, turning to you, he tells them that unless they become like you they cannot "inherit the kingdom of God" (11:38). You hear him speak beautiful words about those who are blessed and you hear him call you and others "to be the light of this people" (12:14). As you and the other survivors of the darkness gather around Jesus, you hear him call for all the children to be brought to him. He asks you to sit on the ground in front of him. As you look up at this man in the white robe with a luminous face, he asks everyone to kneel. You hear him pray in language more beautiful than you have ever heard or imagined, words like the songs of unknown birds and the whisper of wind through great trees. Then he looks directly at you and calls you to come to him. When you do so, he places his hands on your head, and it seems as if his heart speaks directly to your heart. He embraces and kisses you. As you look up, you see angels of fire descending from the sky. The angels embrace and kiss you and all the other children with you, and you all become beings of light.[6]

Now, imagine what your life will be like from this moment on.

Among the things Jesus teaches you and the others who have survived the cataclysmic destruction is that you should cease from fighting with one another—"There shall be no disputations among you, as there hitherto have been" (11:22, 28). He condemns such conflicts as originating with "the devil, who is the father of contention, and [who] stirreth up the hearts of men to contend with anger, one with another" (v. 29). This reminds us of President Hinckley's statement "that war is the devil's own game."[7] (It is interesting to note that "contention" and "war" are linked not only in the scriptures but also in the addresses of modern prophets.[8])

---

6. Gordon Thomasson persuasively argues that what happens in Third Nephi amounts to a transfiguration: "When, at the turn of the year after the crucifixion and destruction, the people gather at the temple and Christ comes down, then he prays, and first the children are transfigured (I know of no other name for what occurs to/with the Nephites than to compare what the apostles witness when Elijah and Moses are on the mount with Christ) . . . (3 Ne 17:24–25), and later the adults are similarly blessed (19:14, 25, 30), and finally the testimonies . . . or keys which the children possess [—all this lays] the foundation for consecration (26:14–20). Not only are—I believe—any wounds from those three days directly healed, but both the faith and the keys are confirmed on these survivors to build a perfect society in which none of them will ever suffer such an horrendous event again." Gordon C. Thomasson to Robert A. Rees, May 15, 2007, in author's possession.

7. Gordon B. Hinckley, "We Believe In Being Honest," *Ensign*, October 1990, http://www.lds.org/ensign/1990/10/we-believe-in-being-honest?lang=eng (accessed June 8, 2012).

8. What the scriptures condemn as contention is not verbal disputation but physical violence or the creation of schisms in the Church. In the Book of Mormon, "contention" usually means an armed skirmish or battle. We are told, for example, that Alma and "his guards, contended with the guards of the king of the Lamanites until he slew and drove them back" (Alma 2:33). Here contention means "combat," not argument. This is why it is so often coupled with "war," as

What is significant for our understanding is that Christ is teaching his New World children, both anciently and contemporaneously, that it "is *not my doctrine* to stir up the hearts of men with anger, one against another" (which leads to conflict and war); "but this is my doctrine, that such things be done away" (11:30). In a powerful rhetorical manner, Christ ties the rejection of such contention, anger, and conflict to the first principles and ordinances of the gospel. He does this by repeating the phrase "my doctrine" six times within a few verses. In doing so, he subtly shifts the focus from avoiding contention and conflict (which he says are clearly *not* his doctrine), to the first steps in the process of salvation confirmed by the witness of the Father and the Holy Ghost, which he identifies as "my doctrine" (vv. 32–36). Further, he associates these first principles with becoming "as a little child," a phrase he repeats for emphasis (vv. 37–38).

This doctrine of avoiding contention is fascinating, because in speaking to both adults and children Christ identifies the contention and war-like anger that led to the Nephites' destruction with the adults, and the peace that salvation through him promises with the children. This is confirmed by his teaching his new apostles the beatitudes, including, "And blessed are all the peacemakers, for they shall be called the children of God" (12:9). Having identified these disciples (and by extension all the remaining Nephites) earlier as "children of light," he now gives them a commission: "I give unto you to be the light of this people. . . . Therefore let your light so shine before this people, that they may see your good works and glorify your Father who is in heaven" (vv. 14–16). Later, he connects the higher principles of the gospel—"love your enemies, bless them that curse you, do good to them that hate you, and pray for them who despitefully use you and persecute you"—with the purity and innocence of children—"That ye may be the children of your Father who is in heaven" (vv. 44–45).

Return in your imagination to the scene in Bountiful: Jesus breaks bread and pours wine and gives it to you and all those present and asks all of you to do this often in remembrance of him. You notice as he talks that he repeats the word "always" many times and you make a promise to yourself that you will always remember him and that you will always, as he asks, "hold up your light that it may shine unto the world" (18:24).

---

in "wars and contentions" (Alma 48:20). Jesus warns against the outbreak of such contention—or "conflict"—as a result of doctrinal disputes (3 Ne. 11:28–30).

When Jesus finally ascends into heaven, everyone is so excited that they stay up all night talking about what has happened, telling one another what it felt like to be in his presence. Thus, they bring the light of that immense day into the night.

The next day Jesus returns and quotes Isaiah. Among the words he speaks are these:

> How beautiful upon the mountains are the feet of him that bringeth good tidings unto them, that publisheth peace; that bringeth good tidings unto them of good, that publisheth salvation; that saith unto Zion: Thy God reigneth! (20:40)
>
> And all thy children shall be taught of the Lord; and great shall be the peace of thy children. In righteousness shalt thou be established; thou shalt be far from oppression for thou shalt not fear, and from terror for it shall not come near thee. (22:13–14)

Suddenly you realize that you are fulfilling this ancient prophecy, that you are one of those whose feet are beautiful upon the mountains, one of those called to bring good tidings and publish peace, one of those promised freedom from the kind of terror that so recently enveloped you. Jesus's message to you is that you and others of your generation have been transformed from children of darkness into children of light and that your society has been transformed from a warring to a peaceful people. Looking directly at you, you hear him say, "And now, behold, my joy is great, even unto fullness, because of you, and also this generation; yea, and even the Father rejoiceth, and also all the holy angels, because of you and this generation; for none of [you] are lost" (27:30).

Because of the dramatic transformation from darkness and hatred to light and love, you and the other children of this generation hold in your hearts a remembrance of the absolute terror of that night within a night, of that darkness at noon, as it were. Because you also hold in your hearts a more vivid memory of being in the presence of divine light, of being blessed by the Lord of Light in the glory of heaven's own fire, you determine and covenant to have peace for the remainder of your days and to pass it on to your children and grandchildren so that it rolls forth like a mighty river for two hundred years.

Had you been a child during this momentous time, imagine what your life would have been like in the coming years.[9] Imagine the stories

---

9. We can get some idea as to how light and love could have transformed these

you would tell to others about that devouring darkness that shrouded you in night and how, in your moment of deepest despair, the light came, first as a voice and then as a ray that blossomed into a person as bright as the sun, and how his light flowed into your eyes and into your heart, making your whole body as luminous as sunlight.

Now imagine that you are older and your life is drawing to a close. As you gather your extended family around you—your children and grandchildren and great-grandchildren—they say, "Grandpa, tell us that story again." You pause for a long moment and then you say, "That was a long time ago, but I remember it as if it were this morning. There are no words in all of the languages, even the beautiful language spoken by our first parents when they came from Jerusalem to this promised land, to tell you what happened or how it felt. But when he embraced me and kissed me, I felt as if my heart was in his heart and his was in mine, as if somehow all the light in the universe was flowing through my veins. The peace in my heart was as full as the great seas over which our people sailed and as vast as the night skies that God showed to our father Abraham. I pray for all of you to feel what I felt then as you embrace the Savior in your hearts and as you feel his peace in your souls." You then take them one by one, as the Lord had taken you and the other children, and you bless them to carry his peace forward.

As their history unfolds for the next two hundred years, especially for a society that depended on storytelling as the Nephites must have, these great events, these powerful personal narratives of light overpowering darkness, would have been told and retold, sung and danced, expressed in powerful poetry, in graphic images, in dramas, in weaving and other expressive forms, told down through the generations.

Of the great transformation among the Nephites, we read that, abiding by the doctrine of Christ, "the people were *all* converted unto the Lord, . . . and there were no contentions and disputations among them, and *every man* did deal justly one with another. And they had

---

Nephite children through Ishmael Beah's *A Long Way Gone: Memoirs of a Boy Soldier* (New York: Farrar, Straus, Giroux, 2007). Beah, who was kidnapped at the age of twelve and, along with hundreds of other children his age, forced to murder others in the war between the government and the Revolutionary United Front rebels in Sierra Leone, speaks of his descent into the dark world of the African killing fields as a time when his "heart was frozen" (126). Through the love and light of caring people, Beah ultimately escaped the horror of his living nightmare and was transformed into a child of light.

all things in common among them; therefore there were not rich and poor, bond and free, but they were *all* made free, and partakers of the heavenly gift." Further, "There was *no* contention in the land, because of the love of God which did dwell in the hearts of the people. And there were *no* envyings, *nor* strifes, *nor* tumults, *nor* whoredoms, *nor* lyings, *nor* murders, *nor* any manner of lasciviousness; and surely there could not be a happier people among *all* the people who had been created by the hand of God" (4 Ne. 1:2–3, 15–17). (Note the rhetorical power of that string of negatives.) As Apostle Orson F. Whitney described it, "For two hundred years peace spread her white wings over . . . the entire people. Nephites and Lamanites, were converted unto Christ, were brethren and sisters, and all socially equal."[10]

Although the Nephite peace lasted for two centuries, it came to an end when the Nephites again began to engage in secret combinations, "began to build up churches unto themselves to get gain, and began to deny the true church of Christ, . . . insomuch that they did receive all manner of wickedness." (The use of "receive" is a telling verb, suggesting that they not only sought wickedness but also passively accepted it when it came to them in its various forms.) As a result, "the wicked part of the people began again to build up the secret oaths and combinations of Gadianton. . . . And it came to pass that the robbers of Gadianton did spread over all the face of the land; and there were none that were righteous save it were the disciples of Jesus" (4 Ne. 1:26–27).

All of this leads them to turn once more to war and its destructive darkness. Even though they know the endgame of spilled blood that destroyed the Jaredites and has plagued their own history, they once more surrender to pride and class divisions, to inequality and injustice, to hatred and war. And so they descend deeper and deeper into darkness for the next two hundred years until, full circle, the Nephites become more degenerate and warlike than the Lamanites. As Mormon states, they become so brutal and depraved that they "are without civilization," a shocking condemnation (Moro. 9:10).

The dramatic narrative in Third Nephi seems particularly compelling for modern readers. By its own account and by the confirmation of modern prophets, we know the Book of Mormon was written for future generations, perhaps especially for our own. As Hugh Nibley

---

10. Orson F. Whitney, "Zion and Her Redemption." In *Collected Discourses*, ed. Brian H. Stuy (Burbank, Calif.: BHS, 1987), 1:364.

says, "Suddenly the Book of Mormon has become as modern as today's newspaper."[11] Or as Stephen Walker says, "History repeats itself with a vengeance in Fourth Nephi, which reads like a twenty-first century news report."[12]

Since the purpose of drama is to engage us intellectually, imaginatively, and spiritually so that we may see ourselves in the distant mirrors of the past, the dramatic narrative presented in Third Nephi places a special burden on us to be among those who work to end war and establish peace. How are we to do this? To begin with, we can accomplish what the Lord and his prophets have urged us to do: "[R]enounce war and proclaim peace, and seek diligently to turn the hearts of the children to their fathers, and the hearts of the fathers to the children" (D&C 98:16). Note the strength of these imperatives: *renounce, proclaim, diligently seek*. Renouncing war does not mean silently sitting by while war does its destructive work. It means using our voices to counter those who argue for and support war. It means supporting those individuals, groups, and organizations committed to ending war. Proclaiming peace is more than hoping or praying for it; it is actively using the energy of our hearts and souls as well as our time and economic means to work for it. As Hugh Nibley elaborates, "'Renounce' is a strong word: we are not to try to win peace by war, or merely call a truce, but to renounce war itself, to disdain it as a policy while proclaiming . . . peace without reservation."[13]

During the First World War, President Joseph F. Smith stated, "For years it has been held that peace comes by preparation for war; the present conflict should prove that peace comes only by preparing for peace, through training the people in righteousness and justice, and selecting rulers who respect the righteous will of the people."[14] In times of war "the righteous will of the people" is often ignored and even silenced. As Chris Hedges says in *War is a Force that Gives Us Meaning*, "States at war silence their own authentic and humane culture. When this destruction is well advanced they find the lack of critical and moral restraint useful in the campaign to exterminate the culture of their

11. Hugh Nibley, *Since Cumorah: The Book of Mormon in the Modern World* (Salt Lake City: Deseret Book Company, 1970), 375.

12. Stephen Walker, "Last Words," in *The Reader's Book of Mormon*, ed. Robert A. Rees and Eugene England (Salt Lake City: Signature Books, 2008), 7.

13. Nibley, *Since Cumorah*, 375.

14. Joseph F. Smith, "Editor's Table," *Improvement Era* 17 (1914): 1074–75.

opponents. By destroying authentic culture—that which allows us to question and examine ourselves and our society, the state erodes the moral fabric. It is replaced with a warped version of reality. The enemy is dehumanized; the universe starkly divided between the forces of light and the forces of darkness."[15]

Another lesson we can learn from the drama presented in Fourth Nephi is that pride leads to social inequality and injustice, discrimination against the poor, violence, and, ultimately, war. Note that it is the reemergence of class distinction that begins the Nephites' rapid descent toward their fatal end: "And now, in this two hundred and first year there began to be among them those that were lifted up in pride, such as the wearing of costly apparel, and all manner of fine pearls, and of the fine things of the world," leading to a "great division among the people" (4 Ne. 1:24, 35).

Thus, an additional step we can take toward ending war and establishing peace is to work for greater economic and social equity, both at home and abroad. President Lorenzo Snow stated that what led to the sustained peace among the Nephites was their willingness to have all things in common:

> When the Church was established among the Nephites, as recorded in the Book of Mormon, this doctrine was preached by them, and practiced nearly two hundred years, resulting in peace, union, great prosperity, and miraculous blessings, greater than were ever experienced by any people of whom we have record. The most remarkable miracles were constantly wrought among them. . . . These extraordinary manifestations of the approbation of God continued so long as they remained one in their temporal interest, or were control[l]ed in their financial matters according to the Order of Enoch.[16]

While the Nephite peace is an ideal beyond our power given the present condition of the world, including our own Mormon and American society, we could at least strive for greater balance so that instead of a large portion of wealth being concentrated in the hands of an increasingly small percentage of the population, there could be a more just and equitable distribution of wealth, resources, and opportunities. At present in the United States the top 1 percent of the

---

15. Hedges, *War is a Force*, 63.

16. Lorenzo Snow, October 7, 1873, *Journal of Discourses*, 26 vols. (London and Liverpool: LDS Booksellers Depot, 1854–86), 16:274.

population holds more than a third of the nation's wealth, and the top 20 percent holds 84 percent—while the bottom half holds just 2.5 percent, and the bottom 40 percent holds just 0.3 percent. According to the U.S. Census Bureau, in 2009 thirteen percent of the population (43.6 million Americans) lived below the poverty line.[17] And a recent report from the Annie E. Casey Foundation shows that 31 million or 42 percent of all children living in the United States "live with families that are at 200 percent of the federal poverty level."[18] We could strive for the kind of society the Nephites enjoyed following Christ's visit by, first, sharing our abundance with the poor, the destitute, and the disadvantaged and, second, by supporting the efforts of governmental and non-governmental organizations committed to eliminating poverty and injustice.

Finally, I would like to suggest that we consider following an even more radical lesson from the Book of Mormon—that we love our enemies. I have been struck in my recent reading of the Book of Mormon by how the Nephites and Lamanites, striving to be Christ-like, respond to their enemies—not with contempt but with compassion, not with loathing but with love. Although some Lamanites and some Nephite dissenters plunder, enslave, and wage all-too-frequent war against the Nephites, the more noble Nephites refuse to respond in kind. In spite of the damage and destruction they experience at the hands of the Lamanites, and in spite of the fact that the Lamanites seek their utter destruction, the Nephites continue to try to heal their fraternal bonds, speaking of the Lamanites as their "beloved brethren," forgiving them easily and often, and continually trying to persuade them to make peace.

This principle is reflected in a 1981 Christmas message from the First Presidency:

> To all who seek a resolution to conflict, be it a misunderstanding between individuals or an international difficulty among nations, we commend the counsel of the Prince of Peace, 'Love your enemies, bless

---

17. "Record Number of Americans Living in Poverty," MSNBC, September 16, 2010, http://www.msnbc.msn.com/id/39211644/ns/us_news-life/ (accessed October 10, 2010). "Wealth Quiz: How Does the U.S. Slice the [Economic] Pie?" *PBS Newshour*, August 12, 2011, http://www.pbs.org/newshour/rundown/2011/08/wealth-how-does-the-us-slice-the-pie.html (accessed August 21, 2011).

18. "News Report Shows Alarming Rates of Poverty among U.S. Children," *PBS Newshour*, August 18, 2011, http://www.pbs.org/newshour/bb/business/july-dec11/childrenpovert_08-18.html (accessed August 20, 2011).

them that curse you, do good to them that hate you, and pray for them which despitefully use you, and persecute you; That you may be the children of your Father which is in heaven." This principle of loving one another as Jesus Christ loves us will bring peace to the individual, to the home and beyond, even to the nations and to the world.[19]

Frances Menlove reminds us that Christ did not say blessed are the peacelovers or peacekeepers, but rather "blessed are the peacemakers."[20] James says, "Righteousness is sown in peace of them that make peace" (James 3:18). Making peace is not a passive activity. It is interesting to note that the scriptures use verbs like "proclaim," "execute," and especially "establish" peace. King Benjamin suggests that making peace should be integral to our lives when he says we should "live peaceably" (Mosiah 4:13).

One might argue that the prolonged peace among the Nephites was possible only because Jesus came and dwelled among them and that we cannot hope for such peace until he comes again; however, such peace was achieved by the people of Enoch and the generations who were born after Christ's visit to the New World. The promise is that we too can have it if we will but choose to do so.

If what turned the hearts of the Nephites from war was the light of Christ, which the prophets tell us is the birthright of all humanity, then that light can shine in and through us as well. As Paul says, "For ye were sometimes darkness, but now are ye light in the Lord: walk as children of light" (Eph. 5:8). Walking in his light, I believe we can work for peace and forge that peaceful messianic future that the scriptures promise. As Stephen Mitchell says, "The messianic dream of the future may be mankind's sweetest dream. But it is a dream nevertheless, as long as there is a separation between inside and outside, as long as we don't transform ourselves."[21] As Abinadi says of Christ, "He is the light and the life of the world; yea, a light that is endless, that can never be darkened; yea, and also a life which is endless, that there can be no more death" (Mosiah 16:9). May we strive for that light and the peace

---

19. "A Christmas Prayer," *Church News*, December 19, 1981, 2.

20. Frances Menlove, "How Mormons Have Helped Perpetuate the War in Iraq: What We Could Do to Help End It," presented August 10, 2007, at the 2007 Sunstone Symposium, Salt Lake City, Utah.

21. Stephen Mitchell, *The Gospel According to Jesus* (New York: HarperCollins, 1991), 11.

it promises. And may we use our understanding of this great dramatic conflict between darkness and light in Third Nephi to once more transform our war-like world into Christ's peaceable kingdom.

Imagine such a world.

As John Lennon sang, "Imagine all the people/Livin' life in peace . . . it isn't hard to do."

5

Pax Sanctorum

F. R. Rick Duran

Does the LDS scriptural corpus offer the broader peace dialogue anything unique? I would respond with a resounding yes, and offer the Book of Mormon as keystone evidence. My premise, simply stated, is that the Book of Mormon is a pacifist manifesto. It affirms the following concepts:

- Peace existed in the past, and is now, in our normal, pre-eschatological times, possible.
- The Christian message, extended to ever-larger groups, produces now, as always, a sustainable irenic existence.
- The Book of Mormon's teachings on attitudes, behaviors, and social justice can work positively on present-day society's hearts and minds.

The Book of Mormon does so in part by lending divine sanction to stories of moral peoples, portrayed as examples worthy of emulation, and removing divine sanction from stories of immoral peoples, whose deeds are presented as cautionary tales to be avoided by the righteous. In sum, the scriptural text delivers a comprehensive pacifist injunction and proffers an optimistic civil construct of possibilities that has been constant throughout each past dispensation and, importantly, has been given again to ours. To fully understand the plates as a divinely originated ethical story delineating the peaceable walk of the moral and faithful, it is critical to identify God's explicit in-text affirmations and disaffirmations.

The LDS community, broadly speaking, already adheres to a number of peaceful tenets. Latter-day Saints understand that they are blessed when their lives are void of disputations and anger. Collectively, their works demonstrate a peaceable walk in which they do "not have a mind to injure one another, but . . . live peaceably, and render to every man according to that which is his due" (Mosiah 4:13). This peaceable walk comes in no small part as individual Latter-day Saints strive to follow Church teachings and read and emulate the teachings of the Book of Mormon. Yet, LDS prophet Spencer W. Kimball once characterized us—saints and citizens—as "a warlike people, easily distracted . . . when enemies rise up, we commit vast resources against the enemy instead of aligning with our God."[1] And few listened.[2]

Furthermore, Latter-day Saints have been well instructed in some of the foundational principles of civil discourse. President Gordon B. Hinckley taught, "In a democracy we can renounce war and proclaim peace. There is opportunity for dissent. Speaking out and doing so emphatically" is not only a "privilege" but also a "right."[3] Elder Quentin L. Cook observed that people of goodwill may not see eye to eye, but they can still be civil: "It is appropriate to disagree, but . . . not appropriate to be disagreeable. Violence and vandalism are not the answer to our disagreements."[4] Finally, President Dieter F. Uchtdorf again counseled members of the church that they should not "vilify and demonize" their rivals, nor "look for any flaw and magnify it," nor justify "hatred with broad generalizations and apply them to everyone" who is different than us. He pointedly taught, "Unfortunately we see today too often the same kind of attitude and behavior spill over into the public discourse of politics, ethnicity, and religion," but he challenges us, "my beloved disciples of the gentle Christ, should we not hold ourselves to a higher standard?"[5]

Admittedly, it is difficult for our LDS community to conjure a world without rivals or enemies, or envision a positive collective vision that will provide solutions for all of humankind's problems, or to conceive of an

---

1. Spencer W. Kimball, "The False Gods We Worship," *Ensign*, June 1976, 3.

2. Consider Hugh Nibley's perspective: "We say, The Prophet! The Prophet! We have got us a Prophet! But when he speaks on the most solemn occasion, the bicentennial of the nation, with the deepest fervor and conviction about the conditions of the time and the course we must take, we give his remarks the instant deep-freeze." Hugh Nibley, *Approaching Zion*, vol. 8 of THE COLLECTED WORKS OF HUGH NIBLEY, ed. Don E. Norton (Salt Lake City: Deseret Book, 1989), 281.

3. Gordon B. Hinckley, "War and Peace," *Ensign*, May 2003, 78–81.

4. Quentin L. Cook, "We Follow Jesus Christ," *Ensign*, May 2003.

5. Dieter F. Uchtdorf, "Pride and the Priesthood," *Ensign*, November 2010. For a more structural discussion on attitudes, behaviors, and inconsistencies in society, see Appendix One.

LDS pacifist manifesto that applies not only to our theology but all humankind. But I suggest that this is precisely the higher standard the Book of Mormon challenges us—and shows us how—to achieve.

Peace Defined

The desire for peace is found not just in the Book of Mormon but throughout the Christian tradition. I choose to call this populace tradition "Pax Sanctorum," or the peace of the saints.[6] The core belief, pacifism, is a foundational Christian principle, revealed in each dispensation, corroded over time through institutional and civic accommodation, but with the possibility to be recultivated, with great effort, in our individual and collective lives. This use of "pacifist" relies both on its original formulation[7] and in the LDS First Presidency's remarks of April 1942: "The Church is and must be against war. . . . The Church . . . cannot regard war as a righteous means of settling international disputes; these should and could be settled—the nations agreeing— by peaceful negotiation and adjustment."[8] This echoes the statement of American Quaker reformer Hanna Barnard, who said in 1805, "It never was his positive will and pleasure, for his rational creatures to destroy one another's lives, in any age of the world."[9] The LDS restoration extended the well-established Christian pacifist tradition by introduc-

---

6. Previous applications of the Latin construct have referenced "Pax Romana"— the absence of violence under brutal Roman rule; "Pax Christiana"—the spread of Christianity; and more recently, "Pax Americana"—world democracy in the American centuries.

7. The term "pacifist" first appears in print on September 9, 1901, in *Die Friedens-Warte* in an article entitled "Friend-of-Peace, Federalist, Pacifist?" by Emile Arnaud who "bespoke the word of his own invention." See Alfred H. Fried, "Pacidemocracy," in *Advocate of Peace* LXXX:10 (November 1918): 304. Merriam Webster defines "pacifism" as (1) "opposition to war or violence as a means of settling disputes; specifically refusal to bear arms on moral or religious grounds," (2) "an attitude or policy of nonresistance."

8. First Presidency address, Conference Report, April 1942, 88–97. Drafted and delivered by J. Reuben Clark, of which President Heber J. Grant afterwards confirmed, "President Clark read a long Address of the First Presidency. We approved and signed it, but he wrote it." See D. Michael Quinn, *Elder Statesman, A Biography of J. Reuben Clark* (Salt Lake City: Signature Books, 2002), 296 and 462, n. 241.

9. *A Narrative of the proceedings in America, of the society called Quakers, in the case of Hannah Barnard* (London: C. Stower, 1804), 120–21.

ing new sacred texts, including the Doctrine and Covenants and Pearl of Great Price, but most notably the Book of Mormon. My objective is to explore this wealth of LDS pacifist scripture, which can enhance our current LDS peace theology.

While Pax Santorum focuses on how believers can live among non-believers and even belligerents, the LDS parlance offers a similar descriptor of peace, built on the same elements and revealed in LDS scripture, yet circumscribing a more homogeneous community of believers—Zion. The Book of Moses describes it this way: "And the Lord called his people Zion, because they were of one heart and one mind, and dwelt in righteousness; and there were no poor among them."[10] Implicit in this Zion-peace are three affirmative societal requirements:

1. Correct attitudes—*one heart and one mind*—or what we might call cultural peace.
2. Proper behaviors—*dwelt in righteousness*—or direct peace.
3. Social justice—*no poor among them*—or structural peace.

This formulation closely parallels a triptych (see Figure 1) developed by Johan Galtung, often referred to as the father of modern peace studies. Galtung observed that in any society, a lasting peace requires all three positive qualities:

1. Attitudes—proper thoughts void of prejudice or malice.
2. Behaviors—proper actions void of injury to people or property, while promoting nonviolent conflict resolution.
3. No contradictions or inconsistencies—resolving structural injustices in access to services, economic inequity, and protection of civil liberties.[11]

---

10. Moses 7:18.

11. Galtung offers two triangles: first, arguing it is necessary to analyze the causes of conflict before violence, during violence, and after violence; second, elaborating three categories of violence as direct, structural, and cultural. See Johan Galtung, "Violence, War, and Their Impact: On Visible and Invisible Effects of Violence," *Polylog: Forum for Intercultural Philosophy* 5 (2004); and as an application, Taleh Ziyadov, "The Galtung Triangle and Nagorno-Karabakh Conflict" *Caucasian Review of International Affairs* 1, no. 1 (Winter 2006): 31–41. Minor modifications by this author to the Galtung triangle include conceptualizing ranges across each triangle point, and reorienting these axes so positive aspects are in the same direction, at the center of the illustration.

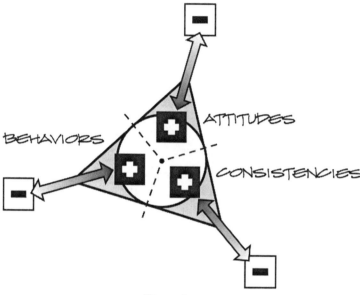

Figure 1

The Book of Mormon provides five discreet examples of robust peace societies, constructed along the three criteria outlined in Moses and by Galtung. First, Nephi rehearses the Prophet Isaiah's archetypal future-oriented peace vision originally proffered to a divided Israel: attitudes ("neither shall they learn war any more"); behaviors ("they shall beat their swords into plowshares"); and social justice ("he shall judge among the nations, and shall rebuke many people") (2 Ne. 12:4, Isa. 2:4). We are then given four additional peace moments unique to the Book of Mormon's thousand-year history:

- The servant-leadership of King Benjamin (Mosiah 4:12–16), whose followers had "not a mind to injure one another" and were protected in righteousness from their enemies for forty-three years (130–87 BCE).
- The nonviolence of the Ammonites (Alma 27:28–29), who knelt down twice to aggressive violence and sustained for decades a pacifist colony, welcoming all.[12]
- The aftermath of the visitation of Jesus Christ to the temple, when "they taught, and did minister one to another; and they had all

---

12. 77–6 BCE (see Hel. 15:8 in 6 BCE), commented on by Samuel eighty years later (see 3 Ne. 6:14 in 29–30 CE).

things in common among them, every man dealing justly, one with another" (3 Ne. 26:19).

- The society of the post-visitation Saints (4 Ne. 1:2–3), who as the "people of Jesus" sustained a peaceable walk for nearly three centuries (32–322 CE).

In sum, the Book of Mormon gives five examples, ranging from the millennial to the historical, that all reaffirm the three Zion-peace metrics illustrated. Therefore, from the Book of Mormon text we can postulate Pax Sanctorum being defined as:

1. The absence of cultural violence and the building of a cultural peace.[13]
2. The absence of direct violence and the creation of a direct peace.[14]
3. The absence of structural violence and the maintenance of a structural peace.[15]

The plates that became the Book of Mormon text contain three necessary elements of a comprehensive LDS pacifist construct: a precise and actionable definition of peace, as discussed above; an allegorical platform[16] on which morality and conflict interact; and an explicit textual commentary for ethical decision-making to aid in discerning our response to conflict.

The Conflict-Morality Grid

The Book of Mormon makes a consistent argument about the relationship between societal morality and the corresponding state of peace or war. Textual indicators of whether a society is at war or peace (or in transition between the two) are usually paired with ethical qualifiers identifying the moral status of the people. The plates contain eighty-nine references to improving or failing morality, 182 wars,[17] and

---

13. See Appendix One for attitude-related themes identified in the Book of Mormon text.

14. See Appendix One for behavior-related themes identified in the Book of Mormon text.

15. See Appendix One for contradiction-related themes identified in the Book of Mormon text.

16. Since by its own admission the Book of Mormon is not a "history" (2 Ne. 5:33), the compilation was purposely selected to be read more allegorically.

17. While several scholars suggest various methods of counting conflicts in the Book of Mormon text (John Sorensen lists Nephite-Lamanite conflicts only in his "Seasonality of Warfare in the Book of Mormon and in Mesoamerica," in

thirty-six periods of peace.[18] Moral conduct qualifiers in the Book of Mormon range from the spiritually lofty to the depraved turpitude of the damned. Conflict qualifiers range from cold stand-offs between massing armies to open war and even genocide. Peace qualifiers range from momentary cessations of conflict (i.e., cold peace) to extended societal harmony. Collectively they delineate two continua along moral-immoral and peace-conflict lines. Together these represent the ethical platform on which the Book of Mormon delineates a contemporary understanding of peace and advances the concept of Pax Sanctorum.

To better visualize this morality-conflict correlation, we can arrange the morality qualifiers vertically and the conflict qualifiers horizontally, thereby defining a two-by-two grid with four distinct cells in which war-peace, morality-immorality mechanics operate. In fact, this Conflict-Morality grid (see Figure 2) is the thematic stage on which the entire Book of Mormon's ethical plot is performed. The aforementioned peace metrics—attitudes, behaviors, and civil liberties—are the catalysts of situational change on this grid; in other words, they describe how peoples move on the grid, representing a change in their moral-ethical conditions. Internal immorality among the believers triggers external retribution from an unbeliever (Morm. 4:5, see also Isa. 13:11, 2 Ne. 23:11).[19] The scriptures—including but not exclusively the Book of Mormon—portray the characteristics of these four cells as a comprehensive construct to evaluate the ethical interplay of morality

---

Warfare in the Book of Mormon, ed. Stephen D. Ricks and William J. Hamblin [Provo, Utah: Foundation for American Research and Mormon Studies, 1990], 462–74), the approach used in this revised census is one conflict per year or season per location, consistent with the text indicating combatants returning during certain periods. Also, the revised census expands Sorenson's original list to include the Jaredite conflicts.

18. The plates contain 183 time markers.

19. On the internal causation of war: "The Book of Mormon, in an earlier time of tribulation, tells us that the warfare the people experienced 'would not have happened had it not been for their wickedness and their abomination' (Helaman 4:11). Mormon provides a list of what those abominations were: pride, oppressing the poor, withholding food from the hungry and clothing from the naked, mocking that which is sacred, denying revelation, murdering, plundering, lying, stealing, committing sexual sin, and creating contention and political dissension (see Helaman 4:11–12)." Kent P. Jackson, "War and Peace—Lessons from the Upper Room," in *To Save the Lost*, ed. Richard Neitzel Holzapfel and Kent P. Jackson (Provo, Utah: Brigham Young University Religious Studies Center, 2009), 35–59.

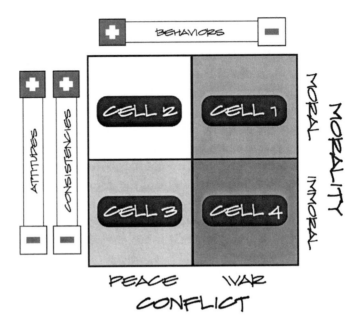

Figure 2

and conflict. John Howard Yoder, Mennonite pacifist scholar, suggests a similar reading of the Christian and Hebrew testaments.[20]

Let's examine each cell in turn.

Cell 4 (Low Morality–High Conflict) is the easiest to understand, and the Jaredites are its quintessential example. Including this plot-interrupting tragedy was final-compiler Moroni's way of reaching for one more bad example of internal-iniquity-induced conflict.[21] Of the sixty-

---

20. As an example of a comprehensive attempt, see John Howard Yoder, *Chapters in the History of Religiously Rooted NonViolence: A Series of Working Papers of the Joan B. Kroc Institute for International Peace Studies* (South Bend, Ind.: University of Notre Dame, 1994).

21. Referencing Moroni's selection of possible polarizing tragedies for inclusion on the plates, Nibley comments, "Nowhere is the process brought into sharper analytical focus than in a history that Moroni inserted between his father's book and his own as the supreme example of the polarizing mania that destroyed his own people. Speaking of another final showdown, which ended in the extermination of both nations, Moroni turns to address us directly: 'And thus we see that the Lord did visit them [when] their wickedness and abominations [not their enemies!] had prepared a way for their everlasting destruction' (Ether 14:25). He wants to make sure we do not miss the point." Hugh W. Nibley, *The Prophetic Book of Mormon*, vol. 8 of THE COLLECTED WORKS OF HUGH NIBLEY (Salt Lake City: Deseret Book, 1989), 435–68.

five Jaredite conflicts described,[22] patricide only marginally surpasses fratricide as the violence of choice for regime-change;[23] all were offensives in which Jaredites "gave battle" (a phrase used only in Ether[24]) internally with "willfulness of their hearts, seeking for blood and revenge" (Moro. 9:23). Yet in his introduction to the open conflict of these Jaredite tragedies, Moroni interjects God's proscription against the shedding of blood "from the beginning of man" (Ether 8:19). He then includes nearly two thousand years and thirty generations of Jaredite conflicts groveling at the bottom of Cell 4 (Low Morality–High Conflict) until with extinction "their bones become as heaps of earth upon the land" (Ether 11:6). The Book of Mormon's endgame at Cumorah is another obvious example of the relationship between low morality and high conflict. Here again Moroni offers God's condemnation against both the attitude of human vengeance and the behavior of violence (Morm. 8:19–20).

Cell 3 (Low Morality–Low Conflict) is a precarious and uneasy existence, able to slip quickly into open conflict or climb more deliberately to higher moral ground. For example, hoping to avoid open conflict, Nephi rehearses Isaiah to his co-wanderers in the wilderness, reiterating promises of peace to a divided and enemy-surrounded House of Israel. The Book of Mormon indicates that Cell 3 peoples who are on a downward moral trajectory are susceptible to open violence, restless to avenge, and hungering for conflict (see Morm. 3:9–10). For those on a moral ascent, Cell 3 is home to survivors, who often linger in post-combat uncertainty, needing to be re-regulated in their religious observance and renourished by the word of God to stabilize their tentative peace (See Mosiah 26:37; Alma 1:28, 4:11–16, 35:9). Cell 3 is thus the plates' transition zone where 182 conflicts and 36 peace moments emerge, and the choice between Word and Sword unfolds (Alma 31:5).[25] As a society's internal moral fiber erodes, that society becomes more susceptible to aggression and violence. The carrier of violence—both aggressor and aggressed—is always

---

22. The Jaredite conflict census includes fifty major conflicts, some of which describe multiple campaigns or multi-day events for a total of sixty-five conflicts described in the text.

23. Of the sixty-five Jaredite conflicts, seventeen clearly involve conflicts among near-relatives (fathers, sons, brothers, cousins, uncles).

24. See for example Ether 7:9, 16–17; 8:3-5; 10:9; 11:15; 13:16, 23, 29–30; 14:3, 11, 13, 16, 26.

25. See also Nephi's proscription of reliance on the armed conflict in 2 Nephi 4:34, 28:31.

declared immoral: "by the wicked the wicked are punished" (Morm. 4:5, Alma 40:13, 2 Ne. 23:15).[26]

Cell 2 (High Morality–Low Conflict) is easy to understand but difficult to achieve. Each of our four Zion moments, previously referenced, are excellent and ethically similar prototypes, where, per Nibley, "the good people never fight the bad people, they never fight anybody."[27] Thus the Book of Mormon, in retelling the Sermon on the Mount and republishing other Old and New Testament pacifist scripture, restores and extends the pacifist theme discernible in Christianity's sacred corpus and history.

The Primitive or Meridian Saints also found their "peace voice" in the Sermon on the Mount and the Master's disarming of Peter, and they believed that they were succeeding at growing a peace culture. With each new adherent, they extended that newly restored pacifism over the next three centuries to overcome civil and imperial violence.[28] They proscribed all believers from combat and defined a cleansing strategy for the delicate walk from military violence back to the sacraments.[29] Many

---

26. Kent P. Jackson notes: "War is from Satan, and peace is from God. In the Book of Mormon, we learn that righteous people never start wars. War sometimes comes upon people who do not deserve it but are subjected to it because of the wickedness of other people. . . . In the Book of Mormon, we learn that those who initiate wars often proclaim high-minded principles, such as the righting of past wrongs (for example, see Alma 54:17–18, 3 Ne. 3:10). Yet the book exposes their true motives to be those most common, but devil-like, human traits: hatred and the desire for power (see Alma 2:10, 43:7–8, 46:4, 51:8; Hel. 2:5)." See Holzapfel and Jackson, *To Save the Lost*, 35–59.

27. Hugh W. Nibley, *Since Cumorah* (Salt Lake City: Deseret Book, 1970), 384.

28. To the cessation of idol-associated violence see Penelope Lawson, trans., *Athanasius: On the Incarnation* (London: Centenary Press, 1944), 37: "He was actually born in Judea, yet men from Persia came to worship Him. He it is Who won victory from His demon foes and trophies from the idolaters even before His bodily appearing—namely, all the heathen who from every region have abjured the tradition of their fathers and the false worship of idols and are now placing their hope in Christ and transferring their allegiance to Him. The thing is happening before our very eyes here in Egypt and thereby another prophecy is fulfilled, for at no other time have the Egyptians ceased from their false worship save when the Lord of all, riding as on a cloud, came down here in body and brought the error of idols to nothing and won everybody to himself and through Himself to the Father."

29. See Roland H. Bainton, *Christian Attitudes Toward War and Peace* (New York: Abingdon Press, 1960), 109. "The approval of the Church was never bestowed on those clerics and monastics who had taken defense into their own hands. St. Thomas

centuries later, the Quakers—representing the best pre-restoration stewards of this primitive pacifism—premised their New Testament-based peace testimony on the concept that for the converted to be ready for the returning pacifist Master, peace—a quality of the millennium and beyond—needed to be practiced in "normal" times.[30] In affirmation of their pacifist tradition, all of the scriptural texts foundational to the early Christians' and Quakers' peace witness are reproduced in the Book of Mormon. In addition to these New Testament stories, the Plates now offered thirty-six new periods of peace.[31] In those periods of peace are ten new and unique examples of nonviolent conflict resolution, including pre-conflict diplomacy, relocation, creating peace spaces, and choosing simply not to contest—behind well-engineered barricades. As well, the Book of Mormon offers sixteen new and unique occurrences of pacifist deportment amid raging interfactional surroundings where a Zion peace is protected irrespective of events and the broader geopolitical atmosphere.[32]

Latter-day revelation to Joseph Smith confirms and extends the teachings of the Book of Mormon in terms of Cell 2. In section 98 of

---

(Acquinas 1225–1274), writing even after the commencement of the crusades . . . held that the clergy should be excluded from military functions, not so much, however, for ethical as for sacramental reasons. . . . He declared that . . . although participation in warfare is legitimate for the Christian, it is not for the clergy because they serve at the altar. For that reason they may not shed the blood of another, but should be prepared rather to shed their own in imitation of Christ. . . . Ten years after the Norman Conquest some of the participants sought counsel from their bishops as to the appeasement of their consciences for the blood they had shed. A council at Winchester in 1076 enacted that he who had killed a man should do penance for a year. He who did not know whether his wounded assailant had died should do penance for forty days. He who did not know how many he had killed should do penance one day a week throughout his life. All archers should do penance thrice for the space of forty days."

30. In 1806, Quaker Thomas Clarkson published a multi-volume work, which included four "Great Tenets" he felt distinguished the Quakers. Among these was their stand on conflict. *A Portraiture of Quakerism taken from a view of the moral education, discipline, peculiar customs, religious principles, political and civil economy, and character of the Society of Friends* (London: Longman, Hurst, Rees, and Orme, 1807), 3:26. For the complete pacifist treatise, see 3:25–113.

31. See Appendix Two. In LDS scholarship, this is the first census of periods of peace from the Book of Mormon text.

32. See Appendix Three for examples of non-violent conflict resolution and pacifist themes in the Book of Mormon text.

the Doctrine and Covenants, given in an atmosphere of frontier violence, God emphasizes the value of laying down one's life for peace, waiting patiently for divine resolution of conflict, and not seeking revenge. The revelation further commands that all Latter-day Saints "renounce war" (move horizontally left on the grid) and "proclaim peace" (move vertically up on the grid) (vv. 14–16). Section 98 not only provides a Restoration-era divine disapproval of violence, but it helps calibrate the pacifist benefits, suggesting a 1,600-fold return on investment (one hundred times, then four times doubled) in choosing a current "non-violent" response over "justified" but more violent third or fourth generation behaviors (v. 28). No other behavior in all LDS scriptural texts promises (or at least quantifies) such a reward.

In another Restoration-era revelation, God repeats his promised protection of the Saints who pursue a nonviolent course.[33] Similarly, in the Book of Mormon, King Benjamin suggests that his people's pacifism and righteousness were their defense against their enemies (Mosiah 2:4); Ammon records that his converts buried their "weapons of rebellion" (Alma 23:13); and Mormon asks *all* latter-day converts to lay down their "weapons of war" (Morm. 7:4).

The ethical geography of the Cell 2–Cell 3 border has been where most ethicists have shown interest and searched for divine insight. As the newly-Christianized empire lay under siege and internal sin in the fifth century, Augustine looked for a way to hand more swords to more believers. He refined the existing "just war" rationale to provide proper Christian reasons to enter into and guide conduct during conflict. Just war theory encompasses these historical efforts to define the existence and boundaries of an ethical space for Christian believers entering, enduring, and exiting lethal conflict. Delineating this alleged "just war" domain has become an extended historical attempt to find the moral borders for a believer-soldier, and is grounded on the perhaps incongruous premise that sufficient ethical space exists to permit a Christian to choose Sword over Word and operate violently without risking moral self-destruction. On the Morality-Conflict grid, the search then is for defensible ethical ground (high enough up Cell 3) to ethically conscript the believer as a belligerent, yet leave for these conscripts enough reasons to believe their sovereign is safeguarding their soldier-soul, when

---

33. Ten months later, God reiterates the non-violent message in Doctrine & Covenants 105:13–14 that was introduced in 98:16.

in fact scripture asserts that such a seeker-citizen would avoid militancy and conscription altogether and look for nonviolent solutions.

The Book of Mormon text, which groups all combative factions in equal disregard, seems to suggest that this narrow ethical strip does not actually exist. In grid-construct, the portrayal of just war theory—what Nibley called "the poor shabby philosophy of St. Augustine"[34]—is somewhat problematic. Traditional "just war" formulation *rarely* relates the cause of advancing external conflict to internal morality of the aggressed; whereas the Book of Mormon *always* links the external conflict of the advancing belligerent force with the internal morality of the aggressed. Furthermore, each time any sort of title of liberty is waived as a belligerent-recruitment strategy, we are told explicitly that the people are morally "down" (i.e., lower Cell 3). Each of the following four title-of-liberty examples identifies an associated iniquity verse:

- "The people of Limhi began to drive the Lamanites before them" (Mosiah 20:11), with allusions to title of liberty causes, but "the Lord was slow to hear their cry because of their iniquities (Cell 3 or Cell 4), and the Lord "did not see fit to deliver them out of bondage" (Mosiah 21:15; clearly Cell 4).

- In internal conflict against Amalickiah, Moroni raises the title of liberty (Alma 46:10–12) when "the affairs of the people of Nephi (were) exceedingly precarious and dangerous," "quick to forget . . . quick to do iniquity, and be led away by the evil one" (vv. 7–8) (that is, Cell 4).

- Later: "Dissenters, rather than be smitten down . . . by the sword, yielded to the standard of liberty" and were compelled (i.e., chose as a preferable alternative) to "hoist the title of liberty . . . and take up arms in defense of their country" (Alma 51:20) at a time when there "began to be a contention among the people," "hitherto the cause of all their destruction," and Moroni had "wars and contentions among his own people" (vv. 2, 16, 22) (internal immorality, high conflict, Cell 4).

- To rescue Pahoran—"not . . . a traitor to the freedom and cause of his country"—Moroni began with "a small number of men" and "did raise the standard of liberty in whatsoever place he did enter, and gained whatsoever force he could in all his march" (Alma 62:1, 3–4) at a time when "there had been murders, and contentions, and

34. Boyd Jay Petersen, *Hugh Nibley, A Consecrated Life* (Salt Lake City: Greg Kofford Books, 2002), 211.

all manner of iniquity among the people of Nephi" and "many had hardened, because of the great length of the war," which included the death penalty for dissenters (vv. 9, 40–41).

Thus each example clarifies that the title of liberty was never God's justification for lethal conflict, and was always applied in conditions of low moral standards and internal societal unrest of the aggressed.

In evaluating the several hundred conflicts and pacifist moments in the Book of Mormon text, the premise is clear and consistent— namely, that the Book of Mormon provides a pacifist manifesto where the highly moral always avoid conflict. Taken in the whole, all thirty-six periods of peace in the Book of Mormon are, in grid terms, up and left (Cell 2), with clear sanction from God, whereas all 182 violent conflicts are down and right (Cell 4) and are void of divine support.

Ethical Motion

What we might call the peace qualifiers—metrics of a society's attitudes, behaviors, and social justice—are the change catalysts, explaining motion across the morality-conflict grid and suggesting a litany of ministerial possibilities for us all. Each peace metric achieved, freedom won, or injustice overcome improves societal morality and buffers us in God's conditionally promised protection. Each peace freedom revoked or ignored, drifts our society toward greater susceptibility to violent conflict and apart from divine sanction.

The plates are both explicit and comprehensive on these mechanics. Cataloging the moral drag from Cell 2 to Cell 3 are eighty-nine texts characterized by language such as "because of internal iniquity" or "had it not been for," inserted by sorrowing prophets, awakened participants, or final compilers, always in close narrative- and causal-proximity to the 182 violent conflicts of Cell 4. To cite a multi-generational example from the record of Zeniff's people:

- Zeniff, "deceived," "over-zealous" (Mosiah 7:21), and "slow to remember" (9:3), conceives of territorial aggression, fails miserably (7:24)—"all because of iniquity" (11:2, 29).[35]

---

35. For a discussion of how being "over-zealous" allowed Zeniff to be deceived "by cunning and craftiness" (Mosiah 7:21), see Cecil O. Samuelson, "Appropriate Zeal," *BYU Magazine*, Winter 2011, available online at http://magazine.byu.edu/?act=view&a=2722 (accessed July 20, 2012).

- Zeniff's son Noah "did not keep the commandments of God" (Mosiah 11:2, 29), exploits (vv. 3–13), and philanders (vv. 14–15).
- Noah's son Limhi, inheritor of these missteps and in a quagmire of conflict, concludes of this immorality-caused violence: "[G]reat are the reasons which we have to mourn; for behold how many of our brethren have been slain, and their blood has been spilt in vain, and all because of iniquity. For if this people had not fallen in transgression the Lord would not have suffered that this great evil should come upon them" (Mosiah 7:24–25).
- A well-seasoned Gideon suggests higher moral ground can be found if they choose a nonviolent path to conflict resolution (i.e., silent nocturnal departure).[36]

Limhi's re-establishment of proselyting freedoms created the missionary environment for Ammon's great success among otherwise violent belligerents. In contrast, the plates contain only descriptors of divine approval and high moral ground surrounding the thirty-six periods of peace and the ten occurrences of nonviolent conflict resolution (both in Cell 2).[37]

The Book of Mormon contains a powerful moral fulcrum—what Erasmus earlier described as the choice between Word and Sword.[38] Reveling in his people's successful conversion and its associated pacifist walk, Ammon reminded his original Nephite naysayers that their previously proposed alternative—a bias divulged only later in the text—was first-strike, violent, ethnic cleansing:

"And moreover they [our brethren] did say: Let us take up arms against them, that we destroy them and their iniquity out of the land, lest they overrun us and destroy us" (Alma 26:25).

The Book of Mormon leaves little room for such first-strike policies, and argues instead that the preaching of the word of God is a more powerful alternative. As Kent P. Jackson reminded us, "The only time righteous people in the Book of Mormon enter 'enemy' lands is when they do so to

---

36. See Mosiah 20:17, where Gideon suggests, in a period of high pre-conflict tension, that the aggressor king "forbear." Gideon then declares, "Let us put a stop to the shedding of so much blood" (Mosiah 20:22). See also Mosiah 22:3–9.

37. See Appendix Three.

38. See Desiderius Erasmus, *The Education of a Christian Prince*, trans. Lester K. Born (New York: Octagon Books, 1963).

teach their brothers and sisters the gospel."[39] Military force for the succession of open violence is not a straight line to lasting peace and morality; Moroni's limited military effectiveness (movement from Cell 4 to Cell 3) needed Helaman and his brethren's "no less serviceable" (Alma 48:19) pastoral re-regulation (movement from Cell 3 to Cell 2) to achieve lasting peace.[40] Indeed, Moroni's own captains thought military victory was too elusive for so corrupt a society. With each military failure, they were quick to doubt *not* the military capabilities of their conscripts, but their aggregate morality (Alma 59:11–12). President Spencer W. Kimball put it bluntly in 1976 when he asserted the Saints' "affirmative" assignment, to forsake the things of the world as ends in themselves, to leave off idolatry and press forward in faith, "to carry the gospel to our enemies, that they might no longer be our enemies."[41]

Most treatments of religion and conflict discuss the "holy war" or "jihad," in which participants feel very right and behave very violently. Those following closely will notice the absence of any discussion here about this Cell 1 (High Morality–High Conflict) behavior, simply because there are no Book of Mormon examples of divine sanction of aggressive societal violence involving the spiritually convinced. To the highly moral societies documented on the plates, violent conflict is both inconceivable (Cell 1) and unnecessary (Cell 2).

The Book of Mormon, perhaps more than the Bible, operates with the explicit assumption that its lessons are specifically applicable—even targeted—to our modern condition. It also contains a universal call to repentance, pointing toward universal templates of morality and righteousness that can be described as Pax Sanctorum. The personal tragedy of violence, and thus the warning against its allure, occupies the plates' opening narrative. Long before armies mass on armies, Nephi records his first violence—personally damaging and tragic—an omen to those who may ponder following spiritual promptings into acts of violence.

---

39. Jackson, "War and Peace," 35–59.

40. See Alma 31:5 and the stirring narrative of the prophet-brothers Nephi and Lehi found in Helaman chapters 4–5.

41. Spencer W. Kimball, "The False Gods We Worship," *Ensign*, June 1976, 3. See also Alma 26:23–26. Kent P. Jackson notes: "The Book of Mormon shows that missionary work among intractable foes is a more successful means of neutralizing their threats than is waging war against them (see Alma 31:5; Hel. 5:20–52, 6:37)." See Holzapfel and Jackson, *To Save the Lost*, 35–59.

Not trained in violence in his youth, never entertaining violence, he justifies his act on the grounds of providential urging. Of the family's minor and major transgressions, S. Kent Brown comments: "the darkest act that hung about their family was Nephi's killing of Laban. To be sure, the Lord had directed Nephi's act. Even so, taking the life of another person . . . would have placed Nephi's family on unfamiliar ground. On the chance that this deed might somehow bring a stain on the family, Lehi offered 'burnt offerings.'"[42] Decades later, Nephi's penitential psalm voices a struggle to regain a nonviolent peace; he cries, "Why am I angry because of my enemy?" (2 Ne. 4:27). The intrafamilial conflict becomes so intense that the tribe splits into two, spawning generations of war. Nephi records that one of his first acts—even before building a temple—was to "make many swords" (2 Ne. 5:14), thus accepting violence as inevitable and divine protection as improbable or insufficient. The sword of Laban thus accompanied him not only physically but also metaphorically all those years. His brother Jacob recorded tragically, decades after the split, that the Nephites' "lives passed away like as it were unto us a dream, we being a lonesome and a solemn people, wanderers, cast out from Jerusalem, born in tribulation, in a wilderness, and hated of our brethren, which caused wars and contentions; wherefore, we did mourn out our days" (Jacob 7:26). Within a generation, war consumed the hearts and minds of the people, so much that "nothing short" of "preaching and prophesying of wars, and contentions, and destructions," with the associated judgments of God, would prick the people's hearts (Enos 1:23). The plates thus contain powerful narratives of ethical motion in both directions, with perhaps some of its most poignant passages outlining the pervasive and depressing results of violence.

Conclusion

Latter-day Saint leaders have cautioned against civil violence, political vandalism, disagreeable disagreement, and ill feelings harbored due to ethnicity or religion. As a people, as a Church, we possess no holy texts or prophetic directives that would carry us to open conflict. To the contrary, we have latter-day books of scripture that we collectively lift

---

42. S. Kent Brown, *Voices from the Dust: Book of Mormon Insights* (American Fork, Utah: Covenant Communications, 2004), 9.

up "as an ensign of peace, and make a proclamation of peace unto the ends of the earth" (D&C 105:29). We know very well this ensign of peace on a personal level. But how is it extended to a societal level? Can we scale our spiritually pacifist demeanor to a broader society?[43]

The God of the plates still expects Latter-day Saints to "make proposals for peace unto those who have smitten you, according to the voice of the Spirit which is in you" (D&C 105:40), and our broader proposal "bond and free, . . . Jew and Gentile" (2 Ne. 26:33) may be the extension of these peace metrics, as restored and exemplified in the Book of Mormon.[44] Our Pax Sanctorum proposal is thus the unique and consistent message of the plates:

- Societal protection lies in a relationship with God.
- Conversion elicits a peaceable walk.
- Pacifism is the code of conduct of full conversion.
- Nonviolence begets world salvation.
- These societal promises are extended to all.

Through all 182 conflicts, the Book of Mormon consistently renounces war as a moral failure of society, and then more thoroughly proclaims peace as God's promised preference. The thirty-six periods of peace underscore—with unique stories—this pacifist wisdom and walk.

Our injunction as Saints is to improve the world's morality by understanding the "peaceable walk" in all our LDS sacred texts, and extend that message outside of our "synagogues" (Moro. 7:1, 4).

Pax Sanctorum.

---

43. For a previous proposal see Russell M. Nelson, "Blessed Are the Peacemakers," *Ensign*, November 2002, 39–42.

44. For a seventeeth-century example of referencing the most unlikely recipients of the Christian message, see "Remonstrance of the Inhabitants of the Town of Flushing to Governor Stuyvesant, (December 27, 1657)," which reads "The law of love, peace and liberty in the states extending to Jews, Turks and Egyptians, as they are considered sonnes of Adam, which is the glory of the outward state of Holland, soe love, peace and liberty, extending to all in Christ Jesus, condemns hatred, war and bondage" (as quoted in Kenneth T. Jackson and David S. Dunbar, eds., *Empire City, New York Through the Centuries*, Kenneth T. Jackson, David S. Dunbar [New York: Columbia University Press, 2002], 34). The phrase may have found common usage, based in part on a Pentecost Monday (1523) sermon by Martin Luther, "The Turk and Jew, too, believe in God, but without means and mediator." In *The Sermons of Martin Luther* (Grand Rapids, Mich.: Baker Books, 2000), 3:342.

Appendix One

The following three sections contain Book of Mormon textual examples of pacifist attitudes, behaviors, and social inconsistencies, aligning with Galtung's peace triptych model.

Attitudes (thoughts, perceptions, or stereo-types). Themes include:

A1. They prize peace over war, as a means of solving problems between parties (Mosiah 29:36, Hel. 3:2).

A2. They understand being "promised" blessings is attained only by personal action, not by pre-selection (1 Ne. 14:2).

A3. They negatively associate the father or author of contention (3 Ne. 11:29).

A4. They enter open combat with great reluctance (Alma 48:23).

A5. They believe zealous behavior leads to bad results (Mosiah 7:21, 9:3).

A6. They believe direct revelation trumps all rationales—but believe this has happened only once (on a personal basis and the historian was also the perpetrator) and nothing similar has happened in this dispensation (Morm. 7:4).

A7. They link all humankind to their God in a personal and familial manner (Mosiah 25:11; Alma 23:3, 26:31–32).

A8. They express sorrow for the wicked, their opponents, in a non-vengeful manner, empathetic of their (both physical and spiritual) conditions (Mosiah 21:29, 25:9, 27:28; Alma 48:23).

A9. They understand that individual peace in a society aggregates to societal peace (Alma 24:16).

A10. They understand war comes upon a society only when evil exists within that society (Mosiah 7:24, 29:27; Alma 10:27, 46:18, 60:40; Hel. 11:34; Ether 8:19; Moro. 8:27).

A11. They feel active proselyting to and among hostile peoples is the best and most effective means of establishing peace (Alma 31:5).

A12. They understand contention and conflict are destructive societal processes (Morm. 8:19).

A13. They call war "work of death" (Alma 43:37–38, 44:20, 60:7; Hel. 4:5) and "murder" (Alma 23:3, 24:25, 27:23, 55:19).

A14. They realize war has a personal impact on its participants—not the least of which is hastening death before repentance and in its detrimental psychological impacts (2 Ne. 4:15; Mosiah 25:11; Alma 24:12, 28:14).

A15. They know personal correct actions and attitudes in society are the best defense to war (1 Ne. 2:23; Alma 44:4, 46:21, 48:17, 50:22)

A16. They feel the righteous have no desire nor need for open conflict (Alma 24:6, 48:16; 4 Ne. 1:15, 34; Morm. 8:20).

A17. They understand negative peace does not last—peace-making needs to be followed by moral improvement in society (Alma 48:19).

A18. They understood God acting, allowed man to remain passive (1 Ne. 21:25).

Behaviors (actions, visible and verifiable). Themes include:

B1. They understand that non-violent means were an effective means of conflict resolution (Mosiah 20:19–21:1).

B2. They encourage spying and information gathering if it supplants or minimizes open conflict (Mosiah 9:1; Alma 2:21, 43:30, 56:22).

B3. They exercise moving and relocation (e.g., to the north, away to Egypt, Lehi leaving Jerusalem, Nephi leaving the landing area) as a conflict avoidance strategy (Mosiah 22:2).

B4. They are cautious never to be the aggressor, never to offer the first strike (Alma 35:14).

B5. Actual combat comes from external sources (e.g., Babylon, Assyria, Lamanites, for "by the wicked are the wicked punished"), but the causes are always internal to society (Alma 50:25, 60:16; Hel. 4:11).

B6. They understand open conflict loses any perceived moral superiority (if there ever were any) when defense becomes offense (Mosiah 4:4, Alma 55:19).

B7. They understand that expanded and protracted conflict eventually involves, detrimentally, non-combatants (Alma 3:2, Morm. 4:14).

B8. They communicate or dialogue with their belligerents as a means of shortening open conflict and loss of combatants (Alma 54:4–57:1).

B9. They deploy non-violent conflict intervention—e.g., an emissary sent to explain a misunderstanding or prevent an open conflict (Mosiah 20:26).

B10. They use oaths and negotiations as a means of ending and thereby shortening open conflict (1 Ne. 4:37, Alma 44:20).

B11. They use just war rationales to solicit combatants, not to substantiate right actions (Mosiah 20:11, 21:15; Alma 46:10, 13, 20, 36, 51:20, 62:1–4).

Contradictions (misapplications, inequities of societal justice). Themes of societal structure include:

C1. Promoting human rights and civil liberties diminishes a conflict atmosphere (Alma 30:7, 11; 3 Ne. 26:19; 4 Ne. 1:2; Morm. 1:13).

C2. Functional societies do not use open conflict as a means of resolving issues (Mosiah 29:36).

C3. Economic improvement and trade diminishes a conflict atmosphere (Hel. 5:15).

C4. Pre-conflict situations usually include constricting the civil rights of some class within society (women, poor, religion, voting, assembly) (Mosiah 29:26–29, Alma 2:2–3).

C5. Open conflict devolves societal structures, causing a reversion to tribal structures (3 Ne. 7:2, 14; Ether 13:25, 14:2).

C6. Open conflict usurps human rights (Alma 25:5, 30:23, 43:8, 60:27; Hel. 7:4).

C7. War results from unresolved internal societal issues (Alma 14:6).

C8. Positive peace, with its diminished societal contradictions, creates a lasting peace (Alma 30:7, 11).

C9. Social equality promotes peace (Jacob 2:17, Alma 5:55).

Appendix Two

Periods of Peace in the Book of Mormon

1.	Jacob 7:23–24	"peace and the love of God was restored again"
2.	Omni 1:3	"had many seasons of peace"
3.	Omni 1:18	"did unite together"
4.	Words of Mormon 1:15–16	"with . . . the holy prophets . . . did once more establish peace"
5.	Mosiah 1:1	"continual peace all the remainder of his days"
6.	Mosiah 10:1	"again began to possess the land in peace"
7.	Mosiah 18:21	"hearts knit together in unity and in love one towards another"
8.	Mosiah 20:13–26	"pacified towards them . . . returned . . . in peace to their own land"
9.	Mosiah 21:20–22	"no more disturbance . . . until"
10.	Mosiah 29:43	"continual peace through the land."
11.	Alma 1:28, 33	"continual peace again," "much peace"

12. Alma 3:25, 4:5   "began to establish peace"
13. Alma 16:1   "no wars nor contentions for a certain number of years"
14. Alma 16:12   "three years . . . continual peace"
15. Alma 23:3, 13   "laid down the weapons of their rebellion, all their weapons of war"
16. Alma 25:13–14   "bury their weapons of war"
17. Alma 28:4–6   "returned again to their land . . . great mourning and lamentation"
18. Alma 30:2   "began to be continual peace"
19. Alma 46:37–38   "began to have peace again in the land and . . . maintain peace"
20. Alma 48:19–20   "free from wars and contentions among themselves . . . four years"
21. Alma 49:30   "continual peace among them, and exceedingly great prosperity"
22. Alma 50:23–24   "never was a happier time . . . peace"
23. Alma 62:11   "having restored peace"
24. Alma 62:42   "once more peace established"
25. Helaman 2:1   "established again peace"
26. Helaman 3:32   "continual peace and great joy"
27. Helaman 6:14   "have great joy and peace"
28. Helaman 11:21   "began in peace . . . exceedingly great peace"
29. Helaman 16:13   "again . . . peace in the land"
30. 3 Nephi 1:23   "again . . . peace in the land"
31. 3 Nephi 6:9   "continual peace"
32. 3 Nephi 11:29   "spirit of contention is not of me"
33. 4 Nephi 1:2, 4   "no contentions and disputations among them . . . still peace"
34. Ether 7:27   "no more wars"
35. Ether 9:15   "peace in the land for the space of two years"
36. Ether 10:3   "brought peace again"
37. Ether 10:17–29   "never could be a people more blessed"

Appendix Three

Wars Averted by Non-Violent Conflict Resolution

1. 2 Nephi 5:34   left to avoid conflict
2. Omni 1:12–13, 20–23   left to avoid conflict

3. Mosiah 18:33   left to avoid conflict
4. Mosiah 19:6–20   retreat
5. Mosiah 20:19–21:1   "pacified towards us"
6. Mosiah 22:6–11   left to avoid imminent conflict, defeat
7. Mosiah 24:23   God delivered them . . . left to avoid conflict
8. Alma 24:20–25   refused to fight
9. Alma 27:2–3   refused to fight
10. Alma 53:14–16   still pacifist (64 BC), 26 years later

Pacifism Themes Introduced via Unique Book of Mormon Accounts

1. 1 Nephi 4:10   "never at any time have I shed the blood of mankind"
2. 2 Nephi 26:32   "commanded . . . they should not contend one with another"
3. Mosiah 4:14   not have a mind to injure, neither fight
4. Mosiah 17:19   God (not man) executes vengeance
5. Alma 23:6, 7, 13   "laid down weapons of their rebellion" against God, brethren
6. Alma 38:4   commends . . . did bear stoning with patience
7. Helaman 5:51   convinced . . . "did lay down their weapons"
8. 3 Nephi 6:13–14   received railings . . . "not turn and revile again"
9. 3 Nephi 11:30   "stirring up . . . not of my doctrine"
10. 4 Nephi 1:38, 16   people of Jesus did not smite again . . . "not a happier people"
11. Mormon 3:15   "vengeance mine, I [God] will repay"
12. Mormon 7:4   converts "must lay down your weapons of war"
13. Mormon 7:4   "save it be that God shall command you"
14. Mormon 8:20   "man shall not smite" . . . not judge . . . vengeance is God's
15. Ether 8:22, 24   vengeance is God's
16. Ether 14:21–24   God (not man) executes vengeance, destruction

Part II

Historical & Cultural Perspectives

6

Zion as a Refuge from the Wars of Nations

Mark Ashurst-McGee

It has been noted that the Book of Mormon, with its tales of an-nihilated civilizations, conveys a profoundly pessimistic view of the world.[1] The Book of Mormon and the revelations of Joseph Smith that followed described a world full of religious, socio-economic, and politi-cal contention that would eventually escalate into violence, warfare, and destruction. While other religious and political reformers in antebel-lum America attempted to redeem the nation, Smith instead attempted to forge a new society. A full understanding of Latter-day Saint atti-tudes and approaches toward issues of war and peace requires therefore a careful examination of some of Smith's earliest revelations bearing of the subject, particularly those reflecting on the establishment of Zion and its relationship to the wars of the nations.

Joseph Smith's style of reform can be compared to that of other types of early American reformers. The moralist reformers of his day sought to improve society with new laws, while institutionalist reform-ers sought to ameliorate social problems through building institutions such as schools and prisons. These moralists and institutionalists had a relatively optimistic view of society. Instead of finding errors internal to American society itself, moralists believed they could solve any problems that *beset* society by perfecting its incomplete body of law. The institu-tionalists, meanwhile, labored to *maintain* a society that was still structur-ally sound though in need of some repair. Abolitionists, feminists, and utopianists held a more pessimistic view. Probing the flaws located deep

---

1. See, for example, Richard Lyman Bushman, *Joseph Smith: Rough Stone Rolling* (New York: Alfred A. Knopf, 2005), 84–88.

within society, they felt the need to fundamentally alter cultural beliefs and attitudes.[2] Joseph Smith and the Mormons—like the Shakers, the Harmonists, and other utopians—took the most pessimistic of reformist stances. They withdrew from the larger society. Early Mormons did not attempt to redeem the United States through either politics or persuasion. In fact, Smith's 1831 revelation of God's law instructed the Saints to deal with outsiders as little as possible (D&C 42).[3] Brigham Young later recounted Joseph Smith teaching this principle to a group of elders in 1833: "Never do another day's work, nor spend another dollar to build up a Gentile city or nation."[4]

The model for a Mormon Zion was set in Joseph Smith's "new translation" of the Bible when he dramatically expanded the verse recounting Enoch's walk with God. In calling Enoch to leave home and preach the gospel, the Lord empowered him with his spirit such that "fear came on all them that heard him." When Enoch returned to the land of Cainan, to which God's people had emigrated, he became the leader of the people of God and infused the entire land with the same protective power by which he had preached abroad. Enoch thereby protected Cainan when enemy nations came to war against it:

> And he spake the word of the Lord, and the earth trembled and the mountains fled. . . . And all nations feared greatly, so powerful was the word of Enoch. . . . There also came up a land out of the depths of the sea. And so great was the fear of the enemies of the people of God that they fled and stood afar off and went upon the land which came up out of the depths of the sea. And the giants of the land also stood afar off. (Moses 7:13–15)[5]

---

2. Here I follow the taxonomy of Steven Mintz in his book *Moralists and Modernizers: America's Pre-Civil War Reformers*, THE AMERICAN MOMENT series, ed. Stanley I. Kutler (Baltimore: Johns Hopkins University Press, 1995).

3. February 9, 1831; see especially verses 9, 36, 45, 62, 67, and 89. All quotations from the Doctrine and Covenants are as transcribed in Revelation Book 1, in Robin Scott Jensen, Robert J. Woodford, and Steven C. Harper, eds., *Manuscript Revelation Books*, facsimile edition, first volume of the Revelations and Translations series of THE JOSEPH SMITH PAPERS, ed. Dean C. Jessee, Ronald K. Esplin, and Richard Lyman Bushman (Salt Lake City: Church Historian's Press, 2009) [hereafter MRBf]. See MRBf, 94–105.

4. Brigham Young, February 3, 1867, *Journal of Discourses*, 26 vols. (London and Liverpool: LDS Booksellers Depot, 1854–86), 11:294–95.

5. All quotations from the Book of Moses are from Kent P. Jackson, ed., *The*

Formerly threatening nations and races feared Enoch to the point that they abandoned their own homelands in order to emigrate even further from Cainan. The Lord thus protected Cainan by increasing the territorial distance between her and the rest of the world. He furthermore "blessed the land" of Cainan and sent a curse of "wars and bloodsheds" among her enemies. Finally, the Lord "came and dwelt with his people" and he named them "Zion." Now, more than ever, "the fear of the Lord was upon all nations, so great was the glory of the Lord which was upon his people." Zion's borders needed no defense. The fear of God's glory kept enemy powers at bay and his curse occupied them with wars among themselves. As Enoch exclaimed: "Surely, Zion shall dwell in safety forever" (vv. 15–20). In time, Zion was taken up into heaven (vv. 18–20). Here was the theoretical extremity of a territorial separation of the righteous from the wicked. Significantly, Enoch's Zion provided the model for the Zion Joseph Smith meant to build. In fact, in Smith's Enoch expansion, Enoch beheld in vision that a new Zion would be established in the last days, and the Lord explained to him, "Then shalt thou and all thy city meet them there" (vv. 61–64).

Smith originally planned to establish the land of Zion and build the city New Jerusalem in the unorganized territory west of the United States. From New York, over a thousand miles away, the Indian country beyond the organized states had seemed like a land beyond Gentile dominion. The missionaries sent to the "Lamanites" were unaware of the federal laws forbidding white residence on Indian land.[6] Ezra Booth reported Oliver Cowdery's claim while traveling through Ohio that he was going to "the place where the foot of a white man never trod."[7] Isaac McCoy, a Baptist minister laboring among the Shawnee, wrote that the Mormons "came here so ignorant of laws, regulating intercourse with the Indian tribes, that they expected to pass on into the Indian territory, procure lands of the Indians, aid them in adopting habits of civilization,

---

Book of Moses and the Joseph Smith Translation Manuscripts (Provo, Utah: Religious Studies Center, Brigham Young University, 2005), 164–69.

6. Regarding these laws, see "Removal of Intruders on Indian Lands," in Francis Paul Prucha, *American Indian Policy in the Formative Years: The Indian Trade and Intercourse Acts, 1790–1834* (Lincoln: University of Nebraska Press, 1962), especially 139–47.

7. Ezra Booth to Ira Eddy, December 6, 1831, in *Ohio Star* (Ravenna, Ohio), December 8, 1831, 1.

and attach them to their party."[8] When the Mormons learned the hard way that this Indian country was administered by a federal agency and an army, migration plans were redirected to western Jackson County, Missouri, where they attempted to stake out Zion's territory as close to the Indians as possible. Smith prophesied that Zion would grow in size and power as America and the nations of the world fell to ruin. In the short term, Smith's plan was to fill Jackson County with his followers and eventually assume control of the local government offices through ordinary democratic channels. Once effectively in power, the Mormons could make a political space for themselves in which to live by divine law.[9]

While Smith originally intended to build Zion outside of the organized states, Zion was never meant to be completely isolated from the world. Zion's international relations began with her proselytizing program. The gathering revelations received on the eve of the exodus from New York to Ohio mandated the agenda of sending elders to "all nations" (D&C 35:13, 36:5, 38:33).[10] Several subsequent revelations affirmed the global reach of Zion's missionaries. As one prophecy assured, "she shall be an ensighn unto the People. & these shall come unto her out of every Nation under heaven" (64:42).[11] Zion thus existed not merely apart from, but in a dynamic relationship with, the worldly nations. Mormon missionaries would journey out of Zion to preach the gospel to the nations and converts would gather out from the nations to settle in Zion.

Mormon elders carried not only the primitivist message of the restored gospel, but also a millenarian warning of wars to befall the nations—including the United States. In March 1831, a month after arriving in Ohio, Smith dictated a revelation instructing the Saints how to escape this impending violence:

> not many years hence ye Shall hear of wars in your own lands wherefore I the Lord hath said gether ye out from the Eastern lands, . . . & with one heart & with one mind gether up your riches that you may

8. Isaac McCoy, statement, November 28, 1833, in "The Disturbances in Jackson County," *Missouri Republican* (St. Louis, Mo.), December 20, 1833.

9. See Mark Ashurst-McGee, "Zion Rising: Joseph Smith's Early Social and Political Thought" (PhD diss., Arizona State University, 2008). See especially chapter 6: "Zion Nationalism."

10. December 7, 1830; December 9, 1830; January 2, 1831; MRBf, 62–67, 66–69, 68–75.

11. September 11, 1831; MRBf, 188–95.

purchase an inheritance which shall hereafter be appointed you & it shall be called the New Jerusalem a land of peace a City of refuge a place of safety for the saints of the most high God ... & there shall be getherd unto it out of evry Nation under Heaven & it shall be the only people that shall not be at war one with another. (D&C 45:63–69)[12]

Smith's eschatology thus established another dynamic geopolitical relationship between Zion and the nations: Zion would be a refugee territory in the midst of a world of warring nations.

In addition to having occupied her enemies with war, God had protected the primitive Zion by blessing Enoch with the ability to speak God's word with overwhelming power and by infusing the entire city of Enoch with the fearsome majesty of his presence. This March 1831 revelation, in which the Lord announced himself as "the God of Enoch & his Brethren," promised such divine protection to the end-time Saints if they would build up a Zion in Missouri: "the glory of the Lord shall be there & the terer of the Lord also shall be there insomuch that the wicked will not come unto it." Then, the revelation continued, as God endowed his people with his power, "it shall be said among the wicked let us not go up to battle against Zion for the inhabitants of Zion are terible wherefore we cannot stand." The Lord admonished his people to build Zion quietly at first, that when her enemies realized what was happening, "it may be terible unto them that fear may seize upon them & they shall stand afar off & tremble & all nations shall be afraid because of the teror of the lord & the power of his might" (D&C 45:11, 67, 70, 72–75).[13] Establishing a spatial demarcation of Zion's territory, even starting in state of Missouri, would not require a land war but would happen by the sheer terror of God's glory.

When Smith returned to Ohio from his first journey to Missouri, he similarly prophesied, "Zion shall flourish & the glory of the Lord shall be upon her ... & the days shall come when the Nations of the Earth shall tremble because of her & shall fear because of her terrible ones" (D&C 64:41–43).[14] Echoing the book of Deuteronomy, another revelation prophesied of the day when a pair of Zion's terrifying warriors could set "tens of thousands to flight" (D&C 133:58).[15] As the

---

12. Circa March 7, 1831; MRBf, 114–25.
13. See ibid.
14. September 11, 1831; MRBf, 188–95.
15. November 3, 1831; MRBf, 204–15; compare with Deuteronomy 32:30.

nations came to fear Zion and flee from her, a flourishing Zion could fill the resulting territorial vacuum without any of the violence and bloodshed of conquest.

Over time, Smith came to identify the temple as the locus of God's presence, his power, and the empowerment of his people.[16] In August 1833, a revelation promised the Missouri Saints that if they would build the New Jerusalem temple, Zion would "prosper and sp[r]ead herself and become very glorious very great and very terable [terrible], and the nations of the earth shall honor her, and shall say surely Zion is the City of our God, and surely Zion cannot fall neither be removed, out of her place" (D&C 97:18–19).[17] With the power of God, therefore, peaceful Zion would preserve and even spread its territory without a single act of aggression.

As the plague of international conflict spread, Zion would serve as a neutral territory and safe harbor for any wishing to escape the destructions of war—there was thus a certain space for Gentiles in Zion. As mentioned, Smith prophesied that the wars would proliferate until Zion would be "the only people that shall not be at war one with another." At this extreme moment of worldwide conflict, Smith declared, "every man that will not take his sword against his neighbor must needs flee unto Zion for safety & there shall be gathered unto it out of every nation under heaven" (D&C 45:68–69).[18] So it was the *violence of war* that would drive people to the *peace of Zion*. Here was another dynamic geopolitical relationship—perhaps even a dependency.

Smith's prophecy of civil and global war traced the trajectory of destruction to its extremity—the "full end of all Nations"(D&C 87:6).[19] Conversely, as another revelation asserted, Zion would continue to grow like the stone in Nebuchadnezzar's dream until it "filled the whole

---

16. On the developing concept of the endowment of power, see Gregory A. Prince, *Power from on High: The Development of Mormon Priesthood* (Salt Lake City: Signature Books, 1995), 115–48.

17. August 2, 1833; MRBf, 318–23.

18. Circa March 7, 1831; MRBf, 114–25. Those willing to live by the sword would die by the sword. As a subsequent revelation affirmed, "the wicked shall slay the wicked" (D&C 63:33). August 30, 1831; MRBf, 180–89.

19. December 25, 1832; MRBf, 290–91. As Smith described it in his letter to the *American Revivalist, and Rochester Observer*, God would "break them in peaces like a potters vessel." Smith to N. C. Saxton, January 4, 1833, in Dean C. Jessee, comp. and ed., *Personal Writings of Joseph Smith*, rev. ed. (Salt Lake City: Deseret Book, 2002), 294–98.

Earth" (D&C 65:2).[20] After the destruction of the United States and all other nations, Zion would be left standing as the sole sovereign in the Americas. Similarly, the Jews in old Jerusalem would eventually be left standing as the sole sovereigns in the eastern hemisphere.[21] The Lord would make peace for the peaceful by sweeping the violent from the earth with the besom of destruction—as he had in the Americas in the meridian of time.[22] These revelations gave the Saints a view of the world as a place that was contentious and prone to violence, warfare, and destruction. With this view on the world, the Saints were not on a mission to save it. Zion would serve as a refuge only for the peaceful.

The Mormon plans for a peaceful conversion of Jackson County, Missouri, into the central region of Zion were dashed in 1833 when the earlier settlers forcibly expelled them. They resented the Mormon community's solidarity, its growing numbers, and the swagger of overzealous Zion nationalists. When the Mormons became a real political threat, the early settlers drove them out with rifles and whips. The magnitude of their losses in land and improvements required the Mormons to seek aid from the state of Missouri in returning to the county. Joseph Smith had to accommodate the Zion project to the broader political landscape. The effort to "redeem" Zion led to a tenuous reengagement with American political culture—culminating in Smith running for President—but basically ended when he was assassinated and the Mormons left the United States bound for northern Mexico. Understanding the original Zion agenda as conceived by Mormonism's founding prophet goes far toward explaining the faith's nearly century-long contention with America.

---

20. October 30, 1831; MRBf, 196–97. Compare with Daniel 2:35. Smith's instructions on the plat for the City of Zion instructed church leaders to "fill up the world in these last days" with similar cities. See Plat of city of Zion, c. June 24, 1833, Church History Library, Salt Lake City, Utah.

21. On Smith's eschatology of Jewish deliverance, see, for example, Doctrine and Covenants 45:24–59 (March 7, 1831; MRBf, 114–125), Doctrine and Covenants 133:12–14 (November 3, 1831; MRBf, 204–15), and Smith to N. C. Saxton, January 4, 1833. See also Steven Epperson, *Mormons and Jews: Early Mormon Theologies of Israel* (Salt Lake City: Signature Books, 1992).

22. See Third Nephi and Fourth Nephi in the Book of Mormon.

*   *   *

The significance of Joseph Smith's original theology of Zion goes beyond mere antiquarian interest. The establishment of Zion—and all it entailed—constituted the formative worldview underlying Mormonism's early revelations, which in turn became canonized scripture for the Church of Jesus Christ of Latter-day Saints. Indeed, the Zion worldview pervades the revelations that make up the current edition of the Doctrine and Covenants, a book studied by millions of Latter-day Saints in Sunday School, seminary, and other religious classes, and considered by the faithful to be the word and will of the Lord in modern times. The Doctrine and Covenants is also an important component of the personal devotional study of Church members; many of those members have adopted the revelations' stark millenarian outlook. Some Latter-day Saints even still yearn to return to Jackson County, Missouri. The Zion revelations still powerfully inform Mormon religiosity.

The contemporary LDS Church cultivates a peaceful society within its bounds, and its members generally behave peacefully toward others, but it does not play the role of a peace-*maker* in the world. While occasionally adopting a position on certain domestic issues in the United States, where it is headquartered, the Church is generally unwilling to take a political stance—much less pursue a robust peace mission—when it comes to global affairs. There may be many explanations for this, but in large part this is because the Church wants to maintain good relations with all governments and have its missionaries and temples placed in as many countries as possible. While the Church did take a vocal position against international communism during the Cold War, it did so primarily because of the impediments that communist governments placed on proselytizing and the religious freedoms of Church members. The Church today is not trying to fix the world so much as it is trying to find the "elect" who are willing to repent and be baptized, embrace and live the gospel, and—though ungathered spatially—be saved spiritually; even the Church's impressive humanitarian effort was until recently considered to be part of its core mission to "proclaim the gospel." In short, the Church remains apolitical on global matters of war and peace because it is more committed to evangelism and the salvation of individuals and families than it is to peace among the nations. It is not a peace church, but a missionary church, an identity shaped in large part because of the millenarianism present in the early revelations. Any genuinely Mormon pacifist agenda, therefore, bears the burden of finding a way to come to terms with the worldview and resultant church mission that pervade the revelations of the religion's founding prophet.

7

Fall from Grace:
Mormon Millennialism,
Native Americans, and Violence

Jennifer Lindell

In the winter of 1849 Old Bishop, a Ute Indian, was murdered by a group of three young Mormon men. The men eviscerated the corpse and dropped the body into a nearby river where it soon surfaced. The incident kicked off months of brutal fighting between Mormon settlers and local Native Americans along the Provo River. The issue was settled on the frozen Utah Lake in February 1850, when Mormon militiamen and federal soldiers chased down and exterminated their native foes "one by one, leaving a grisly trail of blood and bodies on the ice."[1]

Only twenty years before this gruesome episode, Mormon missionaries had approached Indian tribes with news of their unique and chosen place in the providential history revealed to Joseph Smith. That the Indians' exalted status remained a key component of Mormon cosmology at the time of the massacre upon the frozen lake makes the incident all the more troubling. More than troublesome, though, Old Bishop's murder and the resulting violence were also representative of a larger national pattern. During the 1830s, America experienced an upwelling of religious zeal that assumed political and military form by the 1850s. Precursors to the Civil War included contention over states' rights and increased racial violence. The turn to arms as a solution to racial issues is well documented for the eastern and southern United States as well as the Kansas-Nebraska region prior to the Civil War. Lesser known is the

---

1. This account of Old Bishop's murder is recounted in David Bigler, *The Forgotten Kingdom: The Mormon Theocracy in the American West, 1847–1896* (Spokane, Wash.: The Arthur H. Clark Company, 1998), 69–71.

parallel but distinct pattern of violent paternalism that existed among the Mormons in Utah at the same moment in history.

Unlike most American faiths of the 1800s, the early LDS Church had a specific scriptural and theological framework that helped define interactions with Native Americans. This framework did not include violence or warfare, yet those elements still emerged. Several factors caused Mormons to disregard teachings from both their scriptural canon and their church leadership during Utah settlement. First, lived experience among tribes on the American frontier altered their original romantic conceptions of Native Americans. These alterations were reinforced in the press and from the pulpit as charged rhetoric increasingly turned Indians from "brothers" into "Others." As sociologist Armand Mauss has argued, Mormon conception of Indians shifted from the religious to the practical, which enabled justification of violent treatment of Native Americans.[2] Early idealistic notions were overshadowed by the realities of survival in a harsh environment, resulting in increasingly punitive and violent Mormon-Indian interactions. By 1860, millennial conceptions of Native Americans had been sublimated to economic and political concerns, and Mormons had become more "American" than "Mormon" in their perceptions of a racial "Other."

Idealistic Origins

The Book of Mormon highlighted a pivotal role for Native American tribes in ushering in the Second Coming of Christ. Native salvation was a necessary precondition to the millennial reign. One of the most important tenets of Mormon millenarianism was the redemption of the remnants of Israel, including the Indian tribes, associated with gathering those remnants to Zion. Joseph Smith received multiple revelations about gathering the Lamanites. One March 1831 revelation promised that "before the great day of the Lord shall come . . . the Lamanites shall blossom as the rose" (D&C 49:24). This revelation indicated that the redemption and uplift of the Indians would have to occur before Christ would return.

---

2. See Armand L. Mauss, "From Lamanites to Indians," chap. 3 in *All Abraham's Children: Changing Mormon Conceptions of Race and Lineage* (Urbana: University of Illinois Press, 2003).

Early Mormons were also exposed to providential conceptions of Native Americans in Parley P. Pratt's 1837 millenialist pamphlet *A Voice of Warning and Instruction to All People*. Pratt used his booklet to address Native Americans and reassert the promises made in the Book of Mormon. He informed them that their "redemption draweth nigh" now that the record of their true history had been unveiled. Pratt's desire for Indian redemption was clear as he told readers that the "gathering of Israel will be the greatest day for Revelation and Miracles, that the world ever witnessed."[3] Pratt thus reinforced—and helped further establish—the prevailing understanding of the gathering of the Indians as a necessary precondition of the millennium.

In addition to Pratt's influential writings, the broader Mormon press contributed to the ideological framework for early understandings of Indians and their significance in Mormon millennial prophecy. Newspaper editors honed in on the crucial role of Native American tribes to the Second Coming. One relevant series ran in early 1836 and linked the federal Indian Removal Act with Mormon millennial hopes. The Removal Act of 1830 required the relocation, forcibly if necessary, of all tribes east of the Mississippi to western territories. The United States instituted the removal to free up land and resources on the eastern seaboard, but the Saints viewed these removal efforts as fulfillment of the gathering prophecy. The *Messenger and Advocate*, one of the first Mormon newspapers, lauded the federal government for its part in congregating the Indian tribes. In an editorial, Oliver Cowdery informed readers that government action around the Removal Act made possible "according to scripture, the gathering of the elect of the Lord, out of every nation of earth; and bringing them to the place of the Lord of hosts, where the city of righteousness shall be built."[4]

Practical Experience

Faith in Indian redemption was evident throughout the 1830s to mid-1840s in LDS writings, pamphlets, and the press. However, deep convictions about Indian spiritual possibilities did not prevent Mormons

---

3. Parley P. Pratt, *A Voice of Warning and Instruction to All People* (New York City, 1837), 190, 127.

4. "The Indians," *Latter Day Saints' Messenger and Advocate* 2, no. 4 (January 1836): 245.

from experiencing troubles with actual Indians. As persecutions drove the Mormon community further west, clashes with local tribes over use of resources were prevalent, even before the full exodus to Utah. In 1846, Brigham Young negotiated a temporary stay on Omaha lands in Indian Territory. Less than nine months later, the Omaha complained to their federal Indian agent that the Mormons were "killing game and laying waste much of the land."[5] Confrontations between Mormon settlers and the Omaha escalated as Mormons continued to use (and, in the Indians' minds, abuse) the land. The Omaha launched retaliatory attacks on Mormon livestock, and Mormons responded with corporal punishment and petty violence. The two groups also clashed over cultural issues. In the winter of 1847, two Mormon men desecrated Omaha graves by stealing buffalo robes and other articles with the intention of selling them.[6]

Miscommunication and misunderstanding permeated Omaha-Mormon interactions at Winter Quarters and only exacerbated the violence caused by resource competition. When Mormons and Indians came into direct conflict over resources such as land, timber, and game, survival came first for Mormons. Consequently, a general disregard for religious imperatives concerning Native Americans was born.[7] At Winter Quarters and other pre-migration frontier settlements, Mormon millennial tendencies clashed with frontier realities, and spiritual concerns were shed. The Saints would carry this attitude of self-interest and self-preservation, along with disdain for natives, with them into the intermountain West.

As the Saints began to populate the Wasatch valleys, religious sentiments about Native Americans took a backseat to more practical concerns regarding self-protection. As Mormons expanded into Indian land and appropriated limited resources, native tribes faced impoverishment and starvation. As Native American historian Ned Blackhawk has demonstrated, Mormons "undercut Ute subsistence patterns" by disrupting "valley ecologies."[8] The already vulnerable non-equestrian tribes reacted

---

5. Robert A. Trennert Jr., "The Mormons and the Office of Indian Affairs: The Conflict over Winter Quarters, 1846–1848," *Nebraska History* 53, no. 3 (Fall 1972): 390.

6. Lawrence G. Coates, "Cultural Conflict: Mormons and Indians in Nebraska," *BYU Studies* 24, no. 3 (Summer 1984): 299.

7. Trennert, "The Mormons and the Office of Indian Affairs," 398.

8. Ned Blackhawk, *Violence over the Land: Indians and Empires in the Early*

by preying on Mormon settlements. Depredations such as theft or destruction of livestock and grain became common as tribal leaders targeted Mormon towns as sources of food supplies. In a precarious situation themselves, Mormons called for swift retribution to these raids.

There was little sympathy for the Indians' plight. Far from earlier ideals of shared affinity, retaliatory attacks became the norm. John D. Lee recorded in his diary on March 6, 1849, that thirty men had set out for the Utah Valley to "call the Indians to an account for killing Some of our catle." After the vigilante group discovered "10 Beeves hides & 3 calfs skins," they killed four Indian men.[9] These deaths warned nearby Indians what they could expect for encroaching on Mormon property. In May of 1851, Hosea Stout mentioned that the Indians of Tooele Valley were being troublesome so "a party is going out tonight against" them. As in previous disciplinary campaigns, the Indians were dealt with harshly and decisively; at least sixteen Indians were slain.[10] A letter from Brigham Young published in the December 13, 1851, edition of the *Deseret News* publicly affirmed this punitive policy: "we are compelled for our safety to keep a good lookout, and sometimes chastise them a little" when the Indians "steal our horses, kill our cattle, sometimes disturb the quiet . . . of our settlements."[11] Mormon readers were to understand that it was acceptable to react to occurrences of theft with violence to protect their property. Based on the number and similarity of reports, no Saints seemed troubled by the disproportionate punishment being handed out to local tribes.

Mormon newspapers, as participants in public discourse concerning Indian policy and attitudes, reinforced private biases against Native Americans. Stories in the press served to fortify common stereotypes of Indians as "numerous, savage, and bold cowards" during the settlement period.[12] The accounts that were disseminated publicly in the pages of the *Deseret News* contained graphic detail that left no doubt of the

---

American West (Cambridge, Mass.: Harvard University Press, 2006), 237. See also Jared Farmer, *On Zion's Mount: Mormons, Indians, and the American Landscape* (Cambridge, Mass.: Harvard University Press, 2008), especially chapter 2.

9. John D. Lee, *A Mormon Chronicle: The Diaries of John D. Lee, 1848–1876*, ed. Robert Glass Cleland and Juanita Brooks (San Marino, Calif.: Huntington Library, 1955), 100.

10. Ibid., 398–400.

11. Brigham Young to David Adams, *Deseret News*, December 13, 1851.

12. George Cannon to Joseph Cain, extract, *Deseret News*, November 16, 1850.

Indians' depravity and ruthlessness and seemed designed to inspire antipathy in Mormon readers. For example, a sensationalistic article from mid-November 1850 described the murder of three travelers by Indians in which the bodies were mutilated and scalped.[13] Articles like this provided additional rationale for the sustained violence against Indians.[14]

Ratcheted Rhetoric

The longer the Saints stayed in the Great Basin, the more intensely public rhetoric established the neighboring Indian as the "Other." To justify their continued violence and mistreatment of native populations, Mormon pioneers had to make Native Americans worthy of contempt and hatred. Rather than encouraging harmonious ideals of redemption, Brigham Young and other leaders often resorted to fear, distrust, and violence as ways of coping with Indian difference. In particular, Mormon leaders sanctioned self-defense. In a sermon on July 31, 1853, Young informed the congregation that they should always be prepared for an Indian confrontation. Even women working in the fields were to arm themselves with "a good butcher knife in your belt." Young himself swore that if a hostile "band of Indians come round my house . . . I am good for quite a number of them. If one hundred should come, I calculate that only fifty" would make it to the next house. Young's sermon strengthened the messages about the dangerous nature of local Indians and the importance of violent protection that were initially carried in the press. The Mormon public absorbed these feelings about Native Americans, and learned they must always be on the alert for unpredictable, dangerous, and untrustworthy Indians. Young ended this particular sermon with one last reminder that Mormons must "be always on hand to meet [the Indians] with death, and send them to hell."[15]

Along with being depicted as untrustworthy and dangerous, Native Americans were portrayed as inferior because of their nomadic lifestyle and lack of civilization. These differences were more emphatically depicted as the Saints spent more time in the Salt Lake region. Indians

---

13. Ibid. "Indian Difficulties," *Deseret News*, October 15, 1853.

14. See, for example, *Deseret News*, June 14, 1851; October 1, 1853; and November 12, 1853.

15. Brigham Young, July 31, 1853, *Journal of Discourses*, 26 vols. (London and Liverpool: LDS Booksellers Depot, 1854–86), 1:167.

required rescue from their primitive and barbaric ways, and Young's patronizing attitude was evident in his suggestions for Mormons to "instruct [Native Americans] in the arts of civilized life, teach them to plant and sow, reap and mow, raise stock, build homes, [and] make farms."[16] Traditional Indian ways were not good enough or valid in Young's eyes. He advocated that Saints adopt Indian children into their homes so "they have the same opportunities and privileges as the white children," implying that an Indian upbringing was deficient.[17] He also promoted the idea that Mormon missionaries should marry Indian women to lift them and their descendants out of degradation. Many missionaries carried ethnocentric assumptions that Indian culture was underdeveloped. To Thomas Brown, the Indians were degraded and pitiable in their current condition. They needed Mormon intervention to help them "quit [their] savage customs."[18]

Conclusion

Over the first decade of Great Basin settlement, when faced with increasing competition and hostility, Mormon understandings of Indians were transformed. Millenialist tendencies languished as more immediate and practical concerns, including the safety and continuation of the Mormon kingdom in the West, were reflected in a more stereotypical view of natives as dangerous, treacherous, and degraded. Negative perceptions fed into and escalated physical and verbal attacks. Violence became an acceptable reaction when Mormon interests were threatened.

Brigham Young adopted his famous policy of feeding the Indians rather than fighting them in early 1854, after several years of confrontations with local natives. This policy served the Saints well and affirmed the generally peaceable nature of the Mormon community as a whole. The years leading up to this policy, however, revealed circumstances under which early Latter-day Saints could resort to warfare. When community safety or sustainability was threatened, especially by a supposedly inferior group of people, early pioneers felt justified in respond-

---

16. Brigham Young, Heber C. Kimball, and Jedediah Grant, "Thirteenth General Epistle," *Deseret News*, October 31, 1855.

17. Ibid.

18. Thomas Brown, *The Journal of the Southern Indian Mission Diary of Thomas D. Brown*, ed. Juanita Brooks (Logan: Utah State University Press, 1972), 25.

ing with violence. Although this violence was eventually tempered, that it existed at all reflects the prevailing militant attitude toward racial differences that existed in nineteenth-century American society at large.

Like their American contemporaries, most Mormons held deeply ingrained assumptions of native inferiority. The attitude of white superiority over Native Americans, combined with contempt, disdain, and paternalistic tendencies, was an accepted and unquestioned aspect of mid-1800s America. Much like white southerners who used racial differences to excuse violence against African Americans, Mormons relied on the same rationalization to exonerate themselves for crimes against Native Americans. Leaders purposely stressed the differences between Mormons and Native Americans, and Indians became "Others" defined by their lack of civilization or religious enlightenment. In the Mormon collective imagination, then, Indians had descended from potential Saints to definite savages by the early 1850s. Lived experience trumped religious ideals.

8

Negotiating War and Peace in Korea: A Comparison of U.S. Military and Korean Latter-day Saints

Ethan Yorgason

For many Latter-day Saints, issues of war are somewhat abstract and remote. Terrorism could strike, but war's more generalized violence is quite unlikely to be close to home. The situation is different in Korea. War's widespread violence has been avoided for more than half a century, but South Korea has been on high alert during that time. The war with North Korea has not officially ended, and a fragile armistice and a heavily armed border secure an uncomfortable peace. If direct hostilities began again, South Korea would almost surely suffer devastating loss of life and physical destruction.

Yet the presence and moderate success of the LDS Church in South Korea (approximately 83,000 members, with an activity rate around 20 percent)[1] owe much to war, especially the Korean War and its aftermath. American LDS soldiers performed much of the earliest missionary work. The war's dislocations also likely created many of the social conditions that fostered rapid LDS growth.[2] While growth has slowed somewhat over the past decade, the American presence persists

---

1. The Church of Jesus Christ of Latter-day Saints, Church Historical Department, *Deseret News 2011 Church Almanac* (Salt Lake City: Deseret Morning News, 2011), 564; estimates of Korean activity rates come from informal discussions with Church leaders in Korea.

2. Spencer J. Palmer, *The Church Encounters Asia* (Salt Lake City: Deseret Book, 1970); Lanier R. Britsch, *From the East: The History of the Latter-day Saints in Asia, 1851–1996* (Salt Lake City: Deseret Book, 1998).

as the U.S. government continues to view South Korea as strategically vital. Approximately 28,000 U.S. troops remain, which is down from the 35,000–45,000 of previous decades. American military members are thus still an important, if no longer central, part of the country's LDS landscape. An English-speaking LDS district exists in large measure to serve military personnel and their families. Although the English and Korean members typically form separate congregations, members of the two groups often literally rub shoulders each Sunday as they share meetinghouses within the Mormon Church's overlapping congregational schedules.

This paper attempts in a preliminary way to convey how Mormons in Korea, both Koreans and those associated with the U.S. military presence, view issues of war and peace generally and in relation to tensions on the Korean peninsula particularly. It also attempts to modestly comment on the development within Mormonism of what the social-anthropologist Arjun Appadurai has called diasporic public spheres.[3] Such formations, Appadurai argues, increasingly connect publics across national boundaries, having the potential to create new conversations among those who have migrated and those who have not.

The paper is based on in-depth interviews during late 2010 with twenty-six individuals—virtually all are active members of the Church and belong to either a Korean congregation or a U.S. military congregation that jointly shared a single meetinghouse.[4] This research was not intended to systematically capture or statistically represent the viewpoints of all LDS members in Korea. Nevertheless, I hope it points to some important ways of thinking among members in Korea: basic

---

3. Arjun Appadurai, *Modernity at Large: Cultural Dimensions of Globalization* (Minneapolis: University of Minnesota Press, 1996), 21–23.

4. I interviewed eight females and eighteen males. Thirteen interviewees were raised in Korea, while fourteen were associated with the official U.S. presence in South Korea either directly or indirectly, such as by belonging to the family of a U.S. military member. (One interviewee fit both Korean and American categories.) The Koreans clustered in the age groups of the early 20s, late 40s to early 50s, and over 55. Four had served in South Korea's military, and two continued to be linked to it (though not through active-duty service). Most of the interviews with Koreans were conducted through the translations of Kim Young Won, an LDS student at Kyungpook National University; a few of the Korean interviewees chose to respond in English. The Americans' ages were almost all between the late 20s and early 40s. Nine were active-duty U.S. military personnel, virtually all consisting of mid-level officers.

similarities and differences between Koreans and Americans on war and peace, as well as hints on how Mormonism's multi-national and diasporic condition contributes to the negotiation of these thoughts. The paper emphasizes four issues. American and Korean Mormons hold largely similar viewpoints on the first two: living in a tense Korean peninsula and the role of the military in war and peace. The groups diverge somewhat on the last two issues: the contribution of Mormonism to matters of war and peace and issues of nation and culture.

Living on the Korean Peninsula

Victor Cha and David Kang wrote, "Put two people in a room to discuss North Korea and three different opinions will emerge—all likely to be charged with emotion, if not outright vitriol."[5] Indeed, I found many different viewpoints among interviewees, especially Americans, as to North Korea's ultimate intentions. For example, some claimed that North Korea's communism was evil and sought domination; others made assertions about the irrationality of individual North Korean leaders. Some posited that interpreting North Korean actions through these same leaders' desire to remain in power bespoke of a certain (if perverse) rationality, while others suggested how the desire for cultural/political sovereignty and a sense of defending itself from outside threats may have led North Korea to take frequent risky and provocative actions. One might argue that North Korea operates as a Rorschach test for American attitudes and ideologies toward foreign policy. In the absence of solid information about North Korea and in the presence of a media discourse that paints the North Korean government as crazy and unpredictable, Americans often project their anxieties about danger within the world onto North Korea.[6]

Even if they disagreed about the particulars, however, all American interviewees felt North Korea poses a danger to the peninsula and needs to be kept in check. To most, however, this danger did not imply worry about living in South Korea. Many servicemen noted that they were comfortable enough with the situation to bring their families with

---

5. Victor D. Cha and David C. Kang, *Nuclear North Korea: A Debate on Engagement Strategies* (New York: Columbia University Press, 2003), 1.

6. See Bruce Cummings, *North Korea: Another Country* (New York: New Press, 2003).

them to Korea. The combined United States and South Korean deterrence was doing its job. As one serviceman noted, South Korea has experienced incredible economic and political progress over the past sixty years. "You couldn't have done that in a dangerous location," he claimed. With a few exceptions, the Koreans agreed. While North Korea might engage in the occasional provocative act, the likelihood of a major war is quite low, they argued. There was little to be gained from worrying about war. A handful of both Koreans and Americans argued that the North Korean government was not going to jump into a war under current circumstances. In the words of one Korean, "If war should break out, North Korea must be prepared to lose everything, and they are not foolish enough to just let that happen."

One of the Koreans who disagreed with this viewpoint argued that ordinary South Koreans underestimate the threat, reasoning from the common (though questionable)[7] assumption that North Korea's military is vastly superior to South Korea's:

> Generally, people doubt that the war's really going to break out. But those who work in the military or in that sort of field don't think that way. Most citizens have forgotten about the Korean War since there haven't been any [continued hostilities]. . . . However, realistically comparing the two countries' tactics, and judging from North Korea's way of controlling its people, the war may break out.

A U.S. serviceman was similarly worried that nearly sixty years without all-out war had made Koreans forget the dangers. He argued that an unstable communist dictatorship next door *should* set people on edge:

> I don't think you can sit and go . . . "Okay, Korea is peaceful." It's not like living in Canada. It's not like living in Europe, or Argentina, or Chile, or Brazil, where you don't have a country that is just completely communist, with a dictatorship who's a little unbalanced.

Almost all the people I interviewed agreed that whatever the threat level to peninsular peace may be, it originates from North Korea. It seemed to be taken for granted—except by one Korean who suggested that the U.S. and North Korea ought to make more concessions to each other—that neither South Korea nor the United States sig-

---

7. See Roland Bleiker, *Divided Korea: Toward a Culture of Reconciliation* (Minneapolis: University of Minnesota Press, 2005); See also Cha and Kang, *Nuclear North Korea*.

nificantly contributed to the instability. This viewpoint, of course, does not distinguish Mormons from the majority of non-Mormon South Koreans and Americans. The viewpoint is nevertheless significant, since one might argue that it overlooks the possibility that all parties, to greater or lesser degrees, contribute to the ongoing impasse.[8] With that thought in mind, we might conclude that their Mormonism has done little to encourage Latter-day Saints in Korea to counter the (perhaps universal) tendency to assign aggressive tendencies and blame for conflict almost exclusively to the other side. The following sentiment, expressed by a Korean, was typical: "Except for the U.S. Army's military strength, war would have already taken place. The North, I conjecture, might have taken over."

The Military's Role in War and Peace

As the preceding quotation illustrates, a second idea that almost all interviewees agreed upon was that military deterrence is the key reason active war has not returned. All the Americans believed that the primary rationale for the U.S. presence in South Korea was to help maintain peace. A couple of interviewees framed the presence in a broader geopolitical context, adding that a second (and for one a secondary) objective was to maintain stability, freedom, and democracy in the larger East Asian region through a show of force. Likewise the Koreans, while noting some small problems with having a foreign military heavily stationed within their country, felt the U.S. military has played a vital role in maintaining the peace. Quite a few interviewees added that successful future peacekeeping would require South Korea to increase its military and economic strength.

While those I interviewed generally felt the military contributed to peace in this particular context, several spoke in more qualified terms about the role of militaries in creating peace throughout the world more generally. All of the Americans felt nations needed to have strong militaries as deterrents to outside aggression. One soldier who had recently served combat duty in Iraq argued that militaries are necessary in a world of greed and power:

> I believe in the good of man. . . . [But] I'm also a bit of a realist, and I understand that not all men are good. And so it is kind of a weird situa-

---

8. See Cummings, *North Korea* and Bleiker, *Divided Korea*.

tion to be in, because I can tell you war's no fun. I can't imagine a worse anything ever to exist on earth. But at the same time I realize there are people who are going to use it as a tool to get what they want.

Most U.S. military interviewees thus expressed ideas consistent with the international relations philosophy of realism, but they also frequently added warnings about militarism in ways that parallel Christian just war doctrine. A couple made strong statements about how the U.S. military's subservience to civilian leadership allows the military to work ultimately to peaceful ends. A couple others, in partial contrast, worried about the tendency they thought a few U.S. military leaders had to rely on militaristic solutions. A few more spoke of the dangers of seeing the military as a primary way to solve a country's problems. One quipped about how the military *should* be regarded: "It's your last tool in the shed."

While some U.S. military members pointed theoretically to militarism's dangers, most deferred to their leaders' judgments specifically about when and where to wage war. This attitude, clearly a part of the broad U.S. military ethos, seems consistent with an interpretation of citizen-state relations many Mormons hold: individuals are to support the military objectives of their nation. One interviewee put it this way:

I really try not to question the military and their choices of who or where we're going, who we're going to help, or why we're there, because I don't think it's really up to us to choose why we're there. . . . I think there are probably strategic things for a bigger picture that maybe we can't see.

While a couple of military members seemed unsure as to whether the United States' war in Iraq was appropriate, for example, they gave the U.S. government the benefit of the doubt and spoke of the chance for real freedom that they said U.S. military action often confers on another country.

Two servicemen, in particular, told of searching within Mormon teachings for more specific guidance on when to engage in conflict. They noted how hard it would have to be, or had been, to point their weapon at the "enemy" (a point almost all the military members raised). One found particular guidance in Doctrine and Covenants 98, which enjoins Mormons to thrice forgive enemies who don't ask forgiveness before putting the issue of retribution in the Lord's hands. The other acknowledged many possible and perhaps contradictory lessons in the scriptures, but felt that the U.S. military's recent use of counterinsurgency doctrine brought it closer to the Book of Mormon's message, taught through Nephi and Lehi's mission to the Lamanites, that preaching the gospel is more powerful than warfare.

Mormonism's Role in War and Peace

While holding generally similar opinions on the role of militaries in maintaining peace and the individual's responsibility to follow their government into war, Koreans and Americans differed somewhat on how their faith contributes to understanding war and peace. Many of the Americans I interviewed readily referenced distinctively Mormon understandings; Koreans generally did not. Some of the Americans spoke quickly of the Book of Mormon, with its prominent stories of war and the religious-military leaders who waged it. One spoke of the importance of a prophet in identifying what is permissible in specific situations. He added that the Book of Mormon's story of the Ammonites helped him understand that war can be required to protect the innocent:

> The story of the Ammonites is really what kind of sealed my view of the world. . . . There's this people who were enemies of the Nephites, and the missionaries went there. . . . They repented of their sins, they threw away their weapons of war, and then the Nephites, the entire nation of Nephites, voted to protect them from the people who were trying to kill them. And I feel that's very similar to what America has the obligation and opportunity to do right now, . . . to step up [for] those people who aren't capable of protecting themselves from those who seek to destroy them.

Many of the Americans spoke about how their faith teaches them to protect and provide freedom, particularly religious freedom. They drew inspiration from the Book of Mormon's Captain Moroni, for example, who rallied his people to militarily defend themselves against threats of tyranny from both inside and outside their country. And then, whether recognizing the size of the logical step they were taking or not, the interviewees usually applied the story to U.S. military action.

Although I cannot develop a full argument here, I believe that freedom has become something of a fetishized concept within American Mormon cultural discourse. That is, Mormons rarely consider carefully what freedom within and between the earth's huge variety of societies entails, yet they invoke the goal of freedom to justify a variety of means. If freedom is indeed fetishized within American Mormonism, it is probably unsurprising that virtually all of the Americans I interviewed for this research believed that the United States stands for freedom. They argued that while military force in any situation is gravely unfortunate, U.S. military action does at least bring opportunities for freedom to countries lacking it. Nevertheless, while they found this viewpoint about freedom entirely consistent with their Mormonism, they differed a bit on whether the viewpoint originated primarily from their faith. A few thought the primary reason for their strong feelings about spreading freedom was their Mormonism. But many U.S. military members insisted that, even if their own LDS faith gave them a bit more theological insight, many of their non-LDS military colleagues just as strongly yearned for and wanted to defend freedom.

When asked how their faith contributes to war and peace, most Koreans I interviewed responded with *religion's* general role in promoting forgiveness, peace, loving others, unity, and prayer. Some surmised that if religion had been legal in North Korea, Korea would be unified now. But only when I specifically pressed on how *Mormon* doctrines apply to possible conflicts between North and South Korea did a few mention such things as Helaman's stripling warriors, Captain Moroni (who was framed in terms of protecting peace rather than fighting for freedom), and the twelfth article of faith's injunction to sustain civil authority. In other words, Koreans did not turn *quickly* to specifically Mormon scriptural war narratives. One long-tenured Church member even made the argument that the Old Testament's and Book of Mormon's stories of war were not applicable these days. Instead, the Church member suggested we should love as Christ did: "we ought to think about the doctrine of Jesus Christ. Jesus Christ said love endless[ly] and forgive endless[ly]—seven times seventy. If we apply [this] to our North Korean people, we can make peace."

Beyond that, about forty percent of the Koreans also suggested that Mormonism and even religion generally offer little toward creating peace between nation-states. Religion, some asserted, has been as much a force for conflict historically as for peace. A few insinuated that the question is basically irrelevant since Mormonism has such a small presence in Korea. Some of the Koreans implied that Mormon teachings were powerful on the individual level, but did not help societies deal with one another. (One American who is not directly in the military made a similar argument; perhaps different opinions owe as much to a military/non-military split as to an America/Korea split.)

Thus a strong tendency existed among many interviewees, especially U.S. military members, to view Mormonism and the military as working hand in hand toward peace and freedom between countries. Some others, particularly Koreans, sought to decouple the two views somewhat, arguing that Mormonism offers either insufficient conceptual resources or an insufficient social/political presence to affect peacemaking on that scale. A couple of both Korean and American interviewees partially delinked Mormonism and the military in a different way. They asserted that the ultimate power to maintain peace lies within Mormonism. They pointed to promises they feel the Lord has made regarding war on the Korean Peninsula, specifically in relation to the LDS temple in Seoul. A story circulates among Mormons in South Korea that the Lord—initially through LDS Apostle Gordon B. Hinckley, and subsequently through Apostles Boyd K. Packer, Henry B. Eyring, and Hinckley (as LDS president)—has promised that faithful attendance at that temple will prevent war. For some Latter-day Saints in Korea, then, the best contribution Mormons can make toward peace in Korea is attending and praying within the temple.

One final point oriented directly toward Mormonism deserves mention. The interviews indicated that most U.S. servicemen felt great value in providing Christian service through the military. (My sense is that while *service* was often foremost on many military members' minds, in some contexts the *Christian* part of the phrase came to the fore.) They felt great satisfaction in helping the poor, the unlucky, and the threatened, whether from violence, natural disaster, or even life's more mundane challenges. While most did not feel that Mormonism, with its service orientation, uniquely qualified them to regard the U.S. military as such a service organization, it was clear that seeing the military in this way helped them link their identity as Latter-day Saints with their identity as soldiers.

Nation and Culture

Viewing the military as a service organization also seemed to allow U.S. soldiers to overcome worries about U.S. imperialism. Most felt that the United States has a special role to play in the world, particularly as the world's only current superpower. Some attributed this belief to their Mormonism, though I was surprised that a fair number did not make a connection or made only a weak connection. Thus, for example, several justified this special role by asserting that, for the most part, the U.S. military went only where invited within the world and left countries better off than they had been before. There was only modest support for a possible Mormon-centered interpretation: that America's dominant position within the world's structure of power derived from promises revealed through the Lord to modern prophets.

While their viewpoints typically accommodated American geo-political exceptionalism, most of the Americans' perspectives were not oriented solely around their country. With one or two exceptions, each military member spoke of the strong sense of responsibility they felt, not only to carry out their duties as U.S. soldiers, but also toward the Korean people. For example, one said:

> [M]y dedication to the people of Korea is just as real [as to the United States, his community, and family]. . . . If I had to fight and I died here in Korea for the people, that's what I'm prepared to do, as I know that all those soldiers that I serve with [are]. . . . And I think a lot of that is more along the lines of the gospel; you develop a sense of love and compassion for the people that you serve. And because of that, you can't help but to love the people of Korea, because you've committed yourself that you're willing to die for them if the cause should arise.

Thus a few explicitly noted their willingness to die for the people of South Korea, if need be, because of their respect for Korean people.

However, the specific micro-social situation afforded through Mormonism's weekly meeting schedule—Koreans and U.S. military personnel attending church services in the same building—did not nec-essarily strengthen this sentiment. To be sure, some of the Americans thought rubbing shoulders weekly with Korean Mormons helped them strengthen their regard for Koreans, but others felt that the church con-tact partially hindered developing a sense of love. A few frustrations over the way the meetinghouse is shared and over the culturally dif-ferent approaches to communication marked the relationship between these particular Korean and the English-speaking congregations. (To be fair, and especially since the interview period, the congregations have noticeably attempted to improve the relationship.) Some of the Americans felt their appreciation for Koreans and sense of support from Koreans grew more readily outside of church—for example, while riding public transportation, at work, or in service/social situations that brought U.S. military families together with Koreans.

On the other side of the relationship, the Koreans I interviewed did not mention frustrations between the two congregations. But neither did they think that their Sunday interaction with American soldiers had much effect on their feelings toward the U.S. military presence in Korea. One young Korean member noted that seeing U.S. military members with their families at church weakened some previously negative feelings toward the American military, but most Koreans said they simply looked at the U.S. military members as fellow Saints and friends, not soldiers.

This admittedly idiosyncratic relationship between the two congregations reminds us that challenges can always exist in relationships, especially those marked by cultural difference, even when both sides have strong incentives to make the relationship work. On more official levels, miscommunication and misunderstanding similarly persist within the strong South Korea-United States military alliance.[9] The South Korean citizenry exhibits a slow, long-term, and generational decline in support for the alliance. Nevertheless, public opinion toward the alliance fluctuates frequently, often in reaction to specific events.[10] In South Korea, as in other countries where the United States has military bases, specific frustrations sometimes arise over the physical presence of U.S. troops. These frustrations are particularly common in host countries, such as South Korea, that have recently moved toward a democratic political culture and are highly nationalistic.[11]

While a few Korean Mormons noted that some Koreans dislike the U.S. military, my interviewees did not share the disdain. Most of these Korean Mormons expressed gratitude for America's actions in Korea and saw the United States as a trusted ally. At the same time,

9. Victor D. Cha, "Mistaken Attribution: The United States and Inter-Korean Relations," *Asia-Pacific Review* 9, no. 2 (2002): 45–60.

10. Dong Sun Lee, "Democratization and the US-South Korean Alliance," *Journal of East Asian Affairs* 7 (2007): 469–99. Hyun-Wook Kim, "Domestic Events, Ideological Changes and the Post-Cold War US-South Korea Alliance," *Australian Journal of International Affairs* 63, no. 4 (2009): 482–504.

11. Ibid. See also Alexander Cooley, "Democratization and the Contested Politics of U.S. Military Bases in Korea: Towards a Comparative Understanding," *IRI Review* 10, no. 2 (2005): 201–31.

many hinted that they wanted something different from the relationship eventually, envisioning a more self assertive and independent South Korea.[12] All, except a couple of younger interviewees, held the nationalistic view of all Koreans belonging to the same family and strongly desired reunification of North and South Korea. A couple of Koreans wondered whether the United States shared the same objective. (Indeed most, though not all, of the American Mormons I interviewed were fairly agnostic toward Korean reunification.) A few Korean interviewees suggested that in addition to protecting South Korea, the United States was likely also seeking profit and regional dominance through its presence in the country.

Americans look at South Korea's prospects for peace mostly through the immediate North Korean threat, but Koreans take a longer view. While recognizing the North Korean challenge, they also believe that a more fundamental geopolitical challenge preceded and will persist far beyond today's troubles. Korea sits between three of the world's most powerful states: Japan, China, and Russia, each of which historically desired to control Korean territory in some manner.[13] Most South Koreans believe that adding the United States to the equation has given South Korea a temporary respite from geopolitical contests with its near neighbors. But most also regard U.S. interest in Korea as a long-term complication to the situation rather than a path to a permanent solution. Many of my Mormon Korean respondents felt that the key for peace in Korea's future was for South Korea to gain economic and military strength. It would then not need to rely so heavily on the United States and would restore its national pride. As one interviewee put it,

> There is no eternal friend, there is no eternal enemy. . . . I'm hoping for a day when we won't need U.S. troops any longer. . . . One way for a fox to beat a wolf is to be friends with a tiger. But we can't live like a fox forever. I hope our country will be Korea, a republic that's as strong as a wolf.

South Korean Mormons have strong loyalty toward their church, an institution popularly identified by Koreans as generally American-oriented. They doubtless understand the reasons this stereotype exists.

---

12. See also Lee, "Democratization and the US-South Korean Alliance."

13. Chung Min Lee, "Reassessing the ROK-US Alliance: Transformation Challenges and the Consequences of South Korea's Choices," *Australian Journal of International Affairs* 57, no. 2 (2003): 281–307.

But they do not feel beholden to the image. Virtually all of my interviewees strongly respected the United States and regarded the U.S. military quite highly. Nevertheless, they insisted, their Mormonism had little to do with their political viewpoints. While they believe their country's position in the world has benefitted through its association with the United States (which has been intimately involved with recent episodes of war and peace in Korea), as both Koreans and Mormons who wish to promote peace, they see themselves as decreasingly likely to rely on or even refer to the United States.

Conclusion

Representing twenty-six thoughtful individuals' viewpoints in a short paper is an impossible task. Each had a host of interesting ideas that differed, in ways often subtle and often profound, from those of other interviewees. For many, though not all, Mormonism played an important role in understanding war and peace. Still, I think it is safe to conclude that each person comprehends war and peace in significant measure through their own national background. National differences in interpretation and visions for the future exist. The large overlap in viewpoints between Koreans and American interviewees on many issues, such as the contribution of military deterrence in discouraging North Korean aggression, perhaps reflects their countries' close alliance and worries about a common "enemy" as much, or more, than their shared Mormonism. It was in discussions of Mormonism's role in war and peace that some of the more clear national differences emerged. In particular, Americans were more likely to find Book of Mormon parallels for their own country's challenges in creating peace (and justifications for its warfare) than Koreans were.

In such a way, it appears, a Mormon public sphere spreads through diaspora from the United States to Korea (and likely back to the United States). While some of the conversations on war and peace may have only minimal impact on Koreans, the application that American Mormons make of Book of Mormon narratives to U.S. war efforts likely return in strengthened form to American Mormonism because of the experiences of U.S. military personnel in Korea and elsewhere. As a believing Latter-day Saint with a strong personal interest in how Mormons think about war and peace, I believe these voices from Korea are vital to any LDS conversation on this topic; I especially hope that this volume brings Korean Mormons more directly into the discussion.

While attempting to honestly and fairly represent the views of those I interviewed, I surely have also hinted toward my own ideas. Just as those I interviewed do not agree on every issue, I differ with many I interviewed on several points. I conclude, however, by quoting a U.S. serviceman with whom I think all involved with this project agree: "Human life is incredibly, incredibly sacred. . . . To end a life is a serious thing. . . . And in all its forms it needs to be protected and it needs to be valued for what it is." I hope this shared assumption bodes well for future discussions among Mormons about war and peace.

9

Nonviolent Responses and Mormon Attitudes: Reasons and Realities

Jesse Samantha Fulcher

There has long existed in Mormon culture an expectation that its members will participate in the larger society's politics and social governance. Doctrine and Covenants section 134 is, in some ways, a manifesto for an engaged relationship with government, while the eleventh Article of Faith supports respect for and deference to government. But such respect and deference also raises issues regarding the appropriate extent of Mormon support for and involvement in official acts of war and violence. It can be difficult to criticize violent war—for some, the ultimate sacrifice of a soldier's life seals their support. However, instead of simply hoping to avoid conflict, or supporting those involved in conflict once it arises, it is crucial to seek alternative ways to engage these problems and create lasting solutions. Instead of asking: "Can we avoid this argument?" or "Must we use violent action?" we might ask, "How could we use nonviolent action to create a positive result?" Nonviolent action is not a new concept within Mormonism or in the wider political sphere. The principles and strategies of nonviolent action have been understood and practiced for generations. But despite this prevalence there remains a need in the Mormon community to strengthen the natural but poorly understood links between nonviolent action and Mormon beliefs.

Nonviolence is more than the mere absence of violence. Although this is its most basic and perhaps universal meaning, it is a mistake to treat nonviolence without regard for its complexities. Nonviolence is also the continuation of action, while refusing to conform and resort to violent means. These actions can be either pragmatic or principled, and can come in a range of strategies and motives. Gene Sharp, a fundamental scholar in this field, argues that nonviolent action cannot be considered a singularly coherent concept, but rather that there are differences between the various methods of nonviolence, from private pacifism to active resistance, or what Gandhi called *satyagraha*.[1] From a Mormon perspective, active nonviolence can be used as a means for resisting aggression and effecting change while maintaining personal integrity to gospel principles of love and peace.

Many revolutions are violent, however the Gandhi-led movement for Indian independence was highly strategic and steadfast in its use of nonviolent actions to create change. One example was the twenty-four-day "March to the Sea," where Gandhi famously and illegally harvested salt left by the waves. This march was carefully crafted and executed. Gandhi and his followers (who grew to number in the thousands over the course of the march) acted openly against the government and did so in a way that would continue to gain momentum. He gave speeches in villages as he marched, encouraging the people of India to gain personal independence through their economic decisions (choosing to wear homespun clothes, for example, rather than British manufactures). All the while Gandhi retained an open mind toward his opposition, and wrote letters to inform the viceroy of his motives and actions, which consistently left the door open for the viceroy to change his position.[2] Thus Gandhi strategically used his unwavering principles of nonviolent action to strengthen both his moral and political positions.

Gandhi titled his method and his movement *satyagraha*, meaning "the search for and adherence to truth."[3] The Hindi words *satya* (truth) and *ahimsa* (absence of violence) were the foundation for Gandhi's movement. He described *satyagraha* as a personal journey—an exploration in which he invited others to participate. By undertaking this journey, Gandhi believed he would draw closer to God, who, Gandhi believed, was truth. This is not far from the Mormon understanding of God: "For the word of the Lord is

---

1. Gene Sharp, "The Meanings of Nonviolence: A Typology (Revised)," *The Journal of Conflict Resolution* 3, no. 1 (1959): 41–66.

2. Louis Fischer, *Gandhi: His Life and Message for the World* (New York: Mentor, 1954), 97–99.

3. Joan V. Bondurant, *Conquest of Violence: The Gandhian Philosophy of Conflict* (Berkeley: University of California Press, 1958), 16.

truth, and whatsoever is truth is light, and whatsoever is light is Spirit, even the Spirit of Jesus Christ" (D&C 84:45). Gandhi also believed that the relationship between individuals, both within a movement and with any opposition, is tentative and must be forgiving. Mormons likewise believe that opposition in this world is ultimately short term and that to be forgiving is an essential personal attribute.

Gandhi's second pillar, *ahimsa*, can be translated to mean actions based on a refusal to do harm. This does not mean that there will be no violence; rather the refusal to do harm is so crucial that individuals will invite violence upon themselves rather than use violence toward others. *Ahimsa* is different from a pacifist distancing of the individual from the problem and requires an outpouring of love toward the opposition, reminiscent of Christ exhorting his followers to love their enemies and do good to them that despitefully use them (Matt. 5:44). *Ahimsa* is not apathy, but rather is an active approach centered on love, understanding, and personal enlightenment. Gandhi insisted that *ahimsa* is never about submission: "It means the pitting of one's whole soul against the will of the tyrant."[4] Here then is the greatest challenge of Gandhi's methods: retaining an outpouring of love for the opposition while continuing to pit one's whole soul to one's own cause, or more appropriately to God's cause (D&C 4:2).

To retain a forgiving heart without compromising eternal principles is something that we struggle with from an early age. This is evident in an example from Pine Community School, a small alternative and democratic primary school in Brisbane, Australia. Each year the whole school participates in a learning module entitled "Our Town." Children of all ages, from four to thirteen years old, spend a week making currency, running small businesses and other civic services, and functioning as a town with an elected mayor. One year, the older children had been studying various revolutions and decided to stage a revolution in "Our Town." After consulting with the teachers, one of the older children ran for mayor and, after her election, became a tyrant. The other older children rigged the election, were appointed council members, and also became corrupt. Having thus created an oppressive society, they planned for a younger child who knew of the scheme to foster a revolution among the other younger children on the third day. However the younger children, some of them as young as four, knew their rights and by the end of the first day were marching through the

---

4. Quoted in Bondurant, *Conquest of Violence*, 26.

school shouting "Down with the mayor!" As the tyranny continued, emotions escalated and the younger children wanted to tie the mayor to a tree in the schoolyard, leave her there, and administer other unsavory punishments. These young children sought not simply liberation from oppression but also the violent punishment of the perpetrators—who just hours before were their friends.

The ability to have love for their opposition, while still pitting their whole soul against the opposition, came only after teaching moments with parents, staff, and the older children who talked to the younger children about movements such as Gandhi's. The ability to show love was not a natural reaction by the children in these circumstances, but it was an important one. Consequently, the principal of *ahimsa* was employed by the younger children who agitated successfully for new elections and allowed the former tyrannical mayor to run a shop in "Our Town" for the rest of the week.[5]

Such themes of forgiveness in the midst of a struggle to overcome obstacles are common to Christianity as a whole and specifically to Mormonism. Paul states: "And be ye kind one to another, tenderhearted, forgiving one another, even as God for Christ's sake hath forgiven you" (Eph. 4:32). These instructions when applied actively within political and other disputes result in an understanding for the opposition or, in the case of war, for the enemy. This does not mean that one must acquiesce, or that it is morally necessary to refrain from stating and acting upon one's perception that the opposition is wrong. Rather it implies that individuals should have compassion for all people and must be concerned with their own standing before God (or, in *satyagraha*, their relationship to truth). The eternal truth of Paul's statement is that because of Christ we, and our opposition, are able to be forgiven and consequently, for our own sake, we must show love and forgiveness to all who wrong us. Such sentiments are further reinforced in the revelations of Joseph Smith.[6]

Section 121 of the Doctrine and Covenants declares that priesthood power can only be exercised with persuasion and kindness.[7] Since

---

5. As seen in personal observations of Pine Community School's "Our Town" unit in 2007.

6. See, for example, Doctrine & Covenants 64:9–10.

7. Elder James E. Faust stated that: "this greatest of all powers, the priesthood power, is not accessed the way power is used in the world. . . . Worldly power is often employed ruthlessly. However, priesthood power is invoked only through those principles of righteousness by which the priesthood is governed." See "Power

the priesthood is the greatest power it follows that other powers should be similarly exercised, and that same revelations shows the result: "The Holy Ghost shall be thy constant companion, and thy scepter an unchanging scepter of righteousness and truth; and thy dominion shall be an everlasting dominion, and without compulsory means it shall flow unto thee forever and ever" (D&C 121:46). At the risk of being simplistic, this means that when power is exercised correctly we will not have to keep fighting the same battles.

This is all very well in an academic or philosophical context. However when the opposition takes violent action the decision to act nonviolently becomes more difficult. It is a key characteristic for all forms of nonviolent action, including *satyagraha*, to resist not just society's pressure to resort to violence, but also the individual's natural inclination to view physical action as the strongest and most effective symbols of will.[8] Nevertheless, nonviolent action is not passivism, and does not require us to distance ourselves from an issue. Nonviolence does, however, require creativity to employ action that does not physically harm the opponent while still creating meaningful resistance. Gandhi famously reaching down to illegally harvest salt, for example, was a watershed moment for the Indian independence movement.[9] Such restraint and creativity recall the instructions of King Benjamin when he counseled his people to resist their natural impulses:

> For the natural man is an enemy to God, and has been from the fall of Adam, and will be, forever and ever, unless he yields to the enticings of the Holy Spirit, and putteth off the natural man and becometh a saint through the atonement of Christ the Lord, and becometh as a child, submissive, meek, humble, patient, full of love, willing to submit to all things which the Lord seeth fit to inflict upon him, even as a child doth submit to his father. (Mosiah 3:19)

The younger children who fomented revolution in "Our Town" initially believed the most effective action they could take against a tyrant mayor was physical violence. Eventually they were able to put off the "natural man" and creatively work for a solution that achieved their desired result (a change of governance) while retaining their personal integrity

---

of the Priesthood," *Ensign*, May 1997.

8. Leela Gandhi, "The Spirit of Nonviolence: A Transnational Genealogy for *Ahimsa*," *Interventions* 10, no. 2 (2008): 164.

9. Fischer, *Gandhi*, 99.

and decency—although some of them were initially willing to give up that integrity. These same principles, of seeking for truth and refusing to use violence while creatively resisting oppression, can be applied to everyday matters, including our response to government, our individual relationships, and even our personal responses to war.

Historically, the Mormon community was no stranger to struggles with an oppressive government. The polygamy crisis of the 1880s, for example, put the decency and integrity of the Latter-day Saints to the test. In his *Comprehensive History of the Church of Jesus Christ of Latter-day Saints*, B. H. Roberts recounts the ways in which Mormon families were scrutinized and disrupted to discover and prosecute polygamists. In resistance to this, members of Mormon society strove to hide their family circumstances from public view. In general, the crisis evoked a creative nonviolent response from members of the Mormon community as they developed an elaborate system to hide their most vulnerable men from prosecution, resisting what they considered to be an unjust law.

One particular moment, however, threatened to spill over into violence, and required counsel from Church leaders to help guide the Mormon community into a nonviolent response. Roberts recounts the story of Edward M. Dalton, who returned to his home after evading trial for unlawful cohabitation. While riding through town, he was shot and fatally wounded by a U.S. marshal. Respect for Dalton in the Mormon community, coupled with an overtly biased trial in favor of the marshal, caused great anxiety and disruption within the Mormon community. Elder Heber J. Grant, of the Quorum of the Twelve Apostles, felt he needed to give guidance on the reaction to this incident, so he telegraphed the local leaders and counseled them to "keep order, and not allow Dalton's friends to take the law into their own hands 'as one wrong does not justify another.'"[10] Grant's last thought shows a theme running throughout nonviolent struggles—the unjust actions of the opposition does not require a compromise of the individual's and movement's own principles, which must be held fast in order to achieve a positive and just end.

This period of Mormon history was difficult, not just because of the challenge to Mormon beliefs but also because of the violence that was aimed at the community. In 1885 President John Taylor urged the

---

10. B. H. Roberts, *Comprehensive History of The Church of Jesus Christ of Latter-day Saints* (Salt Lake City: Deseret Book Company, 1930), 6:117–18.

Saints to adhere to correct principles and to do all that was right without resorting to violence. Listing the wrongs of America's society and government, Taylor concluded that as "it is no longer a land of liberty [or] of equal rights . . . we must take care of ourselves as best we may, and avoid being caught in any of their snares. . . . Would you fight them? No, I would take care of myself as best I can, and I would advise my brethren to do the same."[11] While President Taylor's guidance to take care of one's self might seem open to violent interpretations, his preceding remarks regarded the need to avoid violence, so it appears that he anticipated nonviolent means.

Focusing on their own community with a view to protection rather than direct opposition became a form of resistance for the Mormons. Other groups have employed similar principles as a form of active nonviolence. One of these was the Golani Druze. The Druze are a small offshoot of Islam that melds Islam with other cultures and beliefs, including Christianity.[12] Their perceived religious (and political) heterodoxy has made them victims of numerous attacks in the Middle East and elsewhere by those who perceive them as dangerous heretics. No strangers to violent conflict, members of the Druze community in the Golan Heights have historically fought both for Syrian independence against the French and also in the Israeli Defense Force. Yet they chose to wage a nonviolent campaign against Israeli occupation when it appeared that Israelis sought to isolate them from Lebanese Arabs and thus manipulate the Druze in order to gain control of the Golan Heights. The resistance movement that followed was not a movement for independence but a movement for recognition of their beliefs and heritage. As one scholar has stated: "In a region and a conflict sick with violence, the Golani Druze demonstrated the efficiency and power of nonviolence as a method of social struggle which can be utilised by unarmed civilians confronted by overwhelming police and military force."[13]

The experiences and nonviolent actions of the Golani Druze do not represent the actions or attitudes of the entire global Druze community, but rather the experiences of a particular society bound by geography and situation that opted for nonviolence as an effective strategy. The Golani

---

11. Quoted in Roberts, *Comprehensive History*, 6:122–23.

12. R. Scott Kennedy, "The Druze of the Golan: A Case of Nonviolent Resistance," *Journal of Palestine Studies* 13, no. 2 (1984): 48.

13. Ibid., 50.

Druze were very aware of their situation and adopted a highly practical nonviolent stance that would give the best chance for success. Their tactics included a "reverse" strike as Druze workers refused to work for their Israeli occupiers, but completed a major sewer project that had been long denied a Druze village, thus undermining Israeli economic power while solving a problem that had been seen as symbolic of the inequality faced by their community. There were other instances where Druze villages banded together and supported each other through shared resources such as food. These nonviolent actions—in effect, simply "taking care of themselves"—became a means of resisting Israeli forces. Unlike Gandhi's *satyagraha*, the Golani Druze's resistance did not end with a dramatic success. Today, however, the Golani Druze are in a unique situation: both Israel and Syria allow them economic concessions, and the famous Golan Heights apples are sold in both Syria and Israel.[14] The Golan Heights and its Druze are still considered strategic, though now they are now in a strategic position for peace. These are immense achievements in such a fraught political realm.

At first glance, the connection between 1880s Mormons and 1980s Druze may not seem evident, separated as they are by a century and an ocean; but both groups creatively and nonviolently resisted oppressive government efforts. While President Taylor counseled for obedience to constitutional law, he also counseled the Saints to consciously resist the anti-polygamy laws, which the Mormons believed to be unconstitutional. In similar fashion, the Druze's actions in the 1980s were carried out as an obvious and clear act of resistance to Israeli law. Both groups actively resisted by bolstering the cohesion of their respective communities. Thus, both Taylor's advice and the example of the Druze point to ways of using nonviolence to achieve recognition of identity during seasons of confrontation.

While the Indian independence movement, the Mormon polygamy struggle, and the Golani Druze resistance effort all utilized nonviolence and were successful (in varying degrees) where violent means may have failed, nonviolent resistance is not exclusively a weapon of the downtrodden or the politically weak. It is true that those to whom other means of resistance are denied have favored nonviolence. However, nonviolence is a legitimate alternative to violent action regardless of

---

14. Majdal Shams, "Israel and the Golan Heights: A would-be happy link with Syria," *The Economist*, February 19, 2009.

the relative strength of the opposing parties. As the Mormon community continues to gain respect in local, national, and international communities, it should seek ways in which its members can positively, and nonviolently, advocate for and create change.

The area in which pursuing nonviolent action that is both principled and possible will be the most difficult is the international arena. Although attacks on homes and personal lives easily lend themselves to individual nonviolence, international actions that involve decisions of state often leave a void of individual nonviolent influence. Peter Antes states that before the end of the Cold War international politics was "the privileged domain of national planning, . . . a totally secularised world . . . neither religion nor emotion had the right to intervene."[15] In such a world, it is hard to picture the nonviolent role of the individual, especially the religious individual, being of any significance. However, Antes asserts, the fall of the Berlin Wall and the events of September 11, 2001, resulted in increased attention on the individual and his or her influence: "If we consider the world in its current state, the cry for justice from the poor and outcasts is a threat to peace. So listening to them and trying to respond positively means that we are committed to bringing about the necessary conditions for lasting peace both within a society and in the relations between peoples."[16]

Such peace is measured on both an individual and state level, and requires understanding and compassion. In an October 2001 General Conference address, President Gordon B. Hinckley talked of the great change the events of September 11 had wrought and the need to value international neighbors: "I ask particularly that our own people do not become a party in any way to the persecution of the innocent. Rather let us be friendly and helpful, protective and supportive."[17] Here Hinckley implied a way in which individuals could work toward peace, which is very much in line with the views of Antes—or perhaps Antes is in line with Hinckley. In subsequent General Conferences, President Hinckley addressed the issue of war and the individual.[18] Although Hinckley did

---

15. Peter Antes, "The New Politics, History and History of Religions: The World After 11 September 2001," *Diogenes* 50 (2003): 23–24.

16. Ibid., 27.

17. Gordon B. Hinckley, *Discourses of President Gordon B. Hinckley, Vol. 2: 2000–2004* (Salt Lake City: Deseret Book Company, 2005), 107.

18. President Hinckley confronted the issues of war and the individual on multiple occasions. In talking of anti-war sentiment, he stated that it is the

not condemn western involvement in Iraq—and indeed seemed to personally favor it—his focus was on creating love and peace both within ourselves and in our communities.[19] Importantly Hinckley admonished the Mormon community to view those with whom we find differences not as enemies but as equals who require our love and compassion.

Nonviolent action presents a practical alternative to violent conflict for effecting political, social, and cultural change. Wide ranges of nonviolent action have been used historically and are available today; these actions and the principles undergirding them are highly compatible with Mormon doctrine and history. As Joseph Smith said:

> I have no enemies but for the truth's sake. I have no desire but to do all men good. I feel to pray for all men. We don't ask any people to throw away any good they have got; we only ask them to come and get more. What if all the world should embrace this Gospel? They would then see eye to eye, and the blessings of God would be poured out upon the people, which is the desire of my whole soul.[20]

It is this desire for truth, to do good, and to invite others to the truth that makes nonviolence so compatible with Mormon attitudes and beliefs. As the Mormon community continues to deal with different discourses of conflict—from war to social politics—principles of nonviolence provide a way to advocate strongly without compromising eternal truths or personal principles.

---

individual's right to voice their opinion if it is done so lawfully. At the same time he affirmed that we must support our government (Hinckley, *Discourses of President Gordon B. Hinckley*, 180).

19. Ibid., 535.

20. Joseph Smith, et al., *History of the Church of Jesus Christ of Latter-day Saints*, ed. B. H. Roberts, 7 vols., 2nd ed. rev. (Salt Lake City: Deseret Book, 1948), 5:259.

Part III

Notable & Prophetic Voices

10

General Conference Addresses during Times of War

Robert H. Hellebrand

General Conference provides a distinctive means by which leaders of the Church of Jesus Christ of Latter-day Saints communicate with each other and with the world. As an open canon, one that is added to every six months, General Conference addresses may reveal and participate in the development of doctrine even more than the closed books of scripture. An analysis of how Church leaders have spoken about war, for example, reveals an evolving message. As the Church has grown in international standing, the messages of leaders have disengaged from particular political entanglements and gravitated toward the pastoral role of counseling members how to live when war is a reality. In the nineteenth century, Church leaders viewed war from a point of view stemming from their experience with persecution. Then, as the Church grew from a vulnerable provincial group into an international force, leaders increasingly recognized that members of the Church were on both sides of any conflict. As a result, Church leaders backed away from taking direct political positions in favor of offering the gospel as a universal cure to the unrest of the world. Leaders have generally avoided official direction regarding whether or not members should participate in a given war. Interestingly, while the basis and core beliefs of the LDS Church can be found in its scriptures, Church leaders have not often turned to these scriptures when discussing the morality and purpose of war, but rather have generally explained war through the unique prism of Mormon culture, doctrine, and history. In this essay, I examine statements given by LDS leaders in General Conference addresses during the nation's wars of the past century and a half.

The Utah War

Members of the Church of Jesus Christ of Latter-day Saints have often viewed conflicts and wars in their own peculiar way, which sometimes is at odds with the broad historical consensus regarding the origins and rationales of particular wars. For example, most historians would consider the issues of polygamy or theocracy as the primary reasons for the suspicion that led to the Utah War (1857–58). However, Mormon leaders at the time characterized the news of the approaching federal troops as part of the longstanding narrative of persecution of God's chosen people, without mentioning either polygamy or theocracy. This sense of persecution, along with the resultant self-sacrifice, united the early Church against its perceived and real enemies.

Such self-sacrifice was formalized when Brigham Young introduced a "Sebastopol Policy,"[1] perhaps the most memorable element of the Utah War:

> I am decided in my opinion that, if worse comes to worst, and the Lord permits [the United States Army] to come upon us, I will desolate this whole Territory before I will again submit to the hellish corruption and bondage the wicked are striving to thrust upon us solely for our exercising our right of freedom of conscience.[2]

There is no record of Church members protesting Young's assertion that he would "desolate this whole Territory." Rather, to underscore the people's commitment, John Taylor said to the congregation, "All you that are willing to set fire to your property and lay it in ashes, rather than submit to their military rule and oppression, manifest it by raising your hands." No dissenting votes were cast.[3] Other speakers also referred to this dras-

---

1. According to historian Richard Poll, "The 'Sebastopol policy' took its name from the 1855 Crimean War episode in which the Russians blew up their military stronghold in the Crimea before surrendering it to allied British and French forces. To the adult Mormons in Utah, most of whom had experienced rejection in England either as members or missionaries, the Russian action was an admirable precedent." Richard D. Poll, "The Move South," *BYU Studies* 29, no. 4 (Fall 1989): 66.

2. Brigham Young, "Remarks of Thomas B. Marsh," September 6, 1857, *Journal of Discourses*, 26 vols. (London and Liverpool: LDS Booksellers Depot, 1854–86), 5:211.

3. *Deseret News*, September 23, 1857, as cited in Poll, "The Move South," 66. Captain Stewart Van Vliet, an assistant army quartermaster, was sufficiently impressed by the Mormons' commitment to this drastic measure that he recommended that the army and the government seek a peaceful settlement with the Mormons. House Executive

tic strategy.[4] To many of these Mormons, packing up and fleeing was nothing new. They had endured forced removals before. Many (though not all) of these Saints, who had already left behind many of their family members and possessions in the East when they joined the Church, readily accepted one more sacrifice. In March 1858, they abandoned their homes and headed south. Although the record does not indicate that people actually burned their homes or belongings, their willingness to do so was on record. Five days after the removal, Brigham Young explained that persecution was good for the Church:

> Were we to live unmolested, uninterrupted, without persecution and hatred from our enemies . . . we might expect that we [would apostatize] from the truth. Persecution and hatred by those who love not the truth are a legacy bequeathed by the Savior to all his followers; for he said they should be hated of all men for his name's sake. If we had ceased to be persecuted and hated, we might fear.[5]

Young thus connected the Utah War with the persecution of the ancient church. Persecution was an essential part of the story of the Church, as members of the Church sacrificed worldly goods for the gospel's sake. Persecution also helped define their relationship to conflicts such as the Utah War.

The Civil War

Mormons applied a similar prism of persecution to the American Civil War. Church leaders did not discuss states' rights or slavery; they did not take sides regarding the North or South; they did not mention the newly formed Republican Party; nor did they glorify the war or the soldiers' sacrifice in battle. Rather, they saw the cause of the Civil War as directly related to how the Saints had been persecuted and how

---

Documents, 35th Congress, 1st sess., x, no. 71, 24–27, and Senate Documents, 35th Congress, 1st sess., 3:37–38, as cited in Poll, "The Move South," 66 fn.

4. There are at least eighteen references to the necessity of burning down their own homes as a last resort as recorded in the *Journal of Discourses*. Volume 5 alone has Heber C. Kimball on pages 164 and 278; John Taylor on 190 and 247; Brigham Young on 211, 232–35, 337, and 339; George Albert Smith on 221–24; Erastus Snow on 286; and Lorenzo Snow on page 313. There are additional references in volumes 6, 7, 11, and 13.

5. Brigham Young, "Wisdom Manifest in All God's Dealings With the Saints," March 28, 1858, *Journal of Discourses*, 7:42.

the nation had rejected the Gospel. God judged the world by the way it treated the Latter-day Saints, and Church leaders often taught that the war was a direct chastening from a vengeful God. Altogether, the sermons reflect a sense that the Saints were remote observers of terrible strife in their former home, but that they were not directly invested.

Furthermore, leaders emphasized the way in which the conflict was proof of Joseph Smith's prophetic calling, since he had prophesied in 1832 that such a war would begin in South Carolina. Church leaders also noted that Joseph Smith himself had laid out a plan to free the slaves during his presidential campaign of 1844. Consequently, in the mind of some leaders, the country was not only punished for killing Joseph Smith and driving out the Saints, but also suffered lost opportunities for avoiding the calamity by not listening to the prophet in the first place. Daniel Wells, for example, pointed out that the country could have been spared "a fratricidal civil war" and borne only "one-tenth of the expense" if only it had followed Joseph Smith's advice to free the slaves and subsidize slaveholders by the sale of public lands.[6]

Beyond emphasizing the punitive or wasteful nature of the war, some leaders noted that banishment from the United States was a blessing in disguise, as it helped the Saints avoid the conflict. For Brigham Young, Utah was a comfortable shelter from the storm:

> We are infinitely more blessed by the persecutions and injustice we have suffered, than we could have been if we had remained in our habitations from which we have been driven. . . . Had we not been persecuted, we would now be in the midst of the wars and bloodshed that are desolating the nation, instead of where we are, comfortably located in our peaceful dwellings in these silent, far off mountains and valleys. Instead of seeing my brethren comfortably seated around me today, many of them would be found in the front ranks on the battle field. I realize the blessings of God in our present safety. We are greatly blessed, greatly favored and greatly exalted, while our enemies, who sought to destroy us, are being humbled.[7]

Twenty years after the conflict, George Q. Cannon was particularly grateful that God had placed him and his fellow Church members far

---

6. Daniel H. Wells, "The Blessing of Life, Etc.," October 7, 1875, *Journal of Discourses*, 18:97.

7. Brigham Young, "Constitutional Powers, Etc.," March 9, 1862, *Journal of Discourses*, 10:38.

away from the fighting, so that "we should not be compelled to shed the blood of our fellow men."[8]

Indicative of the neutrality they felt regarding the conflict, Brigham Young stated that he welcomed conscientious objectors passing through the territory of Utah, while not finding fault with soldiers who fought for either side:

> Multitudes of good and honorable men become enrolled in the contending armies of the present American war, some to gratify a martial pride, and others through a conscientious love of their country; indeed, various are the motives and inducements that impel men to expose themselves upon the field of battle; but a portion of those who are peaceably disposed, and wish not to witness the shedding of the blood of their countrymen, make good their escape from the vicinity of trouble. It is chiefly this class of men who are now passing through this Territory to other parts, and I think they are probably as good a class of men as has ever passed through this country; they are persons who wish to live in peace, and to be far removed from contending factions. As far as I am concerned I have no fault to find with them.[9]

This was one of the rare occasions where Church leaders brought up the issue of conscientious objection in General Conference.

The Spanish-American War

The Spanish American War was a turning point for the Church. Historian D. Michael Quinn has compellingly argued that it was during this war, shortly after Utah obtained statehood, when the Church aligned itself with the United States politically. He noted that although some Mormons, notably Apostle Brigham Young Jr., opposed the war, the First Presidency of the Church expressed that LDS support of and participation in the war was the Saints' patriotic duty: "War has been declared, and we have it to meet. Our citizens are called upon to enlist, and Utah is asked to furnish cavalry and batteries of artillery approximating 500 men. We trust that the citizens of Utah who are Latter-day Saints will be found ready to respond with alacrity to this call which is

---

8. George Q. Cannon, "The Saints a Peculiar People, Etc.," October 9, 1881, *Journal of Discourses*, 22:327–28.

9. Brigham Young, "Necessity for Watchfulness, Etc.," October 6, 1863, *Journal of Discourses*, 10:248.

made upon our State." This charted a new course for Mormons in relation to national wars, and marked a significant departure from the LDS leadership's view just three decades prior. As Quinn notes, "From 1898 onward, the official position of the First Presidency would be to decry war, but to support any declaration of war by the government and to urge Church members to support the conduct of war by their government on the basis of the twelfth article of faith."[10]

The Spanish American War provided a glimpse at a distinctive turning point in LDS/US relations. Church leaders did not relish a war with Spain, but they were fully on board with supporting U.S. policy at this time. At no other time had LDS leaders so fully identified themselves as American, as the Church had evolved from being a provincial outcast in its early days and would gain a worldwide presence later on.

The World Wars

For the First and Second World Wars, Church leaders followed the general American trend and began each war as isolationists, but when the United States entered these wars, they supported the cause of the American forces. Before American involvement in the Second World War, the most outspoken proponent of isolationism was J. Reuben Clark, who found fault with both sides of the conflict. He noted soon after the outbreak of European hostilities in 1939, "There are always deceit, lying, subterfuge, treachery, and savagery, in war, on both sides. There was in the [First] World War. It is not always the other power that commits atrocities."[11] When the Allied forces dropped bombs on Hiroshima and Nagasaki, Clark was shocked at the lack of outrage from the general American public. He recalled the rules governing war, which restricted attacks on unarmed civilians and cities with their libraries and museums. Many of these rules were disregarded during World War I and particularly World War II, culminating in the use of these atomic weapons. Clark growled:

---

10. D. Michael Quinn, "Conscientious Objectors or Christian Soldiers: The Latter-day Saint Position on Militarism," *Sunstone*, March 1985, 17–18.

11. J. Reuben Clark Jr., *Report of the Semi-Annual Conference of the Church of Jesus Christ of Latter-day Saints*, October 1939 (Salt Lake City: Church of Jesus Christ of Latter-day Saints, semi-annual), 9 (hereafter cited as *Conference Report*).

As the crowning savagery of the war, we Americans wiped out hundreds of thousands of civilian population with the atom bomb in Japan, few if any of the ordinary civilians being any more responsible for the war than were we, and perhaps most of them no more aiding Japan in the war than we were aiding America. Military men are now saying that the atom bomb was a mistake. It was more than that: it was a world tragedy. . . . And the worst of this atomic bomb tragedy is not that not only did the people of the United States not rise up in protest against this savagery, not only did it not shock us to read of this wholesale destruction of men, women, and children, . . . but that it actually drew from the nation at large a general approval of this fiendish butchery.[12]

Church leaders must have struggled as they tried to reconcile their basic message regarding war. On the one hand, they held a deep aversion to war and violence, along with a belief in universal peace and unity. On the other hand, they held a basic loyalty to the United States and the principles of democracy. These forces pulled in opposite directions. There were always deep reservations about the war, no matter how strong the pull of patriotism. David O. McKay, for example, wrestled with the apparent incompatibility of the Church's support of the war with the Savior's teachings to love enemies:

We see that war is incompatible with Christ's teachings. The gospel of Jesus Christ is the gospel of peace. War is its antithesis, and produces hate. It is vain to attempt to reconcile war with true Christianity. In the face of all this, I shall seem inconsistent when I declare that I uphold our country in the gigantic task it has assumed in the present world conflict, and sustain the Church in its loyal support of the government in its fight against dictatorship.[13]

Leaders such as McKay explained their support for the American cause in terms of the centrality of free agency in LDS theology, and contextualized it as an extension of the premortal "war in heaven" between God and Satan. Democracy stood for freedom, while totalitarianism stood for oppression and compulsion. However, Church leaders also recognized that they were growing into a worldwide church, with many faithful German Saints in Germany as well as in Utah. The lack of enmity with the German people by Church leaders was notably distinct from the anti-German sentiment in the American public at large. Leaders

---

12. J. Reuben Clark Jr., *Conference Report*, October 1946, 89.
13. David O. McKay, *Conference Report*, April 1942, 70–74.

also pointed out that war could be a starting point for missionary work, allowing American Mormons to intermingle with European comrades. An official statement by the First Presidency in 1940 reiterated that the Church had a relationship with people on both sides of the war:

> Our brethren and sisters are found on both sides of this terrible struggle. On each side they are bound to their country by all the ties of blood, relationship, and patriotism. . . . The Saints on either side have no course open to them but to support that government to which they owe allegiance. But their prayers should go up day and night that God will turn the hearts of their leaders towards peace, that the curse of war may end. As always happens in such cases, each side claims to believe it is in the right. Each claims to feel it is fighting for its very existence.[14]

During World War II, Richard L. Evans offered that conscientious objection could be a righteous option in some circumstances, while he indicated that he did not believe so in this particular war:

> There have been some who have urged the Church and its members to declare themselves conscientious objectors. There may be some merits in this position. Perhaps we should reserve the right so to declare ourselves at some future time. I can think of possibilities and circumstances arising under which there could conceivably come some times and conditions for which we might want to reserve that right. But there are two sides to the question. Traditionally this has not been our position. In the century of our existence there is no people of like numbers that I know of anywhere in the world who have a better record for giving service when the call has come than this people.[15]

The Korean and Vietnam Wars

During the Korean War, there were very few direct references to the war in General Conference, but Church leaders saw the general struggle against communism as a crucial chapter in the War in Heaven. According to this formulation, the communist agenda centered on taking away the God-given right of agency. While the Church did not directly address the politics of North or South Korea, Church leaders

---

14. David O. McKay, *Conference Report*, October 1940, 6–7.
15. Richard L. Evans, *Conference Report*, April 1941, 52.

adopted the Cold War thinking of the time. The Church, because of its opposition to communism, had every reason to come down hard against the North Koreans and their backers; however, other principles prevailed. As the war evolved, Church leaders focused more on how gospel principles, rather than war, provided the path to peace.

During the socially turbulent Vietnam era, one may expect that Church leaders would have presented messages emphasizing law and order, and the importance of defending one's country. Boyd K. Packer delivered such a talk, which included a comment to those considering conscientious objection to the war. A former soldier himself, Packer acknowledged the ugliness of war, while asserting that, for him, conscientious objection could not be an option:

> I have worn the uniform of my native land in the time of total conflict. I have smelled the stench of human dead and wept tears for slaughtered comrades. I have climbed amid the rubble of ravaged cities and contemplated in horror the ashes of a civilization sacrificed to Moloch; yet knowing this, with the issues as they are, were I called again to military service, I could not conscientiously object![16]

However, Packer's comment was the exception, not the rule. In fact, Packer's talk was the first in the history of General Conference to outright disparage conscientious objection, and no other talks during the Vietnam era, including others by Packer himself, presented a militant message.

The addresses during the Vietnam conflict are striking for their absence of a law and order theme, which might have been expected in those tumultuous times. Rather, the overwhelming theme of General Conference talks regarded applying gospel principles to our lives regardless of conditions. Soldiers could serve as good examples and as missionaries, individual stories of goodwill could come between nations even while they were at war, and the gospel could provide strength and peace during the most chaotic of times. No General Authorities explicitly took sides in the war or specifically discussed national policy. (When communism was mentioned by leaders, such as Ezra Taft Benson or David O. McKay, it was never in direct connection with the Vietnam War.) In contrast to the discordant protests, fighting, and chaos in the culture at large, the gospel was presented as a soothing balm.

---

16. Boyd K. Packer, "The Member and the Military," *Conference Report*, April 1968, 33–36.

One surprising characteristic of talks from the Vietnam War era was how long it took Church leaders to specifically mention the war. The first reference came in April 1967, following a visit to the area by Elders Gordon B. Hinckley and Marion D. Hanks. With such a controversial topic as the Vietnam War, Elder Hinckley set the tone for how future talks would handle the subject. Speaking two days after Martin Luther King Jr., gave his controversial anti-war speech in April 1967, Hinckley stated, "I am not disposed to discuss the merits of the war, but I would like to say a few things about some of the young men involved in it."[17] Hinckley thus bypassed political ruminations for pastoral advice.

Over the next several years, subsequent speakers followed suit. They never opined regarding the domino theory, or the consequences of getting involved in a foreign civil war. Rather, they spoke of the individual stories of soldiers applying gospel principles in their lives. Elder Hinckley, the most frequent speaker on the topic, often spoke of soldiers who shared the gospel with each other. While acknowledging the horrors of war, Hinckley stated, "Notwithstanding the evil and the tragedy, I see a silver thread shining through the dark and bloody tapestry of conflict. I see the finger of the Lord plucking some good from the evil designs of the adversary. I see coming out of this conflict, as I have witnessed in other conflicts in Asia, an enlargement of the Lord's program."[18] In a similar vein, President David O. McKay commended the fine behavior of LDS soldiers. He related the story of an LDS Marine major who "expressed his strong testimony and asked that I carry to the missionaries the message that he is happy to be in Vietnam fighting to preserve the right of our missionaries to do their more important work."[19] The virtue and integrity of LDS soldiers described from the pulpit stood in stark contrast to the stories of soldiers misbehavior in My Lai and other places as portrayed on the evening news.

While the great majority of talks during the Vietnam War did not discuss American foreign policy, Vaughn J. Featherstone did provide

---

17. Gordon B. Hinckley, "A Challenge From Vietnam," *Conference Report*, April 1967, 51.

18. Gordon B. Hinckley, "A Silver Thread in the Dark Tapestry of War," *Conference Report*, April 1968, 21.

19. David O. McKay, "Priesthood Holders to Be Examples in Daily Life As Representatives of the Most High," *Conference Report*, October 1968, 84–87.

one patriotic note in the months following the close of the Vietnam War in 1975:

> [One] young soldier asked [his parents] if they loved America. He asked how they felt about this great and glorious nation. Both mother and father got a little teary-eyed and said that they loved this country dearly, that it was more precious to them than their own life. "Why didn't you tell me that when I was growing up?" he said. "I never heard you once say that you loved America. You never taught me to love it. I can't tell you what an ungrateful pup I have been. I had to go to Vietnam to find out what the United States of America is all about. I would gladly lay down my life for it. I would have given anything to know how you felt about it when I was growing up."[20]

As the United States was coming to grips with its least successful military exercise in its history, Elder Featherstone reminded his listeners that the efforts were not a total loss—that the war may have strengthened at least one young man's patriotism.

The War on Terror

In the aftermath of the events of September 11, 2001, LDS Church leaders reached out to Muslims, recognizing that people of all faiths were counted among the victims of that day. One year after the events of September 11, Russell M. Nelson delivered a talk that was interpreted in the national media as an official Church statement against the drumbeat of impending war against Iraq. The Associated Press offered a typical headline in the ensuing week, "Mormon Church Takes Anti-War Stance," noting that, "Nelson never directly referred to Iraq or current moves toward war, but he mentioned the conflict in the Middle East."[21] The primary source for this controversy was the fact that Nelson quoted Doctrine and Covenants 98:16, a call to "renounce war and proclaim peace." This particular scripture had been used only rarely in previous General Conference talks.[22] However, beyond that

20. Vaughn J. Featherstone, "But Watchman, What of the Night?" *Ensign*, November 1975, 7.

21. "Mormon Church Takes Anti-War Stance," Associated Press, October 6, 2002, available at Worldwide Religious News, http://wwrn.org/articles/5993/?&section=mormon (accessed April 6, 2011).

22. It is cited only once in the *Journal of Discourses* (George Q. Cannon, 22:328),

statement, there was little in Nelson's remarks that could be characterized as radically pacifist. Nelson did bemoan the fact that his beloved
Holy Land was now the scene of so much violence and that visits to
the area were becoming too dangerous. Nelson taught that the answer
to this violence was the gospel of Jesus Christ, and full application of
the Golden Rule:

> Now, as members of The Church of Jesus Christ of Latter-day Saints,
> what does the Lord expect of us? As a Church, we must "renounce
> war and proclaim peace." As individuals, we should "follow after the
> things which make for peace." We should be personal peacemakers.
> We should live peacefully—as couples, families, and neighbors. We
> should live by the Golden Rule."[23]

Nelson made no call for conscientious objection or any other radical action.
In fact, he reminded his listeners of their civic obligations, presumably to
serve in the war if called upon. Nevertheless, Nelson's talk was understood
in the national media as a highly significant anti-war statement.

On April 6, 2003, two weeks after the United States implemented
its "shock and awe" blitzkrieg against Iraq, President Gordon B. Hinckley
spoke in General Conference. His talk, entitled "War and Peace," currently stands as the culminating statement regarding the Church's stance
on war.[24] Hinckley, the primary spokesperson regarding the Vietnam War
a generation earlier, admittedly struggled with the subject matter as he
stood as president of an international church. He recalled an individual
soldier's tragic story, which he felt represented the contradictions of one
man serving his church for peace and serving his country for war:

> I received a phone call telling me that Staff Sergeant James W.
> Cawley of the U.S. Marines had been killed somewhere in Iraq. He
> was 41 years of age, leaving behind a wife and two small children.
> Twenty years ago Elder Cawley was a missionary of the Church
> in Japan. Like so many others, he had grown up in the Church, had
> played as a schoolboy, had passed the sacrament as a deacon, and had
> been found worthy to serve a mission, to teach the gospel of peace

---

by Cannon again when he was discussing the Spanish-American War in April
1898 and only seven times in the sixty years previous to Nelson's talk. Gordon B.
Hinckley later cited it in his 2003 address, "War and Peace," but that talk was not
viewed as an anti-war statement.

23. Russell M. Nelson, "Blessed Are the Peacemakers," *Ensign*, November 2002, 39.
24. Gordon B. Hinckley, "War and Peace," *Ensign*, May 2003, 78.

to the people of Japan. He returned home, served in the Marines, married, became a policeman, and was then recalled to active military duty, to which he responded without hesitation.

His life, his mission, his military service, his death seem to represent the contradictions of the peace of the gospel and the tides of war.[25]

This contradiction formed the core of Hinckley's sermon. But there was also an increased tone of militarism when compared with other talks of modern Church leaders, including earlier talks from Hinckley himself. There may be several possible reasons. One reason may have been the controversy surrounding the war. Only Vietnam incited so much divisiveness among the public regarding the morality of war. Hinckley undoubtedly saw the potential for this divisiveness to infect the Church, and felt he needed to take a stand. In his efforts, he acknowledged the agency of all people to agree or disagree with the current policies, thus signifying there was no right or wrong answer to this question. At the same time, by mentioning his personal preference that the citizenry support the war effort, he must have known his opinion would hold considerable weight for the majority of his listeners.

Furthermore, by stating unequivocally that the Church had "no quarrel with the Muslim people or with those of any other faith," Hinckley undoubtedly hoped the Church could be a bridge of understanding between many of the world's faiths. Those who committed the attacks did so in the name of their god, although others in the Muslim community adamantly denied that Al-Qaida represented true Islam. While Hinckley did not specifically address these ecumenical issues in this talk, the religious nature of the attacks may have prompted such commentary.

Gordon B. Hinckley's talk in 2003 was significant because it represented the summation of a century and a half of thought regarding how Mormons should view war. As the most direct address regarding war ever delivered by a Church president, it holds a preeminent position in this discourse. It put forward a dual message: to proclaim peace while also defending the Church and its people. While endorsing the pastoral message of recent Church leaders that called for prayers for peace, Hinckley reminded his audience of scriptures that called for a more active role in defending that peace, even by means of war if necessary.

---

25. Ibid.

Conclusion

While leaders of the Church of Jesus Christ of Latter-day Saints have generally not counseled members whether or not to participate in a given war, they have provided much insight into their perceptions regarding the causes of each war. The wars of the nineteenth century produced comments that portrayed a church that had mixed feelings about the United States and one that still felt the sting of the persecution that had chased it across the country. The Utah War produced comments laced with mistrust, while the Civil War yielded observations singed with bitterness. The causes for these wars, as presented by Church leaders, were idiosyncratic and highly church-centric.

The world wars of the twentieth century, on the other hand, spurred comments that indicated the Church was becoming assimilated into the American mainstream. Opinions regarding isolationism and engagement followed national trends, albeit with some uniquely Mormon interpretations. The conflicts in Korea and in Vietnam revealed the anticommunist feelings of many Church leaders, but the overwhelming reaction also reflected a pastoral attention to the healing balm of the gospel, rather than specific politics. Reaction to the War on Terror in the twenty-first century fully acknowledged the implication of leading a worldwide church, with more members outside the United States than inside. The Church could no longer fully assume the American point of view, despite its headquarters still being located in the United States.

Consequently, the official position of the Church, as revealed in General Conference talks, has shifted dramatically during the history of the Church. After nearly two hundred years, the Church continues to struggle with the relationship of the restored gospel to modern warfare in general and the tension between Christian love and defending one's country. However, as many leaders have suggested, these seemingly disparate imperatives may not be diametrically opposed, as defending the United States may allow the peace of the gospel to pervade the world.

11

Pacifist Counselor in the First Presidency: J. Reuben Clark Jr., 1933–1961

D. Michael Quinn

As the recently resigned U.S. Ambassador to Mexico, J. Reuben Clark entered the LDS Church Administration Building in March 1933 to begin twenty-eight years as a counselor to three different Church presidents. In his sixties, this Republican diplomat soon abandoned enthusiastic militarism to become an anti-militarist, anti-imperialist, consistent isolationist, and strident pacifist. Recognized nationally as an "Elder Statesman" for the next three decades, his post-1933 views on international relations would put him at odds with all U.S. presidents, with most Americans, and with most Mormons.

No one would have predicted those late-life experiences from the sentiments and activities of Joshua Reuben Clark Jr., during the six decades following his Utah birth in September 1871. He idolized his father Joshua for serving in the Union Army during America's Civil War.[1] And only one thing kept twenty-six-year-old "Reube" from volunteering in April 1898 to fight in the Spanish-American War: the entreaties by his mother and by his fiancée for him to stay at home in Utah.[2]

Nonetheless, he also had a heritage of conscientious objection. His soldier-father's family belonged to a pacifist German sect, the

---

1. "A History of the Early Life of Joshua Reuben Clark, Sr.," typed document, 2-3, microfilm, Henry E. Huntington Library, San Marino, California; Joshua R. Clark 1865–67 diary, J. Reuben Clark, Jr. Papers, Special Collections, Harold B. Lee Library, Brigham Young University, Provo, Utah (hereafter JRCP).

2. J. Reuben Clark ("Reube") to Joshua and Mary Clark, May 21, 1898, Box 328, JRCP.

Dunkards. His mother was the daughter of a pacifist Quaker who converted to Mormonism.[3] Thus, Clark's grandparents on both sides were conscientious objectors against all wars, but he rejected that heritage during the first sixty years of his life.

As ghostwriter for the U.S. Secretary of State and as legal adviser for the State Department from 1906 to 1913, he wrote justifications for invading *any* country to protect U.S. citizens and business interests—even without a declaration of war.[4] After Europe's "World War" began in 1914, he advocated breaching U.S. neutrality in order to aid Imperial Britain against Imperial Germany. In 1915, he defended the British naval blockade against American ships entering German ports as simply "extralegal." Moreover, he argued that the sale of U.S. munitions to England and France did not violate American neutrality in the least.[5]

In March 1917, Clark wrote a blistering condemnation of pacifists:

> The older I get, the more I see, the more experience I obtain, the more I become convinced that the peace propaganda and the present peace propagandists are both equally impractical and illusory, as also inimical to the interests of this nation. If we get into war, as seems now all but inevitable, we shall have to put some of them in jail, and personally I should like to begin with Mr. Bryan.[6]

This referred to William Jennings Bryan, who had resigned as U.S. Secretary of State to protest President Woodrow Wilson's alleged efforts

---

3. "History of the Early Life of Joshua Reuben Clark, Sr."; Leonard J. Arrington, *From Quaker To Latter-day Saint: Bishop Edwin D. Woolley* (Salt Lake City: Deseret Book, 1976).

4. Frank W. Fox, *J. Reuben Clark: The Public Years* (Provo, Utah: BYU Press; Salt Lake City: Deseret Book, 1980), 196–97. Clark's *The Right To Protect Citizens In Foreign Countries By Landing Forces* was reprinted in David H. Yarn Jr., ed., *J. Reuben Clark: Selected Papers On International Affairs* (Provo, Utah: BYU Press, 1987), 321–24.

5. Fox, *J. Reuben Clark*, 255–60; D. Michael Quinn, *Elder Statesman: A Biography of J. Reuben Clark* (Salt Lake City: Signature Books, 2002), 278–79.

6. J. Reuben Clark (hereafter JRC) to Theodore Marburg, March 3, 1917, folder for American Peace Society, Box 343, JRCP. Clark's 1917 attitude was similar to the decades-later discussion of "radical pacifist" by Robert S. Wood, "War and Peace," in Daniel H. Ludlow, ed., *Encyclopedia of Mormonism: The History, Scripture, Doctrine, and Procedure of the Church of Jesus Christ of Latter-day Saints*, 5 vols. (New York: Macmillan, 1992), 4:1547.

to provoke war with Germany. At the time of this letter, Bryan was continuing his campaign for pacifism.[7]

Although a staunch Republican, Clark wholeheartedly endorsed the Democratic president's message to Congress in April 1917. Wilson famously stated that U.S. entry into "the European War" was necessary because "the world must be made safe for democracy."[8] Despite the prospect of turning his wife into a wartime widow and leaving his four children fatherless, Clark joined the U.S. Army Reserve. There he was commissioned as a major in the Judge Advocate General, where he assisted in formulating a "selective service" program for "conscripting" or "drafting" young men into the armed forces, where 116,000 would die in the European war. Months later, while also serving as "Special Assistant" to the U.S. Attorney General, Clark endorsed imprisoning thousands of German and Austrian nationals. In addition, he argued that the legal restrictions on "enemy aliens" in the United States should be applied to women as well as men.[9]

In view of the above, one can easily imagine Clark's negative reaction to an official editorial by his Church's newspaper in March 1918 (four months after U.S. soldiers began dying in the trench warfare of Northern France): "Governments of, for and by the people are wise when they try to meet, in a spirit of fairness, the scruples of those who by training or instinct are averse to the bearing of arms with which to slay their fellowmen."[10] In his massive collection of personal papers, no comment survives about this *Deseret News* endorsement of conscientious objection. However, there is a good indication in the views he expressed about pacifists only twelve months earlier.

For a decade after the armistice of November 1918 ended the European bloodshed, Clark continued to work for what he regarded as sane militarism, but he had become an isolationist. He attacked the

7. Ernest R. May, *The World War and American Isolation, 1914–1917* (Cambridge, Mass.: Harvard University Press, 1959), 142–56; Louis W. Koenig, *Bryan: A Political Biography of William Jennings Bryan* (New York: G.P. Putnam's Sons, 1971), 502–69.

8. *Encyclopedia Americana: International Edition*, 30 vols. (Danbury, Conn.: Grolier, 2000), 29:335.

9. Fox, *J. Reuben Clark*, 252, 263, 271.

10. "Service for 'Objectors,'" editorial, *Deseret News*, March 27, 1918, 4. For the deaths of U.S. soldiers beginning on November 4, 1917, see "Passing Events . . . Americans in the Trenches in France," *Improvement Era* 21 (December 1917).

League of Nations provision in the Treaty of Versailles and the treaty itself in ghostwritten talks for U.S. Senator Philander Knox. In 1919, Clark told a crowd of ten thousand people in the Salt Lake Tabernacle that Americans would "waste the strength God has given us" by joining "in petty squabbles over a few rods of miserable European blood-sodden soil."[11] A group of Mormons in favor of the treaty publicly denounced his talk as "pro-German" and "traitorous."[12] Such accusations would echo during Clark's subsequent isolationism in the Second World War.

Nonetheless, at this stage of his career, his American isolationism was definitely *not* anti-war. He wrote in 1922: "A treaty outlawing war would only handicap the 'righteous' nations [from] punishing criminal nations and deterring their future misdeeds." His memorandum concluded that "war is a necessary factor in human progress."[13]

It was a surprise in May 1923 when Clark became chairman of the New York Committee for the Outlawry of War,[14] marking a reversal from statements he had made barely a year earlier. As usual, he did not explain his change of views, nor acknowledge that this was a change. He defended his new position with the enthusiasm of a convert, denying that he was a pacifist or utopian dreamer:

> But, as I said in my last letter, ours is not a pacifist movement. We do not proceed toward peace along the path of disarmament; we expect disarmament through the riddance of war, rather than riddance of war through disarmament.... The main thing, however, is that it will be difficult or impossible to start a war once we have so re-ordered the world, and international wars have become as unlawful as domestic wars of

---

11. "Address of Major J. Reuben Clark on Peace," *Deseret News*, September 6, 1919, Section 4, vii.

12. "Brand Clark as Unfair and Illogical," *Deseret News*, September 6, 1919, 5, in which George W. Middleton, Elias A. Smith, George E. Fellows, and Joshua H. Paul criticized his talk as "pro-German, illogical and one-sided," and as "not false merely, but traitorous." For Middleton, Smith, and Paul as devout Mormons, see Andrew Jenson, *Latter-day Saint Biographical Encyclopedia*, 4 vols. (Salt Lake City: Deseret News/Andrew Jenson History, 1901–36), 2:72, 481, 4:61; *Report of the Semi-Annual Conference of the Church of Jesus Christ of Latter-day Saints*, April 1914 (Salt Lake City: Church of Jesus Christ of Latter-day Saints, semi-annual), 86 (hereafter cited as *Conference Report*).

13. JRC, "Criticism of Plan To Outlaw War," 17 January 1922, Box 47, JRCP, with full text in Yarn, *J. Reuben Clark: Selected Papers On International Affairs*, 193–96.

14. Salmon O. Levinson to JRC, 9 May 1923, folder for American Committee for the Outlawry of War, Box 345, JRCP.

revolution. These latter cannot be prevented but [—] as they proceed in the teeth of the law, they are rare and are illegal and criminal.[15]

With such convictions, it is not surprising that he enthusiastically endorsed the U.S. Secretary of State's 1928 Kellogg-Briand Treaty, or Pact of Paris, which outlawed war.[16]

Ten years later, Clark dismissed this treaty, and by implication his own 1923–24 activities as "poetic pseudo-Messianic dreams of universal peace."[17] He readopted his pre-1923 views about the futility of trying to "re-order" the world, and in 1930 refused an invitation to affiliate with the American Peace Society, the nation's oldest organization for pacifism.[18]

What led to Clark's post-1918 ambivalence and stark reversals thereafter? First, like many Americans, he was already disillusioned that a war "to make the world safe for democracy" had resulted in dictatorships: Russia in 1917, Hungary in 1920, Italy in 1922, Bulgaria in 1923, Romania in 1923, Albania in 1924, Yugoslavia in 1929, and Germany in 1933. Second, he was soon persuaded by "revisionist" scholarship from the late 1920s onward that the British government had maneuvered America into World War I through official lies, military collusion, and newspaper propaganda.[19] Third, he correspondingly became convinced that pro-British Americans would say and do *anything* to aid Britain in *every* war it waged. Fourth, he became convinced that imperialism and colonialism inevitably led to a succession of European wars. Fifth, like most Americans, he was stunned by the testimony of Major General Smedley D. Butler to Congress in 1934 about an alleged plot to estab-

---

15. JRC to J.C. Maxwell Garnett, March 11, 1924, folder for American Committee for the Outlawry of War.

16. Fox, *J. Reuben Clark*, 513.

17. JRC to E. Worth Higgins, October 12, 1938, Folder 3, Box 359, JRCP.

18. John J. Esch to JRC, 9 May, 21 July 1930, both in Box 30, JRCP; also the American Peace Society's official periodical *World Affairs* (front and back covers) for its establishment in 1828.

19. For example, Henry Elmer Barnes, *The Genesis of the World War: An Introduction of the Problem of War Guilt* (New York: Alfred A. Knopf, 1926), esp. 654–62; Arthur Ponsonby, *Falsehood in War-Time: Containing an Assortment of Lies Circulated Throughout the Nations During the Great War* (New York: E.P. Dutton, 1928); C. Hartley Grattan, *Why We Fought* (New York: Vanguard Press, 1929); Walter Millis, *Road To War: America, 1914–1917* (Boston: Houghton Mifflin, 1935); James D. Squires, *British Propaganda At Home and In the United States From 1914 to 1917* (Cambridge, Mass.: Harvard University Press, 1935).

lish a military dictatorship in the United States. Butler accused World War I veterans in the American Legion of promoting a *coup d'etat*,[20] another bitter irony of America's 1917 war to protect democracy.

On the other hand, since 1919, Clark had regarded the Versailles Treaty as a vengeful and unjust punishment of Germany for all of Europe's mistakes.[21] After Adolf Hitler announced in 1935 that, contrary to the treaty, he was remilitarizing Germany, Clark told U.S. Senator Hiram W. Johnson that "Germany wrote at least the head note to a great new chapter in European history," adding that he could not blame Germany's dictator for scrapping the Versailles Treaty.[22] By then, he had already acquired English versions of Hitler's triumphal speeches as translated by a Nazi publisher.[23] As president of the Foreign Bondholders' Protective Council in New York City,[24] Clark visited Berlin for six days in August 1937, then again for a few days the following year. He was favorably impressed with living conditions there. During each visit, he met with LDS mission leaders and the Reichbank president Hjalmar Schacht,[25] who was also "the central figure in National Socialist rearmament."[26] After an LDS general authority condemned Nazi territorial acquisitions during the general priesthood meeting of April 1938, President Clark asked the conference: "Has Great Britain ever seen anything lying loose that she did not pick up? France is in no better position. So, brethren, let us be quiet at any rate about the matter."[27]

---

20. Jules Archer, *The Plot To Seize the White House* (New York: Hawthorne Books, 1973).

21. Fox, *J. Reuben Clark*, 288, 290–92.

22. JRC to Hiram W. Johnson, March 18, 1935, Folder 4, Box 352, JRCP.

23. "Clarkana" (the Lee Library's collection of JRC's entire personal library) has *Understanding Germany: Reichskanzler Adolf Hitler Addressing the German Reichstag on May 17, 1933* (Berlin: Liebheit and Thiessen, 1933); *One Year of National Socialism In Germany: Speech Delivered By Chancellor Adolf Hitler In the Reichstag on January 30, 1934* (Berlin: Liebheit and Thiessen, 1934).

24. For President Heber J. Grant's authorizing Counselor Clark to accept this appointment from the liberal Democratic administration of U.S. President Franklin D. Roosevelt, despite its many distractions of time and travel from LDS Church headquarters, see Quinn, *Elder Statesman*, 62–63, 65.

25. JRC 1937 diary, August 4–9; JRC 1938 diary, June 24–27; both in JRCP.

26. Christian Zentner and Friedemann Beduerftig, eds., *The Encyclopedia of the Third Reich*, trans. Amy Hackett, 2 vols. (New York: Macmillan, 1991), 2:831.

27. JRC to general priesthood meeting, April 4, 1938, transcript, Box 151, JRCP.

After his second visit to Nazi Germany, First Counselor Clark reported on its conditions during a meeting of the LDS Presidency in July 1938. His outline included praise: "Germany's chin is up. No direct attack on religion. Young people's standard—what would Fuhrer do?"[28] In view of Clark's frequently stated opposition to the regulation of businesses by the central government, he was also impressed by newspaper reports that "Hitler Champions Business Freedom."[29] Years later, he would say that at least Nazism allowed "private property and individualism," whereas Communism did not.[30] In his report to President Heber J. Grant and Second Counselor David O. McKay in July 1938, Clark added his own observation that there was widespread support of Hitler among German members of the LDS Church. This was the context of his plea to the next General Conference: "Let us not make a great body of the membership of our Church feel that they are outcasts from us because of the acts of their governments."[31] In November 1938, he bitterly warned that U.S. President Franklin D. Roosevelt was trying to get the United States into a war.[32]

A month after the commencement of the Second World War in September 1939, Clark wrote a First Presidency statement that condemned war in general.[33] His own sermon told the October conference that this was an "unholy war" and that Latter-day Saints should expect "deceit, lying, subterfuge, treachery, and savagery" on all sides.[34] In the midst of the hostilities, he stated in General Conference that it was an

28. JRC memorandum, July 18, 1938, Folder 4, Box 215, JRCP.

29. "Hitler Champions Business Freedom," *New York Times*, May 17, 1934, 13; "Hitler Derides Russia For Asking Assistance of Capitalist Nations," *Salt Lake Tribune*, May 17, 1934, 8. The Lee Library's "Clarkana" collection also has *Economic Development of Germany Under National Socialism* (New York: National Industrial Conference Board, 1937), with JRC underlinings and marginal notations.

30. JRC, *Let Us Have Peace* (Salt Lake City: Deseret News Press, 1947), 15.

31. *Conference Report*, October 1938, 136.

32. JRC to James T. Williams, November 21, 1938, Folder 3, Box 359, JRCP.

33. James R. Clark, ed., *Messages of the First Presidency of The Church of Jesus Christ of Latter-day Saints*, 6 vols. (Salt Lake City: Bookcraft, 1965–71), 6:89–91. For explanation of why Heber J. Grant allowed J. Reuben Clark to write the text of Grant's correspondence, of the Church President's talks to General Conferences, and of the First Presidency's messages after April 1933, see Quinn, *Elder Statesman*, 86, with other examples on pages 60, 69, 78, 80–81, 95, 99, 142–43, 209, 218–19, 232, 244–45, 260, 293, 320–21, 333–34, 384, 392, 395, 462 note 241, 475 note 66.

34. *Conference Report*, October 1939, 11–12.

"unrighteous cause" that "began as a war for empire."[35] He privately explained that in this "unrighteous war," Great Britain was trying to preserve its empire and Nazi Germany was seeking empire.[36]

Such statements were a direct assault against the claim that Britain and France had justifiably declared war to "defend freedom" by combatting Nazi aggression against Poland. Instead, he told the General Conference of October 1939: "There are in the Church tens of thousands of faithful members, and in the [US] nation millions of loyal citizens, whose choice would be, because of their German ancestry, that Germany should become the dominant power of Europe, and following that, perhaps of the world."[37] This same year, he also joined the national advisory council of the American Peace Society, which signaled both his embrace of pacifism and his anti-British views.[38] President Clark seemed to emphasize his German ancestry, rather than his English ancestry.

It did no good when Latter-day Saints expressed to him their conviction that Britain must be victorious against Nazism for the benefit of democratic societies. He merely countered: "The Germans appear to have the idea that they are fighting for their lives. And of course England and France, not Germany, declared this war."[39] He wrote this rebuttal to the LDS Relief Society's general president on July 15, 1940, a month after France surrendered and the Nazi army triumphantly entered Paris.[40] In July 1940, he also warned the Young Republicans of Utah that Roosevelt "seemed to be trying to get Japan to go to war with us" as a backdoor way of entering the European conflict.[41] Within seventeen months, this would seem starkly prophetic.

---

35. *Conference Report*, April 1941, 20.

36. JRC to Orval Adams, April 25, 1941, Folder 1, Box 363, JRCP.

37. *Conference Report*, October 1939, 13.

38. JRC to Arthur Deering Call, June 26, 1939, Folder 1, Box 361, JRCP.

39. JRC to Amy Brown Lyman, July 15, 1940, Folder 2, Box 362, JRCP; also JRC to William Cullen Dennis, July 8, 1942 ("it must not be forgotten that Britain and France declared and opened this war"), Folder 1, Box 365, JRCP.

40. "Hitler Takes Nine Days In Drive On Paris," *Deseret News*, June 14, 1940, 2; for Amy Brown Lyman as general president in 1940, see Jill Mulvay Derr, Janath Russell Cannon, and Maureen Ursenbach Beecher, *Women of Covenant: The Story of Relief Society* (Salt Lake City: Deseret Book, 1992), 436.

41. JRC office diary, July 9, 1940, JRCP; Lee Library's "Clarkana" collection has Edwin C. Riegel, *The Aggressor In the White House* (New York: League for Constitutional Government, 1940); also see the non-polemical "Provoking War" chapter in Irwin F. Gellman, *Secret Affairs: Franklin Roosevelt, Cordell Hull, and*

By mid-February 1941, however, Mormons were criticizing what seemed like President Clark's one-sided view of World War II. Signing her full name and address, one LDS woman's letter asked: "Why didn't you tell about the bombing of Amsterdam by those wonderful Germans you seem to admire so much?" Also signing full name and address, another Mormon wrote that "you sounded more like an apostle of the creed of these murderous butchers, the Huns, than an apostle of the L.D.S. church." Still another fully identified Mormon wrote: "I hope you are ashamed of yourself. You should be!"[42] Instead, with clear satisfaction, Clark wrote a former Acting Secretary of State: "I pretty well stirred up all the Anglophiles in this area."[43]

In April 1941, he wrote: "Looking at the long range of history one can find no nation who has been more acquisitive in the matter of territory than has Great Britain; no nation has been more ruthless, not even Germany, than has Great Britain when she took over the Boers of South Africa."[44] By this time, the armies of Nazi Germany and Fascist Italy controlled nearly all of continental Europe from Poland westward to the border of Spain, a neutral but pro-Nazi dictatorship. To another Mormon critic of the Nazis, President Clark cautioned in June 1941 "against your assuming as truth most of the criticism you see leveled against Hitler and his regime in Germany." He added: "Hitler is undoubtedly bad from our American point of view, but I think the Germans like him."[45]

Nonetheless, he knew that this assessment of Hitler's popularity did not apply to millions of Jews[46] and anti-Hitler Germans who had been sent to Nazi concentration camps. His private library even contained a

---

Sumner Wells (Baltimore, Md.: Johns Hopkins University Press, 1995), 247–60.

42. Mrs. J.S. B--- to JRC, February 13, 1941; J--- R. S--- to JRC, February 13, 1941; Z--- B. S---, February 14, 1941; all in Box 223, JRC. For the full text of Clark's speech that caused this outrage among Mormons, see Yarn, *J. Reuben Clark: Selected Papers On International Affairs*, 503–19.

43. JRC to John Bassett Moore, February 18, 1941, Folder 15, Box 223, JRCP.

44. JRC to Alfred M. Landon, April 28, 1941, Folder 11, Box 364, JRCP; also Thomas Pakenham, *The Boer War* (New York: Random House, 1979).

45. JRC to N.L. Nelson, June 24, 1941, 2, 6, Folder 2, Box 363, JRCP.

46. Quinn, *Elder Statesman*, 28, 83, 264, 271, 284, 304, 325–39, 455 note 108, 560 note 44, 561 note 54, 563 note 73, 563 note 76, 564 note 88, 568 note 122, 569 note 137, for how Clark's intense anti-Semitism (especially his belief in an "international Jewish conspiracy") informed his anti-Communist, anti-Democrat, anti-FDR, anti-immigrant, anti-interventionist, anti-Israel, anti-"liberal," pro-German, and pro-Nazi views.

1933 account by an inmate at the "Nazi murder camp of Dachau," plus a 1934 narrative by a survivor of another "torture camp" in Germany.[47] In a 1939 meeting of the First Presidency, Clark had also spoken of those being sent to "concentration camps, with all the horrors that that entails."[48] Prior to his June 1941 letter, the *Deseret News* had also reported on mass executions of Jews in Nazi concentration camps.[49] During that same month of June, Hitler launched an unprovoked invasion of Soviet Russia, despite its "non-aggression" treaty with Nazi Germany.

In August 1941, Clark joined former U.S. President Herbert Hoover and fourteen other Republican leaders in a public appeal against intervention on Britain's behalf. They asked that the "American people should insistently demand that Congress put a stop to step-by-step projections of the United States into undeclared war." They also affirmed that World War II was "not a world conflict between tyranny and freedom," and insisted "that American lives should be sacrificed only for American independence or to prevent invasion of the Western Hemisphere."[50] In response, the San Francisco Press Club immediately editorialized: "Clark denies he's pro-Hitler, but says Red [Russia's] victory would be a calamity for civilization as he knows it, so he's preaching *Heilsolationism* with Hoover."[51] After preserving this criticism in a scrapbook, President Clark warned the following General Conference against "the effort to take our boys across the Water" to participate in World War II.[52]

---

47. Lee Library's "Clarkana" collection has Hans Beimler, *Four Weeks In the Hands of Hitler's Hell-Hounds: The Nazi Murder Camp of Dachau* (New York: Workers' Library Publishers, 1933) and *The Sonnenburg Torture Camp, By an Escaped Prisoner* (New York: Workers' International Relief and International Labor Defense, 1934). Even though these narratives were printed by Communist publishers, Clark's 1939 statement to Presidents Grant and McKay (see following note) showed that Reuben accepted the basic truth of those publications in his private library.

48. JRC office diary, July 21, 1939.

49. "Concentration Camp Prisoners Shot Down," *Deseret News*, November 19, 1938, 2, about a mass execution of Jews at Buchenwald, plus reference to the camps at Sachsenhausen and Dachau; "Death for 700,000 Jews Threatened: Semites Must Get Out or Die, Nazis Declare," *Deseret News*, November 23, 1938, [2].

50. "Fifteen GOP Leaders Demand U.S. Steps Toward War End," *Deseret News*, August 5, 1941, 1; "Fifteen Republicans Score War 'Steps,'" *New York Times*, August 6, 1941, 6.

51. *Scoop Magazine*, editorial, August 1941, 22, in JRC scrapbook, JRCP, emphasis in original.

52. *Conference Report*, October 1941, 15–16.

He wrote a First Presidency letter on October 11, 1941, that informed the director of the U.S. Defense Bond program: "We do not believe that aggression should be carried on in the name and under the false cloak of defense."[53] In November, President Clark acknowledged that he was trying to "suppress" the anti-Nazi writings and speeches of Arthur Gaeth, the former LDS mission president of Czechoslovakia.[54]

Instead of regarding the Pearl Harbor attack of December 7, 1941, as justification for war, Clark had long stated publicly and privately that Roosevelt was goading Japan into attacking the United States so as to provide a reason for defending Britain militarily.[55] Just days after his own son-in-law, Captain Mervyn Bennion, died on the battleship *West Virginia*, Clark drafted a proposed message of the First Presidency about the young Americans who will now "go out with commissions to kill their fellow men ... It is not the Master's way. It is the jungle law of the beasts."[56] In view of the nation's war-fever, President Grant decided not to use Clark's version, and instead published a Presidency message for soldiers throughout the world to avoid "cruelty, hate, and murder."[57]

There was no reference to the option of pacifism or conscientious objection in the First Presidency's official statement on war delivered at the April 1942 General Conference.[58] This seems odd for two reasons.

---

53. Heber J. Grant, JRC, and David O. McKay to William C. FitzGibbon (Defense Savings staff, U.S. Treasury Department), October 11, 1941, copy in Marriner S. Eccles Papers, Marriott Library; also Heber J. Grant journal sheets, August 5, 1942 (for retrospective comment about the 1941 correspondence: "I thank the Lord that President Clark is capable of writing such a fine letter"), LDS Church History Library, Salt Lake City, Utah, with typescript currently available to the public in D. Michael Quinn's research files at the Beinecke Rare Book and Manuscript Library, Yale University, New Haven, Connecticut.

54. JRC office diary, November 17, 1941. For an example of Arthur Gaeth's anti-Nazi views that led to Clark's determination to "suppress" them, see Gaeth, "If Christ Came To Germany," *Deseret News "Church News,"* January 25, 1941, 5–6, which included a photograph of "prisoners in a German concentration camp."

55. JRC office diary, July 9, 1940; *Conference Report*, October 1940, 165; JRC to Gordon W. Clark, October 29–30, 1940, Box 338, JRCP; JRC to Philip Marshall Brown, February 1, 1941, Folder 1, Box 363, JRCP; *Conference Report*, October 1941, 16–17.

56. JRC unused editorial for *Deseret News* (intended as a First Presidency message), Box 208, JRCP.

57. Clark, *Messages of the First Presidency*, 6:139–41 (with quoted phrase on 140).

58. Clark, *Messages of the First Presidency*, 6:148 (for beginning of message),

First, Clark was on the advisory council of the American Peace Society when he wrote it.[59] Second, endorsing the option of conscientious objection in 1942 would merely echo what the First Presidency had previously allowed the *Deseret News* to editorialize while American soldiers were being killed and maimed during the First World War.

However, in January 1943, President Grant approved a letter stating that "the Church leaves this matter of conscientious objecting to war to the individual."[60] Although it lacked the significance of a publicly announced statement, Clark undoubtedly suggested this clarification. In May 1944, he began monitoring the status of Mormons who were confined in special camps as conscientious objectors, and he subsequently arranged for the First Presidency to reimburse the "Peace Churches" for the costs of supporting these pacifist Mormons while incarcerated.[61]

In September 1945, a *Deseret News* editorial, probably written by Clark, praised "the earnest, sincere, loyal conscientious objector, who, because of his religious convictions, asked to be relieved of military service which would necessitate his taking the life of a fellowman." Moreover, the editorial began by criticizing America's "self-styled ultra-patriots" who opposed conscientious objectors.[62] As the First Presidency's secretary Francis M. Gibbons later acknowledged, Clark "harbored deep-felt pacifist views."[63]

His strident pacifism attracted notice among the leadership of both the Church and the nation. In October 1942, Apostle Harold B.

157–62 (portion on military service and war).

59. Heber J. Grant journal sheets, April 6, 1942 ("President Clark read a long Address of the First Presidency. We approved and signed it, but he wrote it"). I have not consulted JRCP since the early 1980s, when I did not think to examine the preliminary drafts for references to conscientious objection. My guess is that Clark's early draft of the 1942 statement would have included some mention of pacifism as an alternative to entering the armed forces.

60. Heber J. Grant journal sheets, January 30, 1943.

61. JRC office diary, May 8, 1944, October 2, 1945; also Mulford Q. Sibley and Phillip E. Jacob, *Conscription of Conscience: The American State and the Conscientious Objector, 1940–1947* (Ithaca, NY: Cornell University Press, 1952); Gordon C. Zahn, *Another Part of the War: The Camp Simon Story* (Amherst: University of Massachusetts Press, 1979).

62. "The Dictates of One's Conscience," editorial, *Deseret News*, September 11, 1945, 4.

63. Francis M. Gibbons, *Harold B. Lee: Man of Vision, Prophet of God* (Salt Lake City: Deseret Book, 1993), 180.

Lee wrote that Counselor Clark privately "denounced the present war as needless and the coming slaughter of our boys as a crime."[64] At that month's General Conference, Clark read another First Presidency message (which he had also written) condemning "hate-driven militarists" and urging the Allies to agree to a negotiated peace.[65] Nearly two years before the Allied invasion of Nazi-occupied France, this proposal would have left Hitler in control of virtually all of continental Europe East of Spain and west of the Soviet Union, plus most of North Africa. It is not surprising that, as of November 1942, U.S. intelligence agents were filing secret reports about Counselor Clark's statements for pacifism and against war. By January 1943, FBI interrogators also found that pro-Nazis in Utah were claiming his private encouragement.[66] At the end of that year, a Salt Lake City Mormon publicly denounced one of Clark's talks[67] as "the most reactionary, critical and near seditious ever delivered in any country during war." Christian N. Lund Jr. added that the LDS Church's First Counselor was "almost welcoming enemy victory."[68]

Undeterred, Clark gave another talk in February 1944 that proclaimed: "We must have a peace based on justice rather than might."[69] In April, the *New York Sun* reported that he was among several men

64. Harold B. Lee diary, October 27, 1942, among excerpts provided to D. Michael Quinn by Lee's son-in-law L. Brent Goates, Salt Lake City.

65. *Conference Report*, October 1942, 7–17 (quote on 15–16); Clark, *Messages of the First Presidency*, 6:170–85 (quote on 183); also Heber J. Grant journal sheets, October 3, 1942 ("Brother Clark practically wrote it all").

66. "Counter Intelligence Weekly Report, for Week Ending 27 November 1942," 6, District Intelligence Office, Ninth Naval District, Naval Investigative Service, Suitland, Maryland; report of Salt Lake City's FBI office on Internal Security and Custodial Detention Case 100-1487, dated January 2, 1943, Records Management Division, Federal Bureau of Investigation, Washington, DC, obtained through a Freedom of Information Act request; also follow-up telephone conversation of D. Michael Quinn with FBI headquarters, December 4, 1980.

67. Printed in full by *Commercial and Financial Chronicle*, November 25, 1943, JRC's talk was officially published as *Some Factors of a Now-Planned Post-War Governmental and Economic Pattern* (Salt Lake City: Deseret News Press, 1943), and reprinted in Yarn, *J. Reuben Clark: Selected Papers On International Affairs*, 521–39.

68. C.N. Lund [Jr.], *Reply to Clark's Speech* (Salt Lake City: Progressive Opinion, [1943]), broadside, LDS Church History Library, also Marriott Library. Concerning Lund's published criticism of Apostle-Senator Reed Smoot in 1919, James B. Allen, "Personal Faith and Public Policy," *BYU Studies* 14 (Autumn 1973): 83, described this critic as a "faithful Mormon."

69. Yarn, *J. Reuben Clark: Selected Papers On International Affairs*, 432.

recommended to form a treaty-conference to arrange for "a peace magnanimous and just."[70] Two months before the D-Day invasion of France, a "magnanimous" treaty would preserve most of Nazi Germany's territorial gains. The ceasefire involved in such treaty-negotiations would also allow Hitler to complete the annihilation of all European Jews—which readers of the *Deseret News* since mid-1942 knew was a goal the Nazis were achieving with poison gas in death-camps like Auschwitz.[71]

In November 1944, J. Reuben Clark advanced from the American Peace Society's advisory council to serve as one of its national directors, a well-publicized position he maintained until death.[72] When a Latter-day Saint sent him the "Roll of Honor" for family members who had served in the U.S. Armed Forces during World War II, Clark caustically replied: "I could say something about the real 'Cause' for which they served and for which some died, but I refrain."[73] However, his wartime pacifism had sometimes sounded more like traditional isolationism: "We ought to cease worrying about Europe; they can stew in their own juice without materially affecting us."[74]

In any event, Clark's pacifism extended beyond the war itself. Months before hostilities had ended, he wrote a proposed message for the First Presidency against "legislation providing for compulsory military training after the war."[75] His draft stated that standing armies

---

70. *New York Sun*, April 1, 1944, in JRC scrapbook.

71. "700,000 Polish Jews Allowed to Die of Disease, Hunger: Nazis Accused of Hastening End for Race; Poison Gas Used," *Deseret News*, June 20, 1942, 2; "Threat To Palestine," editorial, *Deseret News*, July 3, 1942, 4 ("It has been a consistent policy of the Nazis to obliterate the Jews wherever they have gone"); "Poles Charge Schmeling Headed Worst German Camp," *Deseret News*, July 9, 1942, 1, referring to Oswiechim (*Auschwitz* in German), Poland; "Death Decree For All Jews Charged To Hitler: Dr. Wise Claims To Have Proof Of Order," *Deseret News*, November 25, 1942, 3; "All Jews In Five Town Are Slain," *Deseret News*, March 20, 1943, 1; "Death of All Jews In Europe Expected: Hitler Continues Campaign Of Extinction, Says London Investigator," *Deseret News*, April 19, 1943, 2; "Jews Driven To Gulch, Stripped, Killed By Nazis," *Deseret News*, November 17, 1943, 1.

72. The American Peace Society's official periodical *World Affairs* (front and back covers, 1944–61).

73. JRC to Ben L. Rich, August 6, 1946, Folder 6, Box 374, JRCP.

74. JRC to Stephen Abbot, June 30, 1943, Folder 1, Box 367, JRCP.

75. Mark E. Petersen to JRC, February 2, 1945, Folder 7, Box 371, JRCP, concerning plans then being discussed in the Utah Legislature and in Congress.

"always led to a destruction of liberties and the establishment of tyranny," incentivized militaristic options, enhanced "military influence,"
and had "the effect of making the whole nation war-minded," creating
a nation that was "truculent, overbearing, and imperialistic, all provocative of war."[76] In December 1945, with a softened emphasis, the First
Presidency's three-page letter stated those basic views to all "members
of the Utah delegation to Congress, as well as to the Congressional
delegations from other states in which a considerable number of the
members of the Church reside."[77]

In the June 1946 program of the LDS Sunday School conference,
which celebrated the bravery of American soldiers and their victory
in World War II, Clark announced that he declined to "talk about the
subject of the evening." Instead, he gave a personal endorsement of
pacifism: "My ancestors on one side were Quakers. On the other side
they were Dunkards—a closely affiliated group. During the war, they,
with others, have been called the Peace Churches."[78]

Clark wrote that the tragedy of those who did not escape World
War II's horrors "has shaken me to the very roots . . . and grieve[s] me
beyond expression."[79] Nonetheless, his view of Nazi Germany did not
seem to change. He condemned the postwar Nuremberg trials of Nazi
leaders,[80] and never commented on their extermination of Europe's
Jews. He did write that the United States and England attempted "virtually to destroy the German people, a loss which is not only fiendish
in its conception but in its execution. There is no people in the world
to replace the German people."[81] By contrast, within more than 600
boxes of Clark's personal papers, there appears no criticism of Nazi
conduct during the war.[82] The only books in his private library about

76. JRC manuscript draft, February 5, 1945, Folder 7, Box 371, JRCP.

77. George Albert Smith, JRC, and David O. McKay to U.S. Senator Elbert D.
Thomas, December 14, 1945, Thomas Papers, Utah State Historical Society, Salt
Lake City; "Church Opposes Military Bill: Letter Sent Utah Solons December 14,"
Deseret News, January 3, 1946, 1, 5; Clark, *Messages of the First Presidency,* 6:239–42.

78. JRC, "Conference Address," *Instructor* 81 (June 1946): 277.

79. JRC to Phillip Marshall Brown, November 1, 1944, Folder 1, Box 369, JRCP.

80. JRC, *Stand Fast By Our Constitution* (Salt Lake City: Deseret Book, 1962), 72.

81. JRC to Ezra Taft Benson, August 20, 1946, Folder 2, Box 373, JRCP.

82. This seems especially odd in view of Clark's pre-war criticisms of Nazi
Germany. He described Hitler's 1934 purge-trials of fellow Nazis as "an
assassination tribunal" (JRC to Salmon O. Levinson, July 9, 1934, Folder 1, Box

the war criminals of Germany and Japan were gifts to him, not books he purchased.[83]

Clark's only accusation of war crimes was against his own nation's leaders and its armed forces. At the General Conference of October 1946, he first condemned the American military for killing 250,000 German civilians in its two-day firebombing of Dresden, a non-militarized city to which refugees had fled. Then he told the congregation that the United States committed "the crowning savagery of the war" by using atomic bombs against Japanese "men, women, and children, and cripples." He expressed amazement that there was not a general protest in the United States against this, "but that it actually drew from the nation at large a general approval of this fiendish butchery." President Clark declared: "God will not forgive us."[84]

He probably drafted the 1946 letter in which he and new LDS President George Albert Smith complained that conscientious objectors against U.S. participation in World War II "were apparently treated to all intents and purposes as were prisoners of war." Presidents Smith and Clark recited a catalog of stunning abuse:

> many of them were used as human guinea pigs for experimentation in matters relating to starvation (see how little food would sustain them), in matters of nutrition under conditions of extreme cold and rarified atmo-

---

351, JRCP). Prior to his first visit there, he wrote: "The German authorities have, I am very sure, kept all of the bad of Kaiserism (probably jettisoning much of the good); at any rate, they seem to have kept their criminal methods" (JRC to David O. McKay, June 14, 1937, Folder 1, Box 358, JRCP). After his second visit to Nazi Germany, he told a general priesthood meeting that "there are things about it that to me are detestable" (transcript, October 8, 1938, Box 151, JRCP).

83. Lee Library's "Clarkana" collection has a set of the Chief Counsel for the Prosecution of Axis Criminality, *Nazi Conspiracy and Aggression*, 11 vols. (Washington, DC: Government Printing Office, 1946–48), inscribed: "To Pres. J. Reuben Clark with affectionate regards, Ernest L. Wilkinson, 4/14/47"; also the author's presentation copy to JRC of Shinsh Hanayama, *The Way of Deliverance: Three Years With the Condemned Japanese War Criminals*, trans. Hideo Suzuki, et al. (London: Gollancz, 1955).

84. *Conference Report*, October 1946, 88–89. Clark's intensity may have resulted from reading John Hersey's *Hiroshima* (New York: Alfred A. Knopf, 1946); also see David Irving, *The Destruction of Dresden* (London: William Kimber, 1963); "The Bombing of Dresden," in Garold N. Davis and Norma S. Davis, *Behind the Iron Curtain: Recollections of Latter-day Saints in East Germany, 1945–1989* (Provo, Utah: BYU Studies, 1996), 1–45.

spheres, matters relating to the lice-borne plague of typhus, the diseases of jaundice, influenza, atypical pneumonia, malaria, etc.

With ill-concealed outrage, the First Presidency added that "the Government refused to give them any pay, and refused to pay for their dependents, although they were taken away from their dependents and placed under virtual military discipline, almost the equivalent of a prison camp"—even though "at least one C.O. received the Congressional Medal of Honor" for the heroism of enduring such treatment. Of the 7,724 American citizens who were thus imprisoned as conscientious objectors to World War II, "some 9 represented themselves as members of our Church." Second Counselor McKay did not sign this letter of complaint.[85]

In January 1947, Clark came to the aid of a Mormon who had been a wartime pacifist. A local draft board tried to prevent him from serving a full-time mission after his release from the C.O. camp more than a year after the war's end. The First Counselor did what he could to intercede on the young man's behalf.[86]

Despite his lifelong opposition to Marxism and Communism within the United States, Clark joined the minority of pre-1941 isolationists who disputed America's "Cold War" to stop the spread of international Communism after World War II.[87] In April 1947, he opposed military aid to Greece and Turkey in their campaigns against Communist insurgents. That October, he refused to join all other former U.S. ambassadors in signing a public appeal for military aid to China against Mao Tse-tung's Communist forces.[88]

---

85. George Albert Smith and JRC to Howard C. Maycock (local bishop of Springville First Ward), June 25, 1946, in "Conscientious Objectors" file, Folder 2, Box 3, CR 1/33, First Presidency Cumulative Correspondence, LDS Church History Library, with typescript currently available to the public in D. Michael Quinn's research files at Beinecke Library.

86. JRC office diary, January 16, 1947.

87. Without mentioning JRC, Justus D. Doenecke provided the national context in *Not To the Swift: The Old Isolationists In the Cold War Era* (Lewisburg, Pa.: Bucknell University Press, 1979).

88. James W. Gerard telegram to JRC, April 11, 1947, JRC telegraph to Gerard, April 15, 1947, and JRC to U.S. Senator Henry C. Dworshak, April 30, 1947, all in Folder 1, Box 376, JRCP; Gerard telegrams to JRC, October 14, October 29, 1947, JRC telegrams to Gerard, October 14, October 29, 1947, all in Folder 5, Box 376, JRCP.

If anything, Clark became even more strident. In November 1947, he gave a talk in Chicago that was published as a pamphlet by the *Deseret News*. He warned:

> I regret to say, indeed I am almost ashamed to say, that at the moment, our military branches seem in almost complete control of our own government. They appear to dominate Congress, and under the circumstances, we may assume they are in sufficient control of our foreign relations to be able to set the international scene. . . . We are not justified in doubting, on the facts we have, that we of the United States are, for the first time in our history, under a real threat from our military arm, and if the plans of the militarists carry, we shall become as thoroughly militarized as was Germany at her best, or worst.[89]

During General Conference of April 1948, President Clark even equated service in the U.S. armed forces with murder. Speaking of the draft, he warned the priesthood meeting: "You cannot fill the hearts of men with murder and then have a normal world."[90]

A year later, Clark was the only former or current U.S. ambassador to object to ratification of the North Atlantic Treaty and its creation of NATO.[91] He predictably opposed U.S. participation in the Korean War that began in June 1950,[92] and gave the following advice to his cousin about the U.S. Army Reserve: "Get out of the d—- thing as soon as you can."[93] In January 1951, Clark also warned his Church associates to be on guard against any steps toward "a military dictatorship" within the United States,[94] and he probably arranged for that

---

89. Clark, *Let Us Have Peace*, 15–16.

90. *Conference Report*, April 1948, 174.

91. JRC to James W. Gerard, April 14, 1949, Folder 9, Box 379, JRCP; "Gerard Calls Pact Bar To Early War," *New York Times*, May 7, 1949, 4, for his testimony before the U.S. Senate Foreign Relations Committee that J. Reuben Clark's opposition to NATO placed him among the "well-meaning but impractical pacifists, pseudo-liberals, rabid isolationists and, of course, the Communist party with its assorted fronts"; also *Who Was Who In America, Vol. 3* (Chicago: A.N. Marquis, 1960), 319, for Gerard as formerly a U.S. ambassador to Germany.

92. JRC office diary, September 8, 1950; JRC, *Our Dwindling Sovereignty* (Salt Lake City: Deseret News Press, 1952), 32–33, reprinted in JRC, *Stand Fast By Our Constitution* (Salt Lake City: Deseret Book, 1962), 128–29.

93. JRC office diary, June 27, 1950.

94. Harold B. Lee diary, January 2, 1951; also JRC office diary, May 6, 1950, for his similar statement "to the group at [Apostle] Adam Bennion's."

year's *Deseret News* editorial that praised the "pacifist ideal" in the midst of the Korean War.[95]

In April 1951, David O. McKay became LDS president. He was a lifelong internationalist whose disagreement with Clark over American participation in World War II had been publicized by *Time* magazine in 1942, when McKay was Second Counselor.[96] As LDS president, McKay affirmed his views to a non-Mormon that "the Church was militantly opposed to the godless atheism of communism and would not hesitate to oppose force with force if it became necessary."[97] Though he knew of Clark's opposition to the Korean War, President McKay in June 1952 assigned him to speak to LDS young men in support of military service—exactly one year after the *Deseret News* editorial about conscientious objectors.

Reuben began his talk by commenting that "I would not want to spend two years in the service." He then referred to his sympathy with the pacifist view of his Quaker ancestors, and said: "I loathe war, and all that goes with it." Then, having already been demoted to Second Counselor, he dutifully went on to address his assigned topic: "Two Years in the Service Can Be Profitable."[98] Clark's approach to military service against international Communism as making-the-best-of-a-loathsome-situation was hardly the endorsement of the Cold War that the LDS president wanted. A month later, Apostle Harold B. Lee wrote: "Pres. Clark was considerably concerned over the quoted statement of Pres. McKay to the effect that the 'only way to deal with Russia was by force, which was the only language they knew.'"[99]

In 1954, Clark privately replied to the question of what the United States should do concerning French Indo-China, soon to be partitioned into the independent countries of Laos, Cambodia, North Vietnam, and South Vietnam. He wrote U.S. Senator Henry C. Dworshak (a non-Mormon):

---

95. "The Problem of Conscientious Objectors," editorial, *Deseret News*, June 25, 1951, B-2, which nonetheless condemned "the craven draft-dodger" who acted from purely selfish motives.

96. "Mormon Mixup," *Time*, October 19, 1942, 42.

97. David O. McKay office diary, September 19, 1961, McKay Papers, Marriott Library.

98. JRC, "Two Years In the Service Can Be Profitable," *Improvement Era* 55 (August 1952): 568.

99. Harold B. Lee diary, July 11, 1952.

Finally, while unalterably opposed to Communism, I can imagine that an enlightened Communism may be a whole lot better than a decrepit, deficient, corrupt colonial government. I rather feel that that principle could be applied to very much of the situation in the whole Far East.[100]

Four years later, he asked "about the Far East" during a visit to the U.S. State Department. Afterward, he wrote that "they lied whenever it seemed convenient."[101]

Because of Counselor Clark's death in September 1961, the ten percent of LDS youth who opposed the war in Vietnam had no comparable spokesman for pacifism among the general authorities.[102] These young people could turn only to his published statements against war, and didn't have access to his unpublished statements that supported conscientious objectors.[103] The same has remained true for all of America's wars since the 1960s. Pacifism has not died among rank-and-file Mormons, but has had no allies among the highest leaders of the LDS Church since J. Reuben Clark.[104]

---

100. JRC to U.S. Senator Henry C. Dworshak, May 17, 1954, Folder 15, Box 390, JRC; also Fox, *J. Reuben Clark*, 589.

101. JRC to Fred Morris Dearing, August 18, 1958, Folder 6, Box 402, JRCP.

102. Knud S. Larsen and Gary Schwendiman, "The Vietnam War Through the Eyes of a Mormon Subculture," *Dialogue: A Journal of Mormon Thought* 3 (Autumn 1968): 152–62, for 9–13 percent of BYU's students expressing opposition to this war whenever asked in various questionnaires.

103. For example, Gordon C. Thomasson, ed., *War, Conscription, Conscience and Mormonism* (Santa Barbara, Calif.: Mormon Heritage, 1971), 9–12, 29–36, 44–72, 76, 84–85.

104. For example, "The Member and the Military," *Improvement Era* 71 (June 1968): 5, for the talk at General Conference of April 1968 by Boyd K. Packer (then an Assistant to the Quorum of the Twelve Apostles), who condemned conscientious objectors. From 1968 to 1971 (in the middle of the Vietnam War), the First Presidency's only references to conscientious objection were in unpublished letters, signed only by the Presidency's secretary Joseph Anderson and pointedly lacking any of the enthusiastic endorsement by *Deseret News* editorials in 1918, 1945, and 1951. See Gary James Bergera, comp., *Statements of the LDS First Presidency: A Topical Compendium* (Salt Lake City: Signature Books, 2007), xiii–xx (for its comprehensive sources), 94–95 (for its only statements about conscientious objection).

12

The Work of Death:
Hugh Nibley as Scholar, Soldier,
Peace Activist

Boyd Jay Petersen

As historian Stephen Ambrose noted, "There [was] *no* typical GI among the millions who served in Northwest Europe" during World War II. They were "an army of citizen soldiers" from all walks of life.[1] But Hugh Nibley must have been one of the least typical of the bunch. At the age of thirty-two when he enlisted in 1942, he was older than most of the other men. He had graduated with a doctorate in history from Berkeley, and had, for the past four years, been a professor at the Claremont college consortium, teaching history, social philosophy, humanities, German, and Greek. As a student of ancient history and languages, he had spent more time immersed in books and the study of ancient history than in the real world of the present. "I . . . pull myself out of the Old Stuff only with the greatest difficulty," Nibley wrote his mother at that time.[2] Unlike many of his contemporaries, Nibley had no hatred of Germans. He had served his LDS mission in Germany, knew the German language well, and admired the German culture and intellectual heritage. He stated that his "adolescent thinking was all cast in the German mold."[3] Nevertheless, Hugh Nibley ended up as an intelligence officer in the European campaign, attached for most of the war to the 101st Airborne division, driving a

---

1. Stephen Ambrose, *Citizen Soldiers: The U.S. Army from the Normandy Beaches to the Bulge to the Surrender of Germany* (New York: Simon & Schuster, 1998), 22, 468.

2. Hugh Nibley to Agnes Sloan Nibley, March 27, 1942. All correspondence can be found in the Boyd Petersen papers, MSS 7449 L. Tom Perry Special Collections, Harold B. Lee Library, Brigham Young University, Provo, Utah.

3. Hugh Nibley to Paul Springer, n.d., early summer 1946.

jeep onto Utah Beach on D-Day, landing in Holland by glider during Operation Market Garden, and stationed at Mourmelon-le-Grand at the outbreak of the Battle of the Bulge.

Nibley struck a unique pose among the other citizen soldiers. Max Oppenheimer, one of his friends during the war, remembered him as "a very scholarly and dedicated Mormon" who was "never seen without a book in his hands."[4] Another friend, Lucien Goldschmidt, noticed that Nibley was not among the men who told dirty jokes, that he traded the coffee served in the mess hall for powdered lemonade, and that he carried around the Qur'an in Arabic and Thucydides in Greek.[5]

Nibley also stood out for his deeper understanding of warfare than most of his fellow soldiers, having studied ancient warfare in his classical history courses at UCLA and Berkeley. At military intelligence school at Camp Ritchie, he acquired an impressive knowledge of Civil War history while conducting maneuvers near Antietam. He consumed theoretical texts on warfare and learned the tactics, organization, and composition of the German army. Once his training ended, his various field assignments provided what he called a "grand-stand seat" from which he had "the perfect position to observe" the European stage of World War II. As part of an Order of Battle intelligence team, his job was to see the war in overview and to know the strength, disposition, and location of all units of both armies. "I had to know what was going on right from the very beginning," he observed. But his understanding was not just theoretical. Being attached to the 101st Airborne, Nibley also saw combat up close from inside a foxhole, "face all blackened, and clusters of grenades on," carrying his "trusty carbine."[6]

Nibley knew warfare both in theory and practice better than most. The result of that expertise was an unshakable cynicism about war, a belief that war is a "nasty and immoral business." Skeptical of war as World War II began, he grew more and more pessimistic as it continued. Soon after joining the army, Nibley wrote, "I can't possibly see how anything can be settled by the war or after it until somebody gets more sense than

---

4. Max Oppenheimer, *An Innocent Yank at Home Abroad* (Manhattan, Kan.: Sunflower Press, 2000), 248.

5. Lucien Goldschmidt, "Faith of an Observer," 410, compilation of interviews, ca. 1983–84 for a video documentary of the same name aired in 1985, photocopy of typescript in Boyd Petersen papers.

6. Hugh Nibley, "Faith of an Observer," 164.

we have."[7] From Camp Ritchie, he foresaw "that the war will be a long one, with the Devil enjoying increasing 'control over his own dominion.'"[8] At the end of his first course of intelligence training, Nibley wrote: "I still stick to my original conception of the present mess as a long series of heartless and joyless engagements, of endless significance for the future, but very saddening to live through."[9] And after completing his Order of Battle training, he reiterated the same theme: "I am more convinced than ever that this war will bring about no good."[10] His years of combat did not change that opinion, only deepened it.

His learning and experience taught Nibley six truths about war.[11] First, he learned that the men on both sides of the conflict were basically good. Writing from the war front, he noted, "A fantastically large proportion—I'd say around 10%—of our soldiers are surprisingly high-minded and well-behaved."[12] Ten percent is hardly a "fantastically large" percentage, and whether this reflects Nibley's own high standards, his general attitude about the state of society, or his cynical views on the toll army life takes on individual righteousness is not clear. The German soldiers likewise impressed Nibley. As he later wrote, "The POWs we rounded up to interrogate were men just as good as we were, the victims

7. Hugh Nibley to Agnes Sloan Nibley, postmarked November 6, 1942.

8. Hugh Nibley to Agnes Sloan Nibley, postmarked April 28, 1943. Evidently, Nibley is alluding to Moses 6:15: "And in those days Satan had great dominion among men, and raged in their hearts; and from thenceforth came wars and bloodshed; and a man's hand was against his own brother, in administering death, because of secret works, seeking for power."

9. Hugh Nibley to Agnes Sloan Nibley, June 3, 1943.

10. Hugh Nibley to Agnes Sloan Nibley, postmarked September 24, 1943.

11. It is interesting to compare Nibley's attitudes about war with those of J. Reuben Clark, who served as counselor in the First Presidency to Heber J. Grant, George Albert Smith, and David O. McKay. Clark felt that the Treaty of Versailles had been a "vengeful and unjust punishment of Germany for all of Europe's mistakes" and the ultimate origin of World War II. He argued for American neutrality as the European conflict broke out. In 1939, he authored a First Presidency statement that condemned war in general; and in 1944, he encouraged America to strive for "a peace based on justice rather than might." Despite his anti-Communist sentiments, Clark would also later oppose the U.S. military's entrance into the Korean and Vietnamese wars. See D. Michael Quinn's treatment of Clark in Chapter 11 of this volume.

12. Hugh Nibley to Agnes Sloan Nibley, March 3, 1945.

of a terrible circumstance that the devil's game of power and gain had woven around them."[13]

Second, he learned that men on both sides were capable of great evil. In Normandy, he was sickened to discover that "our boys were acting worse than the Germans . . . as far as atrocities were concerned." For example, early in the D-Day invasion, Nibley was astonished to learn that one platoon of American soldiers held a French wedding at gunpoint while the men took turns raping the bride. Hugh called it "absolutely typical," adding "I know much worse things than that that happened."[14] To the nation's shame, Hugh said, "the French were soon preferring [the Germans] to us as a matter of fact and told us that quite frankly."[15] Cynically, he quoted Jacob Christopher Burckhardt: "Behold the soldier—when he is hungry he steals, and when he is full he fornicates. . . . That covers everything."[16] Any hopes Nibley may have had for German virtue died when he later visited Dachau.

Third, he learned that in the military, careers are built chiefly on the battlefield. As a result, ambitious men longed for the continuation of war and gloom pervaded the upper echelons as the war drew to a close. "The war was ending too fast," recalled Nibley. "It meant the end of quick promotions. It meant the slowing down of careers."[17] He later drew on this situation to illustrate the "Mahan Principle"—by which he meant Cain's "great secret" from the Book of Moses "of converting . . . your life [into] my promotion."[18] Just before the Battle of the Bulge, he wrote to Lucien Goldschmidt: "The whole world today is paying the price of a few careers. I have never objected to being the simple-minded implement of other men's greatness, but one can hardly submit to that without becom-

---

13. Hugh Nibley, *Nibley on the Timely and the Timeless* (Provo, Utah: Religious Studies Center, 1978), 300.

14. Hugh Nibley, "Faith of an Observer," 167–68.

15. Ibid., 167.

16. Hugh Nibley to Paul Springer, n.d., ca. December 1945. Burckhardt (1918–97) was a professor of history at Basel University (1858–93), best-known for his works on the Italian Renaissance and on Greek civilization.

17. Hugh Nibley, *Teachings of the Book of Mormon: Transcripts of Lectures Presented to an Honors Book of Mormon Class at Brigham Young University, 1989–90* (Provo, Utah: FARMS, n.d.): Semester 3, Lecture 67, 119.

18. Hugh Nibley, *Nibley on the Timely and the Timeless*, xxiv. Nibley is alluding to Moses 5:31: "And Cain said: Truly I am Mahan, the master of this great secret, that I may murder and get gain. Wherefore Cain was called Master Mahan, and he gloried in his wickedness."

ing the foil of their spite; for when the mighty fight, the mighty clash by proxy. We are the humble abrasive that polishes their armor."[19]

Fourth, Nibley discovered another example of the Mahan Principle, that of "converting life into property—your life for my property."[20] Some businesses were profiting from the war by maintaining interests on both sides of the conflict. "I had to snoop into everything," he remembered. "And I found out all sorts of things I shouldn't have found out. The whole thing was being run as a game for profits." In particular, he discovered incriminating evidence while "mopping up" in Heidelberg at the end of the war that Standard Oil and I. G. Farben "had an equal part on both sides in the war."[21]

Fifth, Nibley gained a firm knowledge that the military is able to control little, but is also capable of supreme chaos and large-scale blunders. On D-Day, he saw firsthand how the weather threw off the carefully planned landing. And when the Allied troops finally did make it to shore, "everything went foul, people being landed on the wrong beach, the wrong things being landed at the wrong time, . . . all sorts of confusion, not getting the things you wanted and the like."[22] As he wrote from Heidelberg at the end of the war, "The Army is no more incompetent than it ever was, only during operations its blunders are strict military secrets: oy! could I write a book, me with my grand-stand seat—always the hotly detached observer."[23]

Finally, the most important lesson Nibley learned from his war years was the utter evil of war. He was haunted by the grisly battlefields of war, later recounting how on D-Day, "I jumped into [a] foxhole and it was full of—ah—spattered with brains, a helmet full of brains, and so forth, and it was just a bloody mess there."[24] He saw first-hand the horror of warfare. "I remember General Bradley said, 'War is waste!' And

---

19. Hugh Nibley to Lucien Goldschmidt, 8 December 1944.

20. Nibley, *Nibley on the Timely and the Timeless*, xxiv.

21. Hugh Nibley, *Teachings of the Book of Mormon*, Semester 3, Lecture 65, 94. To a class of students later, he hinted: "I could tell you stories that would amaze the faculties of eyes and ears, 'chill your young blood, and cause each particular hair to stand on end, like quills upon the fretful porpentine.'" Here Nibley is quoting one of his favorite passages of Shakespeare, *Hamlet*, Act 1.5, where the ghost of King Hamlet is speaking of his existence in hell.

22. Nibley, "Faith of an Observer," 374.

23. Hugh Nibley to Agnes Sloan Nibley, n.d., ca. summer 1945.

24. Nibley, "Faith of an Observer," 156.

166 Boyd Jay Petersen

that's what it is, you see. The utter wastefulness of the thing. But the wrongness of what we were doing was so strong that everybody would cry. People would cry; they would weep! It was so utterly, unspeakably sad! It was so sad you could hardly stand it. That people would do such things to each other."[25]

The lessons learned from World War II caused Nibley to become an outspoken critic of the wars that followed. I only have space here to highlight a very few of his many anti-war statements, but his commitment to pacifism was constant and unwavering. In his 1967 *Since Cumorah*, Nibley argued, war "is never a case of 'good guys versus bad guys,'" but the inevitable fruit of wickedness on both sides. He saw that the Book of Mormon's emphasis on warfare—its studies in "the work of death" as Alma refers to it no fewer than four times and Helaman at least once—is to revolt us, to show us the horrors of war, and, in so doing, warn us to avoid it at all costs. He concluded that the Book of Mormon's authors saw war as "nasty, brutalizing, wasteful, dirty, degrading, fatiguing, foolish, immoral, and above all unnecessary."[26]

In one of his boldest moves, Nibley challenged the position of an LDS apostle on the matter of the justness of war. In 1971 BYU screened the film *No Substitute for Victory*, starring John Wayne and a host of military and political leaders. Apostle Ezra Taft Benson, in his role as former Secretary of Agriculture, was prominently featured in the film. Benson argued that the U.S. should do away with "suicidal limited political objectives and launch a massive military campaign, topple the Hanoi regime, and dictate rather than negotiate the peace terms." As he put it, "Let the communists see what good-natured Uncle Sam can still do when a bully picks a fight with him."[27] With his first-hand experience and abiding cynicism in "massive military campaigns," Nibley wrote a letter to the editor of the *Daily Universe* that appeared on the last day of the film's showing. Nibley argued that there was indeed a good "substitute for victory": namely to "renounce war and proclaim peace" as the Doctrine and Covenants commands. "Renounce is a strong word," he continued. "We are not to try to win peace by war,

---

25. Ibid., 158.

26. Nibley, *Since Cumorah*, 291–92.

27. Footage is available as "John Wayne & Ezra Taft Benson - The Vietnam War" at http://www.youtube.com/watch?v=ZLbu-mgKgiM&feature=related (accessed December 17, 2011).

or merely to call a truce, but to renounce war itself, to disclaim it as a policy while proclaiming (that means not just announcing, but preaching) peace without reservation." He warned, "If we persist in reversing the words of the Savior, 'Who takes up the sword shall die by the sword' (cf. Revelation 13:10) to read, perversely, 'who does not take up the sword shall perish by the sword,' we shall deserve what happens to us."[28]

If anyone questioned Hugh Nibley's loyalty to the Church for taking a position different from that of a senior apostle, it was moot after his anti-war essay "If There Must Needs Be Offense" appeared in the July 1971 *Ensign*. There Nibley argued that the scriptures' laws "forbidding conflict are of a general and universal nature, while those which countenance it all refer to exceptional cases." He concluded that "the most desperate military situation imaginable is still to be met with the spirit of peace and love."

In 1977, he submitted an essay entitled "Uses and Abuses of Patriotism" for a special edition of the *Ensign* celebrating the bicentennial of Declaration of Independence. Evidently, his approach was not patriotic enough, because it was rejected by the editors and the article instead was published in a textbook for American Heritage, a course at BYU introducing students to the fundamentals of U.S. history, politics, and economics.[29] In the essay, he noted how the noble emotion of patriotism can be abused by conspiring politicians to create conflicts. "There is something wrong with this patriotism, which is based on conflict," argued Nibley.[30]

In 1986, he delivered a chilling essay entitled, "Last Call: An Apocalyptic Warning from the Book of Mormon" at the Sunstone Theological Symposium in Salt Lake City.[31] At the symposium, Nibley

28. Nibley, "Renounce War, or, A Substitute for Victory," *Brother Brigham Challenges the Saints*, ed. Shirley S. Ricks, Vol. 13 of THE COLLECTED WORKS OF HUGH NIBLEY (Salt Lake City: Deseret/FARMS, 1994), 267–69.

29. *American Heritage: A Syllabus for Social Science 100* (Provo, Utah: Brigham Young University Press, 1977), 188–97. The *Ensign*'s editors had published President Kimball's "The False Gods We Worship," an essay that struck a similar theme, in the previous June 1976 bicentennial edition. Spencer W. Kimball, "The False Gods We Worship," *Ensign*, June 1976, 3–6.

30. Nibley, *Brother Brigham Challenges the Saints*, 250.

31. Nibley, "Last Call: An Apocalyptic Warning from the Book of Mormon," *Sunstone* 12, no. 1 (January 1988): 14–25; reprinted in *The Prophetic Book of Mormon*, ed. John W. Welch, vol. 8 of THE COLLECTED WORKS OF HUGH NIBLEY

again returned to the theme of warfare in the Book of Mormon, arguing
that war creates false polarizations, persuading people that "everything
evil [is] on one side and everything good on the other." He pointed
to the cycle of war that emerges in the Book of Mormon: the people
become, first, *privatized*, having nothing in common; then *ethnicized*,
learning to hate other nations; then *nationalized*, serving ambitious
men's careers; then *militarized*, storing up weapons; then *terrorized*,
developing organized crime; then *regionalized*, forming organizations
for protection and profit; then *tribalized*, abolishing the central government; then *fragmentized*, forming wandering groups, paramilitary
organizations, and family shelters; then *polarized*, creating great armies;
finally *pulverized*, wiping each other out as the great armies clashed. He
pessimistically added, "It is left for a future generation to take the final
step and become *vaporized*."[32]

Nibley's own experiences in Europe demonstrated that war does
have real consequences for individual lives. At Mourmelon-le-Grand,
he shared a tent with Master Sergeant David Harmon. Harmon told
Nibley about being ordered to assassinate a German officer thought to
have important documents in his possession. Harmon had obeyed the
order, and did indeed find a briefcase crammed with secret documents.
Nevertheless, killing the man in such a calculated way deeply troubled
Harmon. "He'd done a lot of shooting," Nibley recalled, but for some
reason, the fact that he had shot this officer in the head "preyed on
his mind." Harmon gave Nibley the German officer's briefcase, locks
broken and its fine leather stained with blood, but still functional. One
night, Harmon came into the tent, sat down on the bunk, and asked,
"Nibley, if I want to kill myself, it's my own goddamn business, isn't
it?" As calmly as he could, Nibley tried to assure Harmon that killing
himself would affect a lot of other people and was not a good solution.
But "suddenly he whipped out a little Beretta automatic that he had
in his pocket, a little Italian Beretta. Shot himself right through the
head. Blood splattering all over the place. I put towels around his head
and then ran over to the medics but he was dead before that. He just
couldn't stand living with it."[33] For more than thirty years, Nibley car-

---

(Salt Lake City: Deseret Book/FARMS, 1989), 498–532.

    32. Ibid., 530–31.

    33. Hugh Nibley, "Faith of an Observer," 155. In this quoted passage, I have
silently removed the transcriber's ellipses, which indicate not omitted material but

ried that stained briefcase while teaching at BYU. It invariably bulged with books and papers, but its real purpose was to serve as a lasting and tangible symbol of the evils of war.[34]

Nibley also related another incident that happened when a man was ordered to shoot a German soldier. While the 101st Airborne were "mopping up" the town of Carentan searching for any remaining Germans, one of the men noticed someone suspicious looking out of a factory window. Intelligence Officer Major Paul Danahy ordered a small patrol to go into the factory where they captured the man. Major Danahy assumed that since the man was German he must be a spy, so he ordered Sergeant David Bernay to take him out and shoot him. Bernay was, as Nibley remembered, "a fiery little Jew who won a silver star with two clusters; he was no friend of the Nazis." As Bernay escorted the German, they came to a ditch. "Step over the ditch," Bernay ordered in perfect German. Surprised that the American soldier spoke German, the two began a conversation. "Where are you from?" the German asked. "I come from Maximiliansau," Bernay replied. "Maximiliansau! That's just a little place on the Rhine. There was a celluloid factory there," exclaimed the German. "Yes," Bernay said. "Did you know Herr Bernay?" asked the German. "He is my father," replied Bernay. The German exclaimed, "This must be little David!" Nibley pressed the punch line: "It turned out that this man he was about to shoot was his father's close friend. He had managed the factory for David's father, and he was the one who made it possible for the [Jewish] family to escape from Germany and get to New York." The two men "threw themselves at each other" and embraced. Instead of shooting the German, Bernay took him back to the camp where he became a valuable source of intelligence for the Allies.[35]

Incidents like these had a profound effect on Nibley. War was not an abstract idea, a theoretical possibility, or something studied in the classroom—it was a reality he had experienced first-hand in World War II. While his study of the classical world, his training in military

---

pauses in the narration.

34. Ibid., 155.

35. Hugh Nibley, *Teachings of the Book of Mormon*, Semester 1, Lecture 7, 10. The transcript of this narrative misspells Danahy's and Bernay's names; the spelling I use is from a list compiled by George Koskimaki from the official rosters of the 101st Airborne, dated May 31, 1944, just prior to the D-Day invasion. Photocopy in the Boyd Petersen papers.

intelligence, and his close reading of scripture informed his perspective, it was the individual stories of people like Sergeant David Bernay and Master Sergeant David Harmon that convinced him that war is truly the "work of death."

At the conclusion of the War, Nibley wrote to his mother from Germany summarizing his view: "If we must act with the high-handed immorality of the gods, it is only right to have our bluff called and the reins thrust into our hands—but of course there can only be one end to the farce."[36] His experience had borne out vividly what his studies had taught theoretically: there is no way to win an endeavor fraught so thoroughly with evil. The work of death is utterly opposed to the work of the Prince of Peace. No matter how ostensibly justified or how nobly fought, war inevitably and diabolically creates enmity and strife, rupturing the essential unity that should bind us to Christ, and to each other as sons and daughters of God.

---

36. Hugh Nibley to Agnes Sloan Nibley, n.d., ca. August 1945.

13

Eugene England's Theology of Peace

Loyd Ericson

In the first week of August 1964, two U.S. submarines off the north coast of Vietnam in the Gulf of Tonkin falsely reported receiving unprovoked gun and torpedo fire from nearby Communist ships. Within hours of the purported attacks, U.S. President Lyndon B. Johnson ordered retaliation air strikes on Vietnam and three days later used this and other falsified information to ensure the passage of a resolution authorizing military action in Southeast Asia. Over 50,000 American and millions of Vietnamese lives were lost in what became one of the most controversial wars in American history.

Looking back on this event and its surroundings thirty years later, Eugene England pointed to the beginnings of the Vietnam War as being a foundational and life-changing moment in his life, a paradigmatic moment that changed his thinking and religious understanding. He says,

> In 1964 quite suddenly I experienced a dramatic paradigm shift, a kind of sea change in my soul. . . . I had grown up believing, connected to my belief that the Constitution was divinely inspired, that U.S. Presidents did not lie. When I became convinced that President Johnson had lied, with complicity from his advisors and without significant opposition from Congress, but with such dire results for our country, I crossed some line in my soul. As I thought about it . . . I became convinced that I had crossed to a proper place, to a conviction that the Prince of Peace had to do with peace between nations more than with loyalty to one nation.[1]

---

1. Eugene England, "The Prince of Peace," in *Making Peace: Personal Essays* (Salt Lake City: Signature Books, 1995), 226–27. England also recounts this "paradigm changing" account in Eugene England, "Jacaranda," in *Making Peace*, 114; "What

England wrote that he was both heartbroken and angry. While just a few years earlier he considered himself "a patriotic American" who had been a volunteer weather officer for an Air Force bomber squadron, he soon found himself joining up with anti-war movements and other social causes, where he remained a vocal critic of war and an advocate for peace up until his death in 2001.

Raised within a Mormon farming family in southern Idaho during the 1930s and 40s, George Eugene England Jr. recounted his upbringing as having come from a conservative and "rather cold, emotionally reserved, largely Anglo-Saxon famil[y] and Church culture."[2] Shortly after serving an LDS mission to Samoa with his wife Charlotte Ann Hawkins, England went to Stanford University to do graduate studies in English, which eventually led to a professorship in English at the LDS Church-owned Brigham Young University (BYU) in 1974. He continued to teach there for nearly twenty-five years. In 1998, he took up a writer-in-residency position at Utah Valley State College (now Utah Valley University) where he helped establish a Mormon Studies program before passing away in the early fall of 2001 from complications resulting from a brain tumor. While having never served in the leading hierarchy for the LDS Church, England's prolific writings and intellectual pursuits (as well as the respect he earned from students) made him a prominent figure among LDS scholars, thinkers, and general membership. While at Stanford he helped establish *Dialogue: A Journal of Mormon Thought* and later at BYU he began the Association for Mormon Letters, both of which have been and are key venues for Mormon thought, scholarship, and literature.

England's advocacy for peace permeated nearly all of his writings. Whether explicit and pronounced in his sharp criticisms of the war in Vietnam[3] and the popular first war in Iraq,[4] or subtly expressed in his

---

Covenant will God receive in the Desert?" *Sunstone* 96 (September 1994): 27–28; and "'No Cause, No Cause': An Essay Toward Reconciliation," *Sunstone* 121 (January 2002): 32.

2. England, "No Cause, No Cause," 32.

3. For his criticisms of the Vietnam War, see Eugene England, "The Tragedy of Vietnam and the Responsibility of Mormons," *Dialogue* 2:4 (Winter 1967): 71–91; "Can Nations Love Their Enemies? An LDS Theology of Peace," in *Dialogues With Myself: Personal Essays on Mormon Experience* (Midvale, Utah: Orion Books, 1984), 146–47.

4. See Eugene England "On Trusting God, Or Why We Should Not Fight Iraq," *Sunstone* 79 (October 1990): 9–12; and "Late Night Thoughts at the End of

personal narratives and recollections, his writings portray a struggle as his ideals of peace confront the violence of the scriptures and an often unquestioning American nationalism in Mormon culture. He sought out answers to the questions of how Latter-day Saints should follow the conflicting commands to "renounce war and proclaim peace" (D&C 98:16) while at the same time being "subject to kings, presidents, rulers, and magistrates, in obeying, honoring, and sustaining the law" (A of F 12) when a nation one resides in is engaged in war; or how Latter-day Saints should make sense of Jesus' proscription of violence and war when the world around us cries for war, violence, and revenge.

England's "theology of peace" is perhaps best described by what he terms "effective pacifism" where we "must do, in love, whatever we can that will *genuinely create peace*," even if it may require us to "sacrifice our lives."[5] This pacifism though is not strictly pacifist, nor does it imply simply avoiding aggression and absorbing violence. Affirming the possibility of a just war, England believed that war "can be justified under certain conditions"; however, it must be a "purely defensive war," which must not become aggressive or punishing.[6] When a just defensive war is engaged, certain principles must be attained:

> Ultimate concern must be for the character and salvation of those involved rather than apparent right or wrong or justice; revenge is never right, however "justified"; vengeance and bloodthirstiness, very natural dangers even in a just war, must be vigorously resisted, even at great risk, by fighting purely defensive and not insisting on unconditional surrender.[7]

As violence should only be minimally used in defensive measures, war should also not be engaged to implement new forms of government, nor should it be utilized for instilling new systems of beliefs. Furthermore, participation in an unjust war cannot and should not be justified simply by virtue of being in (or even being a leader or member of the military of) a nation fighting such an unjust war. Rather, both citizens and military members are responsible to decide before joining in the fight whether their nation's war is just. Thus England writes, "to whatever degree any participant is *able* to be responsible—either as a

a War," *Dialogue* 24:2 (Summer 1991): 7–9.

  5. England, "Can Nations Love Their Enemies?" 136; emphasis in original.
  6. Ibid., 137.
  7. Ibid., 138.

leader who brings on the conflict or a soldier who can resist an unjust government or who indulges in hatred even in a just cause—he is accountable as a sinner."[8]

While England believed that a defensive war *can* be justified, he also affirmed an important "distinction between what is justified and what is *best*."[9] Thus, while acts of war against our enemies may be deemed just, there are better ways by which we can engage our enemies to create peace without turning to violence—though these ways require more courage and love than is required to *justly* enter into a defensive war. According to England, in Mormonism there "is clearly . . . a higher law, which stands in judgment even on the most justifiable efforts of men to defend themselves with weapons."[10] Even in what is strongly considered a just war, there is the overriding principle that force begets force and that violence against others fails to create true peace. Moreover such "just" violence fuels further hatred and violence between a nation and its enemies. Instead of engaging in violence, we must engage in:

> the central pragmatic concept of the LDS theology of peace—that enemies cannot be defeated, but they can be changed into other than enemies by true principles of love, and God will provide the power to do that if we will trust him and pay the price of trying things his way.[11]

According to England, the first step to engaging our enemies with "effective pacifism" is "to work toward loving our enemies by knowing them like ourselves, by resisting the usual mindless stereotyping" of them as the other.[12] Treating our enemies with love means to see them as human beings—as brothers and sisters. This involves actively learning about their language, cultures, histories, and beliefs. Loving our enemies means to try to understand their needs and why they see us as their enemy. Finally, it includes reaching out to them with charitable aid, to help those in need who may not have been willing to do the same.[13] This is of course not easy:

---

8. Ibid., 140–41; emphasis in original.

9. Ibid., 139.

10. Ibid., 142.

11. Ibid., 144.

12. Ibid., 148.

13. England discusses his involvement and advocacy for the positive effects of charitable donations to enemy nations in Eugene England, "Fasting and Food, not Weapons: A Mormon Response to Conflict," *BYU Studies* 25:1 (1985): 141–55.

To touch the heart of an enemy and heal divisions is difficult—among the most difficult and important of human duties. It requires risk, imaginative effort to overcome suspicion, hard-headed negotiation and calling to repentance at the right moment—followed by an increase in generosity. But each of us has had enough experience at the personal level to sense that it can be done and something of how it could be done between nations.[14]

In order to engage in this effective pacifism, England points out that one side has to be willing to reach out with love first, and asks, "Since we claim to be a Christian or at least morally superior nation, why shouldn't we be first?"[15]

Recounting his early days at Stanford, England wrote about the cultural confrontations he felt as a believing Mormon in the midst of the early and foundational fronts of the anti-war and civil rights movements of the twentieth century. While his religious ideals of peace, equality, and agency placed him approvingly among peers on campus, those same religious ideals seemed to put him at a variance and with distrust among his fellow Saints in the chapel. He remembered, "On campus, among graduate students and anti-war and civil-rights activists, I was that strange, non-smoking, short-haired, family-raising conservative; [in church-settings], I was that strange liberal who renounced war and worried about fair-housing and free speech."[16] This recollection represents well the harsh polarization that largely existed between the conservatism of the Mormon culture at the time and the liberalism of the anti-war and civil rights movements—a polarization that is still prevalent in American and Mormon culture.

Beginning with the Spanish-American War, the LDS Church's position on war moved away from its previous isolationism with a marked skepticism of American government, toward becoming what historian Ronald Walker calls "a part of pluralistic America."[17] With the arrival of the two world wars of the twentieth century, this became even more pronounced. While during times of relative peace, there was a much stronger pacifist-leaning rhetoric employed by Church lead-

---

14. Ibid., 150.

15. Ibid.

16. England, "No Cause, No Cause," 33.

17. Ronald W. Walker, "Sheaves Bucklers and the State," *Sunstone* 34 (July–August 1982): 49.

ers, however "these expressions have largely disappeared during actual wartime conditions—either discarded or privately kept."[18] The First World War saw this trend as Church President Joseph F. Smith transformed from being a critic of the war effort just prior to its congressional declaration, to later becoming a strong advocate and supporter of the American cause. The Church-owned *Deseret News* proclaimed at the beginning of the war, "Whether the United States is rightfully at war does not for the present concern any American. . . . His country is at war, and unless he is ready to give it every ounce of efficient support he can command, his place is not among Americans."[19] With a firm belief that this war would truly bring about global peace, Church leaders ardently asked Latter-day Saints to support the effort with monetary and volunteer service.

The Second World War began with equal pause and reluctance, but was quickly once again embraced by Mormons. While the LDS First Presidency gave a more restrained support (with never fully supporting) this war, they nevertheless stressed patriotism and national loyalty, releasing a statement claiming that when "constitutional law . . . calls the manhood of the Church into the armed service of any country to which they owe allegiance, their highest civic duty requires that they meet that call."[20] Church leaders stressed a religious duty and obligation of a civilian to the state, and again contributed to the war both monetarily and by urging its members to volunteer for the military and civilian service.

Finally, during the rise of the Cold War and American involvement in Korea and Vietnam, the Mormon position on war developed during the three previous wars became further standardized but with an even stronger affirmation of what Walker refers to as "the leadership's growing trust in the American administration's war policies," at one point expressing "its 'complete confidence' in the national government."[21] At BYU during this time, 84 percent of male students expressed a willingness to

---

18. Ibid., 53.

19. Cited in ibid., 49.

20. J. Reuben Clark, *One Hundred and Twelfth Annual Conference of The Church of Jesus Christ of Latter-day Saints* (Salt Lake City: Deseret Book, 1942), 80. This statement is still used to guide the Church in military matters today. See also D. Michael Quinn's chapter on Clark in this volume.

21. Walker, "Sheaves Bucklers and the State," 52.

fight in Vietnam, supported by the claim of other Church leaders that conscientious objection was not a viable option for Latter-day Saints.[22]

While the climate in Mormonism and at BYU was largely in support of the U.S. government and its military actions, England found a very different atmosphere during his time at Stanford University. Along with other universities such as Berkeley, UCLA, Harvard, Columbia, and Michigan, Stanford was at the forefront of the anti-war and civil rights movements. Far from the rather peaceful and nationalistic tendencies at Brigham Young University, Stanford was a regular home to massive and occasionally violent anti-war protests, often resulting in classes being canceled and buildings being temporarily closed.

Intertwined with the draft-burning and anti-war protests at Stanford and across America was the growing civil rights movement of the 1960s. While England was at Stanford, Martin Luther King Jr. was speaking and leading marches and protests for civil rights. Racial frustrations throughout America were becoming violent and accusatory in both directions, culminating in the assassination of King in April of 1968. England recalls the blending of the anti-war and civil-rights movements when writing of his time at Stanford:

> I became involved in the Graduate Student Coordinating Council, Stanford's version of the Free Speech Movement that had developed at Berkeley. . . . We published a newsletter, organized anti-war rallies, and worked to pass local fair-housing laws. We talked a lot about how the university itself, in its involvement in military research and tendency to support the status quo . . . might be contributing directly to such evils as militarism and racism.[23]

While the anti-war movements at Stanford certainly and admittedly influenced England's theology of peace, various statements by Mormon leaders and scriptures also played important roles in his writings on war and peace—despite the tendency of Church leaders and members to lean toward a nationalistic support of what they considered to be just warfare. The statement he cited most frequently came from a General Conference address given in the spring of 1942 by David O. McKay, then a second counselor to ailing Church President Heber

---

22. See Gary James Bergera and Ronald Priddis, *Brigham Young University: A House of Faith* (Salt Lake City: Signature Books, 1985), 180–81.

23. England, "No Cause, No Cause," 32.

J. Grant. Speaking in the first General Conference after the attack on Pearl Harbor, McKay began by directly addressing the war:

> With a number of young men from each of many wards in the Church serving somewhere in the terrible conflict now raging, it is easily understood why our minds are turned toward the deprecation of war, and to the hope for peace. Thoughts of loved ones are pretty closely linked with their soldier boys in army encampments. There are many, too, who should like to know what the attitude of the Church is toward the present war. This is a fitting day and occasion on which to consider this subject.[24]

McKay continued by pointing out the gross incompatibilities between the peaceful teachings of Jesus Christ and violent war, arguing that they cannot and should not be reconciled. However in doing so, McKay made a paradoxical leap from this seemingly unwavering denouncement of war to a Church sponsorship of the Second World War:

> Thus we see that war is incompatible with Christ's teachings. The gospel of Jesus Christ is the gospel of peace. War is its antithesis, and produces hate. It is vain to attempt to reconcile war with true Christianity.
>
> In the face of all this, I shall seem inconsistent when I declare that I uphold our country in the gigantic task it has assumed in the present world conflict, and sustain the Church in its loyal support of the government in its fight against dictatorship.[25]

McKay continued that despite the incompatibility of war and the teachings of Jesus, Latter-day Saints have an obligation to support a war when that war is (1) defending freedom, (2) part of a loyal obligation of a citizen to his nation, and possibly (3) entered into (never begun) as a measure to defend a weak nation from being "unjustly crushed by a strong, ruthless one."[26] For both McKay and England, the conflicting values of Christian love and the desire to defend freedom and live—because of that Christian love—created a paradox for which there was no simple reconciliation or remedy, and thus must be trudged through with faith.[27]

---

24. David O. McKay, *One Hundred and Twelfth Annual Conference of The Church of Jesus Christ of Latter-day Saints* (Salt Lake City: Deseret Book 1942), 71.

25. Ibid., 72.

26. McKay, *One Hundred and Twelfth Annual Conference*, 72.

27. England, "The Prince of Peace," 242. For a more detailed exploration of McKay's complex view of war, see Gregory A. Prince and Wm. Robert Wright,

This address is cited in at least eight different essays by England,[28] each time focusing on McKay's condemnation of war for unjust reasons—with an emphasis placed each time (with direct citation) of McKay's declaration that war cannot be "justified in an attempt to enforce a new order of government, or even to impel others to a particular form of worship, however better the government or eternally true the principles of the enforced religion may be."[29]

Another citation from this era that England frequently used comes four years later during the fall LDS General Conference, just over a year after the bombings of Hiroshima and Nagasaki had already killed over 200,000 Japanese civilians and arguably ended the war against Japan. President J. Reuben Clark, a devout pacifist and first counselor to the newly appointed Church President, George Albert Smith, openly criticized the use of the atomic bombs:

> Then as the crowning savagery of the war, we Americans wiped out hundreds of thousands of civilian population with the atom bomb in Japan, few if any of the ordinary civilians being any more responsible for the war than were we, and perhaps most of them no more aiding Japan in the war than we were aiding America. Military men are now saying that the atom bomb was a mistake. It was more than that: it was a world tragedy. Thus we have lost all that we gained during the years from Grotius (1625) to 1912. And the worst of this atomic bomb tragedy is not that not only did the people of the United States not rise up in protest against this savagery, not only did it not shock us to read of this wholesale destruction of men, women, and children, and cripples, but that it actually drew from the nation at large a general approval of this fiendish butchery.[30]

David O. McKay and the Rise of Modern Mormonism (Salt Lake City: University of Utah Press, 2005), 279–322.

28. See England, "Can Nations Love Their Enemies?" 140; "Healing and Making Peace in the Church and the World," in *Making Peace*, 10; "Why Utah Mormons Should be Democrats: Reflections on Partisan Politics," in *Making Peace*, 102; "'Thou Shalt Not Kill': An Ethics of Non-violence," in *Making Peace*, 172; "Prince of Peace," 242; "The Tragedy of Vietnam," 74; "On Trusting God," 11; and "Late Night Thoughts," 7.

29. McKay, *One Hundred and Twelfth Annual Conference*, 72.

30. J. Reuben Clark, *One Hundred and Seventeenth Semi-annual Conference of The Church of Jesus Christ of Latter-day Saints* (Salt Lake City: Deseret Book 1946), 88. For more of Clark's pacifism and views on war see D. Michael Quinn, *Elder Statesman: A Biography of J. Reuben Clark* (Salt Lake City: Signature Books, 2002),

England used this to show that "Mormon leaders did not hesitate to criticize leaders of the United States as well as those of other countries for ignoring such general [moral] principles and perpetrating the brutalities of the Second World War."[31] Such a citation of a Church leader strongly criticizing national leaders bolstered England's claim that patriotism and nationalism do not rise above gospel teachings, and that national leaders can and ought to be criticized for moral injustices.

Finally, a third general LDS leader that England frequently cited and utilized in his theology of peace is former Church President Spencer W. Kimball. England often appealed to three key messages given by President Kimball. The first of these is from the monthly "First Presidency Message" presented in the LDS Church's official magazine, the *Ensign*. Written to coincide with the United States' bicentennial celebration, Kimball heavily criticized the state of the nation in an article entitled "The False Gods We Worship." He wrote:

> We are, on the whole, an idolatrous people—a condition most repugnant to the Lord. We are a warlike people, easily distracted from our assignment of preparing for the coming of the Lord. When enemies rise up, we commit vast resources to the fabrication of gods of stone and steel—ships, planes, missiles, fortifications—and depend on them for protection and deliverance. When threatened, we become antienemy instead of pro-kingdom of God; we train a man in the art of war and call him a patriot, thus, in the manner of Satan's counterfeit of true patriotism, perverting the Savior's teaching....
>
> We forget that if we are righteous the Lord will either not suffer our enemies to come upon us ... or he will fight our battles for us.... What are we to fear when the Lord is with us? Can we not take the Lord at his word and exercise a particle of faith in him? Our assignment is affirmative: to forsake the things of the world as ends in themselves; to leave off idolatry and press forward in faith; to carry the gospel to our enemies, that they might no longer be our enemies.[32]

Frequently citing this as a whole, England argued that Latter-day Saints need to stop seeing the military as our only defense against our enemies

---

277–317. See also Quinn's chapter in this volume.

31. England, "Can Nations Love Their Enemies?" 141. See also "Healing and Making Peace," 7; "The Tragedy of Vietnam," 89; and "On Trusting God," 10–11.

32. Spencer W. Kimball, "First Presidency Message: The False Gods We Worship," *Ensign*, June 1976, 6.

and instead trust in "God's ability to work miracles" and the Christian message of peace to transform our enemies rather than destroy them.[33]

Another message from Kimball that England often cited came from a May 1981 First Presidency Statement concerning the basing of MX missile systems (ironically also known as "Peacemakers") in Utah and Nevada.[34] Pointing to possible threats to human health as well as environmental and ecological risks, Kimball argued against the placement of these systems in the West, closing with a criticism of the violent nature of the weapons themselves:

> Our fathers came to this western area to establish a base from which to carry the gospel of peace to the peoples of the earth. It is ironic, and a denial of the very essence of that gospel, that in this same general area there should be constructed a mammoth weapons system potentially capable of destroying much of civilization. With the most serious concern over the pressing moral question of possible nuclear conflict, we plead with our national leaders to marshal the genius of the nation to find viable alternatives which will secure at an earlier date and with fewer hazards the protection from possible enemy aggression, which is our common concern.[35]

Finally, England also referenced Kimball's 1981 First Presidency Christmas message, given just seven months after the criticism of the MX missiles, where again, Kimball called for peace between enemies:

> To all who seek a resolution to conflict, be it a misunderstanding between individuals or an international difficulty among nations, we commend the counsel of the Prince of Peace, "Love your enemies, bless them that curse you, do good to them that hate you, and pray for them which despitefully use you, and persecute you; That ye may be the children of your Father which is in heaven" (Matthew 5:44–45). This principle of loving one another as Jesus Christ loves us will bring peace to the individual, to the home and beyond, even to the nations and to the world.[36]

---

33. England, "On Trusting God," 9–10. See also "Can Nations Love Their Enemies?" 143; "Healing and Making Peace," 9; "The Prince of Peace," 243; "Late Night Thoughts," 7; "Fasting and Food, Not Weapons," 11; and "What Covenant Will God Receive in the Desert?" *Sunstone* 96 (September 1994): 28.

34. See England, "Can Nations Love Their Enemies?" 143; "The Prince of Peace," 244; and "What Covenant Will God Receive in the Desert?" 29.

35. "First Presidency Statement on Basing of MX Missile," *Ensign*, June 1981, 76.

36. "First Presidency Christmas Message," *Church News*, 19 December 1981, 2.

When it came to appeals to scripture, the most cited verses in England's theology of peace were those that deal with the story of the "Anti-Nephi-Lehies" in the Book of Mormon. This tells of a group of people known as the Lamanites, who are usually described as wicked and bloodthirsty compared to the more righteous Nephites. Upon converting to the Christian message, the Anti-Nephi-Lehies decide to literally bury their weapons and covenant with God to never use violence again against another:

> And this they did, it being in their view a testimony to God, and also to men, that they never would use weapons again for the shedding of man's blood; and this they did, vouching and covenanting with God, that rather than shed the blood of their brethren they would give up their own lives; ...
>
> And thus we see that, when these Lamanites were brought to believe and to know the truth, they were firm, and would suffer even unto death rather than commit sin; and thus we see that they buried their weapons of peace, or they buried their weapons of war, for peace. (Alma 24:18–19)

When they are eventually tested by an attack by other Lamanites, these Anti-Nephi-Lehies prostrate themselves to the ground and refuse to take up arms, resulting in the deaths of over a thousand of their people. In the process though, many of these attacking Lamanites are emotionally struck by their pacifist victims and decide to also give up their weapons. Following the battle, many of the attackers—in fact, more than the number of those who had been killed—convert and join up with the Anti-Nephi-Lehies.

England pointed out that this "account gives powerful evidence that this ethic that most Christians affirm, but are afraid to try, really *works*." Though, he also admitted, "There is, of course, no suggestion that conversion to the Gospel in itself requires this kind of covenant, but the prophet giving the account clearly views those who were conscientiously capable of such an ethical choice ... with great admiration."[37]

See also England, "The Prince of Peace," 241; "On Trusting God," 9; "Late Night Thoughts," 7; and "What Covenant Will God Receive in the Desert?" 29.

37. England, "The Tragedy of Vietnam," 73. See also England, "Can Nations Love Their Enemies?" 136; "Why Utah Mormons Should Become Democrat," 102; "Thou Shalt Not Kill," 159; and "What Covenant Will God Receive in the Desert?" 32.

While the story of the Anti-Nephi-Lehies seems to argue for a strong pacifist approach for Latter-day Saints, England was also quick to point out (as many Mormons do) that the Book of Mormon itself also offers justifications for violence. The Mormon scripture begins in its first pages with a justification of violence as the young prophet Nephi is instructed by God to behead a wicked leader in order to protect his family and enable them to possess their scriptures and genealogies. Nephi writes that God commanded him to kill in order to bring about God's righteous purposes and to protect the many from perishing in unbelief.[38] This justification of violence is further expanded in the Book of Mormon to justify entering into defensive wars. Led by Captain Moroni, who is highly praised by the Nephite prophet Mormon,[39] the Nephites are said to be supported by God as they fight off Lamanite aggressors:

> They were not fighting for monarchy nor power but they were fighting for their homes and their liberties, their wives and their children, and their all, yea, for their rites of worship and their church. . . . The Lord said unto them, and also unto their fathers, that: Inasmuch as ye are not guilty of the first offense, neither the second, ye shall not suffer yourselves to be slain by the hands of your enemies. (Alma 43:45–46)

England noted that the emphasis here "is on a purely defensive war," and that given the chance, Moroni and the Nephites allowed the Lamanites the opportunity to return to their homes in peace without further punishing them or seeking revenge.[40] He also contended that while both the Anti-Nephi-Lehies' pacifism and Moroni's defensive violence are tenable positions for Latter-day Saints, it is seen from the Book of Mormon that the "sacrifice of these . . . pacifists ended violence, while the 'just' wars of the Nephites did not and were followed by a decline into apostasy."[41]

---

38. For England's take on this account see "Why Nephi Killed Laban: Reflections on the Truth of the Book of Mormon," in *Making Peace*, 131–55.

39. Mormon writes, "Yea, verily verily I say unto you, if all men had been, and were, and ever would be, like unto Moroni, behold, the very powers of hell would have been shaken forever; yea, the devil would never have power over the hearts of the children of men" (Alma 48:17).

40. England, "Can Nations Love Their Enemies?" 137.

41. England, "Thou Shalt Not Kill," 159. See also England, "Why Utah Mormons Should Become Democrat," 102; and "Thoughts on Violence," 73.

Finally, England on several occasions appealed to the Sermon on the Mount in the New Testament to show that this theology of peace is ultimately grounded in the Christian teaching to "Love your enemies, bless them that curse you, do good to them that hate you, and pray for them which despitefully use you, and persecute you."[42]

It should also be noted that England's writings do not only utilize Latter-day Saint sources, but also reflect on and appeal to a wide variety of literature, events, and other sources outside of Mormonism. In fact it is rare to find any essay of his—even those written for non-scholarly Mormon worship—that do not infuse a wide variety of ideas. For example, his essay "The Prince of Peace," originally written as an Easter sermon, weaves together Mormon sources with the Gulf of Tonkin incident, Martin Luther King Jr., Jimmy Carter, Dietrich Bonhoeffer, Walter Wink, Catholic art, and a Japanese Army interpreter to present a message of worship and faith for a local Latter-day Saint congregation.[43]

England's theology of peace, however, cannot be seen simply as being dependent on these statements and scriptures or just influenced by his experience at Stanford, nor should his theology of peace be seen as something that is merely a statement about war. Rather his theology is representative of a general theology of peace that permeates nearly all of his writings, of which his views on war are only one manifestation.

Unlike many Mormon theologies that focus on the ontological status of the world (or what the world really *is*), England's theology of peace focuses on the ethical status of the world (what the world *ought to be*). Rather than emphasizing the material, divine, or metaphysical and philosophical natures and attributes of God and man, England's theology turns to the social and communal relationships of God and his children. Even his essays on the "Weeping God of Mormonism" and the "Perfection and Progression" of God are exercises in peace and reconciliation, and point out that these attributes of God are only truly meaningful in a context of God's relationship to His children and His desire for them to find peace away from their conflicts.[44] England points

---

42. Matthew 5:44. See England, "Can Nations Love Their Enemies?" 135; "Healing and Making Peace," 8; "Thou Shalt Not Kill," 159; "The Prince of Peace," 235; "On Trusting God," 9; "Late Night Thoughts," 7; and "What Covenant Will God Receive in the Desert?" 30.

43. England, "The Prince of Peace."

44. See Eugene England, "The Weeping God of Mormonism," *Dialogue* 35:1 (Spring 2002): 63–80; and Eugene England, "Perfection and Progression: Two

to Enoch's account in the Book of Moses where he questions how it is possible that God, who created all things, could weep.[45] In reply to Enoch's question, God points to humanity and answers,

> Behold these thy brethren; they are the workmanship of mine own hands, and I gave unto them their knowledge [and] . . . gave I unto man his agency; And unto thy brethren have I said, and also given commandment, that they should love one another, and that they should choose me, their Father; but behold, they are without affection, and they hate their own blood.[46]

England blended strictly religious principles and texts, secular philosophies and writings, as well as personal anecdotes elucidating his theology of peace. This underlying theology took many shapes through his essays and narratives, and can be seen as being composed of three separate, but not necessarily distinct, components: forgiveness and trust; nonviolence and an affirmation of life; and the equality of humankind.

In his essay, "Healing and Making Peace, in the Church and the World," England pointed to the cyclical pattern of violence and harm that our desire for retributive justice constantly renews. This is the standard eye-for-an-eye, tooth-for-a-tooth justice that we usually feel when someone has wronged us. It is the source of continued contention between individuals, the sustenance of feuds between families and communities, and is a primary cause of unending conflicts between nations. Citing his friend and fellow scholar at BYU, Hugh Nibley, England argued that the endless violence resulting from this retributive justice is an unfortunate lesson in the Book of Mormon: "The Book of Mormon reinforces . . . the crucial understanding that conflict, including war, occurs only when both sides have sinned. When either side is willing to obey Christ's commands, to lay down their weapons or angry words and stop fighting or competing, even if they thus sacrifice their lives, as Christ did, they stop the violence."[47] According to England, the only way to truly end conflict is not with force, but with forgiveness and trust. President Spencer W. Kimball argued that we need "to carry the Gospel to our enemies, that they will no longer be our enemies" in his 1976 bicentennial address. England added that this should not be inter-

Ways to Talk About God," in *Making Peace*, 43–63.

45. England, "Weeping God," 63.

46. Moses 7:32–33.

47. England, "Healing and Making Peace," 8–9.

preted as simply sending the missionaries over to proselyte our enemies, but rather it should be interpreted as *showing* our enemies the Gospel: "We are to take the gospel to our enemies by *acting* like Christians, by working for and showing consistent mercy." This is because "extending mercy is the *only* hope we have for moving our enemies to give *us* mercy rather than responding to our violence with retribution until we have continuing and escalating war."[48]

Reacting with violence is easy because it keeps us in control; reacting with mercy is difficult because it leaves us vulnerable to the other—just as Christ's unwillingness to react with violence toward his captors made him vulnerable. Though difficult, England said that we need to react with mercy to end the pattern of violence and conflict. Forgiveness and trust "is to be extended not because they *deserve* it but because they *need* it, because they can *become* trustworthy (or loving) by being nurtured in a community of trust and love. We need to extend trust, even if doing so makes us vulnerable to pain and great cost, in order to save our souls."[49]

This act of undeserved forgiveness, mercy, and trust is exemplified by the Anti-Nephi-Lehies, who refused to violently confront the attacking Lamanites. Rather than take the normal recourse of violence that elevated a feud between brothers into a 500-year-old war between nations, they instead chose to act nonviolently and affirm the life of their enemies. For England, this was not just a principle of nations, but one that should also guide our individual lives within our own communities.

Furthermore, according to England, "The scriptures and modern prophets call us to revere life as the most fundamental value, even to sacrifice our own lives to avoid violence as we respond to injustice and evil that threaten us."[50] This affirmation of life, or what England also called a "Mormon theology of life,"[51] must extend to all humanity as "each human by their very existence constitutes an absolute claim on every other human to be treated as an end rather than a means."[52] This right to life, according to England, extends equally to the enemy nation, the unborn

---

48. Ibid., 9.

49. England, "On Spectral Evidence, Scapegoating, and False Accusation," in *Making Peace*, 29.

50. England, "Thou Shalt Not Kill," 158.

51. Ibid., 174.

52. Ibid., 160.

child, and the convicted killer. While critical of pro-life movements that attempt to demonize their opponents, he was also critical of pro-choice movements whose "rhetoric exalts romantic individualism over social responsibility and trivializes the serious life-and-death questions of abortion."[53] Any systemic devaluation of life, whether it be from war, abortion, or the death-penalty does not only injure those it kills, but it also damages everyone as it

> is such a serious violation of our nature, and our given ethical relationship to each other, that to numb our consciences and enable us to do it at all, we mentally dehumanize our victims (calling embryos mere tissue, "like fingernails," or turning state executions into cloaked, depersonalized rituals)—but that of course is itself a violation of our nature and given ethical relationship.[54]

Finally, England's theology of peace affirms equality and freedom for all. Just as the affirmation of life for all is a fundamental value, a "basic principle, consistent throughout scripture and eminently sensible, seems clear enough: God loves us all equally, treats us all equally and liberally, expects and hopes the same for all of us—and asks, *expects*, us to do the same to each other."[55] England's theology of peace lies at the core of the Church's teaching of the gospel and the atonement—that God desires all of his children to be saved. "There are no limit's on God's redeeming love," England wrote, "God struggles with all his power to provide equal opportunity for all who come to the earth."[56] If God loves and respects all of his children, then we ought to do the same—even for those with political views that we are strongly against.[57] This truth of God should force Latter-day Saints to do some self-reflection to ensure that they excise themselves of racism, sexism, and xenophobia.[58]

Six months before resigning from BYU, England lamented that he felt he was being

---

53. Ibid., 164.

54. Ibid., 170.

55. Eugene England, "'No Respecter of Persons': An Ethics of Diversity," in *Making Peace*, 179; emphasis in original.

56. Eugene England, "Responses and Perspectives: The Mormon Cross," *Dialogue* 8:1 (1973): 80.

57. England, "Why Utah Mormons Should Become Democrats," 95. See also "No Cause, No Cause," 33.

58. England, "No Respecter of Persons," 191.

publicly attacked and privately punished [at BYU], not for violating the academic freedom document prescriptions against criticizing Church leaders or opposing Church doctrine, but for violating cultural taboos that are mistakenly made into religious issues, for publicly opposing war, for exposing [his] own and other Mormons' racism and sexism, even for teaching nationally honored but liberal Mormon writers.[59]

Despite his best effort to identify and live a theology of peace, that very effort put him at odds with others. This was a difficult balance that he struggled with maintaining, and England was ever self-critical of the animosity that he at times helped foster while trying to find peace. After making some emotionally charged accusations toward some in the Church whom he felt had wrongly hurt some of his friends, and then learning of the rift he may have created, England recalled feeling "much anguish" and "like a hypocrite." After learning more of those he had accused, he "felt despair that I had, however unwittingly, criticized them and possibly invited others to do so."[60] He remained committed to his theology of peace to the end of his life, though never claiming that he lived it perfectly. Just as in his life-changing days at Stanford, Eugene England was still far too conservative for the liberal academic crowd and yet far too liberal for the conservative Mormon culture he saw as his own.

---

59. England, "No Cause, No Cause," 35.
60. England, "On Spectral Evidence," 38.

Part IV

Personal & Professional Observations

14

An LDS Chaplain's Perspective on Current Conflicts[1]

Eric A. Eliason

In 2004 I served in Afghanistan as a chaplain with the 19th Special Forces of the Utah Army National Guard. Special Forces' mission is to work with and train local indigenous fighters to become well-disciplined infantrymen. To do this, Special Forces soldiers learn languages, adopt customs, and seek to understand the goals and values of those they train. As a chaplain, I provided for the religious needs of the soldiers of all faiths in my unit. One of my roles was to serve as a liaison with local religious leaders. My unit had a large footprint in the area of operation and was spread out among many small firebases close to the Pakistan border where the fighting was taking place. I spent hundreds of hours in helicopters and driving in convoys to visit my soldiers. I spent most of my deployment living, working, and patrolling with soldiers, and had many close interactions with Afghans.

Much of my unit's work had to do with peacemaking and peace-keeping. The mosque reconstruction program and first-ever chaplain training program for Afghan National Army chaplains, developed and implemented by my assistant and me, are featured in a 2006 booklet published by the United States Institute of Peace.[2] When my unit deployed to do counter-insurgency work in the Philippines in 2006–2007, the host country general that we worked with was very enthusiastic about Mennonite NGOs who had come to offer conflict resolution

---

1. Special thanks are due to BreeAnne Madison for transcribing an initial draft of this talk from a recording of my talk.

2. George Adams, *Chaplains as Liaisons with Religious Leaders: Lessons from Iraq and Afghanistan*, Peaceworks no. 56 (Washington, DC: United States Institute for Peace, March 2006).

training. He required all of his officers to take this training because he found that conflict resolution skills were more useful than his soldiers' rifle training nine times out of ten. My unit's experience in Afghanistan and the Philippines mirrors his observations. The hours we spent sitting with tribal elders making friends and helping resolve conflicts actually outnumbered hours spent in firefights by many hundreds to one. However, that occasional hour of battle made the thousands of hours of nonviolent conflict resolution possible. During the one hour of battle, we proved to the Afghan people that we were willing to risk our own lives to protect them from people who would murder and oppress them. Had we not fought, we would not have been taken seriously and would have been rendered ineffective in establishing peace.

Too often conversations about conflicts are framed as "peace vs. war," with people either in one camp or another. I can't accept this framing and want to suggest some alternate frames through which we might want to look at this issue:

- Are we for protecting the weak, or are we for letting bullies have their way?
- Are we for allowing the rape and murder of Afghan women, or are we for stopping it?
- Are we for the democratically elected government of Iraq, or are we for the mass-murdering Ba'athist tyrants who would still be in power if we had stayed home or for the mass-murdering Al Qaeda tyrants that would take over if we go home too soon?

Some may find these frames as reductionist or as unfair in their choice of categories as "peace vs. war," but in my experience these frames better conform to how LDS soldiers think about these issues and better represent the actual dilemmas people face on the ground. The way we frame issues is crucial, as the questions we ask determine, in part, the answers we come up with. So it is particularly important that the frames match the actualities under discussion.

For Latter-day Saints, another issue to consider is the temptation to play the game of dueling General Authority quotes, pitting one prophetic statement against another. Pacifist Latter-day Saints often invoke Spencer W. Kimball's famous talk titled "The False Gods We Worship," interpreting it as an unequivocal statement against maintaining a national defense—even though President Kimball said nothing against maintaining weapons, only against worshipping or putting false trust in them.[3] Selectively appealing to only this one address, however powerful it is, fails to take into account the overwhelming number and nature of General Authority statements during the Cold War. One could cite any number of examples, but one, from David O. McKay, is suggestive: "Force rules in the world today, consequently, our government must keep armies abroad, build navies and air squadrons, create atom bombs to protect itself from the threatened aggression."[4]

A similar dynamic is often applied to how we approach scripture. People frequently consider that their own interpretations are fully informed and deeply contextualized, while belittling contrasting views as proof texting, cherry picking, and ignoring the full narrative context. Recognizing that I am not exempt from this, I will share my own views on what the Book of Mormon reveals about how Latter-day Saints might deal with differences of opinion over violent conflict. In particular, as I approach the Ammonite versus Nephite approach to war, I don't see a conundrum but rather two equally valid ways of approaching matters of war and peace.

The Nephites believed it right to defend their liberty and the liberty of others even unto bloodshed. The Ammonites did not. In today's polarized world, the Ammonites might have called the Nephites "bloodthirsty war mongering murderers of their Lamanite brethren" whereas the Nephites might have called the Ammonites "Lamanite-loving traitors too cowardly to fight for their Nephite brethren." They might have done this, but they didn't. Rather each group followed their religion as their conscience dictated, and supported their brethren who felt otherwise without questioning their intelligence, their honesty, their morality, or religious commitment or orthodoxy. Rather, the people of Ammon willingly gave of their substance to the war effort while Nephites willingly died in battle to protect their brethren who felt constrained not to do the same.

As a chaplain, I was privy to some of the deepest concerns, values, beliefs, and private thoughts that soldiers have about why they go to war. Sometimes, military culture is such that soldiers will talk about being rough and tough and joining up to prove their manhood. But if you get them in their quiet and thoughtful moments, they often talk very differently about why they joined, why they serve, the compassion

---

3. Spencer W. Kimball, "The False Gods We Worship," *Ensign*, June 1976.

4. David O. McKay, *Gospel Ideals* (Salt Lake City: Improvement Era, 1953), 302.

that they feel for people who are under threat, and how honored they feel to be part of an effort to protect others.

I don't think these sentiments are uniquely LDS, but many Mormons view their military service through the additional light and knowledge that we have as Latter-day Saints. I also believe there is a clear vision to be had on what our current war is all about. In doing so, I want to be clear that nothing I say should be taken as an indictment of Islam. We have more to gain than to lose by supporting the free exercise of Islam. We may be unique among Christian denominations in specifically affirming the 1978 First Presidency Declaration that Muhammad (peace be upon him) was at least partly inspired by God.[5] Neither should what I say be taken as a criticism of Afghan culture, which is enterprising, ingenious, and creative. I have had the opportunity to witness tribal councils and the traditional Afghan legal system of the *Pashtunwali* in action on several occasions. Their ability to bring about justice, reconciliation, and forgiveness is something from which our confrontational winner-takes-all legal system could learn a lot. I also hope that nothing I say will be misconstrued as the LDS Church's official position on this or any other conflict. There are many noble pursuits that Latter-day Saints as private individuals may undertake of their own volition that the Church is not officially involved in. Latter-day Saints are encouraged to be anxiously engaged in good causes. There are lots of them out there. My only hope is to suggest that the work of soldiers can be one of the good causes.

We know that the foundation of our existence as children of God has to do with war—the great War in Heaven regarding the proposed conditions of our mortal probation. In Moses 4:1–3, Lucifer said, "Behold, here am I, send me, I will be thy son, and I will redeem all mankind, that one soul shall not be lost, . . . wherefore give me thine honor." The Lord responded: "Because that Satan rebelled against me, and sought to destroy the agency of man, . . . I [the Lord] caused that he should be cast down." Satan's goal to save everyone might sound good. But his means to this end, by destroying agency, was not only wrong but

---

5. "Statement of the First Presidency regarding God's Love for All Mankind," February 15, 1978. This statement is referenced in an April 2006 General Conference talk given by President James E. Faust, entitled "The Restoration of All Things," website of the Church of Jesus Christ of Latter-day Saints, http://www.lds.org/conference/talk/display/0,5232,23-1-602-21,00.html (accessed January 3, 2012).

also impossible under the conditions necessary for our salvation. The satanic tactic of promising that seemingly good ends could be achieved by means that restrict human agency was a lie from the beginning, and is a theme that has popped up in Satan's counterfeits to God's plan many times in world history.

Around the same time as the Restoration, Karl Marx and Friedrich Engels proposed in *The Communist Manifesto* and *Das Kapital* how an inevitable utopia of economic equality would be achieved by the irresistible dialectic workings of history pushed forward—as later elaborated by Lenin—by a small vanguard imposing their "enlightened" will on others. But David O. McKay and Marion G. Romney warned that communism "is Satan's counterfeit plan for the gospel."[6] Heber J. Grant's First Presidency issued a statement explaining, "Communism is based upon intolerance and force, the United Order upon love and freedom of conscience and action."[7] Despite Marxism's appeal to many, its results crushed freedom and creativity, destroyed economies, brought about horrible brutality, and resulted in the massacre of millions, the likes of which the world has never seen before or since—all in the name of human progress. Ezra Taft Benson called the struggle between freedom and communism "a continuation of the war in heaven" on Earth.[8] Indeed, Marxism rested on that original satanic premise of promising salvation through coercion.

Recently, we have again seen this pattern of satanic counterfeits proposing tyranny and destruction of agency as necessary to achieving something good. In 1995, the First Presidency issued "The Family: A Proclamation to the World," which includes the following: "By divine design, fathers are to preside over their families in love and righteousness and are responsible to provide the necessities of life and protection for their families. Mothers are primarily responsible for the nurture of their children."[9] One year later, in a strange parallel, the Taliban rulers of Afghanistan issued the official document, "Decrees Relating to Women and Other Cultural Issues after the Capture of Kabul in 1996." It includes this statement: "Husband, brother, father, have the responsibility for providing the family with the

---

6. Marion G. Romney, "America's Promise," *Ensign*, September 1979, 3.

7. "A Warning to Church Members From the First Presidency," *Deseret News*, July 3, 1936.

8. Ezra Taft Benson, Conference Report, October 1961, 70–71.

9. "The Family: A Proclamation to the World," website of the Church of Jesus Christ of Latter-day Saints, http://lds.org/library/display/0,4945,161-1-11-1,00.html (accessed January 3, 2012).

necessities of life requirements (food, clothes, etc.). Women have the responsibility as a teacher or coordinator in her family."

Any similarities in the ideal of these two proclamations are belied by categorical distinctions between how they should be implemented and enforced. The Taliban says:

- "We request family elders to keep tight control over their families . . . otherwise [they] will be severely punished . . . by the forces of the religious Police."
- "The religious police are allowed to go for control at any time and nobody can prevent them."
- "If a cassette is found in a vehicle, the driver will be imprisoned."
- "To prevent beard shaving . . . they should be arrested and imprisoned until their beard gets bushy."
- "To prevent idolatry . . . monitors should tear up all pictures."
- "To prevent interest in loans . . . criminals will be imprisoned for a long time."
- [In case of] "music and dancing at wedding parties . . . the head of the family will be arrested and punished."
- "To prevent not praying . . . if young people are seen in the shops [during prayer time] they will be immediately imprisoned."

The actuality of life under the Taliban was far more severe than these official statements suggest. Often the Taliban response to the infractions above was not to haul the offenders to jail, but to the Kabul soccer stadium to be shot in the back of the head in a mass public execution.

We may or may not agree with some of the goals expressed, but the more fundamental point is that the Taliban offered only coercion and agency restriction as the primary means to promoting righteousness. Compare the Taliban's methods to what the restored Gospel teaches:

- "Successful marriages and families are established and maintained on principles of faith, prayer, repentance, forgiveness, respect, love, [and] compassion." ("The Family: A Proclamation")
- Rather than urging patriarchs to exercise tight control, mothers and fathers are called "equal partners" and "individual adaptation" is allowed for their respective roles. ("The Family: A Proclamation")
- "I teach them correct principles and let them govern themselves." (Joseph Smith)[10]

---

10. James R. Clark, comp., *Messages of the First Presidency*, 6 vols. (Salt Lake City: Bookcraft, 1965–75), 3:54.

- "If I esteem a man to be in error, shall I bear him down? No, I will lift him up and in his own way too." (Joseph Smith)[11]

Like the fight against communism, the fight in Afghanistan also looks like a continuation of the War in Heaven. Many of the same dynamics were also at play in Iraq. Contrast Article of Faith 11—"We claim the privilege of worshipping Almighty God according to the dictates of our own conscience, and allow all men the same privilege, let them worship how, where, and what they may"—to the views of Abu Musab al-Zarqawi, the terrorist commander behind much of Iraq's violence in the mid-2000s. In his declaration in January 2004, he said, "We have declared a fierce war on this evil principle of democracy and all who should follow this wrong teaching," because it is based "on the right to choose your religion," and that is "against the rule of God."[12] If our only response to such people is outreach and dialogue, what (or whom) exactly would we be willing to compromise to resolve the conflict?

In my experience and by policy, American soldiers in Iraq and Afghanistan spend most of their time trying to prevent the Taliban and Al Qaeda from killing civilians. For our enemies in both conflicts, however, committing atrocities against civilians is not the rare and regrettable exception but a centerpiece of their strategy that they pursue with great enthusiasm. They purposely target women and children, looking for ways to kill more of them and glamorize those who blow themselves up to bring this about. This is far different morally than civilians tragically and inadvertently being killed after taking great measures to ensure that only combatants are targeted.

If I have learned anything from my interaction with Afghans, it is that freedom is not just some abstract principle for discussion in a political science class or something to feel warm and fuzzy about on the Fourth of July. Freedom is a real human condition that makes all the difference in terms of people's happiness, fulfillment, and prosperity. It is worth fighting for. The Doctrine and Covenants is clear that freedom's benefits are not just political and economic but religious as well, and that the Lord not only allows bloodshed to bring about conditions of freedom, but calls it "redeeming" in the case of the American

---

11. Joseph Fielding Smith, comp., *Teachings of the Prophet Joseph Smith* (Salt Lake City: Deseret Book, 1977), 314.

12. "Purported al-Zarqawi Tape: Democracy A Lie," CNN Website, January 23, 2005, http://www.cnn.com/2005/WORLD/meast/01/23/iraq.main/ (accessed June 2007).

Revolution (fought in response to oppression that was orders of magnitude less severe than those experienced by people living under Saddam Hussein or the Taliban). In words that seem written for our day, the Lord says that the principles enumerated in the U.S. Constitution (and by extension, constitutional governments elsewhere, such as those fighting for their lives in Iraq and Afghanistan)

> should be maintained for the rights and protection of all flesh, according to just and holy principles; That every man may act in doctrine and principle pertaining to futurity, according to the moral agency which I have given unto him, that every man may be accountable for his own sins in the day of judgment. Therefore it is not right that any man should be in bondage one to another.
>
> And for this purpose have I established the Constitution of this land … and redeemed the land by the shedding of blood. (D&C 101:77–80)

The great Nephite General Captain Moroni led men into battle for "their homes and their liberties, their wives and their children, and their all, yea, for their rites of worship and their church" (Alma 43:45). If it is noble to fight for your own home and your own family, how much more noble is it to fight for the benefit of strangers in a country far away whose religion is not your own? Is this not the kind of love the Good Samaritan showed the injured traveler on the road to Jericho in Jesus' parable—namely the desire to aid an oppressed stranger in a different country of a different religion at great personal risk?

With this parable in mind, we can see the morality of military service in a clearer light. But we only serve the right by fighting on the right side for the right motives for the right ends by the right means. We do so by winning wars decisively, establishing the principles on which lasting peace can be founded, and by being victorious over tyrants. While tyrants lead their nations to war frequently and almost by definition, free nations going to war against each other is virtually unheard of. So when we fight to help others secure freedoms and overthrow oppressors we "increase the peace" as the saying goes, in the same way a surgeon can increase a person's health by cutting them open. When we appease and allow tyrants to thrive, we increase the chance that they will continue to oppress, destroy, and foment war against each other and us. Is a God of Peace not best served by practicing the most effective means to bring about peace? This is not done by undermining the liberating actions of the armies of democracy but by supporting them in their efforts to be victorious over Satan's plan on earth. In following the example of the Ammonites who refused to take up arms for personal moral reasons, modern pacifist Mormons might also choose to freely support armies that fight on their behalf, even beyond the requisite taxation. We should also recall that the Anti-Nephi-Lehies did not require their children to abstain from fighting, but rather supported them when they chose to be allies with the Nephites and go to war.

*   *   *

As I conclude, I want to reflect on two images from my experience in Afghanistan. The girls pictured here are Afghans whose school was across the street from Camp Blessing firebase in the Pesch Valley. They were not at school by random chance; they were in attendance because their parents decided to send them to school. It was not on our initiative, but theirs. The girls' teachers invited us to visit the school because the girls were afraid of men with guns. All the men with guns they had seen before were Talibs who, as per their policy, killed girls for going to school, as well as their teachers for daring to educate them. The teachers understood that we were there to protect the girls and asked us to help the girls by visiting the school. At the school, we showed the girls pictures of our school-aged daughters and urged them to study hard because they were the future of Afghanistan. Later, women of their mothers' generation specifically thanked us for our presence because they had been a part of a women's education organization whose members were slowly being killed off as the Taliban found them out. They explained that this had stopped since we came. Now the Taliban were on the run, and the women's organization was free again to promote women's issues and send girls back to school.

People have questioned whether it is worth American taxpayer dollars or American soldiers' lives for the United States to be in Afghanistan. They ask why we should bother protecting Afghans, such as these girls, if they are doomed as soon as we leave and the Taliban come back. People will understandably have different value judgments here. But whatever one might think about these issues, there is no denying the fact that for at least one bright shining moment these girls were safer and given more freedom, not because of pacifist protesters waving banners at a rally, or even because Mennonite-provided conflict-resolu-

Photograph by Eric A. Eliason

tion training helped these girls and the Taliban resolve their differences. They were freer and safer because men and women with guns were in their valley ready to kill, if need be, anyone who threatened them.

Our thinking on war could be considerably clarified if we had different words for different kinds of conflicts. If war is defined as a situation where one people attacks another out of vengeance, to gain territory, enslave, rape, pillage, or purposely target civilians, then what moral person could possibly be for it? But if war is when a compassionate people fight to protect the innocent, remove a warmongering tyranny, stop genocide, allow people to form their own government and control their own resources, while risking their own lives to minimize civilian casualties, who could possibly be against it? Even though both scenarios involve similar tools and similar bloodshed, one is as different from the other as life-saving surgery is from sadistic torture. War is a term that has a semantic domain, and it has been stretched too far. This comes from world history, where the first kind of war has been the only kind most have ever known. Only in recent years, and primarily under the leadership of the United States and its allies, has the second type of

Photograph courtesy of David Butow

"war" been waged. It obscures more than it clarifies to call the two endeavors by the same word, but we are limited by the language we have.

Finally, let me re-emphasize what I said at the beginning: some of the aims being pursued today by violence might better be pursued by other means, even in wartime. The Filipino general I met and his Mennonite-trained officers are an example of this. In my Afghan deployment I spent almost every day making friends, helping resolve disputes, and helping rebuild damage that was mostly incurred before Americans got there. American soldiers are likely to spend more time doing real peacemaking, in places where it really matters, than most stateside pacifists could ever dream of. Nevertheless, while nonviolent strategies may be underutilized, there are still many contexts where violence is the moral response.

15

"Renounce War and Proclaim Peace": Personal Reflections on Mormon Attempts at Peacemaking

Gordon Conrad Thomasson

Forty years ago, on Friday, March 16, 1971, Hugh Nibley published his "Renounce War" letter in BYU's *Daily Universe*.[1] That letter quoted from and commented on Doctrine and Covenants 98:16–17, and generated many responses at the time, the most noteworthy of which was what appeared to be an enraged if unenlightened, "Who is Hugh Nibley and what does he know about the scriptures anyway?"

Word of Nibley's letter reached me at the University of California, Santa Barbara, where I was pursuing a master's degree. The news was more than fortuitous, as I was then preparing camera-ready copy for what became *War, Conscription, Conscience and Mormonism* (hereafter WCCM), and with Nibley's permission I included the text of his letter in that volume.[2] During 1966–1968, when I attended Brigham Young University, open opposition to either war in general or Vietnam in par-

---

1. *Daily Universe*, March 26, 1971. See also Hugh Nibley, *Approaching Zion*, vol. 9 of THE COLLECTED WORKS OF HUGH NIBLEY, ed. Don E. Norton (Salt Lake City: Deseret Book, 1989), 267–69. This essay celebrates Nibley (M/SGT, 101st Airborne, Europe) and notes that before World War II he taught at Claremont (where this essay was originally presented) with Dr. Edgar J. Goodspeed. I dedicate it as well to the memory of the late Sister Alyssa Petersen (Private, 311th Military Intelligence Unit, 101st Airborne, Iraq) and her very suspicious death, recalling the words of Nibley's close friend, the intelligence officer Lucien Goldschmidt, to the effect that Nibley found some things U.S. Army intelligence agents were asked to do to be "distasteful." See Boyd Jay Peterson's chapter on Nibley in this volume.

2. Gordon C. Thomasson, ed., *War, Conscription, Conscience & Mormonism* (Santa Barbara, Calif.: Mormon Heritage, 1971), 24–25.

ticular was not without its social costs, as it was in the nation generally. There were economic and even physical risks in 1971 when WCCM was published.[3] A former bishop who previously had imposed considerably upon my friendship told me, quite stiffly, "Of course my company [a national corporation with a household name] would never hire you, nor would I." This sort of comment was not too unusual. During those "war" years, if you were open in your antiwar beliefs then you found out rather quickly who your friends were.[4]

The first printing of WCCM was quickly exhausted—it was always sold at cost—and a reprinting was scheduled at its original publisher, a collective appropriately known as Peace Press, in West Los Angeles. On the night before my book returned to the press, that building was firebombed. All of WCCM's metal printing plates were spread out on the work desk and were destroyed along with the press's equipment and others' work. As a result, since I still had the original 116 numbered pages of camera-ready copy on hand, I added a few more sheets and published the 1972 revised second printing. It was reproduced by a pioneering off-campus copy shop at the University of California Santa Barbara—a roughly 8x12 foot plywood shack known as "Kinko's"—which lacked facilities to collate or bind the book. Consequently, a large number of my friends in the University of California Los Angeles student ward joined me after church one Sunday for a "Shaker Dance"—all of us repeatedly circling around a group of banquet tables to collate the book's pages. I then built a jig and, using a heavy staple gun, handbound and taped each copy.[5]

---

3. I do not use the terms "economic and physical risks" lightly. The gas tank on my brother's car was sugared when I was distributing copies of WCCM across the American Southwest, requiring an engine overhaul in Reno, Nevada. On another occasion all of the fuel injector lines on my locked car were punctured so that they sprayed onto the engine exhaust manifolds and could catch fire. Breaking in to sabotage that car would have required either a master key or considerable lock-picking expertise.

4. It is noteworthy that, apart from Nibley and a precious few others, quite a few people thought I would (and a few thought that I should) be excommunicated for publishing WCCM. The more distant the individual from the gospel and/or church activity, the more sure they were I would be harshly disciplined in a church court, but I never was. Generally speaking, the more "active" or "orthodox" the individuals were who knew me, the less they feared for me.

5. This soon will be reproduced at www.MormonHeritage.org. Since 1967 I occasionally have used "Mormon Heritage" as a non-commercial paper format

By the time I moved to Cornell in the fall of 1973 to pursue my doctorate, demand for WCCM had diminished, and after 1975, with the end of the draft, interest tapered to almost zero. But the best part of that publishing effort was when people contacted me, even years later, explaining that the book had helped them to stay in the Church, or had won understanding for them from family, friends, or local leaders.

A Reading of "Renounce War"

While being a passenger in two severe and normally fatal auto accidents in 1967 and 1968 left me technically classified 4F (physically exempt or ineligible for the draft), the years following 1968 were when my views on war and pacifism really took root and grew. These views were bolstered by a serious study of Doctrine and Covenants 98, from which Hugh Nibley quoted so effectively in his 1971 letter. I begin with the first published version of the revelation in 1835, when it was then numbered section 85. Here follows the relevant text of section 85/98, as set off in a complete numbered paragraph by the publication committee (made up of the "presiding elders" of the Church: Joseph Smith, Oliver Cowdery, Sidney Rigdon, and Frederick G. Williams). The 1981 (current) text is also presented in a parallel column for comparison and contrast.

Covenants and Commandments of the Doctrine and Covenants [1835]	*Doctrine and Covenants [1981]*
3 And I give unto you a commandment, that ye shall forsake all evil and cleave unto all good, that ye shall live by every word which proceedeth forth out of the mouth of God: for he will give unto the faithful, line upon line; precept upon precept: and I will try you, and prove you herewith: and whoso lay-	11 And I give unto you a commandment, that ye shall forsake all evil and cleave unto all good, that ye shall live by every word which proceedeth forth out of the mouth of God. 12 For he will give unto the faithful line upon line, precept upon precept; and I will try you and prove you herewith.

---

for mini-publishing and more formal publishing. To that I am adding www. NewRoseAndCrown.org, named after my ancestor George Thomasson's seventeenth century London stationer's establishment, from which he personally, and as a member of London's Common Council, published and opposed the excesses of both Charles I, Cromwell, and their militaries.

eth down his life in my cause, for my name's sake, shall find it again, even life eternal: therefore be not afraid of your enemies, for I have decreed in my heart, saith the Lord, that I will prove you in all things, whether you will abide in my covenant, even unto death, that you may be found worthy: for if ye will not abide in my covenant, ye are not worthy of me: therefore renounce war and proclaim peace, and seek diligently to turn the hearts of their children to their fathers, and the hearts of the fathers to the children. And again the hearts of the Jews unto the prophets; and the prophets unto the Jews lest I come and smite the whole earth with a curse, and all flesh be consumed before me. Let not your hearts be troubled, for in my Father's house are many mansions, and I have prepared a place for you, and where my Father and I am, there ye shall be also.

13 And whoso layeth down his life in my cause, for my name's sake, shall find it again, even life eternal.
14 Therefore, be not afraid of your enemies, for I have decreed in my heart, saith the Lord, that I will prove you in all things, whether you will abide in my covenant, even unto death, that you may be found worthy.
15 For if ye will not abide in my covenant ye are not worthy of me.
16 Therefore, renounce war and proclaim peace, and seek diligently to turn the hearts of the children to their fathers, and the hearts of the fathers to the children;
17 And again, the hearts of the Jews unto the prophets, and the prophets unto the Jews; lest I come and smite the whole earth with a curse, and all flesh be consumed before me.
18 Let not your hearts be troubled; for in my Father's house are many mansions, and I have prepared a place for you; and where my Father and I am, there ye shall be also.

Of the 1835 publication committee, Oliver Cowdery and Frederick G. Williams had more formal training and better command and understanding of the written English language than many members of the Church in their day, let alone today. Those brethren understood what a paragraph was and should be, and that is reflected in their parsing and punctuation of the original (pre-1835) manuscripts of the revelations.[6]

---

6. Robert J. Woodford, "The Historical Development of the Doctrine and Covenants" (PhD diss., Brigham Young University, 1974), 3:126. The textual sources also are found in Robin Scott Jensen, Robert J. Woodford, and Steven C. Harper, eds., *Manuscript Revelation Books*, facsimile edition, first volume of the Revelations and Translations series of The Joseph Smith Papers, eds. Dean C.

Moreover, the Prophet Joseph Smith was there to guide and correct them regarding content. Consequently, the rationale, integrity and intent of the original section 85, paragraph 3, unquestionably contrasts clearly in style, format, and content with the paragraphs that precede and follow it. In original paragraph 2 (today's verses 4–10), the subject is a discussion of constitutional and unconstitutional laws and a specified necessity of obeying *only* the former ("that law which *is* constitutional," emphasis added)—not a trivial question and assertion of right in an age which would see, among other things, both individuals and local and state governments refusing to honor warrants for runaway slaves.[7] The

---

Jessee, Ronald K. Esplin, and Richard Lyman Bushman (Salt Lake City: Church Historian's Press, 2009), 546–55. Woodford, in his dissertation, was unaware of a manuscript recorded by John Whitmer prior to Frederick G. Williams' copy in the Kirtland Revelation Book, and the copies of today's sections 97, 94, and 98 that were included in a letter written to Missouri and dated the same day. This first known text is in the *Manuscript Revelation Books*, pages 322–31. Their copying reflects substantial care and accuracy.

7. Compare Doctrine & Covenants 101:76–80. Before the Missouri persecutions and conflicts, the Church was still almost entirely a "northeastern" institution, and most members were still culturally "Yankee" and typically anti-slavery. Both slavery and persecution of the Church were frequent concerns in the revelations: see Doctrine & Covenants 38:29 and 45:63–67 (1831), both of which anticipate 87:1–8 (1832). Note that section 87 and revelations preceding it were never seen as an embarrassment nor taken as "failed" prophecies; section 87 was faithfully reproduced in the first edition of the Pearl of Great Price (1857). See also sections 101:10–11 (1833), 130:12–13 (1843), 136:34–36 (1847).

Consider also D&C 134:8 (1835), and its predictable, though to outsiders seemingly radical (in an anti-slavery context), "all men should step forward and use their ability in bringing offenders against *good* laws to punishment" (emphasis added). The Nauvoo Charter, in this regard, simply provided for Latter-day Saints the same rights to oppose extradition that were being exercised by anti-slavery communities against slave-state extradition throughout the north—recall that Missouri was a slave state. On LDS anti-slavery and other related issues see my following entries in the *Oxford Encyclopedia of the Modern World* (Oxford University Press, 2008): "American Civil Religion," 1:112–14, "American Colonization Society," 1:122–23, "Mormonism," 5:277, and "Religion and Politics," 6:352–59; and in the *Encyclopedia of Antislavery and Abolition*, eds. Peter Hinks and John McKivigan (Westport, Conn.: Greenwood, 2007): "Church of Jesus Christ of Latter-day Saints & Antislavery," 1:158–60, "Jubilee," 2:389–90, "League of Nations Covenant, Articles 22 & 23," 2:421–23, and "Moses," 2:482–83; in the *Encyclopedia of American Studies*, eds. George T. Kurian, Miles Orvell, Johnnella E. Butler, and Jay Melching (New York: Grolier, 2001): "Civil Religion," 1:342–44,

original paragraph 4 (today's verses 19–22) just as clearly deals with events in Kirtland. Thus paragraph 3 was conceptually intended to, and in fact does, stand starkly alone.

A more complete reading of the text of "renounce war," then, involves at least every line of the full 1835 paragraph 3—not just the modern verses 16 and 17; and its interpretation is even less ambiguous than editorial space allowed for Nibley's brief but powerful commentary. The stage is set in verses 11–15 of section 98, which emphasize the strength of the commandment explicitly given in today's verse 16; and it is elaborated upon in the verses that follow, which specify the covenant to which we (the Church) are bound (i.e., to "renounce war and proclaim peace") and which, if we do not abide, leaves us "not worthy of Him."

Moreover, the grammatically unambiguous mandatory nature of "renounce war and proclaim peace" is directly followed in that same paragraph by another equally stringent and unqualified parallel commandment that today no one questions: to "seek diligently to turn the hearts of their children to their fathers and the hearts of the fathers to the children. And again the hearts of the Jews unto the prophets; and the prophets unto the Jews." We can't ignore these latter imperatives or rationalize them away any more than we can ignore the command to renounce war and proclaim peace. The grammar of these commandments reflects directly parallel constructions. "Turn the hearts" and "renounce war" are given identical spiritual and structural weight. There are no qualifiers to relieve us of our sacred responsibilities.

The revelation follows with a scenario that was technological nonsense in an age prior to the creation of modern weapons of mass destruction. In 1835 section 85, paragraph 3, we are commanded to renounce, "lest I come and smite the whole earth with a curse." This is contextually similar if not absolutely identical to the biblical cursing to total destruction (cf. 1 Sam. 15:3, 21), which contrasts with many limp modern readings of Malachi 4:4. The result of not obeying the com-

---

"Draft," 2:49–52, and "Mormonism," 3:138–42. See also "Anti-Mormonism," in *Encyclopedia of the United States in the Nineteenth Century*, ed. Paul Finkelman (New York, Charles Scribner's Sons, 2001), 1:99–100 and "Latter-day Saints, The Church of Jesus Christ of," in *Macmillan Encyclopedia of World Slavery*, ed. Paul Finkelman and Joseph C. Miller (New York: Macmillan Reference, Simon & Schuster, 1998), 2:474–76.

mandments in this revelation and the nature of the curse is very clear: that "all flesh be consumed before me."[8]

If there is any doubt about the word "renounce" in Joseph Smith's English, consider the definitions from Noah Webster's first 1828 edition of *An American Dictionary of the English Language.*[9] There is no ambiguity in any of these entries during the language of Joseph Smith's time.

1. To disown; to disclaim; to reject; as a title or claim; to refuse to own or acknowledge as belonging to; as, to renounce a title to land or a claim to reward; to renounce all pretensions to applause.
2. To deny; to cast off; to reject; to disclaim; as an obligation or duty; as, to renounce allegiance.
3. To cast off or reject, as a connection or possession; to forsake; as, to renounce the world and all its cares.

We have renounced the hidden things of dishonesty (see 2 Cor. 4).

Context

Virtually no one disagrees that we should read things "in context." But which of many, even infinite, relevant contexts should most concern us? To begin, I will no more than briefly allude to and reject one assumed but problematic "historical" context for this revelation—the expulsion of the Saints from Jackson County—since there is hard evidence and effective certainty that section 98 was received before news of events in Missouri could have reached the brethren in Ohio by human means and precipitated this revelation. Whitmer and Williams' earliest manuscript texts of the revelation are dated August 6, 1833.[10] The revelation was then copied into a letter along with what became modern sections 97 and 94, and sent on the same day to Independence (Zion). In accord with the dating, there is absolutely *nothing* in the let-

---

8. Compare "lest the whole earth be smitten with a curse and utterly wasted at his coming" (D&C 138:48, "utterly wasted" as in futile, having served no purpose or "laid waste" as in totally destroyed). In English, Malachi 4:5–6 can be compared to our other standard works: Matthew 10:21–22, Luke 1:17, 3 Nephi 25:5–6, Doctrine & Covenants 2:3 (1823), 110:13–15 (1836), 138:47–48 (1918), Joseph Smith—History 1:36–39 (1823).

9. Noah Webster, *An American Dictionary of the English Language* (New York: S. Converse, 1828).

10. Woodford, "Historical Development," 1261.

ter that suggests any conscious awareness of recent events in Missouri. The Lord was aware of the Saints' expulsion, but humans by human means simply could not have known that in Kirtland. Moreover, and quite contrary to unfounded and imagined claims that these revelations followed news of the expulsion, directions are calmly given for further construction to be undertaken in Zion.[11]

Large scale organized violence that might be characterized as "war" against the Saints began in Jackson County in late July 1833. What was then "modern" transportation infrastructure (whether canal boat, some imagined equivalent of the pony express, railroad, or telegraphy) simply did not exist for regular rapid communication between Jackson County and Kirtland in 1833. Kirtland is mentioned in the revelation, but as historian and archivist David Whittaker noted to me, the word "Zion" is conspicuously absent in the text of section 98.[12] As always, historical context is totally dependent upon chronology. Therefore, events in Missouri can be nothing but an independent prophetic witness of the truth of and need for section 98.

But there are other contexts: following the destruction of the Saints' press in Missouri and all but six copies of the Book of Commandments, there was still an increasing demand among the expanding membership of the Church for access to the revelations. While today's section 98 was effectively contemporary with, though not humanly connected to the expulsion events in Missouri, it preceded publication (such as it was) of the Book of Commandments. By the time of Zion's Camp, manuscript copies (of this and other revelations) would have been in the hands of many. As study and understanding of the commandment to "renounce war" grew, it took on monumental and even eternal significance for that generation of Saints. So another context needed for understanding section 98 would be the events leading to creation of the Doctrine and Covenants.

Let us turn to the context of the text itself. How do we read today's verses 16 and 17 (to follow Nibley) in context, let alone the entirety of section 98? Most readers today have never had the opportunity to read the original paragraphing, punctuation, and other sentence divisions as the revelations were first published, nor have they had the opportunity to consider their editors' intentions (in 1835, remember, the editors

---

11. Ibid., 1226.
12. Personal e-mail communication.

were the First Presidency of the Church). Few readers today know that the textual context of verses ("Therefore, renounce war and proclaim peace" v. 16) has changed. In the publication of the 1981 editions of the Book of Mormon, Doctrine and Covenants, and Pearl of Great Price, in order to save space and minimize price, the main points of those books' editorial histories were omitted, namely the original 1833 publication of the revelations in Zion as the *Book of Commandments for the Government of the Church of Christ*, and the enlarged 1835 compilation issued in Kirtland as *Doctrine and Covenants of the Church of Jesus Christ of Latter-day Saints*. Along with adding subsequent revelations prior to the current (1981) edition, other changes include Orson Pratt's division of the text into chapters and verses in 1876, the addition of footnotes in 1879, the reformatting of text into double-column pages, new chapter headings, chronological data, revised footnotes, and an index in 1921. Only by looking at and studying successive editions side-by-side do the weight of these changes and how we consequently read and comprehend these scriptural texts become obvious.

Such reflections on a complex editorial history—not on the scriptures as such, but on their editorial modifications for the assistance of modern readers—are neither neutral nor insignificant when it comes to reading or interpreting these scriptural texts in historical and other modern contexts. Also involved, is the analysis of typographic, grammatical, and punctuation changes to context and setting and insertions of chapter headnotes and other materials interrupting the flow of texts.[13]

---

13. As one example, in my studies of Israelite ritual and calendrical references in the Book of Mormon, I have found numerous cases where the concerns of modern book history matter. For example, the last verse of today's Alma 44 tells us that the eighteenth year of the judges has ended, and the first two verses of chapter 45 describe just what one should find during the Ten Days of Awe, from Rosh Hashanah to Yom Kippur at the new year, which explicitly mark the transition to the "nineteenth year of the reign of the judges." Modern typography and commentary produces an image of a radical stoppage in the flow of the narrative, and yet, when we look at the rituals of antiquity nothing is more logical than to move continuously from the end of one year into another, transitioning precisely through the new year's rituals. Contrast the text itself from the 1830 edition of the Book of Mormon with what you see in recent editions, where you must ignore the modern verse numbers and non-scriptural reader-helps to get the same effect.

Attempts at Peacemaking

In addition to better understanding the divine injunction to "renounce war and proclaim peace," here follow a number of examples of what can be pursued in individual studies, teaching, and research on latter-day peacemaking and pacifism. These include:

- Joseph Smith's employing Zion's Camp as a process of peace education and defusing pro-war sentiments.
- President Brigham Young prophetically blessing the troops of the Mormon Battalion that they would not have to fight or kill enemy troops while they made the longest U.S. infantry march, invasion, and occupation of (Mexican) territories in nineteenth-century U.S. history.
- Apostle Brigham Young Jr. opposing his younger half-brother and nephew (both West Point graduates) and their support of the Spanish-American War.
- The proliferation of Latter-day Saint peace poetry beginning in 1898.
- The change of J. Reuben Clark's attitudes from the time of his World War I military service to his State Department years (especially in his "Clark Memorandum," which opposed U.S. bullying of Latin America, Teddy Roosevelt-style).[14] Subsequently, through his years in the First Presidency, the values he consciously had shared with his ancestors' acknowledged biblical-pacifist Quaker and Dunkard heritage becomes obvious. Those values, combined with his understanding of the gospel, led to his opposing our tying the U.S. to interwar British militarism, and to supporting individual Latter-day Saint conscientious objectors. See especially his essay "Let Us Have Peace,"[15] and the incredibly prophetic 1945–46 letter from the First Presidency opposing peacetime military conscription, where Clark's voice is clearly visible. Much of the latter prophetic document, which reads like a history of the only then-approaching Korean War and Cold War years and their long-term social and political consequences, in future centuries well might be claimed by anti-Mormons to have been written after-the-fact. It is that accurate![16]

---

14. For a much needed non-LDS perspective on J. Reuben Clark, see William Franklin Sands with Joseph M. Lalley, *Our Jungle Diplomacy* (Chapel Hill: University of North Carolina, 1944), 114–15, 170–71.

15. In J. Reuben Clark, *Fast by Our Constitution* (Salt Lake City: Deseret Book, 1962, reprint 1978), 58–83.

16. "Letter of the First Presidency Concerning Military Training," *Improvement Era*, February 1946, 76–77. See also Frank W. Fox, *J. Reuben Clark: The Public Years*

- Latter-day Saint conscientious objectors to war, to war crimes, and to conscription during World War II.
- The role of former (pre-World War II) LDS missionaries to Germany in building toward a post-war peace, under the direction of Elder (and Marine Lieutenant) Dale Clark at SHAEF in London and on the continent.
- Latter-day Saints Helmut Hübener, Karl Heinz Schnibbe, and Rudi Wobbe, and their non-violent opposition to Nazism, anti-Semitism in the Church, and the German role in World War II. Despite all that has been written here, many questions remain.
- Topics only briefly treated in *War, Conscription, Conscience & Mormonism*, in *BYU Studies*, and in *Dialogue: A Journal of Mormon Thought*, among other publications, during and after the Vietnam War, and later discussions of the Iraq and Afghan invasions and wars.
- Eugene England and his work in "Food for Poland" and the consequent opening of LDS missionary work in Poland, as well as his other writings and anti-war efforts.
- The First Presidency's opposition to the basing of the MX Missile.
- Opposition to nuclear testing in the West, and the writings of Emma Lou Thayne, Robert A. Rees, and others in recent decades up to the present.
- The supposed but highly improbable "suicide" of former LDS missionary sister and U.S. Army linguist, Private Alyssa Petersen, within a day of her first refusing to participate in Abu Ghraib-style torture of Iraqi prisoners, and the obvious risk of her probable legal testimony exposing other soldiers, intelligence agents, and "private contractors" to prosecution for war crimes.[17]
- The large number of in-country American troop "suicides" occurring during and after previous conflicts also needs to be studied and compared to combat deaths in Iraq and Afghanistan, as well as

---

(Salt Lake City and Provo, Utah: Deseret Book & BYU Press, 1980); D. Michael Quinn, *J. Reuben Clark: The Church Years* (Provo, Utah: BYU Press, 1983), and the much expanded version of this book published by Signature Books (2002). Especially startling is Clark's opposition to America's use and first use of nuclear weapons in wartime (Quinn, 212–13). See also Quinn's chapter in this volume.

17. This is an especially painful topic for me, as my good friend and former student, the journalist Frank Teruggi, and his colleague Charles Horman were murdered in 1973 by the Chilean military after gathering evidence of U.S. military involvement in the coup that brought the dictator Pinochet to power (treated "artistically" in the Hollywood movie "Missing").

the high incidence of PTSD and other syndromes among veterans, including Latter-day Saints. The effect of in-country suicides on then M/Sgt Hugh W. Nibley might also be considered here.[18]

Toward a Momentary Conclusion

My family and friends have borne a small portion of the costs of war: besides my cousin Gordon O. Thomasson, killed on Morotai Island in 1944, relatives, close friends, and colleagues have been killed in Mexico (1968), Chile (1973), the Sudan (after 1985), and Liberia (after 1990), or have become alienated from the Church. I personally have spent our last four-plus decades of almost continuous wartime history trying to understand the principles of peace and follow my own pacifist commitments (a difficult task in this adrenalin and violence-charged world). Those commitments have motivated my service in Africa and elsewhere, working in healthcare, education and development in the tropics, with refugees from the Liberian uncivil war (twice as president of the international Liberian Studies Association), the extended conflicts in the Sudan, and opposing wars in Southeast Asia, the Mideast and elsewhere, as well as speaking out and writing.[19]

I recently saw an article fatuously claiming that the people of Ammon in the Book of Mormon were not pacifists. I would submit that the argument that the people of Ammon were not pacifists is only true if you change generally understood definitions beyond any common meaning or recognition. Any attempt to call the people of Ammon anything other than pacifist is an exercise in creating a meaningless distinction without a difference.

Absent accurate peace education, Mormons could face potential future tragedies: a repeat, for example, of America's land-grabbing Sac and Fox Indian War of 1832. Some years back my wife and I visited the first-built Euro-American concrete building in the Americas, lo-

---

18. Boyd K. Petersen, *Hugh Nibley: A Consecrated Life* (Salt Lake City: Greg Kofford Books, 2002), 209–10; Hugh Nibley and Alex Nibley, *Sergeant Nibley, Ph.D.* (Salt Lake City: Shadow Mountain, 2006), 209, 211. See also Peterson's chapter on Nibley in this volume.

19. See especially Gordon C. Thomasson, "Mormon Ethics and Peace," in *The Oxford International Encyclopedia of Peace* (New York: Oxford University Press, 2010), 3:56–62.

cated in southern Wisconsin. Behind that building I was surprised to find a separate monument recalling U.S. troops' presence there during that genocidal 1832 war. It listed the names of "white" participants, including Abraham Lincoln, Albert Sydney Johnston—the commanding general in the "Utah War" of 1857—and another soldier in his unit whose name was John D. Lee. Do their wartime experiences help to explain the later actions of these three men?

Following Brigham Young's command to "Take No Life!" the Utah War ended far better than it might have, and certainly better than our LDS spies traveling in the camp of Johnston's Army reported that Johnston and his troops hoped it would.[20] But in 1857 a prophet of God led all the Saints who would follow to avoid the behaviors that their own roots in American culture almost certainly would have dictated. Are we in danger of reversing that dynamic, of following our national culture at the expense of not heeding the prophets and revelations of the gospel?

The letter sent from Kirtland to Missouri on August 6, 1833, containing the revelations in sections 94, 97, and 98, is conclusive as far as its content goes: Doctrine and Covenants 98:11–18 and the command to renounce war and proclaim peace was received by the Saints in Ohio in absolute ignorance of events in Missouri. It was taken for granted by the membership in Ohio, for example, operating in ignorance of events in Missouri, that printing and building could proceed in Zion as it had been. So again, the commandment to "renounce war and proclaim peace" was not an after-the-fact human reaction to the disaster in Independence. Instead the Lord was preparing the Saints in Kirtland then, and, I pray, we and others in the future, as to how they and we should respond as a Church to persecution, aggression, and violence. The Lord will not permit his Church to wage a "holy" war or a crusade in his name, whether against Missourians or anyone else. If such a defense is ever needed, he will provide it. Instead, the Saints have, with section 98, been commanded to begin what will prove to be a long

---

20. Brigham Young's orders were documented based on those issued by the Mormon Commander Daniel H. Wells, dated October 4, 1857. They were found with the capture of the Mormon Major Joseph Taylor, and published in the East. See Leonard J. Arrington, *Great Basin Kingdom: Economic History of the Latter-day Saints, 1830–1900* (Lincoln: University of Nebraska, 1958), 465 note 64.

and ongoing struggle to overcome the human culture of violence and instead renounce war and proclaim and live peace in his name.

APPENDIX

An Introductory Stylistic Analysis of
Doctrine and Covenants 98:11–18:
Renounce War and Proclaim Peace

Today's Doctrine and Covenants 98:11–18 here is shown in part as it was first published and punctuated, as a single coherent paragraph, in "Covenants and Commandments, Part Second" of the 1835 first edition of the Doctrine and Covenants. In the 1835 edition, today's section 98 was numbered section 85, and today's verses 11–18 were only unnumbered potential divisions of that section's actual numbered paragraph 3, on page 217. In 1835, all the revelations had numbered paragraphs and no verse divisions. Original punctuation here is boldfaced and set off by a space being inserted before and after. Other changes are my own: all text in sanserif; division into scansions and line indenting for emphasis of structure or content; text underlining; line numbering and letters outside the left and right margins for easy reference. Comments, etc., in [square brackets] and {braces} are my own. The content of paragraph 3 is clearly distinct from paragraph 2 (today's verses 4–10, on constitutional law), and paragraph 4 (19–22, on issues in Kirtland). On the title page of the 1835, we are told the revelations were selected and compiled for publication by Joseph Smith, Oliver Cowdery, Sidney Rigdon, and Frederick G. Williams, listed as the Church's "Presiding Elders." I am heavily indebted to Brant A. Gardner and Robert F. Smith for their suggestions and critiques.

Line Number

1	And I <u>give</u> unto <u>you</u> a commandment ,		A
		[preamble to covenant, purpose of paragraph]	
2	that <u>ye</u> shall forsake		B
3	all evil		C
4	and cleave	[antithetical parallel of B]	B'
5	unto all good ,	[ant. para. of C]	C'
6	that <u>ye</u> shall live by every <u>word</u>		A'
7	which proceedeth forth out of the <u>mouth of God</u> :		A

```
8   for he will give unto the faithful ,                                    A
9       line upon line ;                                                     D
10      precept upon precept :           [synonymous internal parallels]  D
11          and I will try you ,                                            E
12          and prove you herewith :              [syn. para.]             E
13              and whoso layeth down his life                             F
14                  in my cause ,                                          G
15                  for my name's sake ,          [syn. para.]            G
16              shall find it again ; even life eternal :  [ant. para.]   F'
17          therefore be not afraid of your enemies ,                     F"
                        [conclusion-comfort, ant. para.]
18  for I have decreed in my heart , saith the Lord ,                     A
19      that I will prove you in all things ,                             E
20          whether you will abide in my covenant , even unto death ,  H
21              that you may be found worthy :                           I
22          for if ye will not abide in my covenant ,  [ant. para.]     H'
23              ye are not worthy of me :          [ant. para.]          I'
24  therefore                              [covenant requirements]  J
25  [ I ]      renounce                                                   K
26                  war                                                   L
27          and proclaim                          [syn. para.]           K'
28                  peace ,                        [ant. para.]           L'
29  [ II ]          and seek diligently to turn the hearts               M
30                  of their { 21 } children to their fathers ,          N
31              and the hearts                                           M'
32                  of the fathers to the children .   [reversal]        N'
33  [ III ]         And again the hearts                                 M
34                  of the Jews unto the prophets ;                      O
35                  And the {"hearts of the" implicit here}  [syn. para.]  {M}
36                  prophets unto the Jews , { 22 }       [reversal]     O'
37  lest                                      [disobedience curse]  P
38      I come and smite the whole earth with a curse ,                  Q
39      and all flesh be consumed before me . { 23 }   [syn. para.]      Q'
```

---

21. This first "their" changed to "the" in later editions.

22. The parallels in lines N and O provide emphasis. O is a more specific instance of N.

23. The word "curse" here, followed by "all flesh be consumed before me" appears directly comparable to *herem*, the biblical cursing to total destruction, as in 1 Sam. 15:21, which is unlike modern readings of Malachi 4:4, unless "smite" is read as a death-blow. See note 8 in this essay. Also especially note in D&C 128:17–18 (1842) the words "I might have rendered a plainer translation to this, but it is sufficiently plain to suit my purpose as it stands. It is sufficient to know, in this case, that the earth will be smitten with a curse unless there is a welding-link of

40	Let not your hearts be troubled ,	[obedience blessing]	R
41	for in my Father's <u>house</u> are many <u>mansions</u> , { 24 }		S
42	and I have prepared a <u>place</u> for you ,		T
43	and <u>where</u> my Father and I am ,	[syn. para.]	S
44	<u>there</u> ye shall be also . { 25 }	[syn. para.]	T

---

some kind or other between the fathers and the children."

24. Today's section 76 already was to some degree in circulation at this time.

25. The movement from S to T is specifically from the Father to his children.

16

Doctrine & Covenants 98: The "Immutable" Rejected Covenant of Peace

Ron Madson

"May God give us that ear. May he give us a disposition to read what he has told us. . . . May he give us the will and power to live them, having taken them into our souls."

—J. Reuben Clark[1]

My father served in Patton's infantry in the European theater during the Second World War. It wasn't until the summer of 2002 that he, at the age of 88, told me his war experiences. That evening we sat on the couch listening to the nightly war rhetoric justifying our invasion into Afghanistan and our next target—Iraq. With emotion he told me that, in his opinion, there was no doctrinal, scriptural, or gospel principle that would justify our invasion of these countries. He was certain our faith community would renounce what he considered wars of aggression.

During the past several years, I have had innumerable discussions with other Latter-day Saints regarding "war and peace." My approach has been to invite them to define which doctrines and beliefs govern whether a person is justified, if ever, in supporting a particular war. Those who support our nation's invasion of Iraq and Afghanistan often cite the words of Captain Moroni; or declare our need to "fight for freedom"; or make a cost/benefit analysis; or state our duty to be loyal citizens as required by the Twelfth Article of Faith. And, to reinforce

---

1. J. Reuben Clark Jr., *Report of the Semi-Annual Conference of the Church of Jesus Christ of Latter-day Saints*, October 1948, 82 (hereafter cited as *Conference Report*).

their positions, they often refer to their belief that our Church leaders support all of our nation's wars.

Why do we have such divergent points of view as to what constitutes our "war/peace" doctrine? What shaped my father's theological framework? And how could others with similar experiences, reading the same scriptures, reach entirely different views as to the justness of current conflicts? What doctrines, if any, define when, if ever, we are justified in supporting, let alone participating in, a particular war? And how do we know which sacred texts and examples to draw upon, especially when one can find scriptural "justification" for almost any form of violence?

A Restoration

The Old Testament invokes God's name in sanctioning all manner of violence. One can find therein the necessary vocabulary to support wars of aggression, genocide, and even terrorism. However, Jesus came declaring "it has been said of old" and "it has been written of old," but said that he was here to tell us what God is really like. The words and example of Christ left such an indelible imprint that for three centuries the early Christians denounced all forms of militarism and refused conscription until the Constantinian shift, when within a few decades every soldier in the Roman Empire was required to be Christian. Through the centuries that followed different strains of beliefs in regard to war and peace emerged. Some theologians articulated various "just war" doctrines, and some popes issued war indulgences to help justify the Crusades.[2] Others,

---

2. Pope John VIII declared: "Those who have recently died in war fighting in the defense of the church of God and for the preservation of the Christian religion and of the state, or those who may in the future fall in the same cause, may obtain indulgence of their sins. We confidently reply that those who out of love of the Christian religion, shall die in battle fighting bravely against pagans or unbelievers, shall receive eternal life." (Migne, *Patrologia Latina* 126:816, in Oliver J. Thatcher and Edgar Holmes McNeal, trans. and eds., *A Source Book for Medieval History* [New York: Scribners, 1905], 512). The Christian soldier was thus not only forgiven his sins, but promised paradise for his state service in slaying unbelievers. Pope Urban II likewise helped inspire the first Crusade when he declared: "All who die in battle against the pagan, shall have immediate remission of sins. This I grant through the power of God with which I am invested." Fulcher of Chartes Account of Urban's Speech, Urban II: Speech at Council of Claremont, 1095, from Bongars, Gesta Dei per Francos, 1:382, in Thatcher and McNeal, *A Source Book for Medieval History* , 513–17.

such as the Anabaptists, continued to renounce all forms of violence—despite the whole world being perpetually engaged in "just" wars.

The Restoration gathered many people eager to hear the direct voice of God again. One was Edward Partridge, the first bishop, of whom the Lord said, "his heart is pure before me" (D&C 41:11). His pureness of heart would be acutely tested in July 1833, when he was attacked by an angry and violent mob in Jackson County, Missouri. Bishop Partridge recounted how he and George Simpson were seized from their homes, taken to the public square, and tarred and feathered. Confronted with unprovoked hostility, Bishop Partridge responded with meekness and love:

> I told them that the Saints had suffered persecution in all ages of the world; that I had done nothing which ought to offend anyone; that if they abused me, they would abuse an innocent person; that I was willing to suffer for the sake of Christ ...
>
> Until I had spoken, I knew not what they intended to do with me, whether to kill me, or whip me, or what else I knew not. I bore my abuse with so much resignation and meekness, that it appeared to astound the multitude, who permitted me to retire in silence, many looking very solemn, their sympathies having been touched as I thought; and as for myself, I was so filled with the Spirit and love of God, that I had no hatred towards my persecutors or anyone else.[3]

Bishop Partridge, drawing upon his understanding of the gospel, chose to follow the example of Jesus. His meekness was so remarkable that it "astounded his persecutors." However, just three days after Bishop Partridge had turned away the persecutors, a second mob assembled, demanding the Saints leave Missouri. The persecutions continued as the Saints were driven from their homes. Remarkably, there was little resistance on the part of the Saints. As John Corrill later recalled, "up to this time the Mormons had not so much as lifted a finger, even in their own defence, so tenacious were they for the precepts of the gospel, —'turn the other cheek.'"[4]

---

3. Joseph Smith, et al., *History of the Church of Jesus Christ of Latter-day Saints,* ed. B. H. Roberts, 7 vols. (Salt Lake City: Deseret Book Company, 1976), 1:391.

4. John Corrill, *A Brief History of the Church of Jesus Christ of Latter-day Saints, (Commonly Called Mormons;) Including an Account of Their Doctrine and Discipline; with the Reasons of the Author for Leaving the Church* (St. Louis: By the author, 1839), 19.

Surely God would have instructions for his covenant people on how to deal with their first real encounter with enemies. Resorting to the scriptures could convey seemingly conflicting messages on how to respond to enemies. But the Church now had a prophet who had repeatedly pierced the veil and received direct messages as to what would be required of the saints. Thus, in the midst of these gross injustices, but before the full details were known to him, the Prophet Joseph Smith received two revelations, the first (now section 97 of the Doctrine and Covenants) on August 2, 1833, and the second (section 98) just four days later.

General Counsel Prior to Section 98

The revelations in August 1833 were not the first of relevance to the Saints' troubles. Seeing the calamities that would come upon all creation, when "peace shall be taken from the earth" and the "wicked shall slay the wicked," the Lord instructed his people to: "gather to Zion," "stand in holy places," "take the Holy Spirit to be their guide," "do not kill," do not "trust in the arm of the flesh," and "if your brethren desire to escape their enemies, let them repent of all their sins" (D&C 1:19, 34; 42:18–19; 45:57, 69; 54:3; 63:33; 87:80). In short, when the Saints encountered enemies they were to avoid conflict by gathering, repenting, seeking the spirit, refraining from killing others (no qualifications), remaining in Holy places, and having faith that God would fight their enemies.

Section 97 was received at a time when the Saints had entered into an agreement to withdraw from Jackson County. The Lord promised that Zion would escape the "vengeance" and "scourge" that will "vex all people" if "she observe to do all things whatsoever I have commanded her." The consequence of not observing what the Lord commands was made equally clear: "but if she observe not to do whatsoever I have commanded her, I will visit her according to all her works, with sore affliction, with pestilence, with plague, with sword, with vengeance, with devouring fire" (D&C 97:23, 25–26). Just four days after this admonition, the Lord gave his law governing conflict with both personal and national enemies.

The divine admonitions pertaining to conflict converge unambiguously in section 98. This crucial revelation was not a mere recommendation, but was given and recorded under a "seal and testament" as an "immutable covenant." The language is concise, almost statutory. Section 98 can be partitioned into five distinct parts. The first ten verses are an invitation to keep the law of God even while being subject to governments, which allegiance is conditioned upon one's government allowing the free exercise of faith in keeping the law of God.[5] The next five verses (11–15) lay out an invitation to live by the covenant of peace. The following seven verses (16–22) are promises or curses that are based on obedience or failure to heed these warnings. The next eleven verses (23–33) contain the law as to personal enemies encountered by individuals and families. Finally, the last fifteen verses (34–48) deal specifically with conflicts between nations. Only the last two sections (vv. 23–48) will be addressed here.

The Law as to Personal Enemies

The Lord first instructs us as to our duty in responding to enemies on a personal level. Here is His law: "if men will smite you, or your families, once, and ye bear it patiently and revile not against them, neither seek revenge, ye shall be rewarded" (D&C 98:23). The Mosaic law of vengeance required retribution, but the Lord is inviting us to live a higher law, and with obedience to that law comes a reward and blessings. But note that in the next verse He gives us an insight as to the fallen nature of the lesser law: "But if ye bear it not patiently, it shall be accounted unto you as being meted out as a just measure unto you" (v. 24).

In practical terms, this means if an enemy harms one of our own and then in our wrath, or even out of a sense of justice, we retaliate, the Lord looks upon the acts of both parties as being equally justly deserved—including those who did not give the first offense. By seeking revengeful justice, we in fact fulfill the Lord's words: "It is by the wicked that the wicked are punished," and "the wicked shall slay the wicked" (Morm. 4:5, D&C 63:33). This model does not fit Hollywood's version of the avenging hero who hunts down and destroys the "bad" guys, who get what they deserve in the end; but the Lord's ways are not our ways, neither are His thoughts our thoughts—they are higher. And we are invited to transcend the world and not engage in its cycles of vengeance.

We are then invited to "bear patiently" a second and even a third attack by our enemy, and then warn our enemy to come no more against

---

5. See also Doctrine & Covenants 134:2.

us, for which we will be blessed a "hundredfold." Then, if your enemy "smites" you a fourth time, and only then, if they have escaped the Lord's vengeance, the Lord will "deliver thine enemy into thine hands" (D&C 98:29). But, remarkably, now the Lord invites us to go beyond justification in defending ourselves by choosing to spare our enemy. And if we choose to live this highest law then our posterity will be blessed unto the "third and fourth generation"—perhaps becoming a catalyst for a generational, if not a millennial peace.

Wars between Nations

After providing this pattern for personal conflicts, the Lord declares in the final fifteen verses His law in regard to wars between nations. Parallel to our responses to "personal enemies," the Lord provides the same pattern wherein we are "justified" in engaging national enemies but are also invited to live an even higher law. However, prior to setting forth this parallel pattern, the Lord outlines commandments that act as firewalls to war:

1. Never Take the War to Your Enemies

Like "unto mine ancients," we are commanded that we "should not go out unto battle against any nation, kindred, tongue, or people, save I, the Lord, commanded them" (D&C 98:33). This law is consistent with Mormon's observation, "And it was because the armies of the Nephites went up unto the Lamanites that they began to be smitten; for were it not for that, the Lamanites could have had no power over them," as well as his warning, "Know ye not that ye must lay down your weapons of war, and delight no more in the shedding of blood, and take them not again, save it be that God shall command you" (Morm. 4:4, 7:4). The first firewall is to never take the battle to anyone unless specifically commanded by God to do so—His call, not ours.

2. First Lift a Standard of Peace

The next commandment is that if another nation proclaims war against His people, then His people are required to "lift a standard of peace unto that people, nation, or tongue" (D&C 98:34). Moreover, despite our enemies making their intentions clear, we must, consistent with the law of witnesses, repeat the offering of peace a second and third time so that our enemies cannot mistake our peaceful intentions: "And if that people did not accept the offering of peace, neither the second nor the third time, they should bring these testimonies before the Lord" (v. 35). Once the evidence is presented: "I, the Lord, would give unto them a commandment" (v. 36). In other words, the commandment would not come from humans but directly from God who, unlike us, sees and knows all. With a direct command from God we are then "justified" in engaging the enemy. God directs and "justifies" conflict, not us, and we must patiently offer peace three times before petitioning the Lord—and then await His command.

3. Follow the Same Pattern as Personal Conflict

Once the Lord established that we are never to initiate war, and we are not to react to threats or even proclamations of war, He addressed what we must do when our enemies' words advance to actual attacks. When your enemies have "come upon thee for the first time," their declarations of war are confirmed by deed. Now the Lord sets forth essentially the same "ensample" or pattern that He gave in resolving personal conflicts: "And again, verily I say unto you, if after thine enemy has come upon thee the first time, he repent and come unto thee praying thy forgiveness, thou shalt forgive him, and shalt hold it no more as a testimony against thine enemy. And so on unto the second and third time; and as oft as thine enemy repenteth of the trespass wherewith he has trespassed against thee, thou shalt forgive him, even seventy times seven" (98:39–40).

But what if an enemy does not repent but continues to come upon you? The admonition remains: "And if he trespass against thee and repent not the first time, nevertheless thou shalt forgive him" (v. 41). This command continues unto the second and third assault. Then, if our enemy attacks a fourth time, "thou shalt not forgive him, but shalt bring these testimonies before the Lord; and they shall not be blotted out until he repent . . . and if he do not this, I, the Lord, will avenge thee of thine enemy an hundred-fold" (vv. 44–45).

Note that the Lord does not state that we are to take into our own hands the avenging of our enemies, even after the fourth unprovoked assault, but that we are to narrowly "bring these testimonies before the Lord" and that "the Lord will avenge" us of our enemies. This is the same promise given through Isaiah to King Hezekiah that God would fight Israel's battles if they trusted in Him and did not trust in the "chariots of Egypt" (Isaiah 31:1–3). This is the test. This is the invitation to have complete trust in the Lord. This is the new covenant for the protection of His people in the last days. We are invited to move beyond justification to righteousness by forgiving our enemies and never going out to battle "against any nation" unless we receive a direct commandment. In the meantime, short of a direct revelation, we have been taught how we must respond. And if we choose not to obey we are cursed, being left to our own resources. Relying on the arm of the flesh, we fall into the ancient pattern of retribution played out by those who have pled with us to "be more wise" (Morm. 9:31).

1833–1838: A Case Study

Section 98 issues a covenantal blessing and curse. If we abide by the covenant, we are promised that our enemies will be "delivered into our hands." But if we do not live up to the covenant, then all we endure at the hands of our enemies will be "meted out as a just measure." These principles help explain what happened to the Saints in Missouri from July 1833 through the late fall of 1838. First, the Saints were chased out of Jackson County and relocated in the northern counties of Missouri. Because they did not retaliate to the threats and violence, they were generally seen as victims and public opinion was largely in their favor.[6] Their patience was rewarded, but their resolve did not endure.

After nearly five years of relative peace, there arose competition for land rights tied to the fall elections in 1838. Old fears and prejudices began to arise. The Saints publically trotted out past grievances, fueling

---

6. A number of Clay county leaders, including David Atchison, Alexander Doniphan, and Judge Cameron sympathized with the Mormons, whom they believed had been unjustly persecuted. And as recorded in the *Elder's Journal*, "the saints here are at perfect peace with all the surrounding inhabitants," and many Missourians reached out to assist their Mormon neighbors with goods, land, and employment. See Stephen C. LeSueur, *The 1838 Mormon War in Missouri* (Columbia: University of Missouri Press, 1987), 18–24. See also Leland H. Gentry and Todd M. Compton, *Fire and Sword: A History of the Latter-day Saints in Northern Missouri, 1836–39* (Salt Lake City: Greg Kofford Books, 2011).

a desire for retribution with hyperbolic rhetoric, which coalesced in the formation of the Mormon Danites. Sidney Rigdon conjoined religious with patriotic language to justify "exterminating" all whom opposed the Mormon establishment of Zion. Even though many journals and reminiscences of the Saints do not mention any specific trouble with non-Mormons prior to these orations, the contagion spread to other key Church leaders. Certain members—notably John Corrill, David Whitmer, Oliver Cowdery, and Thomas Marsh—dissented from the rising tide of voices for violence. But members who counseled caution and peacemaking with their non-Mormon neighbors were threatened and silenced.

With reports of injustices done to certain Mormon settlements, the newly formed Mormon militia moved from words to actions. In mid-October Mormon men launched pre-emptive attacks against several non-Mormon settlements—chasing out inhabitants, looting their belongings (then taking the items to the bishop's storehouse), and burning their homes. This went on for at least two weeks. While most of the Mormon militia relished this opportunity, some were sickened by it.[7] But the pillaging was not enough for those seeking to "defend" themselves. They targeted the state militia under the command of Captain Samuel Bogart at Crooked River. The Mormon army considered Bogart's militia a mob, while his men saw themselves as protectors from a Mormon army that was now an aggressor. Shouting "God and Country," the Mormon militia attacked. One man in Bogart's militia was killed and another mutilated as he lay wounded and defenseless on the ground. Most of the others fled in terror and reported exaggerated losses. Upon hearing of these attacks, public opinion swung abruptly against the Mormons. Governor Lilburn Boggs ordered all available state militia to defend the surrounding towns, then issued his infamous

---

7. John Corrill later recollected: "It appeared to me also that the love of pillage grew upon them very fast" (Corrill, *A Brief History*, 38). And Benjamin Johnson recorded the words of future apostle Lyman Wight informing his men that they must pray that "God would damn them [the Missourians] and give us power to kill them." Johnson also observed: "I might say that there was almost a trial of my faith in my pity for our enemies. Among the women was one young married and apparently near her confinement and another with small children and no wagon and the snow already began to fall. So while others were doing the burning and plunder, my mission was of mercy." Benjamin F. Johnson, *My Life's Review* (Independence, Mo.: Zion's Printing and Publishing, 1947), 7, 107.

extermination order—in mimesis to Sidney Rigdon's previous extermination threat.

The conflict was now full blown, as hundreds who had previously supported the Mormons volunteered to defend themselves from what they now saw as a Mormon insurrection.[8] Previously cooperative Generals Alexander Doniphan and David Atchison made no attempt to contact Mormon leaders as they prepared for war. Mirroring the Mormon militia's logic of pre-emptive war, and based on hysteria-induced testimony that the Mormons at Haun's Mill were planning an invasion, a mob decided that they were justified in attacking that settlement. Legislator Charles Ashby, a participant in the slaughter, told the Missouri legislature: "We thought it best to attack them first. What we did was in our own self defense, and we had a right to do it."[9]

Eventually, state militias marshaled in overwhelming force at Far West, where most Mormons prepared for a final grand conflict where the power of the Lord would be manifest as they subdued their enemies. However, seeing the futility of resistance, Joseph and the Mormon militia were persuaded to surrender, have their arms confiscated, and enter into an agreement to leave Missouri. Zion was lost and the Saints did not prevail against their "enemies."

During the build up and final decision to attack non-Mormon settlements, remarkably little reference was made by Church leaders to the Lord's "immutable" covenant in section 98. For all intents and purposes it was as if the revelation never existed. Rather they fell into the violent vocabulary of the Old Testament. Those who actually "denounced war" and made a plea for peace were silenced, threatened, and in some cases cut off for being traitors. Two apostles, Thomas Marsh and Orson Hyde, swore out affidavits condemning what they considered Mormon acts of aggression. In the words of Lorenzo Snow, Marsh "expresses unbounded charity for our enemies—said he did not think they intended us much harm—they were not naturally inclined to wickedness."[10] For

---

8. Arthur Bradford observed: "I did not first approve of the vigilantes, but I finally believed they were right and I joined with them. I am convinced that history does not afford a deeper laid scheme of villainy than that which has just developed itself in regard to the course pursued by that sect." As quoted in LeSueur, *Mormon War*, 146.

9. *Missouri Republican*, December 24, 1838.

10. As quoted in Eliza R. Snow, *Biography and Family Record of Lorenzo Snow* (Salt Lake City: Deseret News Company, 1884), 31.

this Thomas Marsh was threatened, causing him to flee for safety with his family. He was then excommunicated in absentia.

Did the Saints choose to ignore and thereby reject the "immutable" covenant of section 98? The words found in this revelation provide an irrefutable answer: "If" the saints follow the invitation given, then the Lord will "have delivered thine enemy into thine hands" (D&C 98:29), but "if ye bear it not patiently, it shall be accounted unto you as being meted out as a just measure unto you." (v. 24). Despite boisterous bragging about having their enemies delivered into their hands, the Mormons were fully delivered into the hands of their enemies—a punishment "meted out as a just measure." In summation, while non-Mormons persecuted the Saints in 1833, five years later the Saints chose to ignore the words of the Lord and took matters into their own hands, engaging in the very evil they deplored. God's covenant people did not lose Zion because the power of the devil was greater than the Lord's, but because they rejected His word. The Saints were exiled, while Joseph and a few others were sent to Liberty Jail for further tutoring as to what constituted the proper exercise of the priesthood—not just with those in the covenant but with all of God's children (see D&C 121).

Is the Covenant Being Taught Today?

Have we learned our lesson? When faced with conflict do we seek to apply the principles of section 98? Do we even bother to read it, let alone live by it, when we are in the crucible of conflict? Like the Saints in the primitive church, there came a time when we pledged allegiance to our nation and our nation's "enemies" became our enemies. The primitive Saints eventually deeded their allegiance to the Roman Empire, and there came a time when the vast majority of the Latter-day Saints in the United States pledged allegiance to the American Empire. And since doing so, our nation has been engaged in numerous conflicts. So how have we taught and applied this covenant in our generation?

In the October 2002 General Conference, apostle Russell M. Nelson taught that section 98 requires us to "renounce war and proclaim peace."[11] Picking up on this address, CNN reported that the LDS Church had issued a strong anti-war message regarding "current hos-

---

11. Russell M. Nelson, "Blessed are the Peacemakers," *Conference Report*, October 2002.

tilities"—Afghanistan and the proposed invasion of Iraq.[12] The Church public relations department immediately responded that the talk had been misinterpreted as to being applicable to "current hostilities" and that "the Church itself, as such, has no responsibility for these policies, other then urging its members fully to render loyalty to their country."[13]

The following spring, soon after our invasion of Iraq, President Gordon B. Hinckley spoke about "War and Peace" in General Conference. "Modern revelation states that we are to 'renounce war and proclaim peace,'" he said, followed by a subjunctive statement: "we can renounce war and proclaim peace."[14] However, unlike Elder Nelson's address, President Hinckley's statements could not have been misinterpreted as an anti-war message regarding "current hostilities." He did not specifically "renounce" either war.[15] Rather, he made several non-qualified statements regarding how everyone is "under the direction of our respective national leaders" and "subject to the laws of our government," especially soldiers: "Those in the armed services are under an obligation to their respective governments to execute the will of the sovereign. When they joined the military they entered into a contract by which they are presently bound and to which they have dutifully responded."

President Hinckley's reliance on political leaders' judgment was not only based on national allegiance, but also on his belief that "They

---

12. As the Associated Press reported: "The Mormon Church issued a strong anti-war message at its semiannual General conference, clearly referring to current hostilities in the Middle East, advocating patience and negotiation." Also included in the report was this characterization of Nelson's remarks: "'The Golden Rule's prohibition of one interfering with the right of others was equally binding on all nations and associations and left no room for retaliatory reactions,' Nelson said at the meeting Saturday." See "Mormon Church Takes Anti-War Stance," Available through HighBeam Research, http://www.highbeam.com/doc/1P1-68496588.html (accessed April 30, 2012).

13. "Message of Peace Misinterpreted," Mormon Newsroom, http://www.mormonnewsroom.org/article/message-of-peace-misinterpreted (accessed April 25, 2007).

14. Gordon B. Hinckley, "War and Peace," Conference Report, April 2003. Emphasis added.

15. Renouncing war demands that we go further than simply stating war is not nice. Rather it is declaring a resolute "No!" as to a particular war. As Hugh Nibley put it: "'Renounce' is a strong word: we are not to try to win peace by war, or call a truce, but to renounce war itself, to disclaim it as a policy while proclaiming peace without reservation." Letter to Editor, *Daily Universe*, March 26, 1971.

have access to greater political and military intelligence than do the people generally." He then shared his "personal feelings" and "dictates" of his "personal loyalties" in the present situation, which rested on the belief that the invasion of these countries was analogous to the Nephites defending their families and their liberty. And finally, similar to papal decrees during the Crusades (see note 2 above), he offered a latter-day war indulgence: "God will not hold men and women in uniform responsible as agents of their government in carrying forward that which they are legally obligated to do. It may even be that He will hold us responsible if we try to impede or hedge up the way of those who are involved in a contest with forces of evil and repression."

In light of Elder Nelson's and President Hinckley's talks, the principles in section 98 seem to be currently marginalized, if not wholly ignored, in favor of being "under the direction of our national leaders." According to this calculus, attempts to "renounce war and proclaim peace" should not be "misinterpreted" as having application to our "current hostilities." Allegiance to our nation is the controlling principle, and contract law rather than scripture governs those in the military. God will not hold those in uniform responsible for acts done in the name of their government, but "may" hold civilians responsible for "impeding" those who engage in our nation-sponsored wars. Thus, the instructions and formulas found in section 98, including the requirement to inquire of the Lord, are subordinate to our duty to our sovereign. We have adopted de facto the war doctrines of our national leaders.

Have We Rejected the 'Immutable' Covenant?

One might argue that we have not rejected the doctrines found in section 98 by submitting to our nation's wars. However, can we answer any of the following questions in the affirmative?

- Did we, as a faith, lift a "standard of peace" to Afghanistan and Iraq?
- Did we successfully resist exulting in or supporting voices that called for vengeance or promised retribution?
- Did we accept Afghanistan's and Iraq's own standards of peace when they claimed that they had not attacked us nor would they attack us in the future?
- Did we honestly confirm we were in fact attacked by either Afghanistan or Iraq?

- Did we accept their "prayer" for peace?
- Did we sincerely consider living a higher law by turning justice over to God?

In short, did we apply the principles of section 98 to our present conflicts or did we fall back into the same patterns the Saints used during the 1838 Missouri conflict? While Mormons were undeniably assaulted and terrorized by certain Missourians, there was no credible evidence that the citizens the Mormons attacked in Daviess County ever harmed Mormon settlements. In a haunting parallel, hundreds of thousands of innocent Afghans and Iraqis who never personally attacked us have lost their lives since our invasion of their countries.

So the "immutable" covenant of peace offered by our Lord remains largely ignored in our generation. Just as with the Saints in 1838 in Missouri, the voices of dissent to pre-emptive strikes in recent wars were condemned as being disloyal or unpatriotic. Reports of grievances were once again exaggerated or fabricated, and many innocent lives have been lost. Nothing has changed since 1838, other than we have merged our allegiance with our host nation. The "default" position of section 98 is that after we have exhausted every avenue for peace, we await a revelation from God. Instead, we have adopted an inverted "default" position that says: "having no revelation to the contrary, we pledge allegiance to any war our nations endorses." It could be argued that we have gone beyond just ignoring section 98 to engaging in our own "Constantine shift." Therefore, to the extent that we as a faith community have not renounced recent wars or applied the requirements set forth in section 98, we have once again rejected this peace covenant.

Ultimately an Individual Choice

Edward Partridge, John Corrill, Thomas Marsh, and several other early Saints got it right. They refused to retaliate against their "enemies" even if it meant, for some, being marginalized or even cast out of their faith community. Other Saints took longer to reach such clarity. As a voice from the dust, one Mormon militia member, Ebenezer Robinson, sought to tutor us regarding a lesson he and others learned through tribulation:

> Within the space of four months from the time the church made that threatening boast that if a mob came upon us again, we would carry the war to their own houses, and one party or another would be

utterly destroyed, we found ourselves prisoners of war, our property confiscated, our leaders in close confinement, and the entire church required to leave or be exterminated. We admonish all Christian people to let this be a solemn warning to never suffer themselves to make a threatening boast of what they would do under certain circumstances, as we are not our own keepers, and we feel certain that the Lord will not help us fight any such battles.[16]

Have we, like Ebenezer Robinson, with the passing of time, awakened to any realization that we have once again rejected the counsel of the Lord by trusting in the "horses" and "chariots" of Egypt? Fortunately, in one important respect, things have changed since 1838. We have the right and privilege as Church members to exercise individual dissent in both word and deed as to any Church authorities' position regarding a particular war without being cut off from our faith.[17] There are many who refuse to give their allegiance to the "will of our sovereign" when it comes to matters of life and death. Rather, we retain our own sovereign consciences and encourage others to do the same. Our allegiance to any laws of any nation is conditional in that we are required to sustain only those that "secure to each individual the free exercise of conscience" (D&C 132:4). There are many who believe that if section 98 of the Doctrine and Covenants was embraced as our faith's standard, we would have been required—individually as well as collectively—to conscientiously object to the United States' invasions of Vietnam, Afghanistan, and Iraq. Personally, I have no interest in citing any rationale or doctrine, only the words of Jesus when it comes to matters of life and death—accepting no other filter and no other person as my guide, no matter their authority. And least of all, I refuse to abdicate my conscience to my nation—especially when it has adopted a war doctrine that is antithetical to the teachings of Jesus.

In January 2011 I participated with a group protesting Condoleezza Rice's speech at Brigham Young University. While we were protesting outside the Marriott Center, she was telling a capacity stadium that our nation had to engage in pre-emptive wars. Her words were received by what the press called "vigorous clapping," while our small group of no

---

16. "Items of Personal History," *The Return* 2 (February 1890): 210.

17. President Gordon B. Hinckley said: "There is opportunity for dissent. Many have been speaking out and doing so emphatically. That is their privilege. That is their right, so long as they do so legally." *Conference Report*, April 2003, 80.

more then thirty dissidents stood outside in the cold denouncing her message.[18] But I would like to believe the ratio of those applauding her comments to those that protested her remarks does not reflect the same ratio of those of our faith that endorse our nation's current pre-emptive war doctrine.

Leaving aside the jingoistic slogans that are often reflexively accepted as sufficient justifications for any particular war, I return to the original question I have posed to many within our faith: What exactly are the doctrines, principles, and beliefs that govern your personal decision as to whether you would support or denounce a particular war? Does it include the peace covenant, and the accompanying principles and formulas, found in section 98? If not, what doctrines frame your religious training and beliefs? My personal concern is not only that section 98 continues to be ignored by our faith community, but that what we have embraced by default constitutes a rejection of Christ's Immutable Covenant of Peace.

---

18. Kimberly Houk reported, "Vigorous clapping welcomed the former Secretary of State to the campus of Brigham Young University. While Condoleezza Rice spoke on the inside, silent, peaceful protesters were outside holding signs, reading, who would Jesus waterboard?" See "Condoleezza Rice Speaks at BYU," ABC 4 News, January 13, 2011, http://www.abc4.com/content/news/top_stories/story/Condoleezza-Rice-speaks-at-BYU/nX4KbLAu3kmAAQauvYIXyA.cspx (accessed April 30, 2012)

17

War and the Gospel: Perspectives from Latter-day Saint National Security Practitioners

Mark Henshaw, Valerie M. Hudson, Eric Jensen, Kerry M. Kartchner, and John Mark Mattox

I. Introduction[1]

In common with peoples of all religious traditions, Latter-day Saints confront a large array of perplexing questions on how to deal with war. For example, they, like other people of faith, embrace peace on earth as a good to be sought and promoted with all earnestness. At the same time, they recognize war as one of the most enduring—albeit unfortunate—institutions of the present human existence. They acknowledge the difficulties that attend attempts encountered in the quest for peace amid the continual threat of war.

At the same time, Latter-day Saint encounters with questions on peace and war involve a number of unique considerations. First, Latter-day Saints understand the scriptural canon represented by the Old and New Testaments of the Bible to represent a contiguous Christian revelation spanning from the days of Adam to the days of Jesus and His Apostles. Thus, they understand those wars of the Old Testament

---

1. Originally published in *SquareTwo*, 2, no. 2 (Summer 2009), available at http://squaretwo.org/Sq2ArticleHenshawNatSec.html (accessed May 9, 2012). This version appears intact, with only light editing for stylistic consistency. The authors wish to express that the views in this chapter are their own, and should not be construed as necessarily representing the official position of the US government or any of its agencies.

that were divinely appointed to be part of the same divine, salvific plan which includes the hopeful angelic song of peace on earth, good will toward men found in the New Testament (Luke 2:14). Second, Latter-day Saints understand their faith to be a modern, revelatory restoration of ancient Christianity and not merely a denominational manifestation of the predominant Christian tradition, which arose in post-Biblical times. Thus, while there is much of interest to Latter-day Saints in the pacifist and just war traditions that developed in tandem with the predominant Christian tradition, Latter-day Saint discourse on war and peace is not a *product*, per se, of those traditions. Third, Latter-day Saints believe in an open canon of scripture, which allows not only for extra-biblical scripture but also for the receipt of new (and potentially supercessional) revelation by divinely appointed prophets of the modern age. Thus, as new revelations always take doctrinal priority over former revelations, divine instructions regarding the proper response to war may differ from generation to generation without pain of contradiction.

A disproportionate number of Latter-day Saints can be found in the United States national security establishment. These individuals must integrate both doctrine and practice as they face the challenges of their chosen profession. In this essay, we outline what might be considered mainstream views among these Latter-day Saint national security professionals, to the end of enriching and deepening Latter-day Saint discussion of appropriate state use of force by making these views more explicit. Against this backdrop, as one explores discourse on war among Latter-day Saints who find praxis on the subject as national security professionals, several points of reference typically emerge:

- Many such professionals feel that the tenets of their religion give them special reason to be good and supportive citizens. One aspect concerns the Church's emphasis on being "subject" to one's government, and on being good citizens that uphold the law and honor those in positions of governmental authority (D&C 134, A of F 12). Church members are also continually reminded, by those whom they accept as modern prophets, to be politically active—meaning at a minimum to vote and to educate oneself about the societal issues of the day. Military service is considered an honorable career choice for Latter-day Saints. Indeed, ROTC has always been welcome on the campus of Brigham Young University, even during the turbulent 1960s, and patriotism is still considered a virtue.[2]

- The great heroes of the Book of Mormon combine public service, military service, and spiritual service in what is considered an exemplary fashion in Latter-day Saint culture. One second-century BC monarch, King Benjamin, was a great military general as well as the head of state and a Christian prophet. Captain Moroni, a hero for most young Latter-day Saint boys, consulted with Christian prophets to ascertain, by revelation, the tactical movements of his enemies. Several of the greatest generals of ancient America, such as Mormon (from whom the Book of Mormon takes its name) were also prophets. Accordingly, for Latter-day Saint national security professionals there is no necessary conflict between being a person of faith and one who must at times engage in war. Indeed, there appears to be an association: men and women of God fight to preserve and secure what is good and innocent against the forces of evil, and this is a godly act. Moreover, a number of the Church's contemporary presiding officers have served in the militaries of their respective nations, some having attained general officer rank.

- American Latter-day Saints, particularly, find in the Book of Mormon a teleology concerning the United States and its place in world history. The Book of Mormon contains many prophecies concerning the land of America, including its foreordination as a land of freedom and its unique role in preparing the earth for its great eschatological destiny. However, the good therefrom is not limited to Americans: Latter-day Saints believe that the constitutional principles upon which the United States was founded are part of the common heritage of humankind ordained by God (D&C 98:5).

- This apparent "Americo-centricity" notwithstanding, it is not uncommon to find Latter-day Saint national security professionals whose sense of citizenship is more cosmopolitan than parochial. Because of the Church's expansive missionary program, Latter-day Saint young people have extraordinary opportunities to live abroad, learn a second language, and to experience other cultures at the grassroots level for extended periods in ways not usually available

---

2. In a 1991 interview, President Thomas S. Monson of the First Presidency of the Church noted, "Our church has always taught members to obey the nation.... In times of war or stress, we have no hesitancy in following the flag. You won't find any more patriotic group." "Mormons 'follow the flag,'" said President Monson." *The Herald Magazine*, March 12, 1991, 4.

to their non-Latter-day Saint peers. Chalmers Johnson, the noted expert on Asia, once remarked, "Whenever I see a six-foot tall blond kid named Christiansen come through my door speaking flawless Japanese, I know he's LDS."[3] Over 76 languages are taught at Brigham Young University, the most of any university in the nation.[4] Over two-thirds of BYU students speak a second language and have lived abroad for more than a year. Indeed, Latter-day Saints are enjoined by scripture to acquire knowledge of "things which are abroad; the wars and the perplexities of the nations . . . and a knowledge also of countries and of kingdoms" (D&C 88:79). This does not mean, of course, that some individual Latter-day Saints are not ethnocentric and insensitive to other cultures. While one would hope that familiarity with other cultures would breed love and respect, admittedly exceptions exist. However, the types of knowledge and experience necessary to overcome these faults are goods that the Latter-day Saint community imparts liberally to its young people. Thus, patriotism in the Latter-day Saint community aspires to be a patriotism of those who are not unfamiliar with and who are respectful of the peoples of the wider world.

It would, of course, be a gross mischaracterization to suggest that there is a monolithic Latter-day Saint view on war.[5] However, this essay represents an attempt to describe the context in which Latter-day Saint

---

3. Comment made to Valerie M. Hudson in Provo, Utah, in 1990.

4. During the 2002 Winter Olympics held in Salt Lake City, BYU suspended classes for one week to allow students to act as volunteers, including providing translation support for foreign visitors. Although statistics on the number of volunteers were not kept, the Salt Lake Olympic Committee reported that the supply of volunteer translators far outweighed the demand.

5. A symposium held at Brigham Young University in 1993 was the first organized effort to survey the views of LDS national security perspectives on these issues. The proceedings were published in Valerie M. Hudson and Kerry M. Kartchner, eds., *Moral Perspectives on U.S. Security Policy: Views from the LDS Community* (Provo, Utah: David M. Kennedy Center for International Studies, 1995). A second symposium was held in Washington, DC in 2003, and the proceedings published in Kerry M. Kartchner and Valerie M. Hudson, eds., *Wielding the Sword While Proclaiming Peace: Views from the LDS Community on Reconciling the Demands of National Security with the Imperatives of Revealed Truth* (Provo, Utah: Brigham Young University, David M. Kennedy Center for International Studies, 2004). Also relevant are earlier efforts at such articulation, including, for example, Ray C. Hillam and David M. Andrews, "Mormons and Foreign Policy," *BYU Studies* 25, no. 1 (Winter 1985): 1–16.

discourse on war is understood by many contemporary Latter-day Saint national security practitioners. Because the present authors have spent their professional lives operating within the context of United States national security, their views will unavoidably bear the hallmarks of their perspective. Nevertheless, the authors believe that, even within conceptual territory thus circumscribed, substantive and illuminating discussion is facilitated by an acknowledgement of the starting point from which many Latter-day Saint national security professionals begin.

II. Some Unique Aspects of Latter-day Saint Theology Pertinent to National Security

The Historical Context

From its founding in 1830 and throughout the nineteenth century, Latter-day Saints were subjected to regular, and often violent, persecution. The Church's founder, Joseph Smith Jr., was intensely persecuted until the Church relocated from New York, where it was organized, to Ohio, where mounting persecution resulted in its eventual removal to Missouri. While in Missouri, Latter-day Saints became the targets of an executive order by Governor Lilburn W. Boggs on October 27, 1838, stating that "the Mormons must be treated as enemies, and must be exterminated or driven from the State"[6]—an order that was not rescinded until 1976.[7] Some 20,000 Latter-day Saints who survived the Missouri experience trekked across the width of Missouri in the dead of winter to Illinois. During this period, the Latter-day Saints responded violently only when they felt they were either under attack or under imminent threat.[8] Indeed, numerous historical examples can be cited in which

---

6. Executive Order issued October 27, 1838, by Lilburn W. Boggs, Governor of Missouri and Commander-in-Chief of state militia forces. Available at Missouri Secretary of State website, http://www.sos.mo.gov/archives/resources/findingaids/miscMormonRecords.asp?rec=eo (accessed August 14, 2007).

7. Ibid. The most notable example of anti-Mormon persecution occurred three days later when, on October 30, a militia unit of 240 men from Livingston County, Missouri, attacked the Mormon settlement at Haun's Mill in Caldwell County. Eighteen Mormons were killed, including Sardius Smith, a 10-year-old boy who was shot in the forehead at point-blank range.

8. Prominent examples in Latter-day Saint historical literature include the

Latter-day Saints sought for peaceful redress of grievances through lawfully appointed channels. The most prominent occurred in October 1839 when Joseph Smith traveled to Washington DC and personally petitioned President Martin Van Buren, but reportedly was told by the President, "your cause is just, but I can do nothing for you. If I take up for you I shall lose the vote of the Missouri."[9]

After the murder of Joseph Smith on June 27, 1844, the Latter-day Saints were evicted from Nauvoo, Illinois[10] (and from the territorial United States) as officials in the federal government plotted a second "extermination" attempt.[11] After a 1300-mile exodus by foot, wagon, and handcart, they found refuge in the area of the Great Basin (presently the site of Salt Lake City, Utah) and established over 300 settlements extending throughout the intermountain West from Canada to Mexico. However, even in this comparatively isolated region, they were subjected to invasion and occupation by the U.S. Army.

Although the Latter-day Saints were willing, for the most part, to patiently endure injustice while waiting for formal justice to run its long and bureaucratic course, their pacifistic stance did not preclude their taking up arms to defend the United States' security interests. At the very time thousands of exiled Latter-day Saints were crossing the Great Plains and undertaking the largest refugee exodus in American history, some 500 of their number enlisted at the request of the U.S. government to form the "Mormon Battalion" to support the nation from which they had been exiled in its war against Mexico. (The Mormon Battalion's 2000-mile march from Kansas to the California coast continues to hold the record for the longest infantry march in U.S. Army history.)

The latter half of the nineteenth century witnessed Latter-day Saints being deprived of some of their most basic civil and human rights, primarily as the result of their civil disobedience over the issue of polygamy.

"Battle of Crooked River" and the "Haun's Mill Massacre." See Sherrie Johnson, "Persecutions in Missouri," *Liahona*, June 1997, 10.

9. B. H. Roberts, *A Comprehensive History of The Church of Jesus Christ of Latter-day Saints* (Salt Lake City: Deseret News Press, 1912), 2:30, esp. footnote 17.

10. The Latter-day Saints founded Nauvoo in May 1839 after their forced eviction from Missouri. At its peak in early 1845, Nauvoo's population of 12,000 rivaled Chicago's, which had only a few thousand more inhabitants. By the summer of 1846, the departure of the Latter-day Saints left Nauvoo largely deserted.

11. Joseph Smith, et al., *History of the Church of Jesus Christ of Latter-day Saints* (Salt Lake City: Deseret Book, 1984 printing), 7:543–44.

Again, however, the Latter-day Saints responded violently only in those cases in which they either were under actual attack or believed that they were under imminent threat.[12] In the intervening years, institutionalized persecution against the Latter-day Saints in the United States has all but disappeared, and early Latter-day Saint civil disobedience was replaced at the turn of the twentieth century by a strong emphasis on obeying all laws of the land as patriotic citizens. Indeed, large numbers of Latter-day Saints around the world have answered their respective nations' calls to arms in support of national security objectives.

The Theological Context

Latter-day Saint national security practitioners' views on war and peace are informed not only by their Church's unique history but also to its equally unique theology. Latter-day Saints believe that the present human existence is merely a stage (albeit a vitally important one) in their eternal careers. Each person is an eternal being (D&C 93:29, 33), made in the image of God (Gen. 1:27, Moses 2:26), and animated by a spirit (Abr. 5:8) that is the literal offspring of God (Acts 17:28–29), the eternal Heavenly Father of each member of the human race. Prior to living upon this earth, all humankind dwelt as spirits in the presence of God, who ordained that an earth be created for His spirit offspring. There, without memory of their prior existence, they could be tested to assess the character of the life that each would lead and the fitness of each for divine blessings. After death, each would receive an eternal reward predicated upon the degree to which he or she conformed to divinely ordained laws of morality and virtue made known to them while living on the earth (Abr. 3:24–26). Jesus Christ, the firstborn of God's spirit offspring, championed his Father's plan, while Lucifer, another of God's spirit offspring, contested it and sought to usurp God's authority (Moses 4:1–4). What ensued has been termed by Latter-day Saints as a *war*—not of arms, but a very real war nonetheless—in which Lucifer and those spirits who allied themselves with him—a "third part" of all God's spirit children—were banished from heaven and cast down upon

---

12. The Mountain Meadows Massacre constitutes one such example. See Ronald W. Walker, Richard E. Turley Jr., and Glen M. Leonard, *Massacre at Mountain Meadows* (New York: Oxford University Press, 2008).

the earth (where those who had not rebelled against God would shortly be born), to entice humans to evil (D&C 29:36, Rev. 12:1–9).

The Pearl of Great Price, a selection of revelations given to the Prophet Joseph Smith, provides two accounts of this primordial war—one revealed to the Old Testament prophet Moses (Moses 4:1–4), and another revealed to the Old Testament prophet Abraham (Abr. 3:27–28). These accounts clearly document two important Latter-day Saint doctrines relevant to all subsequent discourse on war and peace. First, they acknowledge humans to be endowed by God with personal agency whereby they are empowered to make their own choices, even if those choices entail negative consequences for them or for others influenced or affected by their choices (Moses 7:32, D&C 101:78). Second, they set the stage for the continuation, in the mortal condition, of the primordial war. Just as with the war in heaven, humans find themselves in the position of having to align on the side of good, as best as they are able to discern the good. Latter-day Saint doctrine does not portray death—whether occasioned by war or by other causes—as the great calamity of human existence. Rather, the great calamity is *sin*—the willful choice to act contrary to the dictates of the divine Father's plan, articulated by Him for the salvation of humankind in the primordial age of His spirit offspring's existence.

The Book of Mormon is an important touchstone for placing Latter-day Saint views on war in proper perspective. Interwoven throughout the Book of Mormon is the account of wars between two rival nations, the Nephites and the Lamanites, the latter of which eventually destroys the former. The narrative account of their wars makes abundantly clear that while defensive action is almost always permitted (Alma 43:19, 23, 26, 30, 47; 48:13–16; 51:13, 15, 25), preventive action may not be (3 Ne. 3:21). The intent for which violent action is undertaken always figures prominently in any justificatory calculus (Alma 56:46–47). Indeed, the pacifism of one Book of Mormon group is extolled because it is appropriate to the circumstances (Alma 27), whereas the battlefield heroism of another is equally extolled—again, for its appropriateness under the circumstances (Alma 53:10–18). Mormon provides a lengthy account of a large group of converted Christians who, feeling so convicted with guilt because of numerous murders they had committed in war prior to their conversion, forswore all violence, preferring to "suffer even unto death rather than commit sin" (Alma 24:19). They even went so far as to bury their weapons in the earth as a testimony before God and their fellowman of their pacifistic determination—a decision that cost many of them their lives. In stark contrast stand the children of these pacifists. They had not committed themselves to a life of pacifism and took up arms to defend their parents. Of them, Mormon recounts, these children

> entered into a covenant to fight for the liberty of the Nephites, yea, to protect the land unto the laying down of their lives; yea, even they covenanted that they never would give up their liberty, but they would fight in all cases to protect the Nephites and themselves from bondage. (Alma 53:16–17)

Thus, the Book of Mormon takes the view that the evil of war resides not in violent action itself but in the motive—in the heart—of the perpetrator. Hence, both pacifistic and militant actions can be justified if the motive for action is justifiable and if one's heart is filled with love even for one's enemy. Defense of the nation-state is generally justified, but the most compelling justification for war always is found in defense of moral principle and the security of the institutions most likely to nurture and preserve moral principle: family and church (Alma 46:12–14). The Nephites were taught that it was their sacred duty to defend their families—by the shedding of blood if necessary (Alma 44:5). With respect to the Church, Book of Mormon prophets justify violent action in defense of the right of one's own free religious expression but never for the purpose of suppressing the religious expression of another (Alma 30:7–11).[13] All in all, Book of Mormon prophets view war as a calamity to be strictly avoided, unless no other righteous course is possible. During His post-resurrection visitation to the Book of Mormon peoples, Jesus Christ condemns "contention" in any form as "of the devil," clearly alluding to the primordial war which gave birth to contention in the heavenly realms (3 Ne. 11:29).

The Doctrine and Covenants, another collection of revelations given primarily to Joseph Smith, repeatedly enjoins peacemaking and the love of one's neighbor as second only in importance to the love of God. Furthermore, in the Doctrine and Covenants, the Lord commands his people to "renounce war and proclaim peace" (D&C 98:16). Inasmuch as many of the revelations found in the Doctrine and Covenants were given

---

13. This idea is reaffirmed in the Church's 11th article of faith: "We claim the privilege of worshiping Almighty God according to the dictates of our own conscience, and allow all men the same privilege, let them worship how, where, or what they may."

during the time of the Latter-day Saints' greatest persecutions, it is not surprising that they provide specific revelatory insights concerning how God expects His people to respond to violent action perpetrated against them. One such revelation, given in 1833, enjoins Latter-day Saints to seek peaceful remedies to all grievances—from personal to international—and to extend unqualified and complete forgiveness whenever sincerely sought by an enemy. Moreover, it requires that those being attacked bear with patience a first, second, and even third perpetration of injustice against them. Upon the perpetration of a fourth injustice, they are given divine permission to retaliate, with the understanding that if they forebear, they will be the beneficiaries of unspeakable divine favors both in time and in eternity (D&C 98:23–48). However, even at this late stage, if the enemy were sincerely to repent and make proper satisfaction, forgiveness is required and retaliation strictly prohibited. A subsequent revelation enjoins Latter-day Saints subjected to mob violence to seek redress through constitutionally established means: first, through the judiciary; then, through appeal to the chief executive of the state; and next, through appeal to the President of the United States—a commandment with which Joseph Smith complied in his 1839 visit to Martin Van Buren. After exhausting all legal recourse, the Latter-day Saints—rather than being given permission to take the law into their own hands with respect to violent action—were to rest secure in the promise that God would take up their cause and afford both protection and vengeance as He deemed best and reward the Latter-day Saints for their patience and faith (D&C 101:81–90).

Several of Joseph Smith's successors in the presidency of the Church have articulated the position of the Church with respect to war. For example, as Joseph Fielding Smith, later the tenth President of the Church, observed the unfolding events of World War II, he stated:

> Satan has control now. No matter where you look, he is in control, even in our own land. He is guiding the governments as far as the Lord will permit him. That is why there is so much strife, turmoil, and confusion all over the earth. One mastermind is governing the nations. It is not the president of the United States; it is not Hitler; it is not Mussolini; it is not the king or government of England or any other land; it is Satan himself.[14]

This grim observation served as a reminder to members of the Church that the war engulfing the world at the time was, properly understood,

---

14. Joseph Fielding Smith, *Doctrines of Salvation* (Salt Lake City: Bookcraft, 1956), 3:315.

a mere continuation of the primordial conflict in heaven: Satan can be expected to use violence in an effort to compel humans in their actions, true to his same behavior exhibited before the foundations of the world were laid; and war will be the constant companion of humans until it is abolished by the millennial coming of the Prince of Peace, Jesus Christ.

In an official statement issued in 1942, the Presidency of the Church proclaimed:

> The Church itself cannot wage war, unless and until the Lord shall issue new commands. It cannot regard war as a righteous means of settling international disputes. . . . But the Church membership are [sic] citizens or subjects of sovereignties over which the Church has no control.[15]

The Presidency of the Church acknowledged that, given the Church's international character, Church members unavoidably found themselves praying to the same God but from the vantage point of opposing camps. Nevertheless, righteous members of the Church who answered the call to arms—as indeed they should in response to their highest civic duty—and who conducted themselves as honorably as they could were absolved from responsibility for the shedding of blood. That responsibility necessarily would reside with those duly empowered to engage the nations in war.[16] Indeed, the Church has since provided the following guidance to its members:

> The Lord has said that in the last days there will be "wars and rumors of wars, and the whole earth shall be in commotion, and men's hearts shall fail them" (D&C 45:26).
>
> As members of The Church of Jesus Christ of Latter-day Saints, we are a people of peace. We follow the Savior, who is the Prince of Peace. We look forward to His millennial reign, when wars will end and peace will be restored to the earth (see Isaiah 2:4). However, we recognize that in this world, government leaders sometimes send military troops to war to defend their nations and ideals.
>
> Latter-day Saints in the military do not need to feel torn between their country and their God. In the Church, "we believe in being subject to kings, presidents, rulers, and magistrates, in obeying, honoring, and sustaining the law" (A of F 12). Military service shows dedication to this principle. . . .

---

15. "Message of the First Presidency," delivered in The Assembly Hall, Salt Lake City, Utah, April 6, 1942.

16. Ibid.

If Latter-day Saints must go to war, they should go in a spirit of truth and righteousness, with a desire to do good. They should go with love in their hearts for all God's children, including those on the opposing side. Then, if they are required to shed another's blood, their action will not be counted as a sin.[17]

That, of course, does not mean that the Church has ever welcomed the prospect of war. Indeed, after World War II, the Presidency of the Church forcefully argued against universal conscription in peacetime, decrying the universal training of young men in the arts of war.[18] J. Reuben Clark, a member of the Church's First Presidency, issued a stinging rebuke of national policies which either encouraged war or blurred the distinctions between combatants and noncombatants.[19] At the same time, neither President Clark nor the First Presidency collectively ever advocated civil disobedience in the form of draft dodging or general conscientious objection when called upon by duly constituted authority (though they did not deny the right of any Latter-day Saint to claim conscientious objector status on the basis of personal beliefs, not membership in the Church). For example, over the course of many years, Church authorities consistently counseled Latter-day Saints living behind the Iron Curtain to be good citizens of the countries in which they lived. This exhortation came in spite of the concurrent and scathing denunciations by some Church leaders of the political system then in place behind the Iron Curtain. One prominent example comes from the public pronouncements of Ezra Taft Benson, U.S. Secretary of Agriculture under Dwight D. Eisenhower and later thirteenth President of the Church, who consistently denounced communism[20] as a political ideology but famously implored those under its rule to behave as good Christians without urging them in the slightest to civil disobedience.[21]

The Church's ninth president, David O. McKay, articulated conditions—reminiscent of those found in the traditional Western theory of just war—which he acknowledged as necessary, if not sufficient, grounds

---

17. "War," in *True to the Faith* (Salt Lake City: Church of Jesus Christ of Latter-day Saints, 2004), 183–84.

18. "Letter of the First Presidency Concerning Military Training," *The Improvement Era*, February 1946, 76–77.

19. J. Reuben Clark Jr., "Demand for a Proper Respect of Human Life," *The Improvement Era*, November 1946, 688–89, 740.

20. See, for example, Ezra Taft Benson, "A Witness and a Warning," *Ensign*, November 1979, 31.

21. See *U.S. News & World Report*, October 26, 1959, 76.

for *entering, but not for beginning,* a war. Among these were the defense of the principle of personal agency for oneself and one's countrymen, and *possibly* the defense of another's country from external oppression.[22] He conceded that "In the present stage of morality and spirituality in the world, I do not believe it is possible to eliminate the causes of war."[23] "But," he urged, "even though the causes of war may exist and continue to exist so long as evil continues its eternal struggle with good, it still is possible to prevent war."[24] President McKay thus maintained that that linkage between the causes of war and war itself was merely a contingent one and not a necessary one: war is inevitable only if one surrenders oneself to unbridled passion in preference to self-mastery—the conscious choice of good over evil and the fundamental rule of Christian ethics. By the same token, he taught, "We love peace, but not peace at any price. There is a peace more destructive of the manhood of living man than war is destructive of the body. 'Chains are worse than bayonets.'"[25]

A recent statement by the Church's fifteenth president, Gordon B. Hinckley, incidental to U.S. involvement in Afghanistan and Iraq, sheds further light upon the role of soldiers in the lawful discharge of their military duties:

> I believe that God will not hold men and women in uniform responsible as agents of their government in carrying forward that which they are legally obligated to do. *It may even be that He will hold us responsible if we try to impede or hedge up the way of those who are involved in a contest with forces of evil and repression.*[26]

Individual Right of Conscience

The institutional Church, which now has a presence in almost every nation of the world, may not enjoy the luxury of being able to take sides in specific cases of war. That fact, however, does not preclude individual Church members from supporting or opposing causes in accordance

---

22. David O. McKay, *Secrets of a Happy Life*, ed. Llewelyn R. McKay (Salt Lake City: Bookcraft, 1967), 76–77.

23. Ibid., 82.

24. Ibid.

25. David O. McKay, "Righteousness, Key to Peace," *The Improvement Era*, June 1955, 395.

26. Gordon B. Hinckley, "War and Peace," *Ensign*, May 2003, 78, italics added.

with the dictates of conscience. "The Spirit of Christ is given to every man," the Book of Mormon teaches, "that he may know good from evil" (Moro. 7:16). Thus, since not every *casus belli* labeled as "just" truly embodies a just cause, one is under no obligation to advocate a cause that he or she considers unjust. When, for example, Latter-day Saint youth, Helmuth Hübener,[27] was excommunicated by local Church leaders in Third Reich Germany for his active opposition to the Nazi regime and subsequently put to death by Nazi authorities, the Presidency of the Church posthumously reinstated Huebner's membership in 1946 and thus vindicated actions that the Nazis considered treasonable.

There will always be divergent views, even among individual Latter-day Saints, on what vital issues are at stake and which can best, or only, be resolved by resort to war. However, given the nature of the present existence in which humans are able only, in the words of the Apostle Paul, to "see through a glass darkly," it is their faith that well intended actions which prefer mercy to justice (but which do not deny justice when it fairly asserts its claim) will be mercifully assessed in the day of judgment, when all shall see "face to face," and "know even as [they] also are known" by the omniscient Judge of all (1 Cor. 13:12).

III. Some Latter-day Saint National Security Professional Perspectives on Specific Issues

A number of perennial issues have engaged Latter-day Saint national security professionals. Among these are matters related to the theory of just war, preemptive war, nuclear weapons and deterrence, and the relationship between violence across levels of analysis.

Just War Issues

Now with over fourteen million members in more than 150 countries, many wars and military actions have had Latter-day Saints fighting in the armies of both sides. Taking official positions on the "justness" of any such war would be a politically complex exercise and would certainly complicate what the Church considers to be its primary mission: preaching the gospel of Jesus Christ to all people everywhere. Wars, death, and

---

27. See Rudi Wobbe and Jerry Borrowman, *Three Against Hitler* (Salt Lake City: Deseret Book, 2007).

politics are all temporary, but spiritual salvation is eternal and therefore a higher priority than issuing public judgements on the morality of most military actions. Furthermore, the preaching of the gospel has a strong tendency to dampen violence at all levels of discussion, whether interpersonal or international. The Church is thus sincerely engaged in the peacebuilding process, even though it is not a governmental body.

Latter-day Saint views on the reasons for which wars can righteously be fought can be found explicitly in the scriptural canon. Justifications for bloodshed in the Book of Mormon include the preservation of religious freedom, personal liberties, peace, and family (Alma 46:12).[28] Also implicit in the Book of Mormon is the *jus ad bellum* principle of "comparative justice" (i.e., the idea that although both sides might claim just cause to fight, only the side with the more just cause can possibly have true justification to fight), and even then only as a last resort. However, neither principle can prevent the introduction, by one or another side in a conflict, of false justifications. For example, in the Book of Mormon, an organized crime element called the "Gadianton Robbers"—essentially non-state terrorists—sought to justify its attempted overthrow, mostly by assassination, of the Nephite government on false claims of righting a past injustice.[29] The Book of Mormon also documents some vitriolic correspondence that Captain Moroni received from his Lamanite counterpart, Ammoron, discussing the cause of an ongoing war:

> your fathers did wrong their brethren, insomuch that they did rob them of their right to the government when it rightly belonged unto them. And now behold, if ye will lay down your arms, and subject yourselves to be governed by those to whom the government doth rightly belong, then will I cause that my people shall lay down their weapons and shall be at war no more. (Alma 54:17–18)

The claim was fallacious; the Lamanites had no legitimate right to control the Nephite government and Ammoron knew it: "Moroni . . . knew that Ammoron knew that it was not a just cause that had caused him to wage a war" (Alma 55:1). Ammoron—at that moment the Lamanite leader—was a Nephite traitor who came to power because his brother

---

28. See the entire chapter for a description of how Captain Moroni enshrines these principles on his "Title of Liberty," which he uses to bolster public support for the war.

29. See, for example, Alma 54:16–24 (particular emphasis on verses 1–18 and 24); and 3 Nephi 3: 1–11 (particular emphasis on verse 10).

Amalickiah murdered the Lamanite king. Seizing the Lamanite throne through assassination tends to undercut one's moral authority to issue proclamations as to who rightly should control the Nephite government, and pretty much guts the *jus ad bellum* validity of Ammoron's claim.

Thus, implicit in Latter-day Saint theology is the idea that supposed causes for war require careful scrutiny. Latter-day Saint national security practitioners often find themselves in the position of having to consider how to cope with the injustices that inevitably mingle with just causes for fighting a war.

Latter-day Saints adhere to the principle that the belligerents should have a right intention—that is to say, one which intends the advancement of good, or the avoidance of evil. However, because of the subjective nature of this *jus ad bellum* principle, its empirical assessment is as problematic for Latter-day Saints as it is for other groups. A telling exchange between Captain Moroni and Ammoron demonstrates the difficulty:

> Captain Moroni: "Yea, I would tell you these things [i.e., concerning the illegitimacy of Ammoron's cause] if ye were capable of hearkening unto them; yea, I would tell you concerning that awful hell that awaits to receive such murderers as thou and thy brother have been, except ye repent and withdraw your murderous purposes, and return with your armies to your own lands." (Alma 54:7)

> Ammoron: "if it so be that there is a devil and a hell, behold will he not send you there to dwell with my brother whom ye have murdered, whom ye have hinted that he hath gone to such a place?" (Alma 54:22)

Latter-day Saints can be shown to have encountered the same philosophical difficulties that attend just war theory with respect to justifying civil wars or rebellions against regularly constituted authority as other groups have encountered. On the one hand, civil war and revolution are specifically denounced in an 1834 Church declaration:

> We believe that all men are bound to sustain and uphold the respective governments in which they reside, while protected in their inherent and inalienable rights by the laws of such governments; and that sedition and rebellion are unbecoming every citizen thus protected, and should be punished accordingly. (D&C 134:5)

On the other hand, they recognize cases in which rebellion was not only justifiable, it was divinely inspired. A case in point is the American

Revolution which, according to the Book of Mormon, *was* ordained by God (1 Ne. 13:16–19, D&C 101:76–80). Another case is seen in Captain Moroni's threat at a crucial juncture to overthrow the Nephite government when its perceived neglect of the army during wartime threatened his ability to preserve the Nephite nation against a Lamanite invasion (Alma 60).[30]

The Book of Mormon chronicles some eighty-five armed conflicts, ranging in scale from small skirmishes to civilization-ending multi-year campaigns.[31] Moreover, a number of key figures in the book are professional soldiers—many of them paragons of virtue. Captain Moroni and later Mormon are pre-eminent among these. Captain Moroni, as commanding general of the Nephite armies, oversaw an extended defensive military campaign spanning fourteen years. While the strategies and tactics that Mormon depicts in his account of that particular war are themselves interesting, they clearly are of secondary importance in comparison to Mormon's description of Captain Moroni as an extraordinarily righteous man of impeccable integrity, character, and religious devotion. Mormon opines that "if all men had been, and were, and ever would be, like unto Moroni, behold, the very powers of hell would have been shaken forever; yea, the devil would never have power over the hearts of the children of men (Alma 48:17). Indeed, Mormon—a prophet and exceptionally righteous man in his own right—held Captain Moroni in such high esteem that, although they were separated by four centuries, Mormon named his own son after the famed soldier. Such soldierly examples lead Latter-day Saints to conclude that those fighting in wars to uphold righteous principles can, indeed, enjoy divine approval and that service as a soldier need not be understood necessarily to conflict with one's duty to God.

Although Church doctrine enjoins members to support their respective governments and perform military duties when required, this does not absolve members from moral responsibility for the rectitude of their wartime conduct. The appropriate mood in which to go to war is apparently one of mourning, not exultation or hatred. Moroni mourned that he would be the means of sending so many of his brethren, unprepared, to the next stage of existence (Alma 48:23). Furthermore, mem-

---

30. See Alma 61 for the Nephite head-of-state's response.

31. William J. Hamblin and Stephen D. Ricks, eds., *Warfare in the Book of Mormon* (Salt Lake City: Deseret Book, 1990).

bers acting as soldiers are expected to obey God's commandments to the best of their ability even under the most hostile conditions. As a practical example, Latter-day Saint national security professionals would find themselves generally hard pressed to justify, on theological grounds, individual deviations from the norms of civilized wartime conduct enshrined in the international laws of warfare and the Geneva Conventions. That does not mean, however, that conflicts between law and conscience cannot or do not exist. Again, Captain Moroni stands as the pre-eminent Book of Mormon example. At one point in a protracted war, he is faced with the decision of whether to provide food for enemy prisoners of war or for his own forces, and negotiates an imbalanced prisoner exchange (Alma 54:1–3). The Prophet Mormon—himself the commanding general of the Nephite armies during the war that results in his nation's collapse—stands as another example of one faced with a moral dilemma in the light of *jus in bello* principles. At one point, Mormon finds himself confronted with the choice of whether to resign his post as commander or to remain in charge of an army that has become so morally corrupt— his commands to the contrary notwithstanding—that it had resorted to almost totally depraved behavior, including the systematic rape, torture, and cannibalistic consumption of enemy prisoners of war (Moro. 9). Mormon first resigns his post, but then eventually, but mournfully, picks up the sword again when it becomes clear that the war is going so badly that his nation's existence is threatened.[32] Although these men fight as professional soldiers and wrestle with complex military, social, and political issues, they never forget that they are first and foremost disciples of Jesus Christ, and it is Christian principles that ultimately govern their conduct. Latter-day Saint national security professionals wrestle with the same kinds of issues while at the same time striving to maintain their most fundamental spiritual commitments.

---

32. Despite Mormon's best efforts, he admits to his son in a letter that his fellow Nephites have become so wicked that God will no longer support them in their efforts of self-preservation. The war ends with the Nephites' extermination. Mormon survives the final battle long enough to lament the destruction of his civilization, but is soon hunted down by the Lamanites and killed. His death is recorded by his son Moroni—not to be confused with the earlier Captain Moroni—who also is a professional soldier serving under his father and who survives the final battle as well. He becomes the last surviving Nephite and is the Book of Mormon's final contributor. See Mormon 6, Moroni 9.

Preemptive War

A national security issue that has received much attention during the first decade of the 21st century is the idea of "preemptive war." One year after the September 11, 2001, terrorist attacks on the United States, President George W. Bush issued a new National Security Strategy, which states:

> We will disrupt and destroy terrorist organizations by: direct and continuous action using all the elements of national and international power . . . [and by] defending the United States, the American people, and our interests at home and abroad by identifying and destroying the threat before it reaches our borders. While the United States will constantly strive to enlist the support of the international community, we will not hesitate to act alone, if necessary, to exercise our right of self-defense by acting preemptively against such terrorists, to prevent them from doing harm against our people and our country . . . we recognize that our best defense is a good offense.[33]

It is this issue where significant disagreements among Latter-day Saint national security professionals can be observed. For some, preemptive war marks the beginning of a slippery slope toward a condition warned against by Spencer W. Kimball, twelfth President of the Church. In 1976, he warned that humankind—Latter-day Saints included—were a "warlike people."[34] His warning recalls the declining years of Nephite civilization, during Mormon's generalship. After defeating the Lamanites in two major battles, the Nephites determined to go to battle against the Lamanites, rather than continuing to defend themselves. After this decision to switch to the offensive, Mormon "did utterly refuse from this time forth to be a commander and a leader of this people" (Morm. 3:11). The Nephites persisted in their aggressive desires and as they attacked the Lamanites, were badly beaten and began to be completely destroyed as a people. In explanation for this destruction, Mormon states:

> And it was because the armies of the Nephites went up unto the Lamanites that they began to be smitten; for were it not for that, the Lamanites could have had no power over them. But, behold, the

---

33. President George W. Bush, *The National Security Strategy of the United States of America*, September 2002, available at http://georgewbush-whitehouse.archives.gov/nsc/nss/2002/ (accessed on May 11, 2012).

34. Spencer W. Kimball, "The False Gods We Worship," *Ensign*, June 1976.

judgments of God will overtake the wicked; and it is by the wicked that the wicked are punished; for it is the wicked that stir up the hearts of the children of men unto bloodshed. (Morm. 4:4–5)

However, not all Latter-day Saint national security professionals see the same dangers in preemptive war doctrine. Some of these professionals note that the scriptures demonstrate that there are times when even offensive, or at least preemptive, action is appropriate; and, for this view, they see a scriptural precedent. A first-century BC Book of Mormon figure named Amalickiah tried to overthrow the government of the Nephites and become a totalitarian king. He was prevented from doing so, but then determined to take those who followed him and to ally themselves with the opposing nation of the Lamanites. In this case, though Amalickiah had not committed or even planned an attack, Captain Moroni knew that if allowed to reach the Lamanites, Amalickiah "would stir up the Lamanites to anger against them, and cause them to come to battle against them" (Alma 46:30). Accordingly, Moroni acted preemptively and attacked Amalickiah as he tried to escape to the Lamanites.

The differences between these two approaches may be to some degree definitional, depending on whether one views preemption as defensive or offensive in nature. However, both views understand the same scriptural passages to support their view of the appropriate national security approach.

Less than a month after September 11, 2001, Church President Gordon B. Hinckley stated,

Those of us who are American citizens stand solidly with the president of our nation. The terrible forces of evil must be confronted and held accountable for their actions. This is not a matter of Christian against Muslim. I am pleased that food is being dropped to the hungry people of a targeted nation. We value our Muslim neighbors across the world and hope that those who live by the tenets of their faith will not suffer. I ask particularly that our own people do not become a party in any way to the persecution of the innocent. Rather, let us be friendly and helpful, protective and supportive. It is the terrorist organizations that must be ferreted out and brought down. We of this Church know something of such groups. The Book of Mormon speaks of the Gadianton robbers, a vicious, oath-bound, and secret organization bent on evil and destruction. In their day they did all in their power, by whatever means available, to bring down the Church, to woo the people with sophistry, and to take control of the society. We see the same thing in the present situation. We are people of peace. We are followers of the Christ who was and is the Prince of Peace. But there are times when we must stand up for right and decency, for freedom and civilization, just as Moroni rallied his people in his day to the defense of their wives, their children, and the cause of liberty (see Alma 48:10).[35]

Two years later, after the invasion of Iraq, Gordon B. Hinckley again spoke on the subject of war and specifically the war in Iraq, which had recently begun. He said, "It is clear from [the Book of Mormon] and other writings that there are times and circumstances when nations are justified, in fact have an obligation, to fight for family, for liberty, and against tyranny, threat, and oppression."[36] While the response to the terrorist acts of September 11, 2001, and the war in central Asia may well constitute "times and circumstances" where the obligation described by Gordon B. Hinckley exists, Spencer W. Kimball's warning seems also to apply to the post-9/11 world. Given the present instabilities which typify the international community, it is likely that there will continue to be differing views on this question, both within and among many nations, all of which are home to Latter-day Saints.

Nuclear Weapons and Deterrence

The role of nuclear weapons in U.S. national security and arms control policy is another issue of debate among Latter-day Saint national security professionals. Fewer national security topics evoke more emotional response than issues related to nuclear weapons. Perhaps this is because nuclear weapons are widely seen as a threat to the very existence of life on earth, and therefore no other issue poses such enormous stakes as nuclear weapons. Nor is any other issue so critical to underwriting U.S. national security posture, and that of its friends and allies, than nuclear deterrence and extended deterrence; yet no other weapon system, and its associated targeting strategy, so challenges the basic pre-

---

35. Gordon B. Hinckley, "The Times in Which We Live," *Ensign*, November 2001, 72–74.
36. Gordon B. Hinckley, "War and Peace."

cepts of just war in general, and the Church's doctrinal emphasis on defense and restraint in particular.

The Church rarely takes official positions with respect to specific national security issues. A notable exception to this general practice, however, involves nuclear weapons. In 1981, the Church officially opposed a plan, originated under the Carter Administration, to base the MX missile system in the Utah-Nevada desert.[37] Although the future of the basing plan was already in question when the Reagan Administration entered office earlier that year, the ultimate failure of the Utah-Nevada basing proposal is widely attributed to the Church's opposition.[38] In 2006, the Church opposed the selection of Utah as a repository for nuclear waste, calling upon the federal government "to harness the technological and creative power of the country" to develop alternative disposal options.[39] However, apart from these statements on pressing parochial issues impacting directly on the territory of Utah, the Church has refrained from issuing any official statement on the morality of nuclear deterrence or nuclear weapons and declined to join either the U.S. Catholic Bishops or various groups of Protestant activists in the debates of the 1980s in their pronouncements on the morality of the nuclear freeze or other nuclear arms control proposals. This has not prevented some individual members of the Church hierarchy from issuing personal views on nuclear issues. For example, in the aftermath of the bombings of Hiroshima and Nagasaki, J. Reuben Clark took a highly critical stance with respect to President Harry Truman's decision to drop the bomb, which he called the "crowning savagery of the war."[40]

The Latter-day Saint national security community encompasses a small but eloquent group of scholars who adhere to the absolute pacifist school of thought, just as does the overall Christian community, especially with respect to the morality or immorality of nuclear weap-

---

37. "First Presidency Statement on Basing of MX Missile," *Ensign*, June 1981, 76.

38. The events surrounding this statement are eloquently described in Steven A. Hildreth, "The First Presidency Statement on MX in Perspective," *BYU Studies*, 22, no. 2 (Spring 1982): 215–26.

39. "Church Urges Alternatives for Nuclear Waste," Official Church Statement, dated May 4, 2006.

40. Frank W. Fox, *J. Reuben Clark: The Public Years* (Provo, Utah: Brigham Young University Press, 1980), 589. Originally published in J. Reuben Clark Jr., "Demand for the Proper Respect for Human Life," *Improvement Era*, November 1946, 689. See also D. Michael Quinn's chapter on Clark in this volume.

ons and policies of nuclear deterrence.[41] For these passionate observers, the unthinkably destructive scale of nuclear weapons can never be fully reconciled with the precepts of just war. The destruction anticipated in a nuclear strike would exceed any measure of proportionality, and the scope of destruction could never be so controlled or limited as to avoid vast fatalities among non-combatants, thus failing just war's discrimination criterion. This view is founded upon widely popular assumptions regarding the impossibility of limited nuclear use, and a presumed inability to tailor or control the effects of nuclear weapons so as to limit collateral damage.

Nevertheless, dozens, if not hundreds, of members of the Church work in the nation's nuclear weapons complex as physicists, engineers, support staff, management, or as technical and political advisors, and many more work in the field of nuclear energy production. Still others serve in the military with positions of responsibility for nuclear weapons employment, security, or policy planning, or as civilian contractors supporting the country's nuclear weapons infrastructure. Richard G. Scott, one of the Church's current Twelve Apostles—the second highest leadership body in the Church—spent a career involved in the development of the Navy's first nuclear submarine fleet.[42] Another prominent Church member was former "chief electronics scientist for the nation's nuclear missile work," and subsequently Administrator of NASA.[43] Each of these members of the Church has had to face the challenge of personally reconciling their faith with their responsibilities for the nation's nuclear weapons arsenal. For some, the following five assertions have helped resolve this challenge.[44]

---

41. This minority school of thought is eloquently expressed in three seminal articles: Edwin B. Firmage, "Allegiance and Stewardship: Holy War, Just War, and the Mormon Tradition in the Nuclear Age," *Dialogue* 16, no. 1 (Spring 1983): 47–61; Eugene England, "A Case for Mormon Christian Pacifism," in Hudson and Kartchner, *Moral Perspectives*, 96–103; and Richard Sherlock, "Rooted in Christian Hope: The Case for Pacifism," *Dialogue* 37, no. 1 (Spring 2004): 95–108.

42. "News of the Church: Elder Richard G. Scott of the Quorum of the Twelve," *Ensign*, November 1988.

43. Dale Van Atta, "James C. Fletcher: Knowledge Lights the Way," *Ensign*, April 1984.

44. Not all successfully resolve the nuclear weapons dilemma. Some have concluded that the teachings of the Church, including authoritative interpretations of scripture and a comprehensive reading of official statements, leads to the conclusion that "nuclear weapons and deterrence are not morally sustainable." See Steven A. Hildreth,

First, nuclear weapons have kept the United States safe and secure, and thus have contributed to sustaining the United States as a base for spreading the gospel. Strategic deterrence, based on a robust nuclear arsenal, has been a key component underwriting U.S. national security, as well as U.S. extended deterrence guarantees, to its friends and allies. Nuclear deterrence arguably has kept the nation from being subject to large-scale attack throughout the post-World War II era, and has served as an umbrella to ensure the security of many other countries allied with the United States. The preservation of the nation's territorial integrity and the survival and prosperity of its core institutions have justified the maintenance of a strong nuclear deterrent. For many, the fact that this deterrent has served a defensive posture also helps reconcile support for nuclear weapons with a personal devotion to gospel principles. Gary Stradling, a physicist at Los Alamos National Laboratory, is a prime example of a Church member who has worked through the personal challenge of reconciling his professional responsibilities with his private religious devotion. According to Stradling,

> An essential part of our defensive capability . . . is the U.S. nuclear weapons arsenal. . . . The U.S. nuclear arsenal, designed to deter the Cold War threat of a massive, annihilating attack of the entire Soviet nuclear arsenal, has a powerful capacity to destroy nearly any target in the world. This awesome capability for destruction has held large-scale conventional war at bay for sixty years now.

Stradling is convinced that the U.S. nuclear arsenal has "saved tens to hundreds of millions of lives that might otherwise have been lost in the upward spiral of conventional war."[45]

Second, the development of a robust nuclear deterrence posture is justified by the threat posed to U.S. national security by the nuclear postures of other nations. According to this view, recently articulated by President Barack Obama,[46] as long as other nations with potentially

---

"An LDS Moral Perspective on Security Policy," in Hudson and Kartchner, *Moral Perspectives*, 121.

45. Gary Stradling, "Mass Destruction—Historical and LDS Perspectives," in Kartchner and Hudson, *Wielding the Sword While Proclaiming Peace*, 102.

46. See "Remarks by President Barack Obama," April 5, 2009, Hradcany Square, Prague, Czech Republic. Available at http://www.whitehouse.gov/the_press_office/Remarks-By-President-Barack-Obama-In-Prague-As-Delivered/ (accessed June 21, 2009).

adversarial intentions toward the United States, or its friends and allies, maintain or seek to acquire weapons of mass destruction, the United States will need a credible nuclear deterrent of its own. At present, only Russia retains a nuclear capability sufficient to threaten the existence of the United States as a modern nation. China continues to expand its nuclear arsenal and the range of its delivery systems, while both Iran and North Korea continue to pursue nuclear weapon programs. The international community struggles with uncertain diplomatic efforts to resolve the nuclear challenges. To many Latter-day Saint national security professionals, such circumstances therefore require maintaining a nuclear posture for the defense of the United States and its allies.

Third, while a current debate has arisen with regard to whether advanced conventional weapons can eventually replace roles and missions currently reserved for nuclear weapons, it remains clear that only nuclear weapons enable a nation to hold at risk the full spectrum of essential targets for deterrence purposes. These include, for example, hard and deeply buried targets (such as command and control bunkers), facilities that are heavily defended against conventional means of attack, and storage facilities for chemical and biological agents, which if attacked by conventional means would only result in dispersing lethal agents to surrounding areas, and that can only be fully and confidently destroyed by nuclear strikes. In addition, nuclear weapons carry with them an element of psychological threat that conventional weapons alone cannot convey.

Fourth, while pacifists may disagree, U.S. nuclear strategy in general has evolved toward greater compatibility with principles of traditional just war theory.[47] These precepts require that war be initiated by the proper authority and with the proper cause, and that the conduct of the war be circumscribed by proportionality and discrimination in targeting combatants and avoiding noncombatants. It is the conduct of just war that poses the greatest challenges for reconciling the use of nuclear weapons, because early Cold War targeting strategies were deliberately expansive, prospectively involving the launch of hundreds or even thousands of high-yield nuclear weapons against targets that could not easily be distinguished from civilian countervalue assets. But

---

47. For a more detailed exposition of how nuclear weapons policies relate to just war doctrine, see Kerry M. Kartchner, "Nuclear Weapons and a Moral Defense," in Kartchner and Hudson, *Wielding the Sword While Proclaiming Peace*, 153–69.

over the course of the past several decades, U.S. targeting strategies have become much more discriminate and the weapons much more accurate, while earnest efforts have been undertaken to reduce collateral damage through the development and fielding of "cleaner" weapons and incorporating increasingly limited strike options into U.S. nuclear war plans. The U.S. Department of Energy recently announced that following the completion of the latest round of reductions in the U.S. nuclear weapons arsenal, the number of U.S. nuclear weapons will be at its lowest levels since the 1950s, with new negotiations over a second round of START promising to push that level even lower.[48]

Fifth, the United States has acted responsibly in managing its nuclear stewardship. The United States has engaged in a series of arms control obligations that have helped contain and reduce nuclear arms competitions, and has always honored its nuclear treaty commitments. Furthermore, it has expended considerable resources securing the safety and reliability of its nuclear weapons, thus demonstrating responsible accountability for its nuclear arsenal. These safeguards have helped some Latter-day Saint national security professionals more easily justify support for U.S. nuclear weapon policies.

Several factors are leading to a decline in the relevance of nuclear weapons to U.S. national security. These include steady reductions in the size and composition of deployed U.S. nuclear forces, a deterioration in the U.S. nuclear weapons infrastructure, new threats and an altered threat environment that seem less amenable to nuclear deterrence, growing confidence that conventional supremacy can substitute for nuclear deterrence, and less political support for modernizing or even refurbishing deployed U.S. nuclear weapons. Nevertheless, nuclear weapons will be a key component of U.S. national security strategy for the foreseeable future, and thus will continue to draw general support from those Latter-day Saint national security practitioners who have reconciled their existence with deeply felt gospel principles concerning security and war and a morally sustainable defense.

---

48. U.S. Department of Energy, Office of Public Affairs, "U.S. Nuclear Weapons Strategy Delivered to Congress," July 24, 2007. Available at http://www.defense. gov/releases/release.aspx?releaseid=11163 (accessed May 11, 2012).

The Relationship Between Violence Across Levels of Analysis

One Latter-day Saint national security scholar, Stan Taylor, has eloquently argued that Latter-day Saint theology asserts that the causes of war lie in the human heart.[49] Taylor and Evans note that, in the Book of Mormon, the causes of war are spelled out very plainly; they are not Waltzian Second or Third Levels causes, but old-fashioned First Level causes:

> And we see that these promises have been verified to the people of Nephi; for it has been their quarrelings and their contentions, yea, their murderings, and their plunderings, their idolatry, their whoredoms, and their abominations, which were among themselves, which brought upon them their wars and their destructions. (Alma 50:21)

This linkage between sin at a lower level of analysis and problems at the national and international levels of analysis finds echo in Latter-day Saint theology, including the proclamation on the family, whose ending reads, "Further, we warn that the disintegration of the family will bring upon individuals, communities, and nations the calamities foretold by ancient and modern prophets."[50]

One example of this connection can be found in a recent article, co-authored by five scholars, three of whom are Latter-day Saints. In this study, the authors investigated whether the security of women in a society and the security of the nation-state were linked. That is, if women in a society are very insecure, at significant risk to be victims of domestic violence, rape, murder, honor killings, and so forth, is there any effect at the national level? The study examined 141 nations, examining how physically secure women were, as well as how peaceful the nations were, how compliant with international law, and the relations of the nations with their neighboring states. Though only a correlative study, this analysis showed that the physical security of women was highly predictive of state indicators of peacefulness, and that the physical security of women was a better predictor than variables such as level of democracy, wealth, or presence of particular religions.[51] While

49. Stan A. Taylor and Jeremy O. Evans (2004) "From Whence Come Wars and Fighting Among You? An Integration of Secular and Sacred," in Kartchner and Hudson, *Wielding the Sword While Proclaiming Peace*, 43–56.

50. "The Family: A Proclamation to the World," available at http://www.lds.org/family/proclamation?lang=eng (last accessed May 9, 2012).

51. Valerie M. Hudson, Mary Caprioli, Bonnie Ballif-Spanvill, Rose McDermott, Chad F. Emmett, "The Heart of the Matter: The Security of Women

Latter-day Saint national security scholars and professionals have only just begun to scratch the surface of this topic, they feel they have good doctrinal reason to believe that societies whose homes, schools, and workplaces are not a place of safety for the vulnerable are unlikely to be secure themselves. The fabric of security is woven from the myriad of small threads that comprise the social interactions of the society, and if the threads are red with violence, the garment will be red, as well.

IV. Conclusions

General Operating Premises of Latter-day Saint National Security Practitioners

In sum, the following generalizations suggest themselves as building blocks as a typology for understanding the views commonly found among Latter-day Saint national security practitioners of this era:

- Latter-day Saint theology does not constitute a rigid framework which insists on either an idealist or realist approach to war in the scheme of human existence.
- Instead, it acknowledges the decision to resort to war as a possible expression of God-given personal agency, with both political leaders and individual subjects and citizens bearing responsibility for their responses to that decision.
- It recognizes Satan as the tireless proponent of war and Jesus Christ as the Prince of Peace and that, when humankind submits to the teachings of Jesus Christ, all war will cease.
- In the meantime, however, it holds that humans may expect to be confronted with the decision of whether to participate in war or whether to forego armed resistance—both courses of action entailing the possibility of suffering or death.
- It holds that motive and the feelings of one's heart toward one's enemies are paramount in assessing the praiseworthy or blameworthy character of human action.
- It is not (and by its revelatory nature cannot be) understood as an outgrowth of any of the western philosophical traditions respecting warfare (i.e., holy war, just war, or pacifism), even though there exist points of intersection between it and these philosophical traditions. For example, it recognizes that, in specific instances anciently, God

commanded "holy" war. It holds, in common with the just war tradition, that not all wars are just but that some wars can be. It shares the pacifist aspiration that war, as a human institution, will end.

- Accordingly, these philosophical traditions may illuminate, but cannot circumscribe, Latter-day Saint discourse vis-à-vis war. Indeed, Latter-day Saint theology allows that certain circumstances exist in which one could, with propriety, either engage in war or eschew all violence with equal justification.

- At the same time, it regards one's answering his or her country's call to arms as recognition of one's highest civic duty. Membership in the Church, therefore, cannot constitute adequate justification for conscientious objection, though individual Latter-day Saints may, on personal grounds, attest to being conscientious objectors.

- It regards violence at all levels in society as intertwined, acknowledging that violence within the home and between subnational groups may well be linked to war and conflict at the nation-state level. Furthermore, this linkage means that actions take to decrease violence within society may have a salutatory effect on violence between societies.

- Finally, it allows for a wide range of expression of political opinion with respect to security issues and with respect to the more practical matters of security policy implementation.

Looking Ahead

The perennial issues in national security continue to be debated in universities, government conference rooms, corporate board rooms, and the local diner. As the world security community transforms from the traditional state-on-state conflicts of the last few centuries to conflicts pitting states against global non-state entities such as terrorist and criminal enterprises, the discussions will only continue and intensify.

The continuing discussion leaves the Latter-day Saint community of national security professionals in all nations in a state of perpetual reflection upon eternal principles that can be applied to future situations as they arise. As Elder Robert S. Wood has put it, "The Author and Finisher of the Faith posed a problem rather than specified a solution when he directed us to render unto Caesar the things that are Caesar's and counseled his followers to be in but not of the world. . . . The reconciliation of moral obligation and civic duty persists as a central issue for Christians generally and for Latter-day Saints particularly."[52] Latter-day Saints believe that it is appropriate to consider principles that have been taught by prophets and practiced under divine direction, as these might pertain within the context of existing national policies and procedures. Ancient and modern revelation has provided a number of principles that a loving Heavenly Father seems to expect His children on earth to apply in the face of Satanic contention. These include principles such as defense of essential gospel principles like liberty, or of essential gospel institutions like family and church. Still, faithful Latter-day Saint members of the national security community may take very divergent views on how to apply those principles to specific cases.

Fortunately, there is room for differing views among the Church membership on these matters. In 2003, while discussing the war in Iraq in a general conference, Church President Gordon B. Hinckley stated, "In a democracy, we can renounce war and proclaim peace. There is opportunity for dissent. Many have been speaking out and doing so emphatically. That is their privilege. That is their right, so long as they do it legally." After speaking approvingly of the "contest with the forces of evil," he then continued, "There is much that we can do in these perilous times. We can give our opinions on the merits of the situation as we see it, but never let us become a party to words or works of evil concerning our brothers and sisters in various nations on one side or the other."[53]

Undergirding Gordon B. Hinckley's remarks on the acceptance of divergent views within the Church is the recognition that the Church spans the entire world now and that the Church cannot take a parochial or American-centric view of national security issues. In October 2001, immediately after the attacks of September 11, again when speaking to the entire Church, Gordon B. Hinckley stated, "We are now a global organization. We have members in more than 150 nations. . . . Members of the Church in this and other nations are now involved with many others in a great international undertaking."[54] The Church is not only clearly a global Church, with approximately half of the Church's membership of fourteen million persons located outside of the United States,

---

52. Robert S. Wood, "Rendering Unto Caesar: Moral Responsibility and Civic Duty in a World of States," in Hudson and Kartchner, *Moral Perspectives*, 54–76.
53. Gordon B. Hinckley, "War and Peace."
54. Gordon B. Hinckley, "The Times in Which We Live."

but members of the Church are national security professionals in many nations and members of their militaries. They have been hired to serve the bidding of their respective nations. It may be that future international conflict will bring members of the Church directly into conflict with each other, as has occurred in prior conflicts. Members of the Church can still be faithful members though they face each other across the lines of diplomacy or battle. "War is thus not a relationship between men, but a relationship between states, in which private individuals are only enemies accidentally, neither as men nor as citizens, but as soldiers. . . . Each state can only have as enemies other states, not men."[55] As the Church continues to grow and spread its reach farther across the globe, it will need to continue to espouse a *global* view of war and peace, one in which members can differ in factual application so long as they conform to established Church doctrine and principles.

One of the most important meta-issues apparent in the above discussion of Latter-day Saint thought is the question of how scripture is to be applied in messy contemporary circumstances. Latter-day Saints are enjoined to "liken the scriptures" to their own situations (1 Ne. 19:23), treating the scriptures as one of the most important sources of advice available to humankind. Their faith expects them to "study" things before asking for divine confirmation of rationally obtained conclusions (D&C 9:7–8), with an important part of that study being the scriptures. Yet they are also warned against "wresting" the scriptures for selfish purposes, for such leads to destruction (Alma 41:1). Moreover, they are warned that the answers they receive as private individuals may not be binding on others, for only those with the appropriate divine appointment can make more general pronouncements (D&C 28:2, 7).

Members of the Church will continue to look to the scriptures, the Latter-day prophets, and divine inspiration as they reflect upon what standards and principles should guide in national security affairs. As demonstrated by ancient and modern scripture, it is sometimes difficult to determine from ancient events how eternal principles should be applied to contemporary national security affairs. However, we have identified some principles within Latter-day Saint theology that form a recognizable framework used by Latter-day Saint national security

---

55. Jean-Jacques Rousseau, as quoted in Daphne Richemond, "Symposium on Reexamining the Law of War: Transnational Terrorist Organizations and the Use of Force," *Catholic University Law Review* 56 (Spring 2007): 1005.

professionals in approaching the important national security issues of any time period. Foundational to this framework is the understanding that while peace is preferable to war and Latter-day Saints are enjoined to work for peace, war is part of the backdrop of the present estate of humankind. As a consequence, Latter-day Saints understand that humankind must use its agency in such a way as to safeguard those principles and institutions—family, religion, home, and liberty—that are not only worth defending, but also worth the shedding of blood to preserve for themselves and for the posterity of the whole human family. At the same time, Latter-day Saints must not only proclaim peace, but also build it with energy and effort and heart.

Aftermath

Richard Lyman Bushman

The conference on which this book is based grew out of a conversation between Rick Duran and myself in the gardens at the Huntington Museum in San Marino. Rick was in town on business and suggested we get together. We found that we shared a sense that there were strong anti-war tendencies among Mormons that had not been fully articulated. In private conversations with LDS friends, I had found anti-war feelings running pretty high, but little was said in public. Their fellow Mormons' belief in the necessity and sometimes the nobility of war suppressed such inclinations. The conference was born out of a desire to bring forward the anti-war strains in the Mormon tradition and give a voice to people who hesitated to speak for fear of appearing unpatriotic.

This desire to make a place for anti-war thought was strengthened by the opposition to the Iraq War shared by many Americans. Our inclination to rush to war seemed to have gone astray in that instance, and something needed to be said to check the belief that we can overcome evil by force. When that war was being contemplated, I hoped that Latter-day Saints would be among the number who would caution against shock and awe as a solution to complex international problems but feared that they would instead be all too quick to join in the national crusade against evil. I was immensely encouraged when on visits to Utah I heard many Latter-day Saints expressing strong reservations about the invasion of Iraq. It was those instincts, which I believe are most true to our tradition and beliefs, that we hoped to encourage by holding this conference.

The three major organizers of the conference—Patrick Mason, Loyd Ericson, and myself—all share this perspective. From the outset, we did have an agenda. But we recognized that it would be useless to gather only like-minded souls to ruminate among ourselves on the horrors of war. We are fully aware that most Latter-day Saints do not share our viewpoint and that only by engaging with all the arguments for war could we have any influence.

I soon learned that an LDS position on war has been under constant, high-level discussion for many years by LDS national security professionals and two excellent collections have been published under the auspices of that organization.[1] I learned about this national security group from Professor Valerie Hudson at Brigham Young University, who has been a moving spirit in their gatherings and publications.

I deeply respect these Latter-day Saints. It is one thing to intone high principles of peace and love from the safety of an ivory tower, implying that all those who favor war have fallen from their commitment to the Savior's gospel. It is another to apply gospel principles when sitting in the nation's policy councils and in the war rooms faced with the practical realities of protecting the nation's citizens in a world rife with hatred and the lust for power. It is the people who have a voice in actual decision-making whose understanding of the gospel is most severely put to the test. These are the ones I wanted to hear from, in the hope that my own idealistic view would be able to take into account the complexities of the real life in which they work.

Reading their writings in the collections I alluded to, I have been impressed by their sincere efforts to figure out how the gospel can be made to work. I sensed a kinship with them and felt empathy for the difficulties of their positions. From the readings I have done, I have come to think we begin with the same premises about power, peace, and the Savior's teachings. My own thinking was inspired by the observations of Paul Hammond in one of the national security professionals' volumes. He concludes his essay by asking: "When is the use of military force appropriate and, in particular, morally justified?" He answers: "When it will do more good than harm."[2] That I believe should be the starting point for the discussion of war. Will war do more good than harm?

---

1. Valerie M. Hudson and Kerry M. Kartchner, eds., *Moral Perspectives on U.S. Security Policy: Views from the LDS Community* (Provo, Utah: David M. Kennedy Center for International Studies, Brigham Young University, 1995); Valerie M. Hudson and Kerry M. Kartchner, *Wielding the Sword While Proclaiming Peace: Views from the LDS Community on Reconciling the Demands of National Security with the Imperatives of Revealed Truth* (Provo, Utah: David M. Kennedy Center for International Studies, Brigham Young University, 2004).

2. Paul Y. Hammond, "Security and Morality in a Contingent World," in

It is not an easy question to answer. We know for certain that war will do much harm: property devastated, innocent persons killed and wounded, lives blighted permanently, brutalization and lust for killing instilled in a few, families disrupted, and moral standards lowered. These evils have always ensued in war and can be predicted with certainty.

Hammond then goes on to ask: "Do we understand the situation well enough to be highly confident that our employment of force will achieve the intended results?"[3] I think that is the crucial question and one difficult to answer. As in all government action, the law of unintended consequences invariably comes into play in war. What we rationally predict does not always occur. We cannot know for sure that our employment of force will achieve the intended result. That is why I think we should always err on the side of conservatism, of restraint, of modesty about our capacities to achieve our ends through war. In general I think we should always err on the side of peace, always hold back if possible, always seek alternatives to violence, always stop fighting as soon as possible.

A suitable modesty is called for particularly in view of certain engrained habits in the American character. We Americans have a proclivity to violence in a way that astounds and sobers Europeans. Violence appears constantly in our movies and video games. A recurring American movie plot features the peaceful man who is driven to violence by some wrong against himself or his loved ones. He begins with a reticence, a wish to try every peaceful measure first, even to the point of bearing insults. But then we come to the point where the man of peace is driven beyond the point of restraint. He or his loved ones are wronged so terribly that he must react. That is the most exciting point in the plot in our national dramas. It is how we depict ourselves as a nation in the Declaration of Independence. We are a patient people. Only when "a long train of abuses and usurpations" evince a "design to reduce them under absolute despotism," do we act. We thrill at the moment when Shane finally unpacks his pistols and goes after the villains. Then all manner of violence is warranted, and it is these moments of violent justice that excite us most. We love to reduce our enemies to pure evil and thereby justify the exertion of unfettered force. We show our manhood and our humanity by fighting.

Hudson and Kartchner, *Moral Perspectives*, 151.

3. Hammond, "Security and Morality," 151.

That cultural tendency terrifies many of our allies. How can world leadership be trusted to a people who love violence, who search for justification to unpack their pistols? I think Latter-day Saints should be among those who never delight in violence, who are aware of the evil in ourselves, who know that violent urges must always be checked, who always value peace over war. Especially when the rage for war runs at full throttle, when the affronts of the enemy seem to require that we blast them, we should be the ones to call for reflection and hesitation, aware that rarely can we be confident that force will achieve its intended results.

What I worry about is that as soon as the point of violence is reached, our thinking stops. We short-circuit the debate and all of the violence becomes a fight for liberty. The soldiers say they are fighting for us in Vietnam or Iraq or Afghanistan so that we don't have to fight for our liberties in America. The relationship of the battles in those foreign places to our liberties is no longer problematic but assumed.

There is a good reason for this. Once lives are being sacrificed and the killing begins, we have to have strong reasons. You cannot tell a soldier who has just seen a friend killed that the value of the war is problematic, and that we are not altogether sure that the sacrifice was worth it. You cannot undercut the men in the field that way. We have to make them heroes in a noble cause or their lives were forfeited in vain. I do not know an easy way out of that conundrum. After war begins it almost seems too late to reflect and debate.

Nonetheless, is it in the national interest to curtail debate once the fighting begins? We imagine those scenes in the Book of Mormon where the warring parties fight on and on as the blood flows and their comrades fall simply because they must avenge the killings of one day with more killings the next. In the end, the Jaredite people let every living person fall under the sword until only two fanatical warriors faced one another. Is that the model for our warfare—to fight the enemy until all of them die leaving us as the conquerors?

It is an extreme case, but we too easily fall into that mode of thinking in our movies, in our video games, and in our wars. Nothing but unqualified victory will satisfy us. We cannot consider negotiation lest it appear weak. That is Jaredite thinking at its worst. However we revere our own fallen warriors, we must give ear to those who speak out against war when we are most fully engaged in the struggle. Our respect for our soldiers cannot be allowed to stop our efforts to find peace through negotiation. We wish to be known as peacemakers, not war makers.

The difficulties of speaking against war in time of war are one reason why we need discussions like those conducted in this volume. We must find ways to impede the rush to war well before war begins, and after it starts, discern how to minimize its horrors and direct our actions toward peace.

Contributors

Mark Ashurst-McGee is a historian and documentary editor with the Joseph Smith Papers Project. He holds a PhD in history from Arizona State University and has trained at the Institute for the Editing of Historical Documents. He is a coeditor of the first volume in the Journals series and of the first volume of the Histories series of the Joseph Smith Papers. His essay in this volume is adapted from his doctoral dissertation, "Zion Rising: Joseph Smith's Early Social and Political Thought" (2008), which was awarded the Gerald E. Jones Award for Best Dissertation from the Mormon History Association.

Richard Lyman Bushman is Gouverneur Morris Professor of History Emeritus at Columbia University, and recently visiting Howard W. Hunter Chair of Mormon Studies at Claremont Graduate University. Educated at Harvard College, he earned an AM in history and a PhD in the history of American civilization from Harvard University. His first book, *From Puritan to Yankee* (1967), was awarded the Bancroft Prize. He has also published *Joseph Smith and the Beginnings of Mormonism* (Urbana: University of Illinois Press, 1984), *King and People in Provincial Massachusetts* (1985); *The Refinement of America* (1992); and *Joseph Smith: Rough Stone Rolling* (2005).

Morgan Deane received a BA from Southern Virginia University and an MA in History from Norwich University. He has presented and published papers on Napoleonic warfare, East Asian history, Book of Mormon warfare, and the American Civil War. In 2009 he separated from the military after serving nine years as an infantry riflemen, squad leader, and intelligence analyst. His research interests also include premodern warfare and the application of military theory. He currently teaches history at several schools and is preparing for a PhD program in East Asian history.

F. R. Rick Duran is a member of an LDS peace studies working group formed at the 2008 Peace and Social Justice Conference in Milwaukee, Wisconsin. He has presented his research at various venues, including the 2009 Mormon History Association, where he delivered a paper on the ethical and pacifist reaction to Mormon refugees by the inhabitants of Quincy, Illinois. He is completing a book entitled *Pax Sanctorum: Towards a Latter-day Pacifist Ethic,* based on the premise that the Book of Mormon is a thoroughly pacifist document. He is the managing partner of the Archinomics Group in Winnetka, Illinois, which provides new project strategy consulting in over thirty countries.

Eric A. Eliason is professor of folklore at Brigham Young University. His publications include: *Warrior Ways: Explorations in Modern Military Folklore* with Tad Tuleja; *The J. Golden Kimball Stories*; *Black Velvet Art*; and *Latter-day Lore: A Handbook of Mormon Folklore Studies* with Tom Mould. From 2002–2008 he served as chaplain for the 1st Battalion, 19th Special Forces Group (Airborne) in the Utah Army National Guard. He served in Afghanistan, the Philippines, and at Arlington National Cemetery. He developed the first training program for Afghan Security Forces chaplains and worked closely with Afghan religious and community leaders on peacemaking and reconstruction projects.

Loyd Ericson is a graduate student in Philosophy of Religion and Theology at Claremont Graduate University where he was the founding co-editor of the *Claremont Journal of Mormon Studies*. He is also the managing editor at Greg Kofford Books, co-editor of *Discourses in Mormon Theology: Theological and Philosophical Possibilities*, and an adjunct instructor at Utah Valley University.

Jesse Samantha Fulcher is a young Australian currently undertaking her post-graduate Honours Year in International Relations examining the effects of children on peace building processes and subsequent effects of such processes on children. She works at an independent, democratic, primary school where she facilitates and manages conflict resolution workshops for children, teachers, and parents of the school community.

Robert H. Hellebrand is a mathematics, social studies, and English teacher at Victor Valley High School in Victorville, California. He received his MA in religion at Claremont Graduate University in 2012, where he was an Ahmanson Foundation Fellowship Recipient. His studies focused on the history of Christianity and on Mormon Studies. His essay in this volume was a distillation of his master's thesis.

Mark Henshaw is a senior CIA military analyst and head of the CIA Information Operations Center Analysis Group's Tradecraft Cell. He is an emeritus member of the CIA Red Cell think tank and the creator of CIA's Silent Horizon wargame series, which studies cutting-edge national security challenges. He is the recipient of seventeen CIA Exceptional Performance Awards and the Director of National Intelligence's 2007 Galileo Award. He holds an MA in International Relations from Brigham Young University's David M. Kennedy School of International and Area Studies and an MBA from BYU's Marriott School of Management.

Valerie M. Hudson is Professor and George H. W. Bush Chair at The Bush School of Government and Public Service at Texas A&M University. She has previously taught at Brigham Young, Northwestern, and Rutgers universities. Her research foci include foreign policy analysis, security studies, gender and international relations, and methodology. Her articles have appeared in numerous journals, and she is author or editor of several books, including (with Andrea Den Boer) the award-winning *Bare Branches: The Security Implications of Asia's Surplus Male Population* (2004). Her most recent book (co-authored) is *Sex and World Peace*, published by Columbia University Press.

Eric Talbot Jensen is an Associate Professor at Brigham Young Law School in Provo, Utah, where he teaches Public International Law, U.S. National Security Law, Criminal Law, and the Law of Armed Conflict. Prior to his current position, he spent 20 years in the U.S. Army JAG Corps, serving in various positions including as the Chief of the Army's International Law Branch. He is a graduate of Brigham Young University (BA, International Relations), University of Notre Dame Law School (JD), The Judge Advocate General's Legal Center and School (LLM), and Yale Law School (LLM).

Kerry M. Kartchner is an employee of the U.S. Department of State currently assigned to the Defense Threat Reduction Agency, where he is serving as the Senior Foreign Policy Advisor to the Associate Director for Strategy and Plans. He is also a Distinguished Faculty member in Missouri State University's Graduate Department of Defense and Strategic Studies, where he teaches courses on arms control, strategy, defense planning, and strategic culture. He is the co-editor of a textbook, *Strategic Culture and Weapons of Mass Destruction*, as well as other publications. His PhD and MA in International Relations are both from the University of Southern California.

Jennifer Lindell graduated *magna cum laude* in history and religion from San Diego State University, where she also earned a master's degree in history. She focused her studies on Native American history during her early years and later became interested in the Mormons and their historical interaction with the Native Americans. Her master's thesis focused on Mormons and Native Americans in the Antebellum West. She was accepted as a fellow in the PhD program at University of Pennsylvania where she was awarded a full five-year scholarship to study history and religion. She passed away in May 2011.

Joshua Madson received his undergraduate degree in history from Brigham Young University and JD from J. Reuben Clark Law School. He is a practicing attorney in Alpine, Utah, as well as an independent researcher who has presented at a variety of Mormon conferences. He is a contributor and editor for *The Mormon Worker*, a journal devoted to Mormonism, pacifism, and radical politics. His article, "Don't Torture in My Name," has been highlighted by the National Religious Campaign Against Torture.

Ron Madson is a lawyer in private practice in Alpine, Utah, having earned a BA in English and JD degrees from Brigham Young University. He posts his anti-war and social justice essays with the Mormon Worker blog, and has published four articles in *The Mormon Worker*: "In Defense of Blackwater, Gangs, and Necoons," "Wendell Berry's 'Gift of a Good Life,'" "National Flagophilia," and "12th Article of Faith: Sustaining the Law." He also contributed an essay called "Grandpa's Hat" in *Dialogue: A Journal of Mormon Thought*.

Patrick Q. Mason is Howard W. Hunter Chair of Mormon Studies and associate professor of religion at Claremont Graduate University. He is the author of *The Mormon Menace: Violence and Anti-Mormonism in the Postbellum South* (2011), and numerous articles in fields including Mormon studies, American religion, and religion, conflict, and peacebuilding.

John Mark Mattox is the General Hugh Shelton Chair in Ethics and Visiting Professor at The U.S. Army Command and General Staff College and a Senior Research Fellow at the National Defense University Center for the Study of Weapons of Mass Destruction. A retired U.S. Army Colonel, he is the former Dean of the Defense Threat Reduction University and Commandant of the Defense Nuclear Weapons School. He served on three continents as a field artillery officer and is a veteran of the First Gulf War. He has taught at the United States Military Academy and the University of Maryland.

Boyd Petersen teaches in the English and Literature department at Utah Valley University, where he also serves as the Program Coordinator for Mormon Studies. He has an MA (University of Maryland) and PhD (University of Utah) in Comparative Literature and is the author of the award-winning biography *Hugh Nibley: A Consecrated Life*. He has served on the board of directors for the Association for Mormon Letters, Mormon Scholars in the Humanities, and *Segullah*, a Mormon-themed literary journal, and is the past-president of the Association for Mormon Letters. He currently serves as the book review editor for the *Journal of Mormon History*.

J. David Pulsipher is an associate professor of history at Brigham Young University–Idaho. Educated as an undergraduate at Brigham Young University, Utah, he earned a PhD in American Studies from the University of Minnesota. In 2007–2008 he was a visiting professor and Fulbright scholar at Jamia Millia Islamia in Delhi, India. His research focuses on the intersections of LDS history/theology with just war, peace, and nonviolence traditions.

D. Michael Quinn is an independent scholar in Rancho Cucamonga, California. His last academic appointment was as Beinecke Senior Fellow at Yale University, 2002–2003, when he was also Post-Doctoral Associate in its Department of History. He volunteered for three years of military service during the Vietnam War, while at the same time understanding and admiring America's conscientious objectors: "One of my LDS missionary-friends protested against the war and became a 'draft-dodger' in Canada, while another missionary-friend died as a U.S. soldier invading Cambodia. I respected both Richard W. Glade and Roy Lee Richardson, but grieved for their wartime sacrifices."

Robert A. Rees teaches Mormon Studies at Graduate Theological Union in Berkeley. Previously, he taught at the University of Wisconsin, UCLA, and UC Santa Cruz. Between 1992-1996, Rees was a visiting professor at Vytautas Magnus University in Kaunas, Lithuania, where he was also a Fulbright scholar. Rees has served as editor of *Dialogue* and chair of the Sunstone Foundation. His work has appeared in numerous publications, such as the *Ensign*, *BYU Studies*, *Journal of Book of Mormon Studies*, *Dialogue*, and *Sunstone*. He is the editor of several books, including *Why I Stay: The Challenges of Discipleship for Contemporary Mormons* (2011).

Gordon Conrad Thomasson is an emeritus professor who has taught at numerous institutions. He did graduate study and worked as a research assistant with Hugh W. Nibley at Brigham Young University, and holds a PhD from Cornell. He was principal author, editor, and publisher of *War, Conscription, Conscience and Mormonism* (1971). He was employed in Liberia during its military coup (1980–82) and in the Sudan during a relative lull in its protracted war (1985); and he has also spent time in Kuwait and Mexico. Recent among his publications is an article on the LDS Church for the Oxford International Encyclopedia of Peace.

Ethan Yorgason is an assistant professor of geography at Kyungpook National University, in Daegu, South Korea. Prior to teaching in Korea, he taught at Brigham Young University–Hawaii, I-Shou University (Taiwan), and Syracuse University. His specialties are cultural and political geography. He has also been active researching within Mormon Studies, with a recent emphasis on the cultural geopolitics of Mormonism.

Subject Index

A

Abel, ix–x
Abu Ghraib, 213
Adam, x
Afghanistan, 191–92, 195–97, 199, 213, 231, 247, 270
Al Qaeda, 197
Alexander the Great, 31
al–Zarqawi, 197
Amalekites, 3
Amalickiah, 35
Ambrose, Stephen, 161
Ammonites, xvi, 2–12, 107, 182, 193, 199, 214, 242
  parents, 6
  seek military protection, 2–3
  sons, 3–4, 9, 108, 243
Ammoron, 249–50
Annie E. Casey Foundation, 53
Anti–Nephi–Lehites. *See* Ammonites.
Appleby, Scott, xi, xii note 4
Ashurst–McGee, Mark, xvii, 83–91
Atchison, David, 226 note 6, 228
atomic bombs, 179. *See also* nuclear weapons.
atonement, 23, 26

B

Bailie, Gil, 24–25
Barnard, Hanna, 59
Beah, Ishmael, 49
Benjamin (king), 68, 119, 237
Benson, Ezra Taft, 166, 246
Bible, ix–x, 235
as narrative, 14
Blackhawk, Ned, 96
Bogart, Samuel, 227
Boggs, Lilburn, 227, 239
Book of Mormon, x, xvi, 42, 53, 237, 270
  anti–war text, 14
  battles, 1–2
  Christological reading of, xvi
  historical outline, 15
  larger narrative, 1–2, 14–19
  and LDS Koreans, 107
  as narrative, 27
  number of conflicts, 62–63, 62 note 17, 65 note 22, 65 note 23
  as pacifist manifesto, 57–59
  peace societies, 61
  prohibited war practices, 36
  wars, 22–24, 32–39, 42
Booth, Ezra, 85
Brigham Young University, 172, 187–88, 203, 233, 237–38
Brown, S. Kent, 73
Brown, Thomas, 99
Bryan, William Jennings, 142
Bush, George W., 37–38, 253
  Mormon support for, xv note 8
Bushman, Richard L., xiii, xix, 17, 267–71

C

Cain, ix–x
Calhoun, John C., 5 note 11
Cameron, Judge, 226 note 6
Cannon, George Q., 130–31
Cha, Victor, 103
chaplaincy, 191

China, 32, 259
Christians, early, 66
Civil Rights Movement, 10
Civil War, 34, 129–131
Claremont Graduate University, xiii
Clark, Dale, 213
Clark, J. Reuben, xviii, 141–60, 163 note 11,
    212, 219, 246
    and American Peace Society, 148, 152, 154
    ancestry, 142, 155
    chairman of New York Committee for
        the Outlawry of War, 144
    on Cold War, 157–58
    and conscientious objection, 141
    condemns pacifists, 142
    endorses Pact of Paris, 145
    on Hiroshima and Nagasaki, 132, 156,
        179, 256
    joins U.S. Army Reserve, 143
    pacifist, 145–60
    on Pearl Harbor, 151
    and Spanish–American War, 141–60
    on Treaty of Versailles, 144, 146, 163
        note 11
    and World War I, 142–43
    and World War II, 146–57
Clausewitz, Carl Von, 30–31, 36
Cold War, 37, 90, 123, 134–37, 157–58,
    176, 193, 212
Communist Manifesto, 195
Community of Christ, xiv note 7
conflicts
    global, ix
    number of, ix
conscientious objection, 141
    in General Conference, 131
Cook, Quentin L., 58
Corrill, John, 221, 227, 227 note 7, 232
Coup De'Oeil, 36
Cowdery, Oliver, 85, 95, 206, 227
Crooked River, 227
Cuban Missile Crisis, 37 note 17

D

Dalton, Edward M., 120
Deane, Morgan, xvi, 29–39
Declaration of Independence, 269
"Decrees Relating to Women," 195–96
Doniphan, Alexander, 226 note 6, 228

Druze, Golani, 121–22
Dunkards, 142, 155
Duran, F. R. Rick, xvi, 57–79, 267
Durant, Will, 42

E

effective pacifism, 174–75
Eliason, Eric, xviii, 191–201
Engels, Friedrich, 195
England, Eugene, xviii, 171–88
    on Ammonites, 182
    Brigham Young University, 172, 187–88
    cites David O. Mckay, 177–78
    cites J. Reuben Clark, 179
    cites Spencer W. Kimball, 180–81
    on effective pacifism, 174–75
    establishes *Dialogue*, 172
    "Food for Poland," 213
    on Gulf of Tonkin, 171–72
    and Hugh Nibley, 185
    on just war, 173–74
    Stanford University, 172, 175, 177
    Utah Valley University, 172
    upbringing, 172
    and Vietnam War, 171
Enoch, 84–85, 87
    people of, 54
Erasmus, 71
Ericson, Loyd, xiii, xviii, 171–88, 267
Evans, Richard L., 134
Eve, x
extremist, xii
Eyring, Henry B., 109

F–G

"Family: A Proclamation to the World,
    The," 195–96
Featherstone, Vaughn J., 136–37
Fulcher, Jesse Samantha, xvii, 115
Gadianton robbers, 33, 35, 249
Galtung, Johan, 60
Gandhi, 10, 116–17
Gardner, Brant, 216
General Conference, xvii–xviii, 127–40
Gidgiddondi, 35–36
Girard, René, 16
Grant, Heber J., 120
Gulf of Tonkin, 171

H

Hammond, Paul, 268–69
Hanks, Marion D., 136
Hardy, Grant, 9 note 16, 14 note 2
Harmonists, 84
Haun's Mill, 239 note 7, 288
heaven, 7
Hedges, Chris, 22 note 30, 52
hell, 7
Hellebrand, Robert H., xvii–xviii, 127–40
Henshaw, Mark, 235–66
Hinckley, Gordon B., xv note 8, 46, 58, 109, 123–24, 136, 138–39, 230–31, 247, 254–55, 264
Hiroshima, 132, 179
Horman, Charles, 213 note 17
Hübener, Helmet, 213, 248
Hudson, Valerie M., 235–66, 268
Hussein, Saddam, 38
Hyde, Orson, 228

I–J

Independence Day, 197
Indian Removal Act, 95
Indians, xvii, 85–86, 93–100. *See also* Lamanites
and Mormon theology, 94
Iraq War, xv, 29, 137–39, 197, 213, 231, 247, 255, 267, 270
casualties, 44 note 5
Islam, 194
Jackson County, Mo., 86, 90, 209–10, 222, 226–29
Jackson, Kent P., 26, 66 note 26, 71–72
Jefferson, Thomas, 5 note 10
Jensen, Eric, xix
Jesus Christ, 24
doctrine of, 46–47, 108
visits Americas, 24–25, 42–48
Joan B. Kroc Institute for International Peace Studies, xiii
Johnson, Benjamin, 227 note 7
just war, 4, 6–12 173–74, 220, 248–55

K–L

Kang, David, 103
Kartchner, Kerry M., xix, 235–66
Kellogg–Briand Treaty. *See* Pact of Paris.

Kimball, Spencer W., 58, 72, 180–81, 192–93, 253, 255
King, Martin Luther, Jr., xii note 4, 13
Korea. *See* North Korea, South Korea.
Korean War, 101, 134–35, 176, 212
Lamanites, xvii. *See also* Indians.
foundational narrative, 17
Nephite stereotypes of, 18
LDS Council on Mormon Studies, xiii
Lee, Harold B., 152–53
Lee, John D., 97, 215
Lennon, John, 41, 55
Limhi, 71
Lindell, Jennifer, xvii, xx, 93–100

M

Madson, Joshua, xvi, 13–28
Madson, Ron, xix, 219–34
Marsh, Thomas, 227–29, 232
Marx, Karl, 195
Marxism, 195
Mason, Patrick Q., ix–xx, 267
Mattox, John Mark, 235–66
Mauss, Armand, 94
McConkie, Joseph Fielding, 6 note 14
McCoy, Isaac, 85
McKay, David O., 133, 136, 159, 177–78, 193, 195, 246–47
Messenger and Advocate, 95
Middle East, ix
militant religion, xi
Millet, Robert L., 6 note 14
Mitchell, Stephen, 54–55
Monson, Thomas S., 237 note 2
Mormon (prophet), 16, 36, 224
Mormon Battalion, 212
Moroni (captain), 3–4, 10 note 17, 15–16, 23, 35, 38–39, 69, 107–8, 183, 198, 237, 249–51
Moroni (prophet), 252 note 32
Muhammad, 194
MX missile, 213, 256

N–O

Nagasaki, 132, 179
Native Americans. *See* Indians.
Necessity of Theater, 41
Nelson, Russell M., 137–38, 229–30

Nephi, xvi, 17–18, 34
  kills Laban, 73
Nephites
  foundational narrative, 17–18
  and just warfare, 9–10
Nibley, Hugh, xviii, 30–31, 51, 69, 58 note
  2, 64 note 21, 161–70, 185, 230 note 15
  critiques war, 166–70, 203, 203 note 1, 205
  and D–Day, 165
  enlists in military, 161
  and friendly German soldier, 169
  and Germany, 161
  on "Mahan Principle," 164
  at military intelligence school, 162
  on soldiers, 163
  and truths about war, 163–66
  witnesses friend's suicide, 168
  and World War II, 161–66
Noah (king), 71
nonviolence, 10, 115–16
North Korea, 103
nuclear weapons, 255–260. *See also* atomic
  bombs.
Old Bishop, 93
Order of Enoch, 42

P

pacifism, 1, 3–4
  absolute, 3, 7
  Christian, 59
  definition of, 59
  Mormon, 1
Packer, Boyd K., 109, 135
Pact of Paris, 145
Pahoran, 35, 69
Partridge, Edward, 221, 232
Pashtunwali, 194
Pax Sanctorum, 59
Peace Press, 204
peacemaker, xi
Pearl Harbor, 151
People of Ammon. *See* Ammonites.
Peterson, Alyssa, 213
Peterson, Boyd P., xviii, 161–70
Phillips, R. Douglas, 33 note 9
Pine Community School, 117
Pope John VIII, 220 note 2
positive peace, xix
Pratt, Parley P., 95

preemptive war, 36
Preexistence. *See* War in Heaven.
priesthood, 7–8
Pulsipher, J. David, xvi, 1–12

Q–R

Quaker, 142, 155
Quinn, D. Michael, xviii, 131–32, 141
Rector, Hartman, Jr., 5 note 12
Rees, Robert A., xvi, 41–55, 213
Rice, Condoleezza, 233
Rigdon, Sidney, 227
Robinson, Ebenezer, 232–33
Romney, Marion G., 195

S

satyagraha, 10, 116, 119
scapegoating, 18, 19 note 19
Schnibbe, Karl Heinz, 213
Scott, Richard G., 257
scripture, xiv, xvi, 41. *See also* Book
  of Mormon, Bible, Doctrine and
  Covenants.
Sebastopol Policy, 128
September 11th, 38–39, 123, 137, 255, 264
Sermon on the Mount, x
Shakers, 84
Sharp, Gene, 116
Simpson, George, 221
slavery, 2, 4–5
  and Bible, 2
Smith, Joseph, xii, ix
  on enemies, 124
  martyrdom, 240
  persecution of, 239
  prophecies Civil War, 130
  revelations of, 118, 207
  runs for U.S. President, 89
  sent to Liberty Jail, 229
  style of reform, 83
  travels to Washington, DC, 240
Smith, Joseph F., 51, 176
Smith, Joseph Fielding, 244
Smith, Robert F., 216
Snow, Lorenzo, 52, 228–29
South Korea, 101–14
Spanish–American War, 131–32, 175, 212
Stanford University, 172, 175, 177

story authority, 22 note 29
Stoute, Hosea, 97
Stradling, Gary, 258
stripling warriors. *See* Ammonites, sons.
Sudan, ix

T

Taliban, 195–97, 199
Taylor, John, 121, 128
Taylor, Stan, 261
terrorism, 38–39
Teruggi, Frank, 213 note 17
Thayne, Emma Lou, 213
Thomasson, Gordon C., xix, 46 note 6,
    203–18
Thomasson, Gordon O., 214
Treaty of Versailles, 144, 146

U–V

U.S. Constitution, 198
Uchtdorf, Dieter F., 58
United States
    foreign policy, 29
    poverty, 53
    wealth, 53
United States Military, 39
    LDS soldiers, xv, 101, 197, 245
    troops in South Korea, 102, 105–6
University of California Los Angeles, 204
University of Notre Dame, xiii
Uppsala Conflict Data Program, ix
Utah War, 128–29, 215
utopian societies, 84
Van Buren, Martin, 240, 244
Vietnam War, 135–37, 171, 176–77, 270
Voice of Warning and Instruction to All People, 95

W

Walker, Stephen, 51
*War, Conscription, Conscience and
    Mormonism*, 203–5
War in Heaven, ix, 194, 241
War is a Force that Gives Us Meaning, 52
weapon of love, 10–12
Weigley, Russell, 30
Wells, Daniel, 130
Whitmer, David, 227
Whitney, Orson F., 50
Whittaker, David, 210
Wight, Lyman, 227 note 7
Williams, Frederick G., 206
Winter Quarters, 96
Wobbe, Rudi, 213
Wood, Robert S., 263–64
Woodruff, Paul, 41
World War I, 51, 132–34, 142–43, 176
World War II, 5 note 13, 132–34, 146–57,
    161–66, 176, 213, 219, 246, 248
Wright, N.T., 14, 22 note 29

Y–Z

Yoder, John Howard, 64
Yorgason, Ethan, xvii, 101–14
Young, Brigham, 84, 96–99, 128, 130, 131,
    212, 215
Young, Brigham, Jr., 131, 212
Zeniff, 70
Zion, xvii, 25, 66–67, 83–91
    requirements of, 60
Zion's Camp, 210, 212

Scripture Index

Old Testament

Genesis 1:27 — 241
Genesis 18 — 27
1 Samuel 15:3 — 208
1 Samuel 15:21 — 208
Isaiah 2:4 — 61
Isaiah 13:11 — 63
Isaiah 31:1–3 — 226
Malachi 4:4 — 208, 217 note 23

New Testament

Matthew 5:9 — x
Matthew 5:39 — x
Matthew 5:44 — 117
Matthew 10:34 — x
Matthew 26:52 — x
Luke 2:14 — 236
Acts 17:28–29 — 241
1 Corinthians 13:12 — 248
Ephesians 2:13–20 — 26
Ephesians 4:32 — 118
Ephesians 5:8 — 54
James 3:18 — 54
Revelation 12:1–9 — 242
Revelation 13:10 — 167

Book of Mormon

1 Nephi 2:22 — 18
1 Nephi 2:23 — 76
1 Nephi 3:1–4 — 18
1 Nephi 4:1–26 — 18
1 Nephi 4:10 — 79
1 Nephi 4:37 — 76
1 Nephi 11:24–26 — x

1 Nephi 12 — 23 note 33
1 Nephi 13:16–19 — 251
1 Nephi 13:40–41 — 24
1 Nephi 14:2 — 75
1 Nephi 17:44 — 20
1 Nephi 19:23 — 265
1 Nephi 21:25 — 76
2 Nephi 4:15 — 75
2 Nephi 4:27 — 73
2 Nephi 4:34 — 65 note 25
2 Nephi 5:14 — 18, 73
2 Nephi 5:21–22 — 19
2 Nephi 5:33 — 62 note 16
2 Nephi 5:34 — 78
2 Nephi 11:4 — 24
2 Nephi 12:4 — 61
2 Nephi 23:11 — 63
2 Nephi 23:15 — 66
2 Nephi 25:25–27 — 24
2 Nephi 26:1 — 24
2 Nephi 26:32 — 79
2 Nephi 26:33 — 74
2 Nephi 28:31 — 65 note 25
2 Nephi 32:6 — 24
Jacob 1:10 — 18, 35
Jacob 2:17 — 77
Jacob 3:7 — 20
Jacob 7:23–24 — 77
Jacob 7:26 — 73
Enos 1:23 — 73
Jarom 1:13 — 23 note 33
Omni 1:3 — 77
Omni 1:12–13 — 78
Omni 1:18 — 77
Omni 1:20–23 — 78

Words of Mormon 1:13 — 18, 35
Words of Mormon 1:15–16 — 77
Mosiah 1:1 — 77
Mosiah 1:16 — 18
Mosiah 2:4 — 68
Mosiah 3:19 — 119
Mosiah 4:4 — 76
Mosiah 4:12–16 — 61
Mosiah 4:13 — 54, 57–58
Mosiah 4:14 — 79
Mosiah 6:7 — 23 note 33
Mosiah 7:1 — 23 note 33
Mosiah 7:21 — 70, 70 note 35, 75
Mosiah 7:24 — 75
Mosiah 7:24–25 — 71
Mosiah 9:1 — 76
Mosiah 9:3 — 70, 75
Mosiah 10 — 20 note 20
Mosiah 10:1 — 77
Mosiah 10:12 — 18
Mosiah 10:17 — 18, 20 note 20
Mosiah 10:20 — 20 note 20
Mosiah 11:2 — 70–71
Mosiah 11:3–15 — 71
Mosiah 11:29 — 70–71
Mosiah 12:13–17 — 17
Mosiah 16:9 — 55
Mosiah 17:19 — 79
Mosiah 18:21 — 77
Mosiah 18:33 — 78
Mosiah 19:6–20 — 79
Mosiah 19:29 — 23 note 33
Mosiah 20:11 — 69, 76
Mosiah 20:13–26 — 77
Mosiah 20:17 — 71 note 36
Mosiah 20:19–21:1 — 76, 79
Mosiah 20:22 — 71 note 36
Mosiah 20:26 — 76
Mosiah 21:15 — 69, 76
Mosiah 21:20–22 — 77
Mosiah 21:29 — 75
Mosiah 22:2 — 76
Mosiah 22:3–9 — 71 note 36
Mosiah 22:6–11 — 79
Mosiah 24:23 — 79
Mosiah 25:9 — 75
Mosiah 25:11 — 75
Mosiah 26:37 — 65
Mosiah 27:28 — 75

Mosiah 29:26–29 — 77
Mosiah 29:27 — 75
Mosiah 29:36 — 75, 77
Mosiah 29:43 — 77
Alma 1:28 — 65, 77
Alma 1:33 — 77
Alma 2:2–3 — 77
Alma 2:10 — 66 note 26
Alma 2:21 — 76
Alma 2:23 — 31
Alma 2:33 — 47 note 8
Alma 3:2 — 76
Alma 3:3 — 22 note 28
Alma 3:6 — 19
Alma 3:11 — 17
Alma 3:25 — 78
Alma 4:5 — 78
Alma 4:11–16 — 65
Alma 5:55 — 77
Alma 9:16 — 17
Alma 9:17 — 17, 25
Alma 10:27 — 75
Alma 14:6 — 77
Alma 16 — 31
Alma 16:1 — 78
Alma 16:2–3 — 37
Alma 16:2–4 — 31
Alma 16:12 — 78
Alma 17:1 — 10 note 17
Alma 17:14–15 — 19
Alma 21:2–25:9 — 21 note 24
Alma 21:3 — 21 note 26
Alma 21:17 — 17, 25
Alma 22:29 — 34
Alma 23:3 — 75, 78
Alma 23:5 — 17, 25
Alma 23:6–7 — 79
Alma 23:13 — 78–79
Alma 23:13–15 — 21 note 26
Alma 23:23 — 68
Alma 23:24 — 21 note 26
Alma 24:6 — 76
Alma 24:12 — 75
Alma 24:16 — 75
Alma 24:18 — 26
Alma 24:18–19 — 182
Alma 24:19 — 242
Alma 24:20–25 — 79
Alma 24:25 — 25, 75

Alma 24:28 — 22
Alma 25:1–2 — 10 note 17
Alma 25:5 — 77
Alma 25:13–14 — 78
Alma 26:23–26 — 72 note 41
Alma 26:25 — 71
Alma 26:31–32 — 75
Alma 27 — 242
Alma 27:2–3 — 21 note 26, 79
Alma 27:23 — 75
Alma 27:28–29 — 61
Alma 28:4–6 — 78
Alma 28:14 — 75
Alma 30:2 — 78
Alma 30:7 — 77
Alma 30:7–11 — 243
Alma 30:11 — 77
Alma 30:23 — 77
Alma 30:59–43:44 — 21 note 24
Alma 31:5 — 65, 72 note 40, 72 note 41, 75
Alma 35:9 — 65
Alma 35:14 — 76
Alma 38:4 — 79
Alma 40:13 — 66
Alma 41:1 — 265
Alma 43 — 32–33
Alma 43–44 — 34
Alma 43:6 — 21 note 24
Alma 43:7–8 — 66 note 26
Alma 43:8 — 77
Alma 43:19 — 242
Alma 43:23 — 242
Alma 43:26 — 242
Alma 43:30 — 4 note 9, 33, 35, 76, 242
Alma 43:37–38 — 75
Alma 43:44 — 21 note 26
Alma 43:45–46 — 183
Alma 43:47 — 242
Alma 44:4 — 76
Alma 44:5 — 243
Alma 44:20 — 75–76
Alma 44:22 — 22 note 28
Alma 46 — 38
Alma 46:4 — 66 note 26
Alma 46:7–8 — 69
Alma 46:10 — 76
Alma 46:10–12 — 69
Alma 46:12 — 249
Alma 46:12–14 — 243

Alma 46:13 — 35, 76
Alma 46:18 — 75
Alma 46:20–21 — 76
Alma 46:30 — 30, 254
Alma 46:30–32 — 38
Alma 46:33 — 34
Alma 46:34–35 — 4 note 8
Alma 46:36 — 76
Alma 46:37–38 — 78
Alma 47 — 38
Alma 47:1–6 — 21 note 26
Alma 48 — 34, 38
Alma 48:1–3 — 21 note 26
Alma 48:7–8 — 35
Alma 48:11–14 — 3 note 7
Alma 48:13–16 — 242
Alma 48:14 — 36
Alma 48:16 — 76
Alma 48:17 — 76, 183, 251
Alma 48:19 — 72, 76
Alma 48:19–20 — 78
Alma 48:20 — 23 note 33, 47 note 8
Alma 48:21–25 — 9
Alma 48:22 — 23 note 33
Alma 48:23 — 75, 251
Alma 49:30 — 78
Alma 50 — 38
Alma 50:6–16 – 38
Alma 50:11 — 33
Alma 50:22 — 76
Alma 50:23 — 33 note 9
Alma 50:23–24 — 78
Alma 50:25 — 76
Alma 51:2 — 69
Alma 51:8 — 66 note 26
Alma 51:13 — 242
Alma 51:15 — 242
Alma 51:16 — 69
Alma 51:20 — 69, 76
Alma 51:22 — 69
Alma 51:25 — 242
Alma 52:1–4 — 21 note 26
Alma 53:1–6 — 4 note 8
Alma 53:10–17 — 9
Alma 53:10–18 — 242
Alma 53:14–16 — 79
Alma 53:16–17 — 243
Alma 53:20 — 9
Alma 54 — 38

Alma 54:1–3 — 252
Alma 54:4–57:1 — 76
Alma 54:7 — 250
Alma 54:17–18 — 66 note 26, 249
Alma 54:22 — 250
Alma 55:1 — 249
Alma 55:19 — 3 note 7, 75–76
Alma 56:22 — 76
Alma 56:46 — 3 note 7
Alma 56:46–47 — 9, 242
Alma 56:56 — 9
Alma 57:26 — 9
Alma 59:11–12 — 72
Alma 60 — 251
Alma 60:7 — 75
Alma 60:11 — 35
Alma 60:16 — 76
Alma 60:21 — 35
Alma 60:24 — 30
Alma 60:27 — 77
Alma 60:32 — 17
Alma 60:33 — 30
Alma 60:40 — 75
Alma 61:3 — 36
Alma 61:13–14 — 35
Alma 62:1 — 70
Alma 62:1–4 — 76
Alma 62:3–4 — 70
Alma 62:9 — 70
Alma 62:11 — 78
Alma 62:35–38 — 21 note 26
Alma 62:40–41 — 70
Alma 62:42 — 78
Alma 62:42–43 — 23 note 34
Alma 63:14–15 — 21 note 26
Alma 63:14–15 — 23 note 34
Helaman 1 — 32
Helaman 1:14–33 — 21 note 26
Helaman 1:18 — 34
Helaman 1:19 — 37
Helaman 2:1 — 78
Helaman 2:5 — 66 note 26
Helaman 3:2 — 75
Helaman 3:32 — 78
Helaman 4 — 32
Helaman 4:4 — 21 note 26
Helaman 4:5 — 75
Helaman 4:11 — 76
Helaman 4:16 — 23 note 34

Helaman 4:16–19 — 24
Helaman 5:15 — 77
Helaman 5:20–52 — 72 note 41
Helaman 5:50–52 — 23 note 34
Helaman 5:51 — 17, 25, 79
Helaman 5:51–52 — 24
Helaman 6:14 — 78
Helaman 6:37 — 25 note 39, 72 note 41
Helaman 7:4 — 77
Helaman 11:21 — 78
Helaman 11:25–27 — 33 note 11
Helaman 11:28 — 30, 33, 38
Helaman 11:34 — 75
Helaman 14:4 — 43
Helaman 15:8 — 61 note 12
Helaman 15:9 — 25
Helaman 15:15 — 17
Helaman 15:19 — 26
Helaman 16:13 — 78
3 Nephi 1:9 — 43
3 Nephi 1:23 — 78
3 Nephi 3:10 — 66 note 26
3 Nephi 3:19 — 34
3 Nephi 3:20–21 — 3 note 7
3 Nephi 3:21 — 36
3 Nephi 4:24–25 — 33
3 Nephi 6:9 — 78
3 Nephi 6:13–14 — 79
3 Nephi 6:14 — 61 note 12
3 Nephi 7:2 — 77
3 Nephi 7:14 — 77
3 Nephi 8:19 — 43
3 Nephi 8:21–22 — 43
3 Nephi 8:23 — 43–44
3 Nephi 8:25 — 44
3 Nephi 8:6–19 — 43
3 Nephi 9:14–15 — 45
3 Nephi 9:18 — 45
3 Nephi 9:20 — 26
3 Nephi 10:2 — 45
3 Nephi 10:6 — 45
3 Nephi 10:9–10 — 45
3 Nephi 11:3 — 45
3 Nephi 11:10 — 45
3 Nephi 11:19 — 46, 243
3 Nephi 11:22 — 46
3 Nephi 11:28 — 46
3 Nephi 11:28–30 — 47 note 8
3 Nephi 11:29 — 75, 78

3 Nephi 11:30 — 47, 79
3 Nephi 11:32–36 — 47
3 Nephi 11:38 — 45
3 Nephi 12:9 — 47
3 Nephi 12:14 — 45
3 Nephi 12:14–16 — 47
3 Nephi 12:44–45 — 47
3 Nephi 18:24 — 48
3 Nephi 20:40 — 48
3 Nephi 22:13–14 — 48
3 Nephi 26:19 — 62, 77
3 Nephi 27:30 — 48
4 Nephi 1:2 — 77–78
4 Nephi 1:2–3 — 50, 62
4 Nephi 1:4 — 78
4 Nephi 1:15 — 76
4 Nephi 1:15–17 — 50
4 Nephi 1:16 — 79
4 Nephi 1:24 — 52
4 Nephi 1:26–27 — 50
4 Nephi 1:34 — 76
4 Nephi 1:35 — 52
4 Nephi 1:38 — 79
Ether 7:9 — 65 note 24
Ether 7:16–17 — 65 note 24
Ether 7:27 — 78
Ether 8:3–5 — 65 note 24
Ether 8:19 — 65, 75
Ether 8:22 — 79
Ether 8:24 — 79
Ether 9:15 — 78
Ether 10:3 — 78
Ether 10:9 — 65 note 24
Ether 10:17–29 — 78
Ether 11:6 — 65
Ether 11:15–23 — 65 note 24
Ether 13:25 — 77
Ether 13:29–30 — 65 note 24
Ether 14:3 — 65 note 24
Ether 14:11–16 — 65 note 24
Ether 14:21–24 — 79
Ether 14:26 — 65 note 24
Mormon 1:12 — 23 note 33
Mormon 1:13 — 77
Mormon 3:9–10 — 65
Mormon 3:10–16 — 3 note 7
Mormon 3:11 — 253
Mormon 3:14 — 36
Mormon 3:15 — 36, 79

Mormon 4:4 — 36, 224
Mormon 4:4–5 — 254
Mormon 4:5 — 36, 63, 66, 223
Mormon 4:14 — 76
Mormon 7:4 — 68, 75, 79, 224
Mormon 8:8 — 23
Mormon 8:19 — 75
Mormon 8:19–20 — 65
Mormon 8:20 — 76, 79
Mormon 9:31 — 226
Moroni 7:1 — 74
Moroni 7:4 — 74
Moroni 7:16 — 248
Moroni 8:27 — 75
Moroni 9 — 252
Moroni 9:10 — 50
Moroni 9:23 — 65

Doctrine and Covenants

Doctrine and Covenants 1:19 — 222
Doctrine and Covenants 1:34 — 222
Doctrine and Covenants 4:2 –117
Doctrine and Covenants 9:7–8 — 265
Doctrine and Covenants 28:2 — 265
Doctrine and Covenants 28:7 — 265
Doctrine and Covenants 29:36 — 242
Doctrine and Covenants 35:13 — 86
Doctrine and Covenants 36:5 — 86
Doctrine and Covenants 38:33 — 86
Doctrine and Covenants 41:11 — 221
Doctrine and Covenants 42 — 84
Doctrine and Covenants 42:18–19 — 222
Doctrine and Covenants 45:11 — 87
Doctrine and Covenants 45:57 — 222
Doctrine and Covenants 45:63–69 — 87
Doctrine and Covenants 45:67 — 87
Doctrine and Covenants 45:68–69 — 88
Doctrine and Covenants 45:69 — 222
Doctrine and Covenants 45:70 — 87
Doctrine and Covenants 45:72–75 — 87
Doctrine and Covenants 49:24 — 94
Doctrine and Covenants 54 — 222
Doctrine and Covenants 63:33 — 222, 223
Doctrine and Covenants 64:9–10 — 118
  note 6
Doctrine and Covenants 64:41–43 — 87
Doctrine and Covenants 64:42 — 86
Doctrine and Covenants 65:2 — 88–89
Doctrine and Covenants 84:45 — 117

Doctrine and Covenants 87:6 — 88
Doctrine and Covenants 87:80 — 222
Doctrine and Covenants 88:79 — 238
Doctrine and Covenants 93:29 — 241
Doctrine and Covenants 93:33 — 241
Doctrine and Covenants 97 — 222
Doctrine and Covenants 97:18–19 — 88
Doctrine and Covenants 97:23 — 222
Doctrine and Covenants 97:25–26 — 222
Doctrine and Covenants 98 — 106, 222
Doctrine and Covenants 98:5 — 237
Doctrine and Covenants 98:11–15 — 223
Doctrine and Covenants 98:11–18 —
    205–6, 218
Doctrine and Covenants 98:14–16 — 68
Doctrine and Covenants 98:16 — xix, 51,
    137, 173, 243
Doctrine and Covenants 98:16–17 — 208
Doctrine and Covenants 98:16–22 — 223
Doctrine and Covenants 98:23–48 — 223,
    244
Doctrine and Covenants 98:24 — 223, 229
Doctrine and Covenants 98:28 — 68
Doctrine and Covenants 98:29 — 224, 229
Doctrine and Covenants 98:33 — 224
Doctrine and Covenants 98:34–48 — 223
Doctrine and Covenants 98:35–36 — 225
Doctrine and Covenants 98:39–40 — 225
Doctrine and Covenants 98:41 — 225
Doctrine and Covenants 98:44–45 — 225
Doctrine and Covenants 101:76–80 — 207
    note 7, 251

Doctrine and Covenants 101:77–80 — 198
Doctrine and Covenants 101:78 — 242
Doctrine and Covenants 105:29 — 74
Doctrine and Covenants 105:40 — 74
Doctrine and Covenants 121 — 229
Doctrine and Covenants 121:46 — 119
Doctrine and Covenants 132:4 — 233
Doctrine and Covenants 133:58 — 87
Doctrine and Covenants 134 — 115, 236
Doctrine and Covenants 134:2 — 223
    note 5
Doctrine and Covenants 134:5 — 250
Doctrine and Covenants 138:48 — 208

Pearl of Great Price

Moses 2:26 — 241
Moses 4:1–3 — 194
Moses 4:1–4 — 242
Moses 5 — x
Moses 5:11 — x
Moses 7:13–15 — 84
Moses 7:15–20 — 85
Moses 7:32 — 242
Moses 7:61–64 — 85
Abraham 3:24–26 — 241
Abraham 3:27–28 — 242
Abraham 5:8 — 241
Article of Faith 11 — 115
Article of Faith 12 — 236, 245
Article of Faith 13 — 173

Also available from
GREG KOFFORD BOOKS

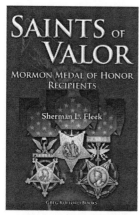

Saints of Valor: Mormon Medal of Honor Recipients

Sherman L. Fleek

Hardcover, ISBN: 978-1-58958-171-5

Since 1861 when the US Congress approved the concept of a Medal of Honor for combat valor, 3,457 individuals have received this highest military decoration that the nation can bestow. Nine of those have been Latter-day Saints. The military and personal stories of these LDS recipients are compelling, inspiring, and tragic. The men who appear in this book are tied by two common threads: the Medal of Honor and their Mormon heritage.

The purpose of this book is to highlight the valor of a special class of LDS servicemen who served and sacrificed "above and beyond the call of duty." Four of these nine Mormons gave their "last full measure" for their country, never seeing the high award they richly deserved. All four branches of the service are represented: five were Army (one was a pilot with the Army Air Forces during WWII), two Navy, and one each of the Marine Corps and Air Force. Four were military professionals who made the service their careers; five were not career-minded; three died at an early age and never married. This book captures these harrowing historical narratives from personal accounts.

Hugh Nibley:
A Consecrated Life

Boyd Jay Petersen

Hardcover, ISBN: 978-1-58958-019-0

Winner of the Mormon History Association's Best Biography Award

As one of the LDS Church's most widely recognized scholars, Hugh Nibley is both an icon and an enigma. Through complete access to Nibley's correspondence, journals, notes, and papers, Petersen has painted a portrait that reveals the man behind the legend.

Starting with a foreword written by Zina Nibley Petersen and finishing with appendices that include some of the best of Nibley's personal correspondence, the biography reveals aspects of the tapestry of the life of one who has truly consecrated his life to the service of the Lord.

Praise for *A Consecrated Life*:

"Hugh Nibley is generally touted as one of Mormonism's greatest minds and perhaps its most prolific scholarly apologist. Just as hefty as some of Nibley's largest tomes, this authorized biography is delightfully accessible and full of the scholar's delicious wordplay and wit, not to mention some astonishing war stories and insights into Nibley's phenomenal acquisition of languages. Introduced by a personable foreword from the author's wife (who is Nibley's daughter), the book is written with enthusiasm, respect and insight. . . . On the whole, Petersen is a careful scholar who provides helpful historical context. . . . This project is far from hagiography. It fills an important gap in LDS history and will appeal to a wide Mormon audience."
—Publishers Weekly

"Well written and thoroughly researched, Petersen's biography is a must-have for anyone struggling to reconcile faith and reason."
—Greg Taggart, Association for Mormon Letters

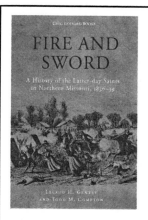

Fire and Sword: A History of the Latter-day Saints in Northern Missouri, 1836-39

Leland Homer Gentry and Todd M. Compton

Hardcover, ISBN: 978-1-58958-103-6

Many Mormon dreams flourished in Missouri. So did many Mormon nightmares.

The Missouri period—especially from the summer of 1838 when Joseph took over vigorous, personal direction of this new Zion until the spring of 1839 when he escaped after five months of imprisonment—represents a moment of intense crisis in Mormon history. Representing the greatest extremes of devotion and violence, commitment and intolerance, physical suffering and terror—mobbings, battles, massacres, and political "knockdowns"—it shadowed the Mormon psyche for a century.

Leland Gentry was the first to step beyond this disturbing period as a one-sided symbol of religious persecution and move toward understanding it with careful documentation and evenhanded analysis. In Fire and Sword, Todd Compton collaborates with Gentry to update this foundational work with four decades of new scholarship, more insightful critical theory, and the wealth of resources that have become electronically available in the last few years.

Compton gives full credit to Leland Gentry's extraordinary achievement, particularly in documenting the existence of Danites and in attempting to tell the Missourians' side of the story; but he also goes far beyond it, gracefully drawing into the dialogue signal interpretations written since Gentry and introducing the raw urgency of personal writings, eyewitness journalists, and bemused politicians seesawing between human compassion and partisan harshness. In the lush Missouri landscape of the Mormon imagination where Adam and Eve had walked out of the garden and where Adam would return to preside over his posterity, the towering religious creativity of Joseph Smith and clash of religious stereotypes created a swift and traumatic frontier drama that changed the Church.

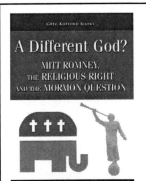

A Different God?
Mitt Romney the Religious Right and the Mormon Question

Craig L. Foster

Paperback, ISBN: 978-1-58958-117-3

In the contested terrain of American politics, nowhere is the conflict more intense, even brutal, than in the territory of public life also claimed by religion. Mitt Romney's 2007–08 presidential campaign is a textbook example.

Religious historian (and ardent Republican) Craig L. Foster revisits that campaign with an astute focus on the never-quite-contained hostility that Romney triggered among America's religious right. Although few political campaign are known for their kindness, the back-stabbing, mean-spirited attacks, eruptions of irrationalism, and downright lies exploded into one of the meanest chapters of recent American political history.

Foster readjusts rosy views of America as the tolerant, pluralistic society against the context of its lengthy, colorful, and bruising history of religious discrimination and oppression against many religious groups, among them Mormonism. Mormons are now respected and admired--although the image hasn't tilted enough to work for Romney instead of against him. Their turbulent past of suspicion, marginalization, physical violence, and being deprived of voting rights has sometimes made them, in turn, suspicious, hostile, and politically naive. How much of this pattern of mutual name-calling stems from theology and how much from theocratic ideals?

Foster appraises Romney's success and strengths—and also places where he stumbled, analyzing an intriguing pattern of "what-ifs?" of policy, personality, and positioning. But perhaps even more intriguing is the anti-Romney campaign launched by a divided and fragmenting religious right who pulled together in a rare show of unity to chill a Mormon's presidential aspirations. What does Romney's campaign and the resistance of the religious right mean for America in the twenty-first century?

In this meticulously researched, comprehensively documented, and passionately argued analysis of a still-ongoing campaign, Craig Foster poses questions that go beyond both Romney and the religious right to engage the soul of American politics.

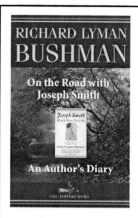

On the Road with Joseph Smith:
An Author's Diary

Richard L. Bushman

Paperback, ISBN 978-1-58958-102-9

After living with Joseph Smith for seven years and delivering the final proofs of his landmark study, *Joseph Smith: Rough Stone Rolling* to Knopf in July 2005, biographer Richard Lyman Bushman went "on the road" for a year, crisscrossing the country from coast to coast, delivering addresses on Joseph Smith and attending book-signings for the new biography.

Bushman confesses to hope and humility as he awaits reviews. He frets at the polarization that dismissed the book as either too hard on Joseph Smith or too easy. He yields to a very human compulsion to check sales figures on Amazon. com, but partway through the process stepped back with the recognition, "The book seems to be cutting its own path now, just as [I] hoped."

For readers coming to grips with the ongoing puzzle of the Prophet and the troublesome dimensions of their own faith, Richard Bushman, openly but not insistently presents himself as a believer. "I believe enough to take Joseph Smith seriously," he says. He draws comfort both from what he calls his "mantra" ("Today I will be a follower of Jesus Christ") and also from ongoing engagement with the intellectual challenges of explaining Joseph Smith.

Praise for *On the Road With Joseph Smith*:

"The diary is possibly unparalleled—an author of a recent book candidly dissecting his experiences with both Mormon and non-Mormon audiences . . . certainly deserves wider distribution—in part because it shows a talented historian laying open his vulnerabilities, and also because it shows how much any historian lays on the line when he writes about Joseph Smith."

-Dennis Lythgoe, *Deseret News*

"By turns humorous and poignant, this behind-the-scenes look at Richard Bushman's public and private ruminations about Joseph Smith reveals a great deal—not only about the inner life of one of our greatest scholars, but about Mormonism at the dawn of the 21st century."

-Jana Riess, co-author of *Mormonism for Dummies*

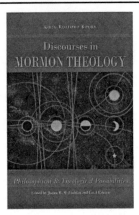

Discourses in Mormon Theology: Philosophical and Theological Possibilities

Edited by
James M. McLachlan and Loyd Ericson

Hardcover, ISBN: 978-1-58958-103-6

A mere two hundred years old, Mormonism is still in its infancy compared to other theological disciplines (Judaism, Catholicism, Buddhism, etc.). This volume will introduce its reader to the rich blend of theological viewpoints that exist within Mormonism. The essays break new ground in Mormon studies by exploring the vast expanse of philosophical territory left largely untouched by traditional approaches to Mormon theology. It presents philosophical and theological essays by many of the finest minds associated with Mormonism in an organized and easy-to-understand manner and provides the reader with a window into the fascinating diversity amongst Mormon philosophers. Open-minded students of pure religion will appreciate this volume's thoughtful inquiries.

These essays were delivered at the first conference of the Society for Mormon Philosophy and Theology. Authors include Grant Underwood, Blake T. Ostler, Dennis Potter, Margaret Merrill Toscano, James E. Faulconer, and Robert L. Millet

Praise for *Discourses in Mormon Theology*:

"In short, *Discourses in Mormon Theology* is an excellent compilation of essays that are sure to feed both the mind and soul. It reminds all of us that beyond the white shirts and ties there exists a universe of theological and moral sensitivity that cries out for study and acclamation."
-Jeff Needle, Association for Mormon Letters

CPSIA information can be obtained at www.ICGtesting.com
Printed in the USA
BVOW081049100113

310160BV00009B/570/P

9 781589 580992